Brain Computer Interfaces and Emotional Involvement: Theory, Research, and Applications

Brain Computer Interfaces and Emotional Involvement: Theory, Research, and Applications

Editor

Claudio Lucchiari

MDPI • Basel • Beijing • Wuhan • Barcelona • Belgrade • Manchester • Tokyo • Cluj • Tianjin

Editor
Claudio Lucchiari
Department of Philosophy
Università degli studi di
Milano
Milan
Italy

Editorial Office
MDPI
St. Alban-Anlage 66
4052 Basel, Switzerland

This is a reprint of articles from the Special Issue published online in the open access journal *Brain Sciences* (ISSN 2076-3425) (available at: www.mdpi.com/journal/brainsci/special_issues/BCI_Emotional_Involvement).

For citation purposes, cite each article independently as indicated on the article page online and as indicated below:

LastName, A.A.; LastName, B.B.; LastName, C.C. Article Title. *Journal Name* **Year**, *Volume Number*, Page Range.

ISBN 978-3-0365-5378-8 (Hbk)
ISBN 978-3-0365-5377-1 (PDF)

Contents

About the Editor

Claudio Lucchiari

Claudio Lucchiari is an associate professor of Cognitive Psychology at the University of Milan where he teaches General Psychology, Mind and Brain and Psychology of Negotiation as part of the Philosophy bachelor's and master's programs.

His research activities focus on cognitive and psycho-physiological aspects of creativity, with a special interest in neuro-cognitive methods aimed at empowering divergent thinking in different populations. He is now developing a line of research focused on the application of cognitive science in the developing of innovative tools, in both educational and professional contexts, to help people to change unhealthy behaviors and improve their cognitive abilities, especially by using BCI devices. He also works on emotions, negotiation and decision making in different domains, including economics, moral decisions, health psychology, conflicts, medical decision making, and consumer choice.

He has authored more than 50 scientific papers, six books and several essays in various books.

Preface to "Brain Computer Interfaces and Emotional Involvement: Theory, Research, and Applications"

This reprint is dedicated to the study of brain activity related to emotional and attentional involvement as measured by Brain–computer interface (BCI) systems designed for different purposes. A BCI system can translate brain signals (e.g., electric or hemodynamic brain activity indicators) into a command to execute an action in the BCI application (e.g., a wheelchair, the cursor on the screen, a spelling device or a game). These tools have the advantage of having real-time access to the ongoing brain activity of the individual, which can provide insight into the user's emotional and attentional states by training a classification algorithm to recognize mental states.

Pietro Aricò, Nicolina Sciaraffa and Fabio Babiloni broadly introduced this topic addressing the potential applicability of BCI in everyday applications. Indeed, the success of BCI systems in contemporary neuroscientific research relies on the fact that they allow one to "think outside the lab". The integration of technological solutions, artificial intelligence and cognitive science allowed and will allow researchers to envision more and more applications for the future. The clinical and everyday uses are described with the aim to invite readers to open their minds to imagine potential further developments.

Abeer Al-Nafjan, Khulud Alharthi and Heba Kurdi investigated the feasibility of building a lightweight emotion detection system using a small EEG dataset size with no involvement of feature extraction methods while maintaining decent accuracy. The results showed that by using a spiking neural network, it's feasible to detect the valence emotion level using only 60 EEG samples with 84.62% accuracy.

Yasuhisa Maruyama and colleagues, instead, focused their contribution on data analysis, describing an independent component method to analyze EEG signals. They showed that is possible to identify neural correlates of emotional states in the source space. The results suggest that specific cortical areas correlate with low and high emotional valences in accordance with Russell's valence–arousal model.

Zhipeng He and colleagues critically reviewed the state of the art of affective BCI application (aBCI). Starting with the idea that multimodal systems will probably be the standard for future applications, they described and analyzed three types of multimodal aBCIs (combination of behavior and brain signals; hybrid neurophysiology modalities and heterogeneous sensory stimuli systems) reporting the pros and cons of each.

The work conducted by Choong Wen Yean and colleagues offers an interesting perspective. The authors tried to apply a BCI-based emotion detection system in stroke patients. The possibility to estimate the patient's emotional state in a difficult situation could be very important for whoever takes care of patients and supports their rehabilitation. Using a bispectrum feature method to analyze EEG signals, they reported promising results about the possibility and efficacy of their system in clinical settings.

Mihaly Benda and Ivan Volosyak's contribution covers the relevant issues of artefacts in online applications. They provided a system to filter online movement artefacts in order to increase peak detection. In particular, the authors proved the efficacy of their online filter in determining objective user fatigue using alpha peak detection. The described artefact-removal methods could be extended to emotion detection.

Coherent with previous work, Dong-Hwa Jeong and Jaeseung Jeong described a BCI system aimed at discriminating attentive and resting states. Indeed, attention level is a basic parameter used to make estimations, which is potentially useful in a variety of contexts, and could also support emotional estimation thanks to its association with arousal. In particular, the authors described and tested a portable in-ear EEG device coupled with an Echo State Network model reporting promising outcomes.

Dong-Her Shih, Kuan-Chu Lu and Po-Yuan Shih used a BCI system to evaluate the attentional level of people engaged in e-commerce activity. They showed that time pressure limits attention, suggesting that targeted strategies are needed in order to improve the online shopping experience. Emotional detection capabilities would offer vital data to marketers.

Mina Kheirkhah and colleagues, finally, researched patients with peripheral facial nerve paralysis. The authors proved that it is possible to use MEG data and machine learning to provide a good estimation of emotions even for people with severe problems in encoding and decoding emotions. Future studies will test the possibility of also using simpler devices in this critical setting.

Claudio Lucchiari
Editor

brain sciences

MDPI

Editorial

Brain–Computer Interfaces: Toward a Daily Life Employment

Pietro Aricò [1,2,3,*], Nicolina Sciaraffa [1,2] and Fabio Babiloni [1,2,3,4]

1 Department of Molecular Medicine, Sapienza University of Rome, Piazzale Aldo Moro, 5, 00185 Rome, Italy; nicolina.sciaraffa@uniroma1.it (N.S.); fabio.babiloni@uniroma1.it (F.B.)
2 BrainSigns srl, Lungotevere Michelangelo 9, 00192, Rome, Italy
3 IRCCS Fondazione Santa Lucia, Neuroelectrical Imaging and BCI Lab, Via Ardeatina, 306, 00179 Rome, Italy
4 College of Computer Science and Technology, Hangzhou Dianzi University, Hangzhou 310018, China
* Correspondence: pietro.arico@uniroma1.it

Received: 6 March 2020; Accepted: 8 March 2020; Published: 9 March 2020

Abstract: Recent publications in the Electroencephalogram (EEG)-based brain–computer interface field suggest that this technology could be ready to go outside the research labs and enter the market as a new consumer product. This assumption is supported by the recent advantages obtained in terms of front-end graphical user interfaces, back-end classification algorithms, and technology improvement in terms of wearable devices and dry EEG sensors. This editorial paper aims at mentioning these aspects, starting from the review paper "Brain–Computer Interface Spellers: A Review" (Rezeika et al., 2018), published within the Brain Sciences journal, and citing other relevant review papers that discussed these points.

Keywords: passive brain–computer interface (pBCI); EEG headsets; daily life applications

---

A brain–computer interface (BCI) was originally defined as "a communication system in which messages or commands that an individual sends to the external environment do not pass through the brain's normal output pathways of peripheral nerves and muscles". For example, in an electroencephalogram (EEG)-based BCI, the messages can be directly decoded by specific EEG features [1]. In 2012, Wolpaw and Wolpaw [2] widened the meaning of the brain-computer interface, defining it as "a system that measures Central Nervous System (CNS) activity and converts it into artificial output that replaces, restores, enhances, supplements, or improves natural CNS output and thereby changes the ongoing interactions between the CNS and its external or internal environment", suggesting the possibility of employing this technology for different applications and targeting different kind of potential users, starting from completely locked-in people (e.g., amyotrophic lateral sclerosis, ALS), in which BCI can be used in its original meaning, or in other words in an "active" way (Active BCI), in which the user voluntary modulates his/her brain activity to generate a specific command on the surrounding environment (i.e., to replace and/or restore lost or impaired muscular abilities, [3–5]), coming to healthy users in daily life applications. In particular, BCI for healthy users could be used to enhance human–surroundings interaction. In this regard, the BCI (i.e., passive BCI, pBCI, [6–13]) is able to derive its outputs from arbitrary brain activity arising without the purpose of voluntary control (i.e., implicit information on the user states), for example, workload, attention, emotion, and most in general task-induced states that can only be detected with weak reliability using conventional methods such as subjective (e.g., questionnaires) and/or behavioral (e.g., reaction times) measures [14]. Systems based on pBCIs can directly use in a closed loop this information about the user states to automatically modify the behavior of the interface that the user is interacting with (i.e., adaptive automation), or just to inform, even in real-time, the user himself/herself or other people about dangerous human behaviors (e.g., overload [15], or loss of vigilance [16,17]) that could increase the human error probability and consequently induce possible unsafe situations.

Several giant leaps have been made in the BCI field in the last years, from several points of view. For example, many works have been produced in terms of *front-end* graphical user interfaces (GUIs), as deeply reported in the review paper "Brain–Computer Interface Spellers: A Review" recently published in the Brain Sciences journal. In this regard, "*throughout the years, scientists have worked on spelling systems to make them faster, more accurate, more user-friendly, and, most of all, able to compete with traditional communication methods*" [18].

In this particular regard, a huge effort has been made even in *back-end* algorithms (i.e., classification techniques) running under BCI systems [19], allowing for high discrimination accuracy (e.g., target vs. no-target, low workload vs. high workload) together with high information transfer rates (ITRs) and by using less and less features (i.e., EEG sensors). In this regard, machine-learning and deep learning approaches based on the analysis of physiological data went through a rapid expansion in the last decade since such methodologies are able to provide the means to decode and characterize task relevant brain states (i.e., reducing from a multidimensionality to one dimensionality problem) and to distinguish them from non-informative brain signals (i.e., to enhance Signal to Noise Ratio). In this regard, Aricò and colleagues have published a few review papers demonstrating the maturity and effectiveness of this kind of technique by testing BCI systems in daily life applications [20,21]. Figure 1 shows BCI concept and related potential fields of application.

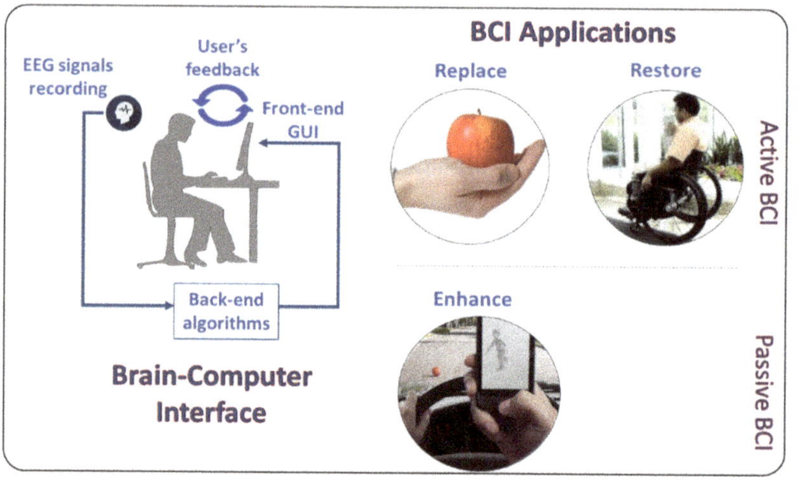

Figure 1. The brain–computer interface concept and related applications that could be realized in an *Active*, and a *Passive* meaning.

Last, but not least important, enhancement in technology is related to EEG recording headsets that could finally allow BCI systems to enter the market, especially for daily life applications. In recent years, many companies have been moving to develop more wearable and minimally invasive biosignal acquisition devices. With particular regard to EEG systems, current effort is being made to develop dry sensors (i.e., not requiring any conductive gel), or to eventually use water-based technology instead of the classic gel-based technology, allowing high signal quality and higher comfort (e.g., [22]). There is a common opinion that gel-based electrodes still have to be considered the gold standard [23,24], however, the gap between wet and dry electrodes is being more and more reduced [25]. Several attempts are already present in the literature about the comparison and validation of these innovative dry EEG electrodes. In this regard, recently Di Flumeri and colleagues [25] published a paper aiming to assess the level of maturity achieved by the EEG dry electrodes industry by comparing three different types of dry electrodes with traditional ones (i.e., gel-based). The results of this work highlighted the high level of quality achieved by dry EEG solutions, since all the tested electrodes were able to guarantee the same quality levels of the wet electrodes, allowing at the same time significantly reduced times of montage and improvement in the users' comfort.

In conclusion, because of the leaps and bounds performed in terms of front-end interfaces and back-end algorithms of BCIs, and the huge technology improvement in terms of wearable devices and dry EEG sensors, we can infer that BCIs are not too far from leaving the labs, and entering the market as a new consumer product.

Acknowledgments: This work was supported by the European Commission by Horizon2020 projects "HOPE: automatic detection and localization of High frequency Oscillation in Paediatric Epilepsy"(GA n. 823958); "WORKINGAGE: Smart Working environments for all Ages" (GA n. 826232); "SIMUSAFE": Simulator Of Behavioral Aspects For Safer Transport (GA n. 723386); "SAFEMODE: Strengthening synergies between Aviation and maritime in the area of human Factors toward achieving more Efficient and resilient MODE of transportation" (GA n. 814961), "BRAINSAFEDRIVE: A Technology to detect Mental States during Drive for improving the Safety of the road" (Italy–Sweden collaboration) with a grant from the Ministero dell'Istruzione dell'Università e della Ricerca della Repubblica Italiana.

Conflicts of Interest: The authors declare no conflicts of interest.

References

1. Wolpaw, J.R.; Birbaumer, N.; McFarland, D.J.; Pfurtscheller, G.; Vaughan, T.M. Brain-computer interfaces for communication and control. *Clin. Neurophysiol.* **2002**, *113*, 767–791. [CrossRef]
2. *Jonathan Wolpaw and Elizabeth Winter Wolpaw, Brain-Computer Interfaces—Jonathan Wolpaw*; Elizabeth Winter Wolpaw—Oxford University Press: Oxford, UK, 2012; pp. 1–424.
3. Abiri, R.; Borhani, S.; Sellers, E.W.; Jiang, Y.; Zhao, X. A comprehensive review of EEG-based brain-computer interface paradigms. *J. Neural Eng.* **2019**, *16*, 011001. [CrossRef] [PubMed]
4. Aloise, F.; Aricò, P.; Schettini, F.; Salinari, S.; Mattia, D.; Cincotti, F. Asynchronous gaze-independent event-related potential-based brain-computer interface. *Artif. Intell. Med.* **2013**, *59*, 61–69. [CrossRef] [PubMed]
5. Pichiorri, F.; Morone, G.; Petti, M.; Toppi, J.; Pisotta, I.; Molinari, M.; Paolucci, S.; Inghilleri, M.; Astolfi, L.; Cincotti, F.; et al. Brain-computer interface boosts motor imagery practice during stroke recovery. *Ann. Neurol.* **2015**, *77*, 851–865. [CrossRef]
6. Di Flumeri, G.; Borghini, G.; Aricò, G.; Sciaraffa, P.; Lanzi, N.; Pozzi, P.; Vignali, S.; Lantieri, V.; Bichicchi, C.; Simone, A.; et al. EEG-Based Mental Workload Neurometric to Evaluate the Impact of Different Traffic and Road Conditions in Real Driving Settings. *Front. Hum. Neurosci.* **2018**, *12*, 509. [CrossRef]
7. Blankertz, B.; Acqualagna, L.; Dähne, S.; Haufe, S.; Schultze-Kraft, M.; Sturm, I.; Uščumlic, M.; Wenzel, M.A.; Curio, G.; Müller, K.R. The Berlin brain-computer interface: Progress beyond communication and control. *Front. Neurosci.* **2016**, *10*, 530. [CrossRef]
8. Cartocci, G.; Maglione, A.G.; Vecchiato, G.; Di Flumeri, G.; Colosimo, A.; Scorpecci, A.; Marsella, P.; Giannantonio, S.; Malerba, P.; Borghini, G.; et al. Mental workload estimations in unilateral deafened children. In Proceedings of the Annual International Conference of the IEEE Engineering in Medicine and Biology Society, EMBS, Milan, Italy, 30 August–3 September 2015; pp. 1654–1657.
9. Zander, T.O.; Kothe, C. Towards Passive Brain-Computer Interfaces: Applying Brain-Computer Interface Technology to Human-Machine Systems in General. *J. Neural Eng.* **2011**, *8*. [CrossRef]
10. Valeriani, D.; Cinel, C.; Poli, R. Brain-computer interfaces for human augmentation. *Brain Sci.* **2019**, *9*, 22. [CrossRef]
11. Vecchiato, G.; Borghini, G.; Aricò, P.; Graziani, I.; Maglione, A.G.; Cherubino, P.; Babiloni, F. Investigation of the effect of EEG-BCI on the simultaneous execution of flight simulation and attentional tasks. *Med. Biol. Eng. Comput.* **2016**, *54*, 1503–1513. [CrossRef]
12. Astolfi, L.; Toppi, J.; Borghini, G.; Vecchiato, G.; He, E.J.; Roy, A.; Cincotti, F.; Salinari, S.; Mattia, D.; He, B.; et al. Cortical activity and functional hyperconnectivity by simultaneous EEG recordings from interacting couples of professional pilots. In Proceedings of the Annual International Conference of the IEEE Engineering in Medicine and Biology Society, EMBS, San Diego, CA, USA, 28 August–1 September 2012; pp. 4752–4755.

13. Sciaraffa, N.; Borghini, G.; Aricò, P.; di Flumeri, G.; Colosimo, A.; Bezerianos, A.; Thakor, N.V.; Babiloni, F. Brain Interaction during Cooperation: Evaluating Local Properties of Multiple-Brain Network. *Brain Sci.* **2017**, *7*, 90. [CrossRef]
14. Zander, T.O.; Jatzev, S. Context-aware Brain-Computer Interfaces: Exploring the Information Space of User, Technical System and Environment. *J. Neural Eng.* **2012**, *9*, 016003. [CrossRef]
15. Borghini, G.; Aricò, P.; di Flumeri, G.; Sciaraffa, N.; Colosimo, A.; Herrero, M.-T.; Bezerianos, A.; Thakor, N.V.; Babiloni, F. A new perspective for the training assessment: Machine learning-based neurometric for augmented user's evaluation. *Front. Neurosci.* **2017**, *11*, 325. [CrossRef]
16. Di Flumeri, G.; De Crescenzio, F.; Berberian, B.; Ohneiser, O.; Kramer, J.; Aricò, P.; Borghini, G.; Babiloni, F.; Bagassi, S.; Piastra, S. Brain–Computer Interface-Based Adaptive Automation to Prevent Out-Of-The-Loop Phenomenon in Air Traffic Controllers Dealing With Highly Automated Systems. *Front. Hum. Neurosci.* **2019**, *13*, 296. [CrossRef]
17. Sebastiani, M.; Di Flumeri, G.; Aricò, P.; Sciaraffa, N.; Babiloni, F.; Borghini, G. Neurophysiological Vigilance Characterisation and Assessment: Laboratory and Realistic Validations Involving Professional Air Traffic Controllers. *Brain Sci.* **2020**, *10*, 48. [CrossRef]
18. Rezeika, A.; Benda, M.; Stawicki, P.; Gembler, F.; Saboor, A.; Volosyak, I. Brain–computer interface spellers: A review. *Brain Sci.* **2018**, *8*, 57. [CrossRef] [PubMed]
19. Schettini, F.; Aloise, F.; Aricò, P.; Salinari, S.; Mattia, D.; Cincotti, F. Self-calibration algorithm in an asynchronous P300-based brain–computer interface. *J. Neural Eng.* **2014**, *11*, 035004. [CrossRef] [PubMed]
20. Aricó, P.; Borghini, G.; Di Flumeri, G.; Sciaraffa, N.; Colosimo, A.; Babiloni, F. Passive BCI in operational environments: Insights, recent advances, and future trends. *IEEE Trans. Biomed. Eng.* **2017**, *64*, 1431–1436. [CrossRef] [PubMed]
21. Pietro, A.; Gianluca, B.; Gianluca, d.; Nicolina, S.; Fabio, B. Passive BCI Beyond the Lab: Current Trends and Future Directions. *Physiol. Meas.* **2018**, *39*. [CrossRef]
22. Von Lühmann, A.; Müller, K.-R. Headgear For Mobile Neurotechnology: Looking Into Alternatives For Eeg And Nirs Probes. In Proceedings of the Berlin Brain Computer Interface View Project M3ba: Mobile, Modular, Multimodal Biosignal Acquisition: Hybrid Eeg-Nirs For Neurotechnology Out Of The Lab View Project pr, Graz, Austria, 18–22 September 2017; pp. 496–501.
23. Tallgren, P.; Vanhatalo, S.; Kaila, K.; Voipio, J. Evaluation of commercially available electrodes and gels for recording of slow EEG potentials. *Clin. Neurophysiol.* **2005**, *116*, 799–806. [CrossRef]
24. Lopez-Gordo, M.A.; Sanchez Morillo, D.; Pelayo Valle, F. Dry EEG electrodes. *Sensors* **2014**, *14*, 12847–12870. [CrossRef]
25. Di Flumeri, G.; Aricò, P.; Borghini, G.; Sciaraffa, N.; Di Florio, A.; Babiloni, F. The dry revolution: Evaluation of three different eeg dry electrode types in terms of signal spectral features, mental states classification and usability. *Sensors* **2019**, *19*, 1365. [CrossRef] [PubMed]

brain sciences

MDPI

Article

Lightweight Building of an Electroencephalogram-Based Emotion Detection System

Abeer Al-Nafjan [1], Khulud Alharthi [2,3] and Heba Kurdi [2,4,*]

1 Computer Science Department, Imam Muhammad ibn Saud Islamic University, Riyadh 11432, Saudi Arabia; annafjan@imamu.edu.sa
2 Computer Science Department, King Saud University, Riyadh 11543, Saudi Arabia; m.khloud@tu.edu.sa
3 Computer Science Department, Taif University, Taif 26571, Saudi Arabia
4 Mechanical Engineering Department, Massachusetts Institute of Technology (MIT), Cambridge, MA 02139, USA
* Correspondence: hakurdi@mit.edu or hkurdi@ksu.edu.sa; Tel.: +966-11-805-9637

Received: 20 August 2020; Accepted: 23 October 2020; Published: 26 October 2020

Abstract: Brain–computer interface (BCI) technology provides a direct interface between the brain and an external device. BCIs have facilitated the monitoring of conscious brain electrical activity via electroencephalogram (EEG) signals and the detection of human emotion. Recently, great progress has been made in the development of novel paradigms for EEG-based emotion detection. These studies have also attempted to apply BCI research findings in varied contexts. Interestingly, advances in BCI technologies have increased the interest of scientists because such technologies' practical applications in human–machine relationships seem promising. This emphasizes the need for a building process for an EEG-based emotion detection system that is lightweight, in terms of a smaller EEG dataset size and no involvement of feature extraction methods. In this study, we investigated the feasibility of using a spiking neural network to build an emotion detection system from a smaller version of the DEAP dataset with no involvement of feature extraction methods while maintaining decent accuracy. The results showed that by using a NeuCube-based spiking neural network, we could detect the valence emotion level using only 60 EEG samples with 84.62% accuracy, which is a comparable accuracy to that of previous studies.

Keywords: brain–computer interface (BCI); electroencephalogram (EEG); EEG-based emotion detection; spiking neural network; NeuCube

1. Introduction

Brain–computer interfaces (BCIs) are technologies used to provide a direct interface between sensors and the brain. BCIs have been identified as an emerging technology in many trend reports [1,2], and the number of BCI devices is expected to grow rapidly [3]. BCIs use responses from brain activities in humans or animals to activate external devices. The feedback delivered and captured by these devices bypasses the motor functions of a user or subject, thereby preventing interference. In this regard, nascent brain activities are objectively translated to this device, which in turn interprets them.

Many BCI systems and platforms have been developed and deployed over the past decade. However, most platforms were implemented based on proprietary solutions or developed to solve specific domain problems. In an interdisciplinary field of research, BCI studies have sought to leverage recent advances in its interdisciplinary relationship with other fields and foster a range of applications in various fields, such as signal processing, neuroscience, machine learning, and information technology. Figure 1 illustrates the basic components of a BCI system.

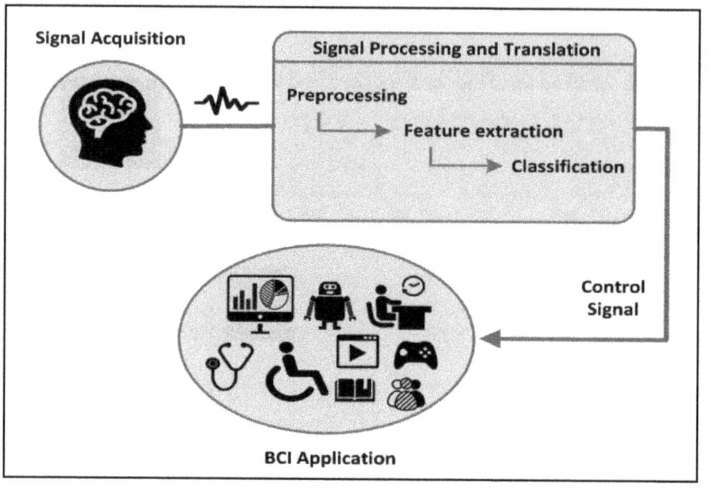

Figure 1. Basic components of a brain–computer interface.

BCI systems are designed to translate brain activities into control commands using a device that stimulates brain activity, thereafter providing an assessment of neurological function or sensory feedback. Sensory feedback is recorded, decoded, and eventually translated into a measurable neurophysiological signal, effector action, or behavior. Basically, any BCI system can be described by traditional processing pipelines, which include the following processing stages [1]:

1. Signal acquisition: This step deals with the measurement of brain signals using a particular type of sensor device. Furthermore, it involves different noninvasive neuroimaging methods that have been employed in BCI studies. These noninvasive techniques include electroencephalography (EEG), magnetoencephalography (MEG), functional magnetic resonance imaging (fMRI), functional near infrared (fNIR), and positron emission tomography (PET). All these methods have been reported as accepted. and safe imaging procedures used in research facilities and hospitals in clinical and nonclinical contexts. However, EEG is used most often in BCI research experimentation because the process is noninvasive to the research subject and minimal risk is involved. Moreover, the devices' usability, reliability, and cost-effectiveness, along with the relative convenience of conducting studies and recruiting participants afforded by portability, have been cited as factors influencing the increased adoption of this method in applied research contexts. Yet, these advantages are often accompanied by challenges such as low spatial resolution and difficulty in managing signal-to-noise ratios.
2. Signal processing and translation: This BCI process includes the following steps:
   - Signal preprocessing: This step deals with the filtering of acquired signals and removal of noise. Basically, signals are amplified, filtered, digitized, and transmitted to a computer.
   - Feature extraction/selection: This step deals with the analysis of digital signals to discriminate relevant signal characteristics. The signals are then represented in a compact form suitable for translation into output commands through selecting a subset and reducing the dimensionality of features.
   - Feature classification: The subsequent signal features are fed into the feature translation algorithm, which translates the features into a control signal for the output device or into commands that accomplish the user's intent.
3. Application/ feedback: The control signal from the signal processing and translation stage causes changes in the environment, device, or feedback mechanism of the EEG system. Many EEG-based

BCI systems have been developed that have targeted different applications and shared the same goal of translating users' intent into actions without using peripheral nerve impulses and muscles.

Recently, EEG-based emotion detection has garnered increased attention in both research and applied settings. It cuts across several application areas, including medical and nonmedical, and several disciplines such as clinical neurology, rehabilitative therapy, neurobiology, electronic engineering, psychology, computer science, medical physics, and biomedical engineering [3]. Most of these studies have proposed building an EEG-based emotion detection system with an EEG dataset larger than 300 samples, which has involved several feature extraction methods; by contrast, in the present study, we aim to propose a building process for an EEG-based emotion detection system that is lightweight in terms of a smaller EEG dataset size and with no involvement of feature extraction methods—all without compromising accuracy.

EEG-based emotion detection has promising potential applicability in numerous fields, where the ability to build such applications requires a sufficient size of EEG dataset and different feature extraction methods. This emphasizes the demand for a lightweight building process for an EEG-based emotion detection system with a smaller EEG dataset size and no feature extraction methods involved. Thus, investigations on the feasibility of promising tools and algorithms to maintain the high accuracy of EEG-based emotion detection systems—while learning from a smaller-sized preprocessed EEG dataset with no feature extraction methods involved—are highly encouraged.

Spiking neural networks (SNN) is the third generation of neural networks. It more closely mimics natural neural networks than artificial neural networks (ANN), as a neuron in SNN will fire when the accumulated stimuli reach above a threshold value, which makes SNNs more biologically realistic than ANNs [4].

Inspired by the fast information processing of spiking neural networks (SNNs) [5] as well as the results of studies that have used a NeuCube-based SNN as a classifier, which is an SNN architecture for spatio- and spectro-temporal brain data proposed in [6,7], we proposed an EEG-based emotion detection system that uses a NeuCube-based SNN as a classifier, with an EEG dataset of fewer than 100 samples [5,7,8]. The method was applied to address the following objectives: (i) to investigate how the SNN architecture NeuCube's connectivity, learning algorithms, and visualization of the learning processes inside the SNN helped in classification and analysis of functional changes in brain activity when using EEG technique to recognize emotion states; (ii) to build an EEG-based emotion detection system using an EEG dataset of fewer than 100 samples and no feature extraction methods, with a NeuCube-based SNN as a classifier, and without compromising accuracy. Overall, our proof-of-concept work towards emotion detection and classification using NeuCube-based SNN shows promise and will provide the basis for continued research in this direction.

The remainder of this paper is organized as follows: Section 2 introduces the main concepts of this study with background details; Section 3 explores and reviews related studies in the field of EEG-based emotion detection and SNN-based EEG classification; Section 4 illustrates our proposed system, the acquisition of EEG data, the experiments, and the evaluation design; Section 5 reports the experimental results; and Section 6 presents the conclusion.

2. Background

In this section, we introduce an overview of EEG-based emotion detection systems and applications, SNNs, and NeuCube-based SNNs.

2.1. EEG Correlates of Emotion

Emotions play a critical role in human interactions with the outer world and are considered an important factor in human actions and behaviors. Therefore, the detection and recognition of emotion-related information have become attractive research topics, such as in human–computer interaction (HCI) and affective computing studies and have opened a wide space for multiple applications. Such applications range from visualizing a user's emotional state to initializing a computer action based on this emotion, e.g., verbal feedback, or stimulating mini-games to initialize an application-dependent action, e.g., an e-learning application that can adjust the course to the current emotional state of the student [3,9].

Emotions can be measured objectively using various approaches, such as speech, gesture, body posture, or facial feature analyses, and also through physiological measurements that take advantage of sensors in direct contact with the user's body, such as heart rate, skin temperature, skin conductivity, and brain activity. One advantage of using physiological measurements to indicate the emotional state of users is that users lack the ability to manipulate their emotional state, which is hidden in these measurements, as they can do with other approaches [9].

EEG largely captures electrical activity by means of electrodes placed at specific locations on the scalp [10], following the international 10–20 system depicted in Figure 2. The emotional state that EEG-based emotion detection systems are intended to recognize is usually defined according to the 2-D arousal–valence emotional model; this model, proposed by Russell (1980), can map discrete emotion labels into the arousal–valence coordinate system [3], as shown in Figure 3.

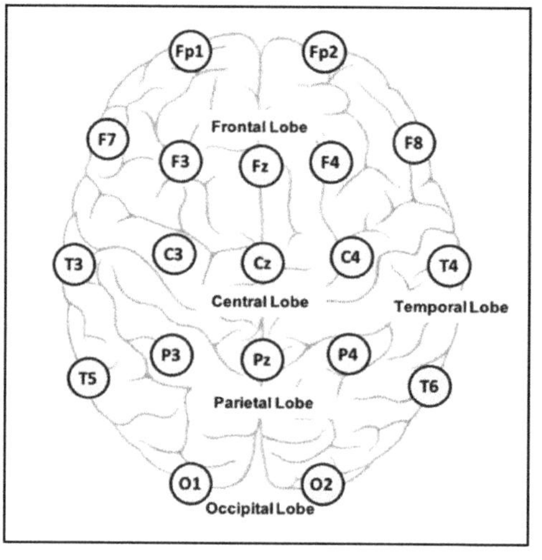

Figure 2. 10–20 system of electrode placement.

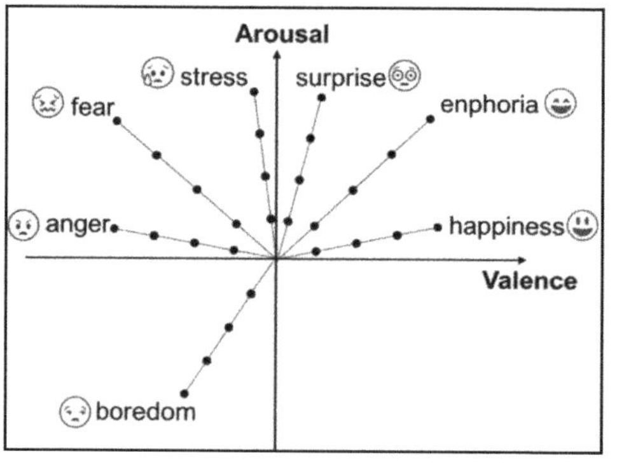

Figure 3. Arousal–valence emotional model.

2.2. EEG-Based Emotion Detection Applications

EEG-based emotion detection has been applied in numerous medical and non-medical fields. Consequently, numerous EEG-based BCI emotion detection systems and application have been developed that target different application areas. These applications are employed for both healthy individuals and unhealthy study participants. They all share the same research approach of using objective methods to determine affective emotional states.

In the following, we provide an overview and recent examples of applications that have been developed and studied for EEG-based emotion detection systems, categorizing them into five main areas including Medical and healthcare, Recreation, leisure and entertainment, Marketing, BCI aid and assistance, and Cognitive load estimation.

Medical and healthcare: This category includes research work that studies participants with medical conditions by comparing their affective state with the control group and experiments are conducted in clinical settings. These studies have suggested novel approaches for assisting, enhancing, mentoring, and diagnosing debilitative conditions of the study participants by using an EEG-based emotion detection technique. Medically related studies have detailed how EEG-based emotion detection systems are used to understand, diagnosis, and assess medical conditions. They have explored the relationship between symptoms and affective states in medical conditions such as disorder of consciousness [11], schizophrenia [12], Parkinson's disease [13], and autism [14,15].

Recreation, leisure and entertainment: This category included studies that proposed EEG-based emotion detection in gaming and other associated entertainment domains. For example, they were used for observing the relationship between multimedia data (music/video) and human emotions. The results were then used to explore the effects of these multimedia data on emotional affective states for different gender and age groups. In gaming research, some work sought to detect gamers' affective states in order to adapt to specific game's features such as level of difficulty, punishment, and encouragement. All of these were investigated using an EEG-based emotion detection system. Research groups in the HCI community have started pushing boundaries by trying to determine the extent of their ability to peer into a user's brain, if even roughly. Considering the minimally invasive nature of these devices and how they barely interfere with the day-to-day activities of a physically challenged person, researchers decided to further push the boundaries to ascertain the advantages that may accrue following what insight they may get in different application areas. Studies have explored BCI controlled recreational applications, such as games [16], virtual reality [17], brain-controlled art and music [18,19], and multimedia data tagging system [20,21].

Marketing: This category included studies that sought to understand consumer responses to market stimuli. During sales, a customer's emotions can be strongly influenced by the perception of his/her surroundings. Recognition of emotional responses reveal true consumer preferences and can improve and assist the (buying) process. An EEG-based emotion detection system helps in the marketing of products to potential buyers by offering personalized information to the user through an understanding of individual preferences. These individualized preferences can then be extrapolated to other customers with a view to making tailored advertising preferences [22,23].

BCI aid and assistance: These research studies aimed to explore how assistive technologies become more effective by recognizing the affective states of persons. Assistive research studies were used to identify skills, user experience, and limitations of potential users. They were also used to improve behavior, cognition, and emotion regulation. BCI studies began as a move towards incorporating assistive technological solutions for persons with significant physical disabilities. It further drew research enthusiasts when it became apparent that persons with physical disabilities wanted to communicate with others, as well as have some level of control over their environment. The answer was to create computer-based recreational activities. Integrated emotion recognition systems with assistive technologies make them more efficient by recognizing affective state. BCIs were further used to identify users' skills, experience, or limitations. Conversely, they were used to improve behavior, cognition, and emotion regulation [24,25].

Cognitive load estimation: This research work investigated how emotional states support learning processes. They assess an individual's degree of engagement, attention, and cognitive load under different conditions. They also determined how emotions affect the way users consume information in school by assessing their levels of engagement and learning. These studies sought to monitor the alertness of individuals in job performance, security-critical tasks, measuring and estimating alert levels of cognitive load during task performance. Emotion is one of the key elements involved in learning and education; it also affects decision-making, communication, and the ability to learn. Research studies found that an emotional state has the potential to influence one's thinking. Hence, measuring and estimating alertness levels and cognitive load during task performance can be applied in education and learning. This is done so as to assess the degree of engagement, attention, and cognitive load of a user under different conditions. Such cognitive tasks as listening to a lecture, solving logical problems, or workload assessments can benefit from BCI technologies [26,27].

2.3. NeuCube-Based Spiking Neural Networks

SNNs are considered the third generation of neural networks. The main difference between this generation and previous generations is the timing of potential spike firing of a neuron, which mainly depends on the spikes of other neurons. Depending on the input of the spiking neuron, it fires a spike or action potential at certain points in time, which could induce the postsynaptic potential of other spiking neurons according to an impulse response function; thus, information in an SNN is propagated by the timing of individual spikes. The input of the SNN must first be coded into sequences of neuronal spikes (spike trains) [28]. SNNs require a special learning rule, such as spike-timing-dependent plasticity (STDP), which adjusts the strength of a weight in response to the time difference between the pre- and postsynaptic spikes [29]. A significant number of researchers have used SNNs for different EEG-based pattern recognition problems and related them to the nature of information propagation in the SNN, which depends on the firing time of the spike and is close in nature to EEG data [30,31]. This makes SNNs an interesting method because they represent time and space compactly, process information rapidly, and can provide both time- and frequency-based information representation.

SNNs only accept data in forms of spike trains, thus input data should be first encoded into this form using special coding methods. Neurons in SNNs have the ability to generate action potentials or spikes when the pre-synaptic neurons exceed a threshold. Different neurons models have attempted to emulate this semi-biological behavior of SNN such as the spike response model (SRM), the Izhikevich neuron model, and the leaky integrated-and-fire (LIF) neuron. This behavior allows the weights of the SNN to increase if action potentials generated by the neurons decrease, otherwise based on the spike trains which induce the learning process of the SNN [4].

NeuCube is an SNN architecture for spatio- and spectro-temporal brain data, shown in Figure 4. The NeuCube architecture was first proposed by Nikola Kasabov for brain data modelling in [6] and was further developed as a multi-modular software/hardware system for large scale applications [5]. Basically, NeuCube-based SNN classification can be conducted in four steps:

1 Data encoding, in which EEG samples are converted into spike trains using encoding methods such as threshold-based representation (TBR), which generates a spike train whenever changes in the EEG data exceed a specific threshold.
2 SNN cube initialization, in which each neuron in the SNN cube is connected to its nearby neurons, which are within a specific distance threshold.
3 Training the cube using unsupervised learning, in which EEG data in the forms of spike trains are used to modify the initially set connection weights; thus, the same groups of spiking neurons in the SNN cube will be activated when similar input stimuli are presented.
4 Classification, in which the same dataset used for the unsupervised training phase is propagated to the SNN cube to train neurons in the output layer classifier. For each sample, a new neuron in the classifier is generated, and the state of the SNN cube is measured to establish a connection between this new neuron and a specific group of spiking neurons in the SNN cube. The state of the SNN

cube is measured to establish a connection between this new neuron and a specific group of spiking NeuCube parameters, such as the SNN learning rule rate, the encoding method threshold, and the spike firing rate, which can affect the classification accuracy; therefore, an optimization module is proposed in this architecture to obtain the values of some of these parameters, which could lead to enhanced accuracy. The weight of this connection adapts according to the datasets used to link each sample, represented as a neuron in the output layer to specific emotional stimuli (emotion class), represented as a specific group of spiking neurons in the SNN cube.

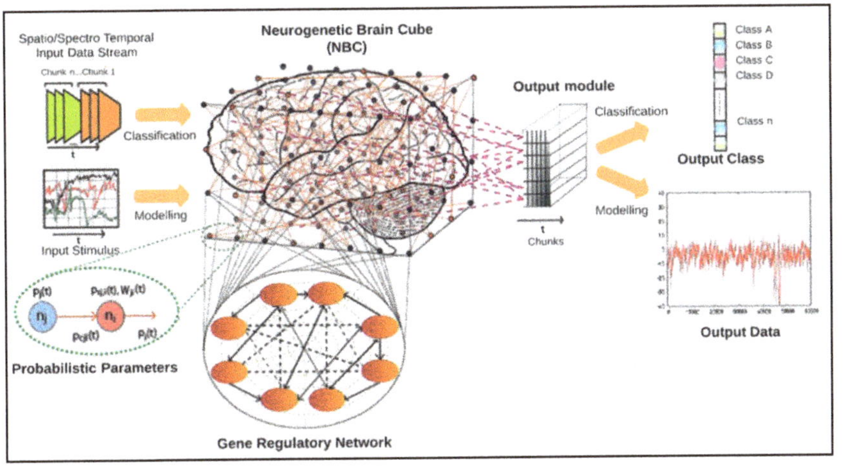

Figure 4. NeuCube model (Source: Kasabov 2012 [6]).

3. Related Works

Several studies have investigated the contribution of various feature selection and extraction methods as well as classification algorithms to the overall performance of EEG-based emotion detection systems. Although the number of research studies on EEG-based emotion recognition has been increasing in recent years, EEG-based emotion recognition still faces challenges, including low signal-to-noise ratios (SNRs), nonstationary signals, and high inter-subject variability that limits effective analysis and processing [32].

In [33], the researchers conducted an experimental study in which they applied EEG-based emotion detection in clinical settings. A total of 26 subjects participated in a music-listening experiment where their EEG was recorded using 32 electrodes while they listened to 16 music clips (30 s each) as stimuli. A total of 416 samples were each labeled with one of the following four emotion classes: joy (positive valence and high arousal), anger (negative valence and high arousal), sadness (negative valence and low arousal), or pleasure (positive valence and low arousal), which followed the 2-D valence–arousal emotion model. The EEG samples were classified using two learning models, namely multilayer perceptron (MLP) and support vector machine (SVM), with four feature types: the power spectrum density of all 30 channels (PSD30), power spectrum density of 24 channels (PSD24), differential asymmetry of 12 electrode pairs (DASM12), and rational asymmetry of 12 electrode pairs (RASM12), computed on each one of the five frequency ranges of the EEG signals. The experimental results showed that SVM obtained the best averaged classification accuracy of 82.29%.

In [10], the researchers developed four learning models, and power spectral features and power spectral asymmetry were extracted from the DEAP dataset. These features fed into all four learning models, which had a deep learning network (DLN) as their main component. The proposed DLN consisted of three hidden layers, an input layer, and three neuron output layers where the three neurons corresponded to the three levels of arousal or valence that had been classified separately in the study.

The first and second learning models consisted of a DLN with 100 and 50 hidden nodes in each layer, respectively, whereas the third learning model used principal component analysis (PCA) to reduce the number of features before feeding them into the DLN with 50 hidden nodes. The last model had the same structure as the third learning model except for its use of the covariate shift adaptation of principal components (CSA) to normalize each input feature, with the average of the previous feature values within a specific rectangular window, before applying PCA. The last model achieved the best classification accuracies for classifying the three levels of valence and arousal of 53.42% and 52.05%, respectively.

In [34], the researcher proposed a real-time emotion classification system. Four emotional classes—low arousal/low valence (LALV), low arousal/high valence (LAHV), high arousal/low valence (HALV), and high arousal/high valence (HAHV)—were classified with accuracies of 84.05% for arousal levels and 86.75% for valence levels using k-nearest neighbors (KNN) (k = 3). The features used with the classifier were extracted from the DEAP dataset by dividing EEG samples into several overlapping windows with widths between 2 s and 4 s, each of which was subsequently decomposed into five frequency bands using discrete wavelet transforms. Finally, entropy and energy were computed from each of these frequency bands and served as a feature vectors.

In [35], the researchers proposed an EEG-based emotion recognition method based on empirical mode decomposition (EMD), which is a data-driven signal processing analysis technique. Their method was used to decompose each EEG signal acquired from the DEAP dataset into eight or nine oscillations on various frequency scales called intrinsic mode functions (IMFs). The first four IMFs of each signal were selected to construct feature vectors according to their contribution to emotion detection determined, using a cumulative variance contribution rate test. Feature vectors were constructed by computing the sample of each one of the IMFs for each EEG signal and then used along with SVM to perform four binary class classifications, namely HAHV/LAHV, LAHV/LALV, LALV/HALV, and HALV/HAHV. This model obtained an average classification accuracy equal to 94.98%.

In [36], the researchers used a deep neural network (DNN) to identify human emotions using the DEAP dataset. Power spectral density (PSD) and frontal asymmetry features were extracted and then fed into the DNN to classify two classes by emotion dimension (arousal and valence), achieving accuracies of 82.0%. and 48.5%, respectively. Moreover, the DNN results were compared with those of a traditional EEG signal classification method, namely random forest (RF) classification, achieving a 48.5% classification accuracy.

In [37], PSD features were extracted in both time and frequency domains. Then, authors proposed the application of a deep convolutional neural network (deep CNN model) in emotion recognition and obtained accuracy of 88.76% and 85.75% on valence and arousal dimension, respectively.

Table 1 presents a comparison of the abovementioned studies with respect to the EEG dataset they acquired, the number and types of extracted features they computed, the number and types of classifiers they used, and the optimal accuracies they obtained.

A considerable number of researchers have taken a further step beyond conventional machine learning techniques to find promising concepts and methods for enhancing the performance of EEG-based emotion detection systems.

In [38], the researchers built an EEG ontology using a specific set of features, and then performed feature reduction by choosing the features most relevant to the emotional state using Spearman correlation coefficients. These coefficients were calculated between the EEG features and two emotional dimensions (arousal and valence). An analysis of variance (ANOVA) test was used to search for differences in activation on different arousal–valence levels. These two tests were computed on the EEG ontology, and then the most relevant features were selected to finalize the classification process with the C4.5 algorithm.

In [39], the authors proposed a special structure for an emotion detection system that builds and trains a separate classifier (SVM) for each EEG channel feature vector, as opposed to building one classifier and training it through the combination of all the channels' feature vectors. A weighted fusion of all these classifiers was used to detect the desired emotional label. This structure was suggested based on several studies that proved that the intensity at which emotional information is processed differs according to different brain areas.

Table 1. Comparison of different conventional studies on electroencephalogram (EEG)-based emotion detection.

Ref.	Dataset	Feature Extraction	Classifier	Accuracy
[33]	Own dataset	4	Multilayer perceptron (MLP) Support Vector Machine (SVM)	82.29%.
[10]	DEAP dataset	2	Deep learning network (DLN)-100 DLN-50 DLN-50 + PCA DLN-50 + PCA + covariate shift adaptation (CSA)	53.42% (valence) 52.05% (arousal)
[34]	DEAP dataset	2	k-nearest neighbors (KNN)	86.75% (valence) 84.05 %
[35]	DEAP dataset	1	SVM	94.98%
[36]	DEAP dataset	2	Deep neural network (DNN), Random forest (RF)	82.0%, 48.5%
[37]	DEAP dataset	1	Deep convolutional neural network (CNN)	88.76% (valence) 85.75% (arousal)

Because of SNNs' fast processing of information [5], they have been used in studies as a classifier, trained using an EEG dataset for various purposes. For example, in [40], an accuracy of 93.28% was achieved using an SNN and delta content extracted by wavelet transform from an EEG dataset, which was collected using the P3 Speller paradigm to classify P300 signals. These results showed that the SNN outperformed other algorithms used on the same dataset. In a recent study [41], the authors proposed using a spiking neural model (SNM) to discriminate EEG signals from motor imagery movements when it is necessary to avoid a long calibration session.

The use of NeuCube, which is an SNN architecture developed for spatio- and spectro-temporal brain data and proposed in [7], encouraged the researchers in [5] to conduct classification experiments based on different EEG datasets. A NeuCube-based SNN classifier was used in [8] to investigate the attention bias of consumers when a specific marketing stimulus was presented by classifying each EEG sample in a dataset of 90 total samples into five classes: alcoholic, nonalcoholic, design, drink color, and brand name. The classifier obtained an accuracy of 90%, which is superior to that obtained by MLP, MLR, and SVM. GO/NOGO cognitive patterns were measured in [42] based on EEG and using a NeuCube-based SNN as a classifier trained on 42 EEG samples. The classifier achieved an accuracy of 90.91%, which was superior compared with other traditional classifiers.

In recent literature, unsupervised novelty detection using SNN approach is proven to have high effectiveness [31,43]. Researchers reported that the SNN approach has a high potential to be explored and used to detect and recognize human cognitive and affective states. In [43], the SNN approach has been used on EEG signals processing and classification, They developed a model to use EEG data in order to provide insight into brain function in depression and to study the neurobiological characteristics of depressed individuals who respond to mindfulness.

In another recent publication [31], researchers built a SNN model for recognizing EEG data and classifying emotional states. Their experimental results showed that the SNN achieved the highest accuracy compared to other conventional approaches due to its processing capability for spatial and temporal data. In their experiments, they used two datasets, DEAP and SEED datasets. With the DEAP dataset, their model achieved accuracies of 74% on arousal, 78% on valence, 80% on dominance, and 86.27% on liking. With the SEED dataset, their model achieved an overall accuracy is 96.67%.

From the above-mentioned review, we concluded as follows. (i) The size of the datasets used in most of these studies was no smaller than 300 EEG samples. For example, in the DEAP dataset, 32 subjects participated in the EEG-recording experiments, in which each had an EEG sample recorded for each 40-s music clip stimulus. (ii) Feature extraction in most of these studies was not a minor task in terms of the number of features as well as the processes underlying their extraction, which emphasizes the need for a sufficient EEG dataset and effective feature extraction method for the accurate classification of emotions from EEG. (iii) EEG-based emotion detection is one of the EEG-based pattern recognition problems. These problems have been solved by several useful machine learning algorithms, and one promising algorithm that has yet to be investigated is SNN. (iv) SNN models have been developed effectively to enhance the analysis and understanding of spatio-temporal brain data and recognize cognitive and affective states. These reasons encouraged us to build an EEG-based emotion detection system with a smaller version of the DEAP dataset using a NeuCube-based SNN as a classifier.

4. Proposed System

In this section, we illustrate our methodology along with implementation details of our proposed solution. It consists of three stages: the construction of smaller versions of the DEAP dataset, classification with the NeuCube-based SNN classifier, and evaluation of the trained classifier's accuracy. Figure 5 shows the structure of the proposed solution model. Using this model, we performed four experiments, each of which used different sample sizes.

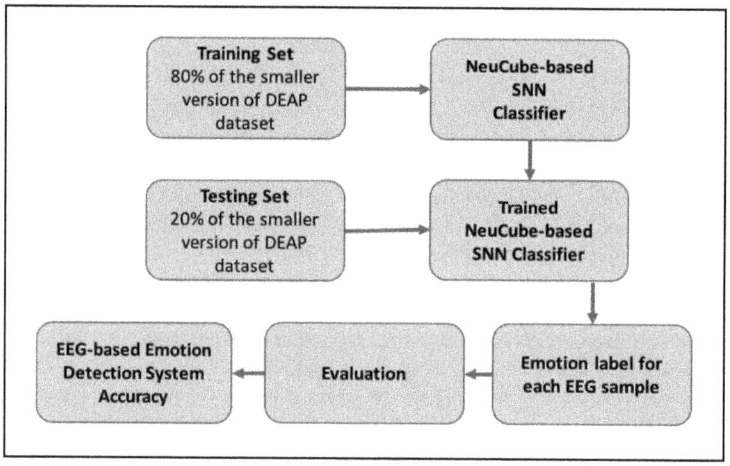

Figure 5. The proposed solution.

4.1. Dataset

The DEAP dataset is a multimodal benchmark dataset for the analysis of human affective states [44]. The EEG and peripheral physiological signals of 32 participants were recorded as each watched 40 1-min excerpts of music videos. Participants rated each video in terms of the levels of arousal, valence, like/dislike, dominance, and familiarity.

The sampling rate of the original recorded EEG data of 512 Hz was down-sampled to a sampling rate of 128 Hz with a bandpass frequency filter that ranged from 4.0–45.0 Hz, and the electrooculogram (EOG) artifacts were eliminated from the signals using a blind source separation method, namely independent component analysis (ICA).

In this study, we injected the preprocessed data directly into the learning model without being subjected to any feature extraction or selection process. The two EEG channels of FP1 and FP2 obtained good accuracy in [34], as did F3 and C4 in [35]; thus, we only used FP1, F3, C4 and C3 channels as the raw features of the dataset. We selected the EEG data points according to the accuracy achieved in [35] by selecting 1152 EEG data points from 34 s to 42 s, and related this selection to the participants' emotional stability in this segment of the 1-min music video stimuli.

We constructed four datasets with two different sizes, 60 and 40 samples, and we performed two binary classifications, one for valence levels and one for arousal levels, for each of these datasets to enable us to measure the classification accuracy corresponding to the dataset size. We performed four experiments, each of which was performed using one of the smaller-version datasets constructed from the DEAP dataset.

Experiment 1 (60-Exp1) used a 60-sample dataset constructed by selecting the first 10 trial samples of the first six participants, whereas Experiment 2 (40-Exp2) used a 40-sample dataset constructed by selecting the first 10 trial samples of the first four participants. Experiment 3 (60-Exp3) used a 60-sample dataset constructed by selecting 10 trial samples, from the eleventh trial to the twentieth trial, of six participants, starting from the seventh participant to the twelfth participant, whereas Experiment 4 (40-Exp4) used a 40-sample dataset constructed by selecting the first 40 samples of the second 60-sample dataset.

The EEG-based emotion classification proposed in this study was conducted according to the valence and arousal dimensions, with each dimension divided into high (ratings of 5–9) and low (ratings of 1–5) classes; thus, two binary classifications of valence and arousal were included in each of the four experiments.

Table 2 summarizes the description of the original DEAP dataset and this study's datasets, which were constructed from the original DEAP dataset.

Table 2. Description of the DEAP dataset and our smaller versions of DEAP.

Dataset /Dimension	Participants	Samples for Each Participant (Trial × Channel × Data)	Labels
Original DEAP	32	40 × 32 × 8064	1280 × 4
60-samples-Exp1	6	40 × 32 × 8064	60 × 2
40-samples-Exp2	4	40 × 32 × 8064	40 × 2
60-samples-Exp3	6	40 × 32 × 8064	60 × 2
40-samples-Exp4	4	40 × 32 × 8064	40 × 2

4.2. NeuCube-Based SNN Classifier

We performed our experiments using NeuCube v1.3 software implemented in Matlab. The NeuCube is a modular development system for SNN applications on spatio- and spectro-temporal data. It was developed by the Knowledge Engineering and Discovery Research Institute (KEDRI, www.kedri.aut.ac.nz). NeuCube is based on the evolving connectionist system (ECOS) principles and neuromorphic computations. It facilitates building spatiotemporal data machines (STDM) for problem solving such as classification, prediction, pattern recognition, data analysis and data understanding.

NeuCube includes modules for data encoding, unsupervised learning, supervised classification and regression, visualization, pattern discovery, and model optimization. NeuCube facilitates the building of SSN applications, using the following steps: input data transformation into spike sequences; mapping input variables into spiking neurons; deep unsupervised learning spatio-temporal spike sequences in a scalable 3D SNN reservoir; on-going learning and classification of data over time; dynamic parameter optimization; evaluating the time for predictive modelling; adaptation on new data, possibly in an on-line/real time mode; model visualization and interpretation for a better understanding of the data and the processes that generated it; implementation of a SNN model: von Neumann vs neuromorphic hardware systems.

The NeuCube-based classifier was built using the following four steps:

1. Data were encoded into spikes using the threshold-based representation (TBR) method with a 0.5 threshold.
2. The SNN cube was initialized with 1000 spiking neurons and a 2.5 small-world radius, which defined the distance that constrained the number of each neuron's initial connections to its neighboring neurons.
3. Unsupervised training of the cube was performed using a threshold for neuron firing = 0.5 and unsupervised STDP learning rate = 0.01.
4. The output layer classifier was classified with a modulation factor = 0.8 and drift value = 0.005. An architecture of the SNN cube trained using 60 samples is shown in Figure 6a, with the output layer when colored by true labels shown in Figure 6b, and when colored by predicted labels shown in Figure 6c.

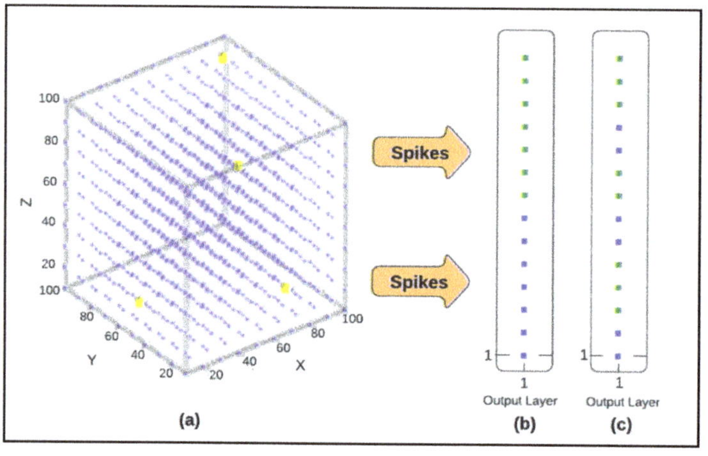

Figure 6. Architecture of the Spiking neural networks (SNN) cube trained using 60 samples (**a**), with the output layer colored by the true (**b**) and predicted (**c**) labels of the samples.

We assigned the NeuCube parameters as the values of the original NeuCube model, but further parameter optimization could lead to better accuracy.

For all the experiments, we divided the dataset into 80% training set and 20% testing set. The 20% of the dataset represent a testing set that has not been used during the training phase and the results are based on these new unseen samples which shows that the model could be generalized to a new subject. We evaluated our system performance by the accuracy of the classification in terms of the number of correctly classified emotions based on the EEG sample over all EEG samples in the testing set.

5. Results and Discussion

We evaluated the proposed system accuracy using four smaller versions of the DEAP dataset by performing a binary classification according to the valence dimension and a binary classification according to the arousal dimension for each version of the dataset. The results of the four experiments are listed below:

60-Exp1: A 60-sample EEG dataset was used to train and test the proposed system, obtaining an accuracy of 66.67% for valence classification and 69.23% for arousal classification. The accuracy of the low valence class was 0%, whereas that of the high valence class was 88.89%. Furthermore, the accuracy of the low arousal class was 100%, whereas that of the high arousal class was 33.33%.

40-Exp2: A 40-sample EEG dataset was used to train and test the proposed system, obtaining an accuracy of 55.56% for valence classification and 66.67% for arousal classification. The accuracy of the low valence class was 0%, whereas that of the high valence class was 83.33%. Furthermore, the accuracy of the low arousal class was 83.33%, whereas that of the high arousal class was 33.33%.

60-Exp3: A 60-sample EEG dataset was used to train and test the proposed system, obtaining an accuracy of 84.62% for valence classification and 61.54% for arousal classification. The accuracy of the low valence class was 0%, whereas that of the high valence class was 100%. Furthermore, the accuracy of the low arousal class was 57.14%, whereas that of the high arousal class was 66.67%.

40-Exp4: A 40-sample EEG dataset was used to train and test the proposed system, obtaining an accuracy of 66.67% for valence classification and 55.56% for arousal classification. The accuracy of the low valence class was 0%, whereas that of the high valence class was 85.71%. Furthermore, the accuracy of the low arousal class was 60%, whereas that of the high arousal class was 50%. Figure 7 presents a comparison of the valence experiments' results; Figure 8 presents a comparison of the arousal experiments' results; and Table 3 presents a comparison of all the experiments in both dimensions.

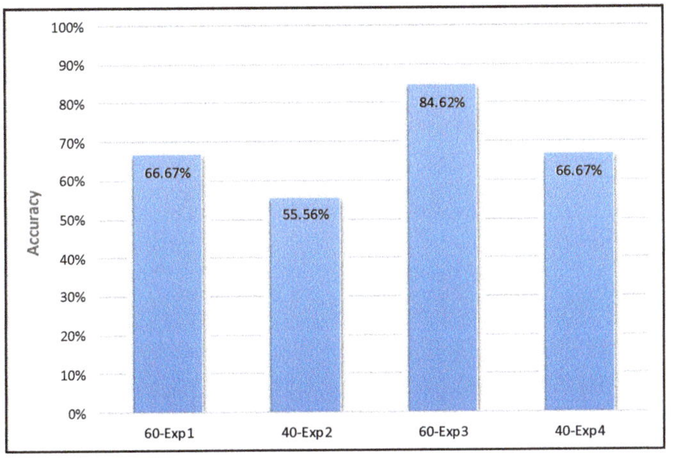

Figure 7. Comparison of the valence experiments' results.

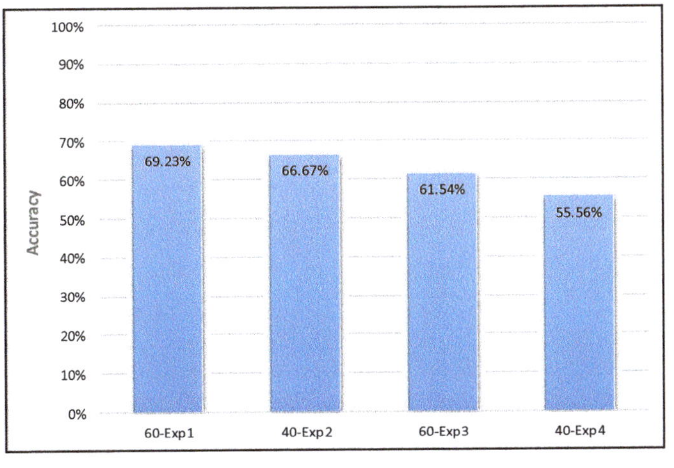

Figure 8. Comparison of the arousal experiments' results.

The classification accuracy obtained in all experiments ranged between 56% and 85%, as shown in Figures 7 and 8, which is comparable to that obtained in previous studies that used the same dataset for EEG-based emotion detection.

Table 3. Comparison of all experiments' results.

Sample Size/Emotion Dimension	Valence	Arousal
60-samples-Exp1	66.67%	69.23%
40-samples-Exp2	55.56%	66.67%
60-samples-Exp3	84.62%	61.54%
40-samples-Exp4	66.67%	55.56%

We used two EEG dataset sizes (60, 40), which were smaller than the datasets used in previous studies, as shown in in Table 3; however, we were able to obtain an accuracy comparable to those studies that used large versions of the same dataset.

These results demonstrate the potential ability of NeuCube-based SNNs as well as SNNs in general to learn to detect emotion from EEGs with a small EEG dataset and to learn relevant patterns in raw EEG datasets without any need to extract the features manually. Using a NeuCube-based SNN in an EEG-based emotion detection system may not improve classification accuracy significantly, but it provides an option for a building process for an EEG-based emotion detection system that is lightweight in terms of a small EEG sample size and with no feature extraction processes involved.

In previous studies, the extraction of relevant features from the EEG dataset involved several complex methods. By contrast, in this study, we did not include any feature extraction method and fed the classifier directly with the EEG dataset; however, we still obtained an accuracy comparable to other studies that used several feature extraction methods on the same dataset, as shown in Table 4 and Figure 9.

Table 4. Comparison with other studies that used the DEAP dataset.

	Study	Dataset Subjects (Trial × Channel × Data)	Feature Extraction Methods	Accuracy Valence	Accuracy Arousal
	Jirayucharoensak et al. [10]	32 (40 × 32 × 8064)	2	53.42%	52.05%
	Luo et al. [31]	32 (40 × 32 × 8064)	1	78%	74%
	Mohammadi et al. [34]	32 (40 × 10 × 8064)	2	86.75 %	84.05 %
	Chen et al. [37]	32 (40 × 32 × 128)	5	88.76%	85.75%
Proposed method	60-Exp1	6 (10 × 4 × 1152)	0	66.67%	69.67%
	40-Exp2	4 (10 × 4 × 1152)	0	55.56%	66.67%
	60-Exp3	6 (10 × 4 × 1152)	0	84.62%	61.54%
	40-Exp4	4 (10 × 4 × 1152)	0	66.67%	55.56%

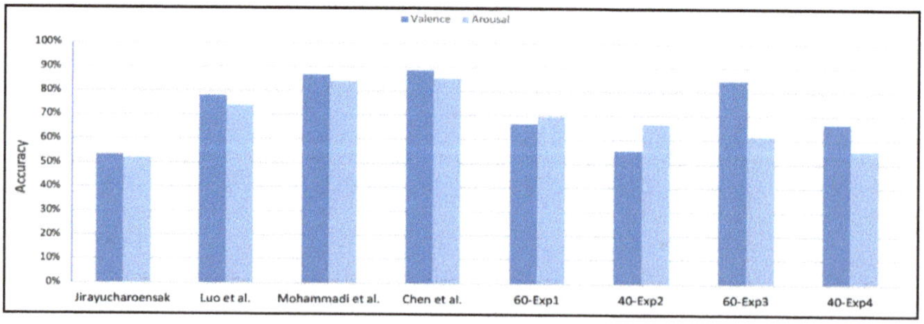

Figure 9. Comparison with other studies that used the DEAP dataset.

We also tested some state-of-the-art traditional machine learning classifiers which included Naïve Bayes, Bayesian Network, Logistics Regression, Decision Tree, Support Vector Machine (SVM)and k-nearest neighbors (KNN). The average classification accuracy obtained in all experiments showed that SVM obtained the highest average accuracy of 62.71% followed by Bayesian network and KNN which achieved average accuracy of 61.88% and 61.46%, respectively.

6. Conclusions

BCI research studies were initially focused on applications for persons with some degree of impaired motor disability. Over the years, many EEG-based BCI emotion detection systems have been developed that targeted different application areas. They all shared the same research approach of using objective methods to determine affective emotional states. In recent times, alternative applications in healthy human study participants have increased. This later research in able-bodied humans has gained popularity for EEG-based BCI investigative research purposes.

In this study, we proposed a lightweight building process for an EEG-based emotion detection system, in terms of small EEG sample size and no feature extraction methods, using a NeuCube-based SNN. We constructed four small versions of the DEAP dataset with 40 and 60 EEG samples to perform two binary classifications according to the valence and arousal emotional dimensions. The results showed that the proposed system obtained a comparable accuracy with that of other studies that used the larger version of the same dataset with the involvement of feature extraction processes.

Although good experimental results have been achieved with our proposed NeuCube-based SNN model, further research and investigation is still needed on how to select, construct and optimize learning models to obtain a higher classification accuracy and robustness model for EEG-based emotion recognition. Therefore, we encourage the investigation of NeuCube-based SNN classifiers and other architectures of SNNs in an EEG-based emotion detection system with respect to: (i) different EEG sample sizes, (ii) different parameters, (iii) with and without a feature extraction method, and (iv) performance of multiclass classification and regression according to the different emotional dimensions.

Author Contributions: K.A. conceived, designed, performed the experiment; analyzed and interpreted the data; and drafted the manuscript. A.A.-N. reviewed and edited the manuscript, and contributed to the analysis and discussion. H.K. supervised this study, and reviewed the manuscript. All authors have read and agreed to the published version of the manuscript.

Funding: This research received no external funding.

Acknowledgments: This research project was supported by a grant from the Research Center of the Female Scientific and Medical Colleges, Deanship of Scientific Research, King Saud University.

Conflicts of Interest: The authors declare no conflict of interest.

References

1. Fernando Nicolas-Alonso, L.; Gomez-Gil, J. Brain computer interfaces, a review. *Sensors* **2012**, *12*, 1211–1279. [CrossRef] [PubMed]
2. Shih, J.J.; Krusienski, D.J.; Wolpaw, J.R. Brain-Computer Interfaces in Medicine. In *Proceedings of the Mayo Clinic Proceedings*; Elsevier BV: New York, NY, USA, 2012; Volume 87, pp. 268–279.
3. Al-Nafjan, A.; Hosny, M.; Al-Ohali, Y.; Al-Wabil, A. Review and classification of emotion recognition based on EEG brain-computer interface system research: A systematic review. *Appl. Sci.* **2017**, *7*, 1239. [CrossRef]
4. Tavanaei, A.; Ghodrati, M.; Kheradpisheh, S.R.; Masquelier, T.; Maida, A. Deep learning in spiking neural networks. *Neural Netw.* **2019**, *111*, 47–63. [CrossRef] [PubMed]
5. Kasabov, N.; Capecci, E. Spiking neural network methodology for modelling, classification and understanding of EEG spatio-temporal data measuring cognitive processes. *Inf. Sci.* **2015**, *294*, 565–575. [CrossRef]
6. Kasabov, N. NeuCube EvoSpike Architecture for Spatio-temporal Modelling and Pattern Recognition of Brain Signals. In *Computer Vision*; Springer Science and Business Media LLC: Trento, Italy, 2012; Volume 7477, pp. 225–243.

7. Kasabov, N. NeuCube: A spiking neural network architecture for mapping, learning and understanding of spatio-temporal brain data. *Neural Netw.* **2014**, *52*, 62–76. [CrossRef]
8. Doborjeh, Z.G.; Doborjeh, M.G.; Kasabov, N. Attentional bias pattern recognition in spiking neural networks from spatio-temporal EEG data. *Cogn. Comput.* **2017**, *10*, 35–48. [CrossRef]
9. Peter, C.; Peter, C.; Urban, B. Emotion in human-computer interaction. In *Expanding the Frontiers of Visual Analytics and Visualization*; Springer: London, UK, 2012; pp. 239–262.
10. Jirayucharoensak, S.; Pan-Ngum, S.; Israsena, P. EEG-based emotion recognition using deep learning network with principal component based covariate shift adaptation. *Sci. World J.* **2014**, *2014*, 1–10. [CrossRef] [PubMed]
11. Pan, J.; Xie, Q.; Huang, H.; He, Y.; Sun, Y.; Yu, R.; Li, Y. Emotion-related consciousness detection in patients with disorders of consciousness through an EEG-based BCI system. *Front. Hum. Neurosci.* **2018**, *12*, 12. [CrossRef]
12. Gica, S.; Poyraz, B.C.; Gulec, H. Are emotion recognition deficits in patients with schizophrenia states or traits? A 6-month follow-up study. *Indian J. Psychiatry* **2019**, *61*, 45–52. [PubMed]
13. Iyer, K.K.; Au, T.R.; Angwin, A.J.; Copland, D.A.; Dissanayaka, N.N. Source activity during emotion processing and its relationship to cognitive impairment in Parkinson's disease. *J. Affect. Disord.* **2019**, *253*, 327–335. [CrossRef]
14. Charpentier, J.; Kovarski, K.; Houy-Durand, E.; Malvy, J.; Saby, A.; Bonnet-Brilhault, F.; Latinus, M.; Gomot, M. Emotional prosodic change detection in autism Spectrum disorder: An electrophysiological investigation in children and adults. *J. Neurodev. Disord.* **2018**, *10*, 28. [CrossRef]
15. Malaia, E.; Cockerham, D.; Rublein, K. Visual integration of fear and anger emotional cues by children on the autism spectrum and neurotypical peers: An EEG study. *Neuropsychologia* **2019**, *126*, 138–146. [CrossRef]
16. Alakus, T.B.; Gonen, M.; Turkoglu, I. Database for an emotion recognition system based on EEG signals and various computer games—GAMEEMO. *Biomed. Signal Process. Control* **2020**, *60*, 101951. [CrossRef]
17. Stavroulia, K.E.; Christofi, M.; Baka, E.; Michael-Grigoriou, D.; Magnenat-Thalmann, N.; Lanitis, A. Assessing the emotional impact of virtual reality-based teacher training. *Int. J. Inf. Learn. Technol.* **2019**, *36*, 192–217. [CrossRef]
18. Feradov, F.; Mporas, I.; Ganchev, T. Evaluation of features in detection of dislike responses to audio–visual stimuli from EEG signals. *Computers* **2020**, *9*, 33. [CrossRef]
19. Proverbio, A.M.; Camporeale, E.; Brusa, A. Multimodal recognition of emotions in music and facial expressions. *Front. Hum. Neurosci.* **2020**, *14*, 14. [CrossRef] [PubMed]
20. Hsu, J.-L.; Zhen, Y.-L.; Lin, T.-C.; Chiu, Y.-S. Affective content analysis of music emotion through EEG. *Multimedia Syst.* **2017**, *24*, 195–210. [CrossRef]
21. Gupta, R.; Abadi, M.K.; Cabré, J.A.C.; Morreale, F.; Falk, T.H.; Sebs, N. A Quality Adaptive Multimodal Affect Recognition System for User-Centric Multimedia Indexing. In *Proceedings of the 2016 ACM on International Conference on Multimedia Retrieval—ICMR '16*; Association for Computing Machinery (ACM): New York, NY, USA, 2016; pp. 317–320.
22. Aldayel, M.; Ykhlef, M.; Al-Nafjan, A. Deep learning for EEG-based preference classification in neuromarketing. *Appl. Sci.* **2020**, *10*, 1525. [CrossRef]
23. Wei, Z.; Wu, C.; Wang, X.; Supratak, A.; Wang, P.; Guo, Y. Using support vector machine on EEG for advertisement impact assessment. *Front. Neurosci.* **2018**, *12*, 76. [CrossRef]
24. Lamti, H.A.; Ben Khelifa, M.M.; Alimi, A.M.; Gorce, P. Emotion detection for wheelchair navigation enhancement. *Robot* **2014**, *34*, 1209–1226. [CrossRef]
25. López-Hernández, J.L.; González-Carrasco, I.; López-Cuadrado, J.L.; Ruiz, B. Towards the recognition of the emotions of people with visual disabilities through brain-computer interfaces. *Sensors* **2019**, *19*, 2620. [CrossRef] [PubMed]
26. Khosrowabadi, R. Stress and perception of emotional stimuli: Long-term stress rewiring the brain. *Basic Clin. Neurosci. J.* **2018**, *9*, 107–120. [CrossRef] [PubMed]
27. Mehmood, R.M.; Lee, H.J. Towards building a computer aided education system for special students using wearable sensor technologies. *Sensors* **2017**, *17*, 317. [CrossRef] [PubMed]
28. Pavlidis, N.G.; Tasoulis, D.; Plagianakos, V.; Nikiforidis, G.; Vrahatis, M. Spiking neural network training using evolutionary algorithms. In *Proceedings of the 2005 IEEE International Joint Conference on Neural Networks*; IEEE: Montreal, QC, Canada, 2005; Volume 4, pp. 2190–2194.

29. Tan, C.; Šarlija, M.; Kasabov, N. Spiking neural networks: Background, recent development and the NeuCube architecture. *Neural Process. Lett.* **2020**, 1–27. [CrossRef]
30. Taherkhani, A.; Belatreche, A.; Li, Y.; Cosma, G.; Maguire, L.P.; McGinnity, T. A review of learning in biologically plausible spiking neural networks. *Neural Netw.* **2020**, *122*, 253–272. [CrossRef]
31. Luo, Y.; Fu, Q.; Xie, J.; Qin, Y.; Wu, G.; Liu, J.; Jiang, F.; Cao, Y.; Ding, X. EEG-based emotion classification using spiking neural networks. *IEEE Access* **2020**, *8*, 46007–46016. [CrossRef]
32. Roy, Y.; Banville, H.; Albuquerque, I.; Gramfort, A.; Falk, T.H.; Faubert, J. Deep learning-based electroencephalography analysis: A systematic review. *J. Neural Eng.* **2019**, *16*, 051001. [CrossRef]
33. Lin, Y.-P.; Wang, C.-H.; Jung, T.-P.; Wu, T.-L.; Jeng, S.-K.; Duann, J.-R.; Chen, J.-H. EEG-based emotion recognition in music listening. *IEEE Trans. Biomed. Eng.* **2010**, *57*, 1798–1806. [CrossRef]
34. Mohammadi, Z.; Frounchi, J.; Amiri, M. Wavelet-based emotion recognition system using EEG signal. *Neural Comput. Appl.* **2016**, *28*, 1985–1990. [CrossRef]
35. Zhang, Y.; Ji, X.; Zhang, S. An approach to EEG-based emotion recognition using combined feature extraction method. *Neurosci. Lett.* **2016**, *633*, 152–157. [CrossRef]
36. Al-Nafjan, A.; Hosny, M.; Al-Wabil, A.; Al-Ohali, Y. Classification of human emotions from electroencephalogram (EEG) signal using deep neural network. *Int. J. Adv. Comput. Sci. Appl.* **2017**, *8*, 419–425. [CrossRef]
37. Chen, J.X.; Zhang, P.W.; Mao, Z.J.; Huang, Y.F.; Jiang, D.M.; Zhang, Y.N. Accurate EEG-based emotion recognition on combined features using deep convolutional neural networks. *IEEE Access* **2019**, *7*, 44317–44328. [CrossRef]
38. Chen, J.; Hu, B.; Moore, P.; Zhang, X.; Ma, X. Electroencephalogram-based emotion assessment system using ontology and data mining techniques. *Appl. Soft Comput.* **2015**, *30*, 663–674. [CrossRef]
39. Li, X.; Yan, J.-Z.; Chen, J.-H. Channel division based multiple classifiers fusion for emotion recognition using EEG signals. *ITM Web Conf.* **2017**, *11*, 07006. [CrossRef]
40. Goel, P.; Liu, H.; Brown, D.; Datta, A. On the use of spiking neural network for EEG classification. *Int. J. Knowl.-Based Intell. Eng. Syst.* **2008**, *12*, 295–304. [CrossRef]
41. Salazar-Varas, R.; Vazquez, R.A. Evaluating spiking neural models in the classification of motor imagery EEG signals using short calibration sessions. *Appl. Soft Comput.* **2018**, *67*, 232–244. [CrossRef]
42. Doborjeh, M.G.; Wang, G.Y.; Kasabov, N.K.; Kydd, R.; Russell, B. A spiking neural network methodology and system for learning and comparative analysis of EEG data from healthy versus addiction treated versus addiction not treated subjects. *IEEE Trans. Biomed. Eng.* **2015**, *63*, 1830–1841. [CrossRef]
43. Doborjeh, Z.; Doborjeh, M.; Taylor, T.; Kasabov, N.; Wang, G.Y.; Siegert, R.; Sumich, A. Spiking Neural network modelling approach reveals how mindfulness training rewires the brain. *Sci. Rep.* **2019**, *9*, 1–15. [CrossRef]
44. Koelstra, S.; Muhl, C.; Soleymani, M.; Lee, J.-S.; Yazdani, A.; Ebrahimi, T.; Pun, T.; Nijholt, A.; Patras, I. DEAP: A database for emotion analysis; using physiological signals. *IEEE Trans. Affect. Comput.* **2011**, *3*, 18–31. [CrossRef]

brain sciences

Article

Independent Components of EEG Activity Correlating with Emotional State

Yasuhisa Maruyama [1], Yousuke Ogata [1,2], Laura A. Martínez-Tejada [1], Yasuharu Koike [1,2] and Natsue Yoshimura [1,2,3,4,*]

1 Institute of Innovative Research, Tokyo Institute of Technology, Yokohama, Kanagawa 226-8503, Japan; maruyama.y.ae@m.titech.ac.jp (Y.M.); y.ogata1110@gmail.com (Y.O.); martinez.l.aa@m.titech.ac.jp (L.A.M.-T.); koike@pi.titech.ac.jp (Y.K.)
2 Department of Advanced Neuroimaging, Integrative Brain Imaging Center, National Center of Neurology and Psychiatry, Kodaira, Tokyo 187-8551, Japan
3 PRESTO, JST, Kawaguchi, Saitama 332-0012, Japan
4 Neural Information Analysis Laboratories, ATR, Kyoto 619-0288, Japan
* Correspondence: yoshimura.n.ac@m.titech.ac.jp

Received: 12 August 2020; Accepted: 23 September 2020; Published: 25 September 2020

Abstract: Among brain-computer interface studies, electroencephalography (EEG)-based emotion recognition is receiving attention and some studies have performed regression analyses to recognize small-scale emotional changes; however, effective brain regions in emotion regression analyses have not been identified yet. Accordingly, this study sought to identify neural activities correlating with emotional states in the source space. We employed independent component analysis, followed by a source localization method, to obtain distinct neural activities from EEG signals. After the identification of seven independent component (IC) clusters in a k-means clustering analysis, group-level regression analyses using frequency band power of the ICs were performed based on Russell's valence–arousal model. As a result, in the regression of the valence level, an IC cluster located in the cuneus predicted both high- and low-valence states and two other IC clusters located in the left precentral gyrus and the precuneus predicted the low-valence state. In the regression of the arousal level, the IC cluster located in the cuneus predicted both high- and low-arousal states and two posterior IC clusters located in the cingulate gyrus and the precuneus predicted the high-arousal state. In this proof-of-concept study, we revealed neural activities correlating with specific emotional states across participants, despite individual differences in emotional processing.

Keywords: brain-computer interface (BCI); electroencephalography (EEG); emotion recognition; independent component analysis (ICA); regression

1. Introduction

Emotion plays an important role in daily life, because it enriches communication. To achieve emotional interaction between human beings and computers, electroencephalography (EEG)-based emotion recognition is gaining attention in brain-computer interface (BCI) studies. For engineering purposes, many studies have performed emotion classification using various types of EEG features [1–3]. In [4], emotion classification based on Russell's valence–arousal model was performed using event-related potentials (ERPs) and event-related oscillations calculated from EEG recorded during affective picture viewing. Russell's valence–arousal model is a widely-recognized model of emotion, and in this model, emotions are represented in the space of two axes: valence (ranging from pleasant to unpleasant state) and arousal (ranging from excited to calm state), as illustrated in Figure 1a [5]. Among many emotion classification studies based on EEG, some studies estimated source activities in the brain and performed classification using only emotion-related source signals [6–9]. Padilla-Buritica and colleagues reconstructed source-level signals from scalp EEG and classified emotions using signals extracted from the selected brain regions [6]. Their results showed improvement of prediction accuracy by estimation of source signals combined with the appropriate selection of brain regions from which features used in the classification analysis were computed. Additionally, in EEG-based emotion recognition studies, identification of common EEG features across individuals is required to create models that can be generalized to various people, although there are large individual differences in emotional processing and many studies tested participant-dependent models [10].

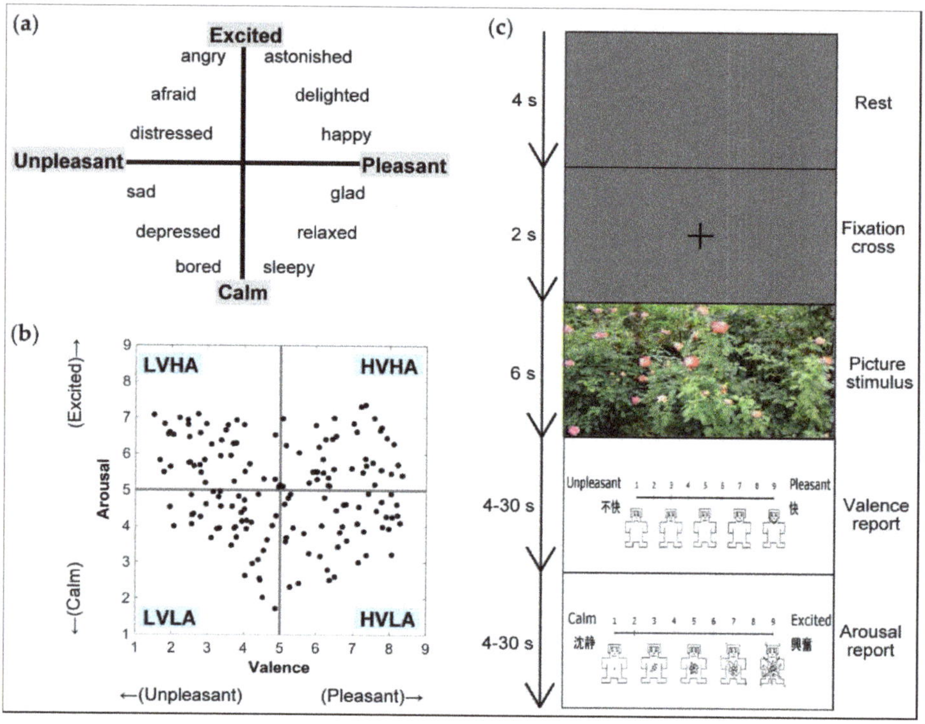

Figure 1. Experimental settings. (**a**) Schema of Russell's valence–arousal model [5]. (**b**) The distribution of the International Affective Picture System normative ratings of the 160 pictures used in the current study. On the valence axis, values of 9, 5, and 1 represent pleasant, neutral, and unpleasant states, respectively. On the arousal axis, values of 9, 5, and 1 represent excited, neutral, and calm states, respectively. HVHA, high valence and high arousal; HVLA, high valence and low arousal; LVHA, low valence and high arousal; LVLA, low valence and low arousal. (**c**) Trial flow. Each trial consisted of 4 s of rest, 2 s of fixation cross presentation, 6 s of picture stimulus presentation, and 4–30 s of reporting of the felt valence and arousal levels. Valence and arousal levels were reported using a computerized visual analog scale with a self-assessment manikin (SAM; [11]). In the valence and arousal reporting scales, the emotions were written in English and Japanese at both ends of the scales.

In addition to emotion classification studies which are based on a limited number of pre-defined emotional categories, several studies have performed EEG-based or electrocorticography (ECoG)-based emotion or mood state regression/correlation analyses to recognize small-scale emotional changes [12–30]. McFarland and colleagues performed canonical correlation analysis (CCA) to predict participants' emotional states from the sensor-level features of EEG recorded during affective picture viewing [22]. Their results showed difficulty in attaining good prediction accuracy in the test set. Similar to the classification analyses, the use of source-level signals might improve the prediction accuracy in regression analysis. However, to the best of our knowledge, no study has identified effective brain regions in EEG-based emotion regression.

To estimate source-level neural activities, independent component analysis (ICA) with subsequent dipole fitting has often been used. ICA is a signal separation method that linearly decomposes multi-channel data into independent signals [31]. The application of ICA to EEG data enables extraction of distinct neural activities that are free from any type of noise and whose activities are independent of each other. Localization of the sources of independent components (ICs) can be performed based on their projections onto the scalp, which allows investigation at the source level. ICA with subsequent source estimation methods has often been applied in EEG studies investigating emotional processing in the brain [32–38], suggesting the suitability of this method for the identification of effective brain regions in EEG-based emotion regression.

Accordingly, this proof-of-concept study elucidated brain regions that recognize small-scale emotional changes by using regression analysis. We applied ICA to EEG data captured during affective picture viewing and then grouped the obtained ICs into IC clusters by a k-means clustering method. In the regression analyses, valence and arousal levels were predicted from theta, alpha, beta, and gamma band power of ICs, since frequency band power has been one of the most popular features in EEG-based emotion classification studies [2]. A leave-one-participant-out approach was used to identify effective features that are common across participants, and emotional state-specific regression analyses were introduced with the aim of improving regression performance based on functional magnetic resonance imaging (fMRI) studies suggesting difference of the neural activities between high- and low-valence states and between high- and low-arousal states [39,40].

2. Materials and Methods

2.1. Participants

Twenty-six healthy human participants (10 females; mean age [standard deviation (S.D.)]: 25.2 [4.1] years) with normal or corrected-to-normal vision participated in this study. All participants were right-handed and had no history of psychiatric or neurological disorders. Data obtained from 1 male participant were excluded from the analysis because of an unacceptably noisy signal. The experimental protocol was approved by the ethics committee of the Tokyo Institute of Technology (Approval No. A17011) and conducted in accordance with the Declaration of Helsinki. The procedures were explained to each participant and written informed consent was obtained prior to the experiment.

2.2. Stimuli

Pictures selected from the International Affective Picture System (IAPS; [41]) were used as stimuli to induce emotion. The IAPS is commonly used in research on emotion. It provides general information on the emotion induced by each picture stimulus, since all IAPS pictures have normative ratings of valence, arousal, and dominance (ranging from controlled to in-control) levels. These ratings are mean values of multiple participants' ratings obtained in previous research. Figure 1b illustrates the distribution of normative ratings of IAPS pictures used in this study in the valence–arousal plane. Both valence and arousal axes ranged from 1 to 9 (9 = pleasant in the valence axis and excited in the arousal axis, 1 = unpleasant in the valence axis and calm in the arousal axis). A value of 5 represented a neutral level in both axes. For this study, pictures covering a wide area of the valence–arousal plane were selected. Hereafter, we refer to values higher or lower than 5 in valence or arousal ratings as belonging to a high or low emotional state, respectively. We selected 160 pictures distributed equally in each of the four quadrants (40 pictures per quadrant: high valence and high arousal [HVHA], high valence and low arousal [HVLA], low valence and high arousal [LVHA], and low valence and low arousal [LVLA]).

2.3. Experimental Task

Participants were positioned sitting in a reclining chair in a sound-attenuated chamber and instructed to look at a monitor positioned approximately 1 m away from their eyes during the experiment. Each trial consisted of 4 s of rest, 2 s of fixation cross presentation, 6 s of picture stimulus presentation, and 2 reporting periods (Figure 1c). During the reporting periods, participants were asked to report the valence and arousal levels they felt during the presentation of the picture stimulus by using a computerized visual analog scale ranging from 1 to 9 (in 0.1-point steps) and a touch pad, within 30 s. The minimum reporting time was set to 4 s to ensure that the participants were reporting accurately, and not perfunctorily. A self-assessment manikin (SAM; [11]) was placed below the visual analog scales to assist the participants in reporting. We instructed the participants not to think about the reporting periods during picture stimulus presentation in order to avoid such thoughts influencing EEG signals during picture stimulus viewing. The experiment consisted of eight sessions, with each session comprising 20 trials. The picture stimuli were presented in a pseudo-random order, so that each of the 4 quadrants (HVHA, HVLA, LVHA, and LVLA) consisted of 5 pictures presented in 1 session, thereby, equalizing the emotions induced by the stimuli across the sessions. Participants were allowed to take breaks of unlimited duration between sessions. Before the experiment, we explained the meanings of the valence and arousal axes to the participants and allowed them to rehearse using three practice picture stimuli that were not used in the subsequent experiment. All images were presented using a 24-inch monitor connected to a computer, and MATLAB R2018b (The MathWorks, Inc., Natick, MA, USA) and Psychophysics toolbox [42–44] were used to control the experimental program.

2.4. EEG Data Acquisition

EEG signals were recorded from 64 channels using a Biosemi Active Two amplifier system with active sensors (Biosemi, Amsterdam, Netherlands) at a sampling rate of 2048 Hz. All EEG channels were attached to the participant's scalp using electrically conductive gel, according to the International 10–20 system, with two reference channels attached to their earlobes.

2.5. EEG Data Processing

EEG data were processed using MATLAB R2018b and EEGLAB 14.1.2 software [45] (Figure 2). First, we set the reference signal as the average of the signals at both earlobes. We applied a high-pass finite impulse response (FIR) filter at 0.5 Hz and a low-pass FIR filter at 45 Hz to the raw continuous 64-channel data to attenuate the noise, and subsequently down-sampled the signal to 512 Hz to reduce the computational cost. To clean the data, we rejected and interpolated noisy channels based on visual inspection after extracting the 6-s epochs of picture stimulus presentation. Then, we removed epochs containing artefacts, such as muscle activities, by visual inspection, and concatenated all the remaining epochs. On average, 1.04 channels were rejected and 5.2% of epochs were removed. Following this preprocessing, we applied adaptive mixture ICA (AMICA, https://sccn.ucsd.edu/~jason/amica_web.html; [46]) to the data after changing the reference to the average of all 64-channel signals and reducing the data dimensions to their rank by principal component analysis. Subsequently, we used the DIPFIT3 function (https://sccn.ucsd.edu/wiki/A08:_DIPFIT) of the FieldTrip toolbox [47] to locate the equivalent current source dipole of each IC, based on boundary element model (BEM) of the Montreal Neurological Institute (MNI) standard brain. To perform the analysis using only ICs originating from brain activity, we identified and extracted the brain ICs. In this evaluation, we excluded ICs whose residual variances in the dipole fitting procedure exceeded 15% [31], those with dipole locations that were localized outside the brain, or those whose characteristics such as power spectral densities (PSDs) and time series activities across epochs (ERP images) did not appear to be brain activities by visual inspection. In total, 212 ICs (between 3 and 14 ICs per participant, mean 8.48) were selected as brain ICs.

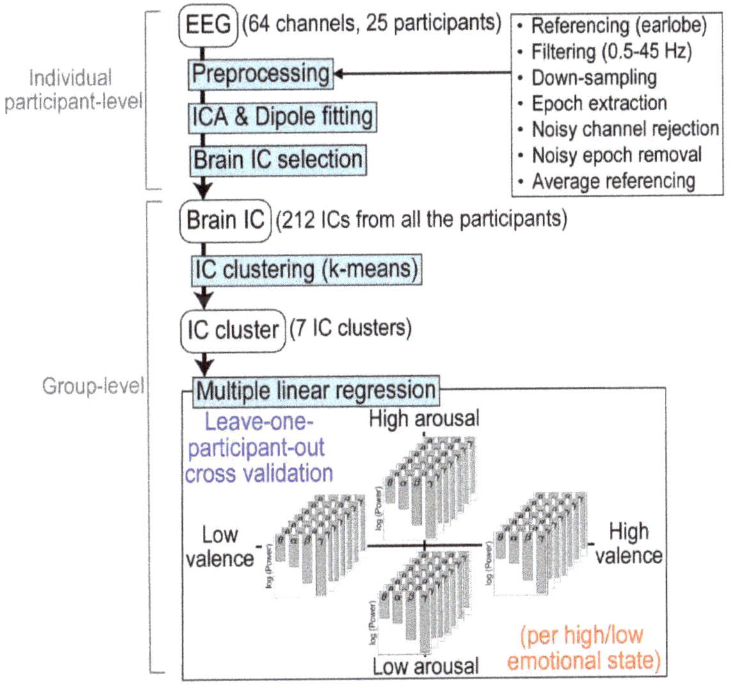

Figure 2. Flow of data processing and analysis. In the regression analysis, valence and arousal levels were predicted by inter-participant regression from logarithms of theta (4–7 Hz), alpha (8–13 Hz), beta (14–30 Hz), and gamma (31–45 Hz) band power of independent components (ICs).

Finally, we conducted a cluster analysis to identify common ICs across participants by using a k-means clustering method in EEGLAB. All brain ICs were clustered by their characteristics, such as scalp topographies, dipole locations, and ERPs in 0–500 milliseconds. To reduce the total number of the dimension, principal component analysis was performed on each of the scalp topography and ERP data, and top 10 and 5 principal components were included in the cluster analysis, respectively. Accordingly, the k-means clustering analysis was performed in the 18-dimensional space (3 dimensions for the dipole locations, 10 for the scalp topography, and 5 for the ERP). The number of clusters (k) was set to a value that we considered to yield plausible clustering results in terms of consistency of characteristics across ICs within the same cluster and distinctness of characteristics between different IC clusters, after several changes in k. The threshold level for outliers was set to 3 S.D., and only IC clusters with ICs present in more than half of all participants (i.e., 13) were reported. IC clusters were labeled using automated anatomical labeling (AAL; [48]) in MRIcron software (http://people.cas.sc.edu/rorden/mricron/index.html; [49]), based on the MNI coordinates of centroids of IC clusters. If the coordinates were judged to be in the white matter by AAL, the nearest labels in the MNI space were reported.

2.6. Regression Analyses

The regression analysis was performed in a leave-one-participant-out manner and per emotional state: high-valence, low-valence, high-arousal, or low-arousal state. We predicted the valence and arousal levels by multiple linear regression with the ordinary least-squares method from logarithms of theta (4–7 Hz), alpha (8–13 Hz), beta (14–30 Hz), and gamma (31–45 Hz) band power of ICs included in the IC clusters. PSDs of 6-s epochs of each IC were calculated by 512-point (1-s) fast Fourier transform (FFT) with a 128-point (0.25-s) overlap, and the Hann window was applied as the window function.

When more than 2 ICs from 1 participant were included in an IC cluster, their PSDs were averaged before logarithmic transformation.

Based on fMRI studies suggesting that some brain regions are differently activated in high- and low-valence (pleasant and unpleasant) states or in high- and low-arousal (excited and calm) states during affective picture processing [39,40], we performed four separate regression analyses for each IC cluster. Specifically, (1) regression of the valence level in a high-valence state (using HVHA and HVLA pictures in Figure 1b, (2) regression of the valence level in a low-valence state (using LVHA and LVLA pictures), (3) regression of the arousal level in a high-arousal state (using HVHA and LVHA pictures), and (4) regression of the arousal level in a low-arousal state (using HVLA and LVLA pictures) were performed. For dependent variables, we used the IAPS normative ratings of each picture stimulus rather than the participants' reports, because some participants' reports were biased to either high- or low- valence/arousal state. In these participants, only a few pictures were included in the other emotional state, based on the participants' reports. In order to ensure adequate sample sizes for the regression analyses and to equalize sample sizes across participants and across emotional states, we determined to use IAPS normative ratings as the dependent variable. The prediction accuracy was evaluated using Pearson's correlation coefficient between predicted variables and IAPS normative ratings. We conducted a leave-one-participant-out cross validation and reported the mean values of Pearson's correlation coefficients obtained with all participants whose ICs were included in the IC cluster. Before regression analyses, all independent and dependent variables for each participant were standardized to mean values of 0 and variances of 1.

2.7. *Identification of IC Clusters Correlating with Emotional State*

We identified IC clusters that exhibited Pearson's correlation coefficients significantly higher than 0 in each emotional state for each dependent variable (valence or arousal level) using a one-tailed one-sample *t*-test. For each combination of the dependent variable and the emotional state, the obtained *p*-values were corrected with the Holm–Bonferroni method to compensate for multiple comparisons across the seven identified IC clusters [50]. As identification of significant IC clusters was performed in two emotional states per dependent variable, the significance level was set to 0.025 (=0.05/2). Furthermore, we calculated the coefficients of the regression model in which successful prediction was obtained to determine the degree of contribution of each frequency band. Statistical tests and calculation of mean correlation coefficients were performed after transformation to Fisher's z values.

3. Results

3.1. *IC Clusters Obtained by ICA and Cluster Analysis*

ICA and cluster analysis by a k-means clustering method resulted in seven IC clusters. The MNI coordinates of their centroids and their labels are presented in Table 1. The average projections of the ICs onto the scalp, their dipole locations in the MNI standard brain, ERPs during 0–500 milliseconds, and PSDs in 1–45 Hz are illustrated in Figure 3. Two anterior IC clusters (IC clusters 1 and 2) were located in the anterior cingulate gyrus and middle cingulate gyrus. Two additional lateral IC clusters (IC clusters 3 and 4) were located in the right and left precentral gyrus. Both of these lateral IC clusters showed prominent alpha peaks in their PSDs. The other 3 IC clusters, clusters 5, 6, and 7, were located in the posterior part of the brain, middle cingulate gyrus, right precuneus, and cuneus, respectively. IC clusters 6 and 7 had specific ERPs, and IC clusters 5 and 6 exhibited alpha peaks in their PSDs.

Table 1. Montreal Neurological Institute (MNI) coordinates and labels of the centroids of independent component (IC) clusters.

Cluster Index	Location of Centroid [1]	MNI Coordinates (X, Y, Z)	Number of Participants	Number of ICs
1	Right anterior cingulate gyrus	(2, 39, −2)	14	21
2	Right middle cingulate gyrus	(1, −5, 32)	14	21
3	Right precentral gyrus	(39, −6, 36)	16	18
4	Left precentral gyrus	(−28, −13, 43)	16	19
5	Left middle cingulate gyrus	(−3, −40, 44)	16	24
6	Right precuneus	(20, −45, 4)	18	19
7	Right cuneus	(6, −84, 16)	19	19

[1] Labels were determined using automated anatomical labeling (AAL; [48]).

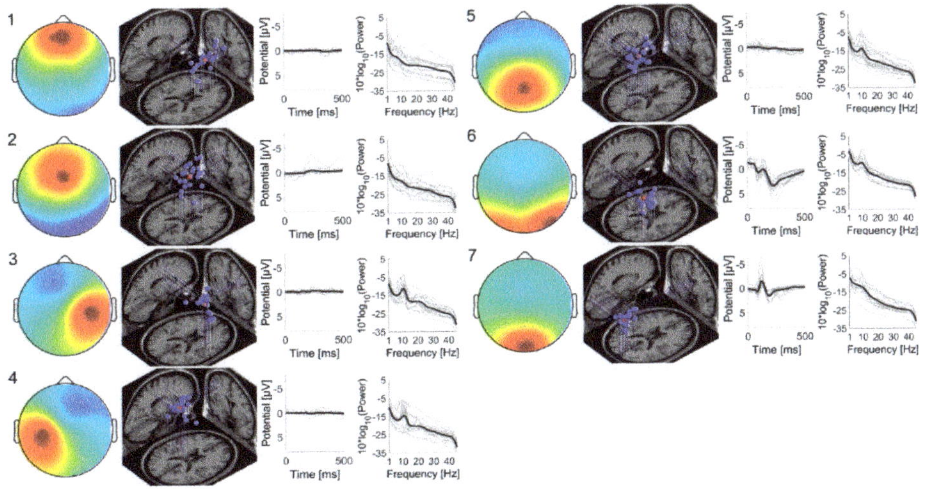

Figure 3. Average projections onto the scalp, dipole locations in the Montreal Neurological Institute (MNI) brain (blue points: each dipole, red points: centroid of dipoles), event-related potentials (ERPs) during 0–500 milliseconds, and power spectral densities (PSDs) in 1–45 Hz of each IC cluster obtained from independent component analysis and cluster analysis by a k-means clustering method in EEGLAB. The numbers from 1 to 7 represent cluster indices shown in Table 1. In the scalp topography maps, the left and right sides represent left and right hemispheres, respectively. The upper and lower sides represent anterior and posterior sides of the scalp, respectively. The red color represents positive weight and the blue color represents negative weight. In plots of ERPs and PSDs, thin gray lines represent data from each IC and thick black lines represent averaged values.

3.2. IC Clusters Correlating with Emotional State

Prediction accuracy (Pearson's correlation coefficient between predicted values and IAPS normative ratings and mean squared error (MSE)) of all IC clusters in the inter-participant regression analysis is shown in Figure 4. Among the 7 IC clusters, 1, 3, 3, and 1 IC clusters reached significance in the regression of the high-valence, low-valence, high-arousal, and low-arousal states, respectively.

In the regression analysis of the high-valence state, IC cluster 7 (with the centroid located in the cuneus) exhibited a correlation coefficient significantly higher than 0 (mean correlation coefficient: 0.095, $p < 0.0005$ in a one-tailed t-test with Holm–Bonferroni correction; MSE: 0.980). Mean (S.D.) regression coefficients of the theta, alpha, beta, and gamma bands were −0.12 (0.01), 0.10 (0.01), 0.03 (0.01), and −0.01 (0.01), respectively (Figure 5a).

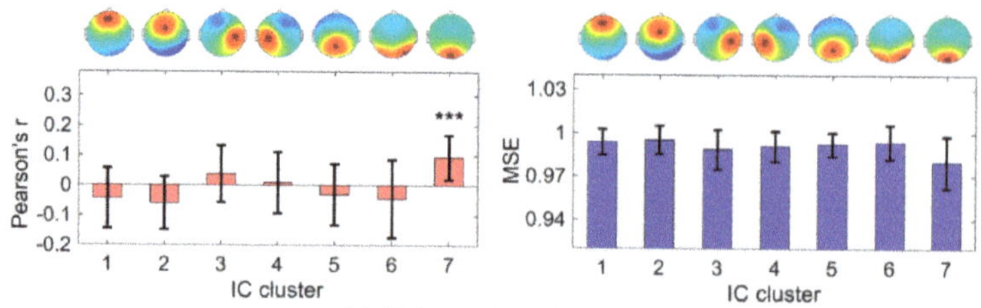

(**a**) Valence (High valence)

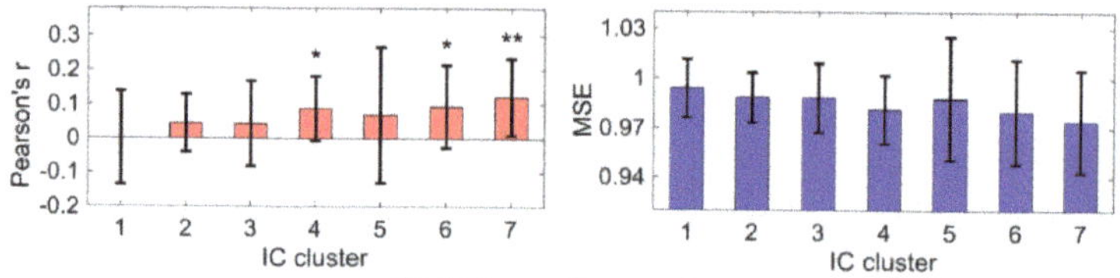

(**b**) Valence (Low valence)

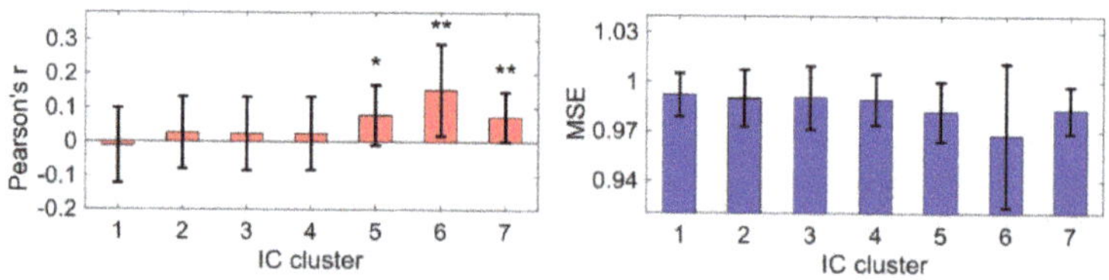

(**c**) Arousal (High arousal)

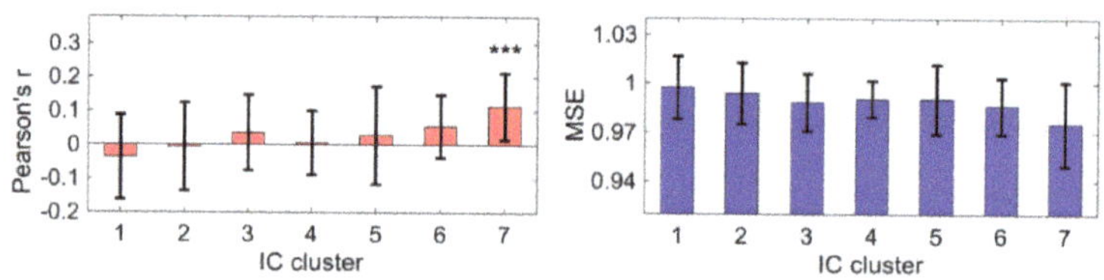

(**d**) Arousal (Low arousal)

Figure 4. Prediction accuracy of the seven identified IC clusters in the inter-participant regression. Error bars represent standard deviations. (**a**) Regression of the high-valence state. (**b**) Regression of the low-valence state. (**c**) Regression of the high-arousal state. (**d**) Regression of the low-arousal state. (Left column) Pearson's correlation coefficient between predicted values and International Affective Picture System normative ratings. (Right column) mean squared error (MSE). * $p < 0.025$, ** $p < 0.005$, *** $p < 0.0005$ in one-tailed one-sample t-tests with Holm–Bonferroni correction.

In the regression analysis of the low-valence state, IC clusters 4 (with the centroid located in the left precentral gyrus), 6 (with the centroid located in the precuneus), and 7 exhibited correlation coefficients significantly higher than 0. Mean correlation coefficients were 0.088 ($p < 0.025$), 0.093 ($p < 0.025$), and 0.121 ($p < 0.005$), respectively, and MSEs were 0.981, 0.980, and 0.974, respectively. The mean (S.D.) regression coefficients of the theta, alpha, beta, and gamma bands were 0.03 (0.01), 0.07 (0.01), −0.04 (0.01), and −0.08 (0.01), respectively, in IC cluster 4 (Figure 5b), −0.10 (0.01), 0.11 (0.01), 0.00 (0.01), and −0.07 (0.01), respectively, in IC cluster 6 (Figure 5c), and −0.10 (0.01), −0.04 (0.01), −0.02 (0.01), and −0.02 (0.01), respectively, in IC cluster 7 (Figure 5d).

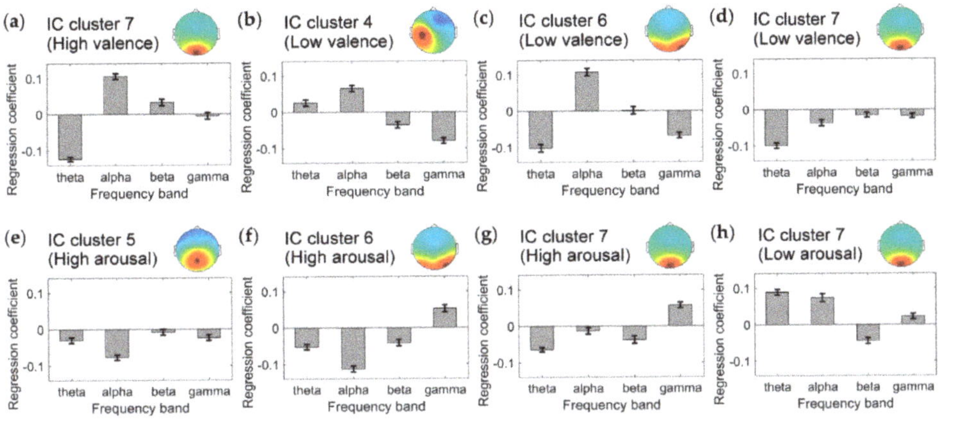

Figure 5. Mean coefficients of the theta, alpha, beta, and gamma bands in the regression model. Larger absolute value of the regression coefficient indicates larger degree of contribution of the frequency band to the regression model. Positive (negative) regression coefficient indicates positive (negative) relationship between the frequency band power and IAPS normative ratings. Error bars represent standard deviations. (**a**) Regression of the high-valence state of IC cluster 7. (**b**) Low-valence state of IC cluster 4. (**c**) Low-valence state of IC cluster 6. (**d**) Low-valence state of IC cluster 7. (**e**) High-arousal state of IC cluster 5. (**f**) High-arousal state of IC cluster 6. (**g**) High-arousal state of IC cluster 7. (**h**) Low-arousal state of IC cluster 7.

In the regression analysis of the high-arousal state, IC clusters 5 (with the centroid located in the middle cingulate gyrus), 6, and 7 exhibited correlation coefficients significantly higher than 0. Mean correlation coefficients were 0.079 ($p < 0.025$), 0.152 ($p < 0.005$), and 0.074 ($p < 0.005$), respectively, and MSEs were 0.982, 0.967, and 0.983, respectively. The mean (S.D.) regression coefficients of the theta, alpha, beta, and gamma bands were −0.03 (0.01), −0.08 (0.01), −0.01 (0.01), and −0.02 (0.01), respectively, in IC cluster 5 (Figure 5e), −0.05 (0.01), −0.11 (0.01), −0.04 (0.01), and 0.05 (0.01), respectively, in IC cluster 6 (Figure 5f), and −0.06 (0.01), −0.01 (0.01), −0.04 (0.01), and 0.06 (0.01), respectively, in IC cluster 7 (Figure 5g).

In the regression of the low-arousal state, IC cluster 7 exhibited a correlation coefficient significantly higher than 0 (mean correlation coefficient: 0.114, $p < 0.0005$; MSE: 0.975). Mean (S.D.) regression coefficients of the theta, alpha, beta, and gamma bands were 0.09 (0.01), 0.07 (0.01), −0.04 (0.01), and 0.02 (0.01), respectively (Figure 5h). The other 3 IC clusters (IC clusters 1, 2, and 3) did not exhibit correlation coefficients significantly higher than 0 for either dependent variable (valence or arousal level).

4. Discussion

In this study, we investigated neural activities that can be recorded from scalp EEG and correlate with emotional states, by using ICA with dipole fitting and regression analysis. We first identified seven IC clusters in the frontal, parietal, and occipital regions in the group analysis. These clusters were distinct from each other in terms of scalp topography, MNI coordinates, and ERPs. Subsequently, inter-participant emotion regression was performed using frequency band power of the ICs included in the seven IC clusters. As a result, the relationship between specific emotional states and four IC clusters was identified in spite of individual differences in emotional processing [51]. In the regression of the valence level, we found that an IC cluster located in the cuneus (IC cluster 7) predicted both high- and low-valence states and two other IC clusters located in the left precentral gyrus and the precuneus (IC clusters 4 and 6) predicted the low-valence state. In the regression of the arousal level, IC cluster 7 was found to also predict both high- and low-arousal states and 2 posterior IC clusters located in the cingulate gyrus and the precuneus (IC clusters 5 and 6) were found to predict the high-arousal state.

Thus, the results suggest that these brain regions are good candidates for effective brain regions in EEG-based emotion regression.

In the regression of the valence level, IC cluster 7 (located in the cuneus) showed significant regression performance in both high- and low-valence states. The cuneus is located in the occipital lobe and is thought to be strongly related to visual function. This IC cluster also exhibited specific ERPs, comprising P1, N1, and P2 in the 100–250 milliseconds range. Based on the ERP and the location, this IC cluster may reflect the activity related to early visual processing. The activity of the visual cortex has been found to be affected by emotion [52]. The regression coefficients of the frequency bands suggest a strong influence of the theta band power. In human EEG studies, increased theta band response to affective picture stimuli than to neutral ones has been reported at the posterior electrodes [53,54], and these theta band modulations were suggested to reflect top-down and bottom-up attentional mechanisms [55,56]. Attention-mediated theta band power change in the visual cortex was also shown in a macaque ECoG study [57]. Thus, the regression model in our study might decode attention-related neural activity. However, our results showed that the direction of the theta band-power influence differed between high- and low-valence states. While theta band power decreased as the pleasantness increased in the high-valence state, theta band power increased as the unpleasantness increased in the low-valence state. (In the valence axis, a value of 1 represents an unpleasant state, and a value of 5 represents a neutral state in the regression model; thus, the negative coefficient indicates a positive correlation with unpleasantness in the low-valence state.) This may indicate different mechanisms of emotional processing in the cuneus between these two emotional states. In addition, IC cluster 6 (located in the right precuneus) significantly contributed to the regression, but only for the low-valence state. The precuneus is located in the parietal lobe and is thought to be involved in visuo-spatial imagery, episodic memory retrieval, and self-processing [58]. In our study, IC cluster 6 had specific ERPs, comprising P300 and the subsequent late positive potential (LPP). Therefore, this IC cluster may represent neural activation related to attention and memory processing, since P300 and LPP are thought to be associated with these processes [59–62]. In particular, a larger LPP amplitude is thought to be associated with increased motivated attention and memory. In a study using simultaneous EEG and fMRI measurements, Liu and colleagues demonstrated that the amplitude of LPP significantly positively correlated with blood-oxygenation-level-dependent (BOLD) signals in the precuneus only in the presentation of high-arousal ("pleasant" and "unpleasant" in their study) pictures [63]. However, we observed significant results in regression analysis of the low-valence state, but not of the high-valence state. This result may be partly due to the "negativity bias"; it has been suggested that unpleasant stimuli induce stronger emotional responses in the brain than pleasant stimuli [64]. Accordingly, although both pleasant and unpleasant stimuli induced emotional responses in the brain, the unpleasant stimuli might induce attention and memory processing more strongly; thus, the activity could be strongly represented in the EEG. In addition, Liu et al. found that the LPP correlated with the BOLD signal in the ventral part of the precuneus in the "unpleasant" condition and in the more dorsal part of the precuneus in the "pleasant" condition. The location of IC cluster 6 in our study is in the ventral part of the precuneus, near the posterior cingulate cortex. Taken together, activity in the ventral part of the precuneus may correlate with the low-valence state. Moreover, IC cluster 4 (located in the left precentral gyrus) also significantly contributed to the regression of the low-valence state. The precentral gyrus is mainly associated with motor function; thus, this IC cluster may be related to motor activity caused by the emotional content of the picture stimuli. One type of the motor activity may be induced through facial muscles, because negative emotions, such as fear, anger, sadness, and disgust, are accompanied by unique facial expressions [65]. Involvement of the precentral gyrus in the low-valence state is in accordance with an fMRI study using affective pictures [39]. The regression coefficients of the frequency bands support the contribution of motor activity to the regression performance. In the regression model, the alpha and gamma bands contributed most significantly; as unpleasantness increased, alpha band power decreased and gamma band power increased. Movement accompanies a decrease in alpha band power in the central area, in a process called event-related desynchronization [66]. A previous human

ECoG study has reported the relationship between gamma band power and movement execution [67]. Accordingly, movement-related activity of IC cluster 4 might correlate with the level of unpleasantness.

In the regression of the arousal level, IC cluster 5 (located in the middle cingulate gyrus; Brodmann area [BA] 31) significantly predicted the high-arousal state. This IC cluster was located in the posterior part of the brain, and the posterior cingulate cortex, including BA31, has been associated with controlling attentional focus [68]. IC cluster 6 located in the right precuneus also significantly contributed to the regression, but only for the high-arousal states. As mentioned above, a study using simultaneous EEG and fMRI measurements demonstrated the contribution of the precuneus to the high-arousal state [63]. In accordance with the results of the current study, they observed no such correlation in the presentation of low-arousal ("neutral" in their study) pictures. Their results suggest that the degree of activation in the precuneus during affective picture viewing correlates with the electrophysiological index of motivated attention and memory, but only in the high-arousal state. The regression coefficients of the frequency bands also supported a contribution of visual attention in IC clusters 5 and 6 to the regression performance. In the regression analysis of the high-arousal state in IC clusters 5 and 6, the alpha band power contributed most significantly. The result suggested that, as arousal level increased, alpha band power decreased. It has been suggested that alpha band power in the parietal–occipital region is associated with visual attention [69]. Taken together, these findings suggest that attention and memory processing are key factors that correlate with the high-arousal states in these two posterior IC clusters. Additionally, IC cluster 7 showed significant regression performance in both high- and low-arousal states. However, as with the valence axis, mechanisms of emotional processing may be different between high- and low-arousal states in the cuneus. Specifically, theta band power decreased as the arousal level increased in the high-arousal state and theta band power increased as the arousal level increased in the low-arousal state.

Among the 3 posterior IC clusters (IC clusters 5, 6, and 7), IC cluster 7 exhibited activity correlating with both high- and low-valence and high- and low-arousal states, while IC clusters 5 and 6 predicted only either half of the valence and/or arousal axes. This may indicate that neural activity responsible for early visual processing correlated with valence and arousal levels regardless of emotional states, while those that process more higher-level information showed emotional state-specific activities. Based on our current results suggesting the existence of neural activities involved in emotion regression only in specific emotional states and fMRI studies showing different neural activities between high- and low-valence states and between high- and low-arousal states [39,40], applying separate regression models to high- and low- valence/arousal states would result in higher prediction accuracy in EEG-based emotion regression analysis. Additionally, although posterior IC clusters correlated with emotional states, 2 anterior IC clusters (IC clusters 1 and 2) did not predict either valence or arousal level. This may be because frontal regions are responsible for more complicated functions than simple visual processing. Frontal regions are thought to have a general role in emotional processing [70] and to be a place of higher cognitive function [71]. Accordingly, in contrast to the posterior IC clusters that seem to be responsible for rather simple functions, anterior IC clusters did not exhibit correlation with emotional states.

Though we identified neural activities correlating with specific emotional states by applying separate regression models per emotional state, there are some potential limitations in this study. The first limitation is the low prediction accuracy. The correlation coefficients were 0.15 at the most in this study. However, this value is higher than that of the previous study performed by McFarland and colleagues, where sensor-level features and whole-axis analyses were used and the correlation coefficients were at most around 0.08 in the test data [22]. Since experimental and analytical procedures were totally different in many respects, it is not possible to directly compare our results with those of the previous study. Nevertheless, our results may suggest the effectiveness of the use of source-level signals in EEG-based emotion regression and/or the existence of neural activities correlating with only specific emotional states. These findings would be useful for establishing regression models that can achieve high prediction accuracy in future research. Moreover, to further increase the prediction accuracy for the real-life application of EEG-based emotion regression, non-linear regression methods may be effective. Specifically, deep neural networks would result in significant improvement of the regression performance [30]. Additionally, use of connectivity and causality measures between brain regions rather than focusing on single brain region would also be beneficial. The second limitation is the dependent variables used in this study. We did not use the participants' reports, but rather utilized IAPS normative ratings to maintain the large sample sizes and to equalize the sample sizes across participants and across emotional states. Though IAPS normative ratings highly correlated with the participants' reports in this study (mean Spearman's rank correlation coefficients across the participants were 0.72 in the valence axis and 0.53 in the arousal axis), IAPS normative ratings may differ from the participants' actual emotion to some extent. Thus, regression performance would be higher if we could use a larger sample and utilize the participants' reports as the dependent variable, though Petrantonakis and Hadjileontiadis reported that using participants' reports instead of IAPS normative ratings did not increase the prediction accuracy in emotion classification [72,73]. The third limitation is the possible effects of visual features of the affective pictures on the regression performance. We found that occipital IC cluster (IC cluster 7) predicted the emotional states; however, the visual cortex processes various visual features. Though the visual cortex has been reported to be involved in emotional processing [52], this IC cluster might respond to physical properties of the pictures rather than the emotional content.

5. Conclusions

In order to identify neural activities that can predict valence and arousal levels, we used ICA followed by the source localization method and inter-participant regression analyses. As a result, 4 IC clusters correlated with certain emotional states in spite of individual differences in emotional processing. The results were physiologically plausible and in line with those of previous studies. Specifically, attention and memory processing might contribute to the significant regression results in three posterior IC clusters. Finally, this study suggested that applying separate regression models based on the target emotional states would help to attain good prediction accuracy in EEG-based emotion regression research.

Author Contributions: Conceptualization, Y.M.; methodology, Y.M.; software, Y.M.; validation, Y.M., Y.O., L.A.M.-T., Y.K., and N.Y.; formal analysis, Y.M.; investigation, Y.M. and L.A.M.-T.; resources, Y.O., Y.K., and N.Y.; data curation, Y.M.; writing—original draft preparation, Y.M.; writing—review and editing, Y.M., Y.O., L.A.M.-T., and N.Y.; visualization, Y.M.; supervision, Y.O., Y.K., and N.Y.; project administration, Y.M., Y.O., and N.Y.; funding acquisition, Y.O. and N.Y. All authors have read and agreed to the published version of the manuscript.

Funding: This research was funded by JST PRESTO (grant number JPMJPR17JA), and in part by JSPS KAKENHI grants (15K16080 and 18K11499).

Acknowledgments: The authors thank the participants for their involvement. The authors also acknowledge the advice on regression analysis and statistical tests received from T. Kawase.

Conflicts of Interest: The authors declare no conflict of interest.

References

1. Kim, M.-K.; Kim, M.; Oh, E.; Kim, S.-P. A Review on the Computational Methods for Emotional State Estimation from the Human EEG. *Comput. Math. Methods Med.* **2013**, *2013*, 573734. [CrossRef] [PubMed]
2. Al-Nafjan, A.; Hosny, M.; Al-Ohali, Y.; Al-Wabil, A. Review and Classification of Emotion Recognition Based on EEG Brain-Computer Interface System Research: A Systematic Review. *Appl. Sci.* **2017**, *7*, 1239. [CrossRef]
3. Alarcão, S.M.; Fonseca, M.J. Emotions Recognition Using EEG Signals: A Survey. *IEEE Trans. Affect. Comput.* **2019**, *10*, 374–393. [CrossRef]
4. Frantzidis, C.A.; Bratsas, C.; Papadelis, C.L.; Konstantinidis, E.; Pappas, C.; Bamidis, P.D. Toward Emotion Aware Computing: An Integrated Approach Using Multichannel Neurophysiological Recordings and Affective Visual Stimuli. *IEEE Trans. Inf. Technol. Biomed.* **2010**, *14*, 589–597. [CrossRef] [PubMed]
5. Russell, J.A. A circumplex model of affect. *J. Personal. Soc. Psychol.* **1980**, *39*, 1161–1178. [CrossRef]

6. Padilla-Buritica, J.I.; Martinez-Vargas, J.D.; Castellanos-Dominguez, G. Emotion Discrimination Using Spatially Compact Regions of Interest Extracted from Imaging EEG Activity. *Front. Comput. Neurosci.* **2016**, *10*, 55. [CrossRef] [PubMed]
7. Martinez-Vargas, J.D.; Nieto-Mora, D.A.; Muñoz-Gutiérrez, P.A.; Cespedes-Villar, Y.R.; Giraldo, E.; Castellanos-Dominguez, G. Assessment of Source Connectivity for Emotional States Discrimination. In *Brain Informatics (BI 2018), Proceedings of the International Conference on Brain Informatics, Arlington, TX, USA, 7–9 December, 2018*; Springer: Cham, Switzerland, 2018; pp. 63–73.
8. Becker, H.; Fleureau, J.; Guillotel, P.; Wendling, F.; Merlet, I.; Albera, L. Emotion Recognition Based on High-Resolution EEG Recordings and Reconstructed Brain Sources. *IEEE Trans. Affect. Comput.* **2020**, *11*, 244–257. [CrossRef]
9. Chen, G.; Zhang, X.; Sun, Y.; Zhang, J. Emotion Feature Analysis and Recognition Based on Reconstructed EEG Sources. *IEEE Access* **2020**, *8*, 11907–11916. [CrossRef]
10. Hu, X.; Chen, J.; Wang, F.; Zhang, D. Ten challenges for EEG-based affective computing. *Brain Sci. Adv.* **2019**, *5*, 1–20. [CrossRef]
11. Bradley, M.M.; Lang, P.J. Measuring emotion: The self-assessment manikin and the semantic differential. *J. Behav. Ther. Exp. Psychiatry* **1994**, *25*, 49–59. [CrossRef]
12. Soleymani, M.; Koelstra, S.; Patras, I.; Pun, T. Continuous emotion detection in response to music videos. In Proceedings of the Face and Gesture 2011, Santa Barbara, CA, USA, 21–25 March 2011; pp. 803–808.
13. Uzun, S.S.; Yildirim, S.; Yildirim, E. Emotion primitives estimation from EEG signals using Hilbert Huang Transform. In Proceedings of the 2012 IEEE-EMBS International Conference on Biomedical and Health Informatics, Hong Kong, China, 5–7 January 2012; pp. 224–227.
14. Garcia, H.F.; Orozco, Á.A.; Álvarez, M.A. Dynamic physiological signal analysis based on Fisher kernels for emotion recognition. In Proceedings of the 2013 35th Annual International Conference of the IEEE Engineering in Medicine and Biology Society (EMBC), Osaka, Japan, 3–7 July 2013; pp. 4322–4325.
15. Jenke, R.; Peer, A.; Buss, M. A Comparison of Evaluation Measures for Emotion Recognition in Dimensional Space. In Proceedings of the 2013 Humaine Association Conference on Affective Computing and Intelligent Interaction, Geneva, Switzerland, 2–5 September 2013; pp. 822–826.
16. Koelstra, S.; Patras, I. Fusion of facial expressions and EEG for implicit affective tagging. *Image Vis. Comput.* **2013**, *31*, 164–174. [CrossRef]
17. Soleymani, M.; Asghari-Esfeden, S.; Pantic, M.; Fu, Y. Continuous emotion detection using EEG signals and facial expressions. In Proceedings of the 2014 IEEE International Conference on Multimedia and Expo (ICME), Chengdu, China, 14–18 July 2014; pp. 1–6.
18. Torres-Valencia, C.A.; Álvarez, M.A.; Orozco-Gutiérrez, Á.A. Multiple-output support vector machine regression with feature selection for arousal/valence space emotion assessment. In Proceedings of the 2014 36th Annual International Conference of the IEEE Engineering in Medicine and Biology Society, Chicago, IL, USA, 26–30 August 2014; pp. 970–973.
19. Zhuang, X.; Rozgić, V.; Crystal, M. Compact unsupervised EEG response representation for emotion recognition. In Proceedings of the IEEE-EMBS International Conference on Biomedical and Health Informatics (BHI), Valencia, Spain, 1–4 June 2014; pp. 736–739.
20. Al-Fahad, R.; Yeasin, M. Robust Modeling of Continuous 4-D Affective Space from EEG Recording. In Proceedings of the 2016 15th IEEE International Conference on Machine Learning and Applications (ICMLA), Anaheim, CA, USA, 18–20 December 2016; pp. 1040–1045.
21. Lan, Z.; Müller-Putz, G.R.; Wang, L.; Liu, Y.; Sourina, O.; Scherer, R. Using Support Vector Regression to estimate valence level from EEG. In Proceedings of the 2016 IEEE International Conference on Systems, Man, and Cybernetics (SMC), Budapest, Hungary, 9–12 October 2016; pp. 2558–2563.
22. McFarland, D.J.; Parvaz, M.A.; Sarnacki, W.A.; Goldstein, R.Z.; Wolpaw, J.R. Prediction of subjective ratings of emotional pictures by EEG features. *J. Neural Eng.* **2016**, *14*, 016009. [CrossRef] [PubMed]
23. Soleymani, M.; Asghari-Esfeden, S.; Fu, Y.; Pantic, M. Analysis of EEG Signals and Facial Expressions for Continuous Emotion Detection. *IEEE Trans. Affect. Comput.* **2016**, *7*, 17–28. [CrossRef]
24. Thammasan, N.; Fukui, K.; Numao, M. An investigation of annotation smoothing for EEG-based continuous music-emotion recognition. In Proceedings of the 2016 IEEE International Conference on Systems, Man, and Cybernetics (SMC), Budapest, Hungary, 9–12 October 2016; pp. 3323–3328.

25. Al-Fahad, R.; Yeasin, M.; Anam, A.S.M.I.; Elahian, B. Selection of stable features for modeling 4-D affective space from EEG recording. In Proceedings of the 2017 International Joint Conference on Neural Networks (IJCNN), Anchorage, AK, USA, 14–19 May 2017; pp. 1202–1209.
26. Thammasan, N.; Fukui, K.; Numao, M. Application of Annotation Smoothing for Subject-Independent Emotion Recognition Based on Electroencephalogram. In *Trends in Artificial Intelligence: PRICAI 2016 Workshops, Proceedings of the Pacific Rim International Conference on Artificial Intelligence, Phuket, Thailand, 22–23 August 2016*; Springer: Cham, Switzerland, 2017; pp. 115–126.
27. Ding, Y.; Hu, X.; Xia, Z.; Liu, Y.; Zhang, D. Inter-brain EEG Feature Extraction and Analysis for Continuous Implicit Emotion Tagging during Video Watching. *IEEE Trans. Affect. Comput.* **2018**. [CrossRef]
28. Reali, P.; Cosentini, C.; de Carvalho, P.; Traver, V.; Bianchi, A.M. Towards the development of physiological models for emotions evaluation. In Proceedings of the 2018 40th Annual International Conference of the IEEE Engineering in Medicine and Biology Society (EMBC), Honolulu, HI, USA, 18–21 July 2018; pp. 110–113.
29. Sani, O.G.; Yang, Y.; Lee, M.B.; Dawes, H.E.; Chang, E.F.; Shanechi, M.M. Mood variations decoded from multi-site intracranial human brain activity. *Nat. Biotechnol.* **2018**, *36*, 954–961. [CrossRef]
30. Yao, Y.; Qing, C.; Xu, X.; Wang, Y. EEG-Based Emotion Estimate Using Shallow Fully Convolutional Neural Network with Boost Training Strategy. In *Advances in Brain Inspired Cognitive Systems, Proceedings of the International Conference on Brain Inspired Cognitive Systems, Guangzhou, China, 13–14 July 2019*; Springer: Cham, Switzerland, 2020; pp. 55–64.
31. Onton, J.; Makeig, S. Information-based modeling of event-related brain dynamics. *Prog. Brain Res.* **2006**, *159*, 99–120. [CrossRef]
32. Liu, J.; Tian, J. Spatiotemporal analysis of single-trial EEG of emotional pictures based on independent component analysis and source location. In *Medical Imaging 2007: Physiology, Function, and Structure from Medical Images*; SPIE: Washington, DC, USA, 2007; Volume 6511, pp. 646–655.
33. Onton, J.; Makeig, S. High-frequency broadband modulations of electroencephalographic spectra. *Front. Hum. Neurosci.* **2009**, *3*, 61. [CrossRef]
34. Lin, Y.-P.; Duann, J.-R.; Chen, J.-H.; Jung, T.-P. Electroencephalographic dynamics of musical emotion perception revealed by independent spectral components. *Neuroreport* **2010**, *21*, 410–415. [CrossRef]
35. Wyczesany, M.; Ligeza, T.S. Towards a constructionist approach to emotions: Verification of the three-dimensional model of affect with EEG-independent component analysis. *Exp. Brain Res.* **2015**, *233*, 723–733. [CrossRef]
36. Rogenmoser, L.; Zollinger, N.; Elmer, S.; Jäncke, L. Independent component processes underlying emotions during natural music listening. *Soc. Cogn. Affect. Neurosci.* **2016**, *11*, 1428–1439. [CrossRef]
37. Shen, Y.-W.; Lin, Y.-P. Challenge for Affective Brain-Computer Interfaces: Non-stationary Spatio-spectral EEG Oscillations of Emotional Responses. *Front. Hum. Neurosci.* **2019**, *13*, 366. [CrossRef] [PubMed]
38. Machizawa, M.G.; Lisi, G.; Kanayama, N.; Mizuochi, R.; Makita, K.; Sasaoka, T.; Yamawaki, S. Quantification of anticipation of excitement with a three-axial model of emotion with EEG. *J. Neural Eng.* **2020**, *17*, 036011. [CrossRef] [PubMed]
39. Nielen, M.M.A.; Heslenfeld, D.J.; Heinen, K.; Van Strien, J.W.; Witter, M.P.; Jonker, C.; Veltman, D.J. Distinct brain systems underlie the processing of valence and arousal of affective pictures. *Brain Cogn.* **2009**, *71*, 387–396. [CrossRef] [PubMed]
40. Viinikainen, M.; Jääskeläinen, I.P.; Alexandrov, Y.; Balk, M.H.; Autti, T.; Sams, M. Nonlinear relationship between emotional valence and brain activity: Evidence of separate negative and positive valence dimensions. *Hum. Brain Mapp.* **2010**, *31*, 1030–1040. [CrossRef] [PubMed]
41. Lang, P.J.; Bradley, M.M.; Cuthbert, B.N. *International Affective Picture System (IAPS): Affective Ratings of Pictures and Instruction Manual*; Technical Report A-8; University of Florida: Gainesville, FL, USA, 2008.
42. Brainard, D.H. The Psychophysics Toolbox. *Spat. Vis.* **1997**, *10*, 433–436. [CrossRef] [PubMed]
43. Pelli, D.G. The VideoToolbox software for visual psychophysics: Transforming numbers into movies. *Spat. Vis.* **1997**, *10*, 437–442. [CrossRef]
44. Kleiner, M.; Brainard, D.; Pelli, D. What's new in Psychtoolbox-3? *Perception* **2007**, *36*.
45. Delorme, A.; Makeig, S. EEGLAB: An open source toolbox for analysis of single-trial EEG dynamics including independent component analysis. *J. Neurosci. Methods* **2004**, *134*, 9–21. [CrossRef]

46. Palmer, J.A.; Makeig, S.; Kreutz-Delgado, K.; Rao, B.D. Newton method for the ICA mixture model. In Proceedings of the 2008 IEEE International Conference on Acoustics, Speech and Signal Processing, Lag Vegas, NV, USA, 31 March–4 April 2008; pp. 1805–1808.
47. Oostenveld, R.; Fries, P.; Maris, E.; Schoffelen, J.-M. FieldTrip: Open Source Software for Advanced Analysis of MEG, EEG, and Invasive Electrophysiological Data. *Comput. Intell. Neurosci.* **2011**, *2011*, 156869. [CrossRef]
48. Tzourio-Mazoyer, N.; Landeau, B.; Papathanassiou, D.; Crivello, F.; Etard, O.; Delcroix, N.; Mazoyer, B.; Joliot, M. Automated Anatomical Labeling of Activations in SPM Using a Macroscopic Anatomical Parcellation of the MNI MRI Single-Subject Brain. *Neuroimage* **2002**, *15*, 273–289. [CrossRef]
49. Rorden, C.; Karnath, H.-O.; Bonilha, L. Improving Lesion-Symptom Mapping. *J. Cogn. Neurosci.* **2007**, *19*, 1081–1088. [CrossRef] [PubMed]
50. Holm, S. A Simple Sequentially Rejective Multiple Test Procedure. *Scand. J. Stat.* **1979**, *6*, 65–70.
51. Hamann, S.; Canli, T. Individual differences in emotion processing. *Curr. Opin. Neurobiol.* **2004**, *14*, 233–238. [CrossRef]
52. Lang, P.J.; Bradley, M.M.; Fitzsimmons, J.R.; Cuthbert, B.N.; Scott, J.D.; Moulder, B.; Nangia, V. Emotional arousal and activation of the visual cortex: An fMRI analysis. *Psychophysiology* **1998**, *35*, 199–210. [CrossRef] [PubMed]
53. Aftanas, L.I.; Varlamov, A.A.; Pavlov, S.V.; Makhnev, V.P.; Reva, N.V. Affective picture processing: Event-related synchronization within individually defined human theta band is modulated by valence dimension. *Neurosci. Lett.* **2001**, *303*, 115–118. [CrossRef]
54. Güntekin, B.; Başar, E. A review of brain oscillations in perception of faces and emotional pictures. *Neuropsychologia* **2014**, *58*, 33–51. [CrossRef]
55. Zhang, W.; Li, X.; Liu, X.; Duan, X.; Wang, D.; Shen, J. Distraction reduces theta synchronization in emotion regulation during adolescence. *Neurosci. Lett.* **2013**, *550*, 81–86. [CrossRef]
56. Uusberg, A.; Thiruchselvam, R.; Gross, J.J. Using distraction to regulate emotion: Insights from EEG theta dynamics. *Int. J. Psychophysiol.* **2014**, *91*, 254–260. [CrossRef]
57. Spyropoulos, G.; Bosman, C.A.; Fries, P. A theta rhythm in macaque visual cortex and its attentional modulation. *Proc. Natl. Acad. Sci. USA* **2018**, *115*, E5614–E5623. [CrossRef]
58. Cavanna, A.E.; Trimble, M.R. The precuneus: A review of its functional anatomy and behavioural correlates. *Brain* **2006**, *129*, 564–583. [CrossRef]
59. Cuthbert, B.N.; Schupp, H.T.; Bradley, M.M.; Birbaumer, N.; Lang, P.J. Brain potentials in affective picture processing: Covariation with autonomic arousal and affective report. *Biol. Psychol.* **2000**, *52*, 95–111. [CrossRef]
60. Schupp, H.T.; Cuthbert, B.N.; Bradley, M.M.; Cacioppo, J.T.; Ito, T.; Lang, P.J. Affective picture processing: The late positive potential is modulated by motivational relevance. *Psychophysiology* **2000**, *37*, 257–261. [CrossRef] [PubMed]
61. Olofsson, J.K.; Nordin, S.; Sequeira, H.; Polich, J. Affective picture processing: An integrative review of ERP findings. *Biol. Psychol.* **2008**, *77*, 247–265. [CrossRef] [PubMed]
62. Hajcak, G.; MacNamara, A.; Olvet, D.M. Event-Related Potentials, Emotion, and Emotion Regulation: An Integrative Review. *Dev. Neuropsychol.* **2010**, *35*, 129–155. [CrossRef]
63. Liu, Y.; Huang, H.; McGinnis-Deweese, M.; Keil, A.; Ding, M. Neural Substrate of the Late Positive Potential in Emotional Processing. *J. Neurosci.* **2012**, *32*, 14563–14572. [CrossRef]
64. Cacioppo, J.T.; Berntson, G.G. Relationship between attitudes and evaluative space: A critical review, with emphasis on the separability of positive and negative substrates. *Psychol. Bull.* **1994**, *115*, 401–423. [CrossRef]
65. Ekman, P. An argument for basic emotions. *Cogn. Emot.* **1992**, *6*, 169–200. [CrossRef]
66. Pfurtscheller, G.; Aranibar, A. Evaluation of event-related desynchronization (ERD) preceding and following voluntary self-paced movement. *Electroencephalogr. Clin. Neurophysiol.* **1979**, *46*, 138–146. [CrossRef]
67. Crone, N.E.; Miglioretti, D.L.; Gordon, B.; Lesser, R.P. Functional mapping of human sensorimotor cortex with electrocorticographic spectral analysis. II. Event-related synchronization in the gamma band. *Brain* **1998**, *121*, 2301–2315. [CrossRef]
68. Leech, R.; Sharp, D.J. The role of the posterior cingulate cortex in cognition and disease. *Brain* **2014**, *137*, 12–32. [CrossRef]
69. Foxe, J.J.; Snyder, A.C. The Role of Alpha-Band Brain Oscillations as a Sensory Suppression Mechanism during Selective Attention. *Front. Psychol.* **2011**, *2*, 154. [CrossRef] [PubMed]

70. Phan, K.L.; Wager, T.; Taylor, S.F.; Liberzon, I. Functional Neuroanatomy of Emotion: A Meta-Analysis of Emotion Activation Studies in PET and fMRI. *Neuroimage* **2002**, *16*, 331–348. [CrossRef]
71. Etkin, A.; Egner, T.; Kalisch, R. Emotional processing in anterior cingulate and medial prefrontal cortex. *Trends Cogn. Sci.* **2011**, *15*, 85–93. [CrossRef]
72. Petrantonakis, P.C.; Hadjileontiadis, L.J. A Novel Emotion Elicitation Index Using Frontal Brain Asymmetry for Enhanced EEG-Based Emotion Recognition. *IEEE Trans. Inf. Technol. Biomed.* **2011**, *15*, 737–746. [CrossRef] [PubMed]
73. Petrantonakis, P.C.; Hadjileontiadis, L.J. Adaptive Emotional Information Retrieval From EEG Signals in the Time-Frequency Domain. *IEEE Trans. Signal Process.* **2012**, *60*, 2604–2616. [CrossRef]

brain sciences

MDPI

Review

Advances in Multimodal Emotion Recognition Based on Brain–Computer Interfaces

Zhipeng He [1], Zina Li [2], Fuzhou Yang [1], Lei Wang [1], Jingcong Li [1], Chengju Zhou [1] and Jiahui Pan [1,*]

[1] School of Software, South China Normal University, Foshan 528225, China; zhipenghe@m.scnu.edu.cn (Z.H.); fuzhouyang@m.scnu.edu.cn (F.Y.); wezard@m.scnu.edu.cn (L.W.); lijingcong@hotmail.com (J.L.); cjZhou@scnu.edu.cn (C.Z.)

[2] School of Computer, South China Normal University, Guangzhou 510641, China; zina@m.scnu.edu.cn

* Correspondence: panjiahui@m.scnu.edu.cn

Received: 20 August 2020; Accepted: 26 September 2020; Published: 29 September 2020

Abstract: With the continuous development of portable noninvasive human sensor technologies such as brain–computer interfaces (BCI), multimodal emotion recognition has attracted increasing attention in the area of affective computing. This paper primarily discusses the progress of research into multimodal emotion recognition based on BCI and reviews three types of multimodal affective BCI (aBCI): aBCI based on a combination of behavior and brain signals, aBCI based on various hybrid neurophysiology modalities and aBCI based on heterogeneous sensory stimuli. For each type of aBCI, we further review several representative multimodal aBCI systems, including their design principles, paradigms, algorithms, experimental results and corresponding advantages. Finally, we identify several important issues and research directions for multimodal emotion recognition based on BCI.

Keywords: emotion recognition; multimodal fusion; brain–computer interface (BCI); affective computing

1. Introduction

Emotion is a general term for a series of subjective cognitive experiences. Emotions consist of a set of psychological states generated by various feelings, thoughts and behaviors. People convey emotional information constantly during the process of communication; emotion recognition plays an important role in interpersonal communication and many aspects of daily life. For example, recognizing the emotional states of patients with emotional expression disorders would be helpful in supplying better treatments and care. Emotion recognition is also an indispensable aspect of humanization in human-computer interaction. The advent and development of portable noninvasive sensor technologies such as brain–computer interfaces (BCI) provide effective methods for achieving humanization in human-computer interactions.

A BCI consists of technology that converts signals generated by brain activity into control signals for external devices without the participation of peripheral nerves and muscles [1]. Affective BCI (aBCI) [2] originated from a research project in the general communication field that attempted to create neurophysiological devices to detect emotional state signals and then to use the detected information to promote human-computer interaction. aBCI uses techniques from psychological theories and methods (concepts and protocols), neuroscience (brain function and signal processing) and computer science (machine learning and human-computer interaction) to induce, measure and detect emotional states and apply the resulting information to improve interaction with machines [3]. Research in the aBCI field focuses on perceiving emotional states, modeling of emotional processes, synthesizing emotional expression and behavior and improving interactions between humans and machines based on emotional background [4]. In this study, we focus primarily on emotion recognition in aBCI systems.

In emotion-recognition research, one of the most important problems is to describe the emotional state scientifically and construct an emotional description model. Emotional modeling involves establishing a mathematical model to describe an emotional state, which can then be classified or quantified by an aBCI system. Establishing an emotion model is an important aspect of emotional measurement because it allows us to make more accurate assessments of emotional states. Many researchers have proposed emotional representation methods; these can be divided into discrete emotional models and dimensional emotional models.

For discrete emotion model, emotional states are composed of several basic discrete emotions, (e.g., the traditional concept of "joys and sorrows"). Ekman [5] suggested that emotions include sadness, fear, disgust, surprise, joy and anger and that these six basic emotions can form more complex emotional categories via combined patterns. However, this description neither describes the connotation of emotion scientifically nor enables a computer to analyze emotional state from a computational point of view. The dimensional emotional model maps emotional states to points in a certain space. Different emotional states are distributed in different positions in space according to their different dimensions; the distances between locations reflect the differences between the different emotional states. In the previous research, the valence-arousal, two-dimensional emotion model proposed by Russell [6] in 1980 is the most widely used. The model divides emotion into two dimensions: a valence dimension and an arousal dimension. The negative half of the valence dimension axis indicates negative emotion, while the positive half indicates positive emotion. The largest difference between this model and the discrete emotion model is that the dimensional emotion model is continuous; thus, it has the advantage of being able to express emotion within a wide range and can be used to describe the process of emotion evolution.

The aBCI system has achieved great progress in paradigm design, brain signal processing algorithms and applications. However, these BCI systems still face some challenges. On one hand, it is difficult to fully reflect emotional state based on a single modality because emotion information is easily affected by various noises. On the other hand, some modality is easy to disguise, and it is difficult to reflect the true emotional state, e.g., detecting an accurate expression does not always represent a person's true emotional state, because a person can disguise an expression. Automated emotion recognition is still impractical in many applications, especially for patients with affective disorders.

From a human performance perspective, emotional expression is mainly divided into the neurophysiological level and the external behavior level. By collecting and analyzing behavioral data and brain image data, we can reveal the relationship between behavior and neural activity and construct theoretical models that map emotion, behavior, and the brain. Therefore, emotion recognition can be based on images, voice, text and other easily collected physiological signals (e.g., skin impedance, heart rate and blood pressure). Nonetheless, it is difficult to use these signals to accurately identify complex emotional states. Among all the types of signals that can be useful in identifying emotional states, electroencephalogram (EEG) data have been widely used because they provide a noninvasive and intuitive method for measuring emotion. EEGs data are the preferred approach for studying the brain's response to emotional stimuli [7]. EEGs can record neurophysiological signals and they objectively reflect the activity of the cerebral cortex to a certain extent. Studies have shown that different brain regions participate in different perceptual and cognitive activities; for example, the frontal lobe is related to thinking and consciousness, while the temporal lobe is associated with processing complex stimulus information, such as faces, scenes, smells and sounds. The parietal lobe is associated with the integration of a variety of sensory information and the operational control of objects, and the occipital lobe is related to vision [8].

We assume that multimodal emotion recognition based on EEG should integrate not only EEG signals, an objective method of emotion measurement, but also a variety of peripheral physiological signals or behaviors. Compared to single patterns, multimodal emotion processing can achieve more reliable results by extracting additional information; consequently, it has attracted increasing attention. Li et al. [9] proposed that in addition to combining different input signals, emotion recognition should include a variety of heterogeneous sensory stimuli (such as audio-visual stimulation) to induce emotions. Many studies [10,11] have shown that integrating heterogeneous sensory stimuli can enhance brain patterns and further improve brain–computer interface performance.

To date, a considerable number of studies on aBCI have been published, especially on emotion recognition based on EEG signals. In particular, with the development of modality fusion theory and portable EEG devices, many new technologies and applications of emotion recognition have emerged. However, there are few comprehensive summaries and discussions of multimodal EEG-based emotion recognition systems. With this problem in mind, this paper presents the concepts and applications of multimodal emotion recognition to the aBCI community. The main contributions of this paper are as follows:

Therefore, in this study, we present the concepts and applications of multimodal emotion recognition to the aBCI community clearly. The main contributions of this study are as follows:

(1) We update and extend the definition of multimodal aBCI. Three main types of multimodal aBCI were devised: aBCI based on a combination of behavior and brain signals, aBCI based on various hybrid neurophysiology modalities and aBCI based on heterogeneous sensory stimuli;
(2) For each type of aBCI, we have reviewed several representative multimodal aBCI systems and analyze the main components of each system, including design principles, stimuli paradigms, fusion methods, experimental results and relative advantages. We find that emotion-recognition models based on multimodal BCI achieve better performances than do models based on single-modality BCI;
(3) Finally, we identify the current challenges in the academic research and engineering application of emotion recognition and provide some potential solutions.

The remainder of this paper is organized as follows: Section 2 briefly introduces the research basis of emotion recognition and the overall situation of related academic research. Section 3 focuses on data analysis and fusion methods used for EEG and behavior modalities, while Section 4 describes the data analysis and fusion methods used for EEG and neurophysiology modalities. Section 5 summarizes the aBCI based on heterogeneous sensory stimuli. Finally, we present concluding remarks in Section 6 and provide several challenges and opportunities for the design of multimodal aBCI techniques.

2. Overview of Multimodal Emotion Recognition Based on BCI

2.1. Multimodal Affective BCI

Single modality information is easily affected by various types of noise, which makes it difficult to capture emotional states. D'mello [12] used statistical methods to compare the accuracy of single-modality and multimodal emotion recognition using a variety of algorithms and different datasets. The best multimodal emotion-recognition system reached an accuracy of 85% and was considerably more accurate than the optimal single-modality correspondence system, with an average improvement of 9.83% (the median was 6.60%). A comprehensive analysis of multiple signals and their interdependence can be used to construct a model that more accurately reflects the potential nature of human emotional expression. Different from D'mello [12], Poria [13] conducted a horizontal comparison between multimodal fusion emotion recognition and single-modality emotion recognition on the same dataset with regard to accuracy based on a full discussion of the current situation of single-modality recognition methods. This study also strongly indicated that efficient modality fusion greatly improves the robustness of emotion-recognition systems.

The aBCI system provides an effective method for researching emotional intelligence and emotional robots. Brain signals are highly correlated with emotions and emotional states. Among the many brain measurement techniques (including EEG and functional magnetic resonance imaging (fMRI)), we believe that multimodal aBCI systems based on EEG signals can greatly improve the results of emotion recognition [14,15].

The signal flow in a multimodal aBCI system is depicted in Figure 1. The workflow generally includes three stages: multimodal signal acquisition, signal processing (including basic modality data processing, signal fusion and decision-making) and emotion reflection control. These stages are described in detail below.

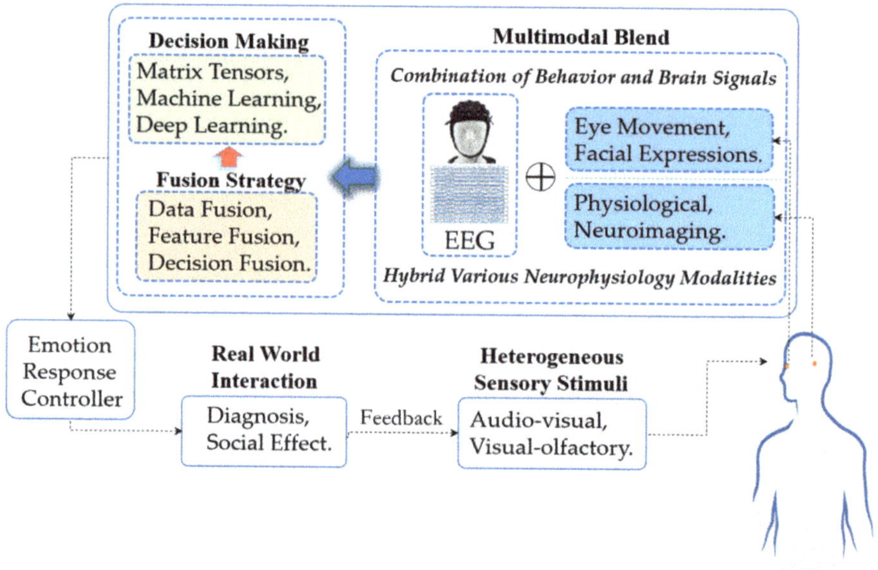

Figure 1. Flowchart of multimodal emotional involvement for electroencephalogram (EEG)-based affective brain–computer interfaces (BCI).

(1) In the signal acquisition and input stage, modality data from combined brain signals and behavior modalities (such as expression and eye movement) or various hybrid neurophysiology modalities (such as functional Near-infrared spectroscopy (fNIRS) and fMRI) induced by heterogeneous sensory stimuli (such as audio-visual stimulation) during interaction with other groups or by certain events are captured by the system's signal acquisition devices. At this stage, multimodal aBCI can be divided into three main categories: aBCI based on a combination of behavior and brain signals, aBCI based on various hybrid neurophysiology modalities and aBCI based on heterogeneous sensory stimuli. For each type of multimodal aBCI, the principles are further summarized, and several representative aBCI systems are highlighted in Sections 3–5.

(2) In signal processing, obtaining pure EEG signals containing emotional signals is critical. For neurophysiological signals, the preprocessing process is to denoise and remove artifacts from the collected original signals. For image signals such as expressions, irrelevant information in images is eliminated and information representing emotional state is restored and enhanced. In the stage of modalities fusion, we can use different fusion strategies, including data fusion, feature fusion and decision fusion. In decision-making, emotional state decision output can select spatial tensors [16,17], machine learning [18,19], or deep learning methods [20,21], as the final classification decision-maker.

(3) Multimodal aBCI systems output relevant emotional states. If the task involves only emotional recognition, it does not require emotional feedback control; the feedback occurs through a relevant interface (such as diagnosis). However, if the task involves social effects (such as wheelchair control), the user's state information needs to be included directly in the closed-loop system to

automatically modify the behavior of the interface with which the user is interacting. Many aBCI studies are based on investigating and recognizing user' emotional states. The applied domains for these studies are varied and include such fields as medicine, education, driverless vehicle and entertainment.

2.2. The Foundations of Multimodal Emotion Recognition

2.2.1. Multimodal Fusion Method

With the development of multisource heterogeneous information fusion, fusing features from multiple classes of emotional states may be important in emotion recognition. Using different types of signals to support each other and fusing complementary information can effectively improve the final recognition effect [22]. The current mainstream fusion modalities include data-level fusion (sensor-layer fusion), feature-level fusion and decision-level fusion.

Data-level fusion [23]—also known as sensor layer fusion—refers to the direct combination of the most primitive and unprocessed data collected by each sensor to construct a new set of data. Data-level fusion processing primarily involves numeric processing and parameter estimation methods. It includes estimation techniques (linear and nonlinear) and uses various statistical operations to process the data from multiple data sources.

Feature-level fusion [24,25] involves extracting a variety of modality data, constructing the corresponding modality features and splicing the extracted features into a larger feature set that integrates the various modality features. The most common fusion strategy cascades all the modality feature data into feature vectors and then inputs them into an emotion classifier.

Decision-level fusion [26,27] involves determining the credibility of each modality to the target and then coordinating and making joint decisions. Compared with feature-level fusion, decision-level fusion is easier to carry out, but the key is to gauge the importance of each modality to emotion recognition. Fusion strategies adopted at the decision level are based on statistical rules [28] (e.g., sum rules, product rules and maximum-minimum-median rules), enumerated weights [29,30], adaptive enhancement [31,32], Bayesian inference and its generalization theory (Dempster–Shafer theory [33], dynamic Bayesian networks [34]) and fuzzy integrals [35].

2.2.2. The Multimodal Open Database and Its Research on Representativeness

The open database is convenient for objective comparison of algorithms; for this reason, much research has focused on the emotion database. To enhance an intuitive understanding of the EEG-based multimodal emotion data sets, we summarize the characteristics of the popular databases in Table 1.

Current research on EEG-based multimodal emotion recognition uses different induction materials and acquisition equipment and lacks objective evaluation of the algorithms. Therefore, to objectively evaluate the performances of different algorithms, the related studies were compared on the same open databases. Table 2 lists the representative multimodal emotion recognition research based on open datasets. However, to provide readers with a more comprehensive understanding of multimodal emotion research, the case studies in Sections 3 and 4 are no longer limited to open datasets.

Table 1. Databases based on EEG for multimodal emotion recognition.

Database Access	Modality	Sub.	Stimuli	Emotional Model/States
DEAP [36] www.eecs.qmul.ac.uk/mmv/datasets/deap/	EEG, EOG, EMG, GSR, RSP, BVP, ST, facial videos	32	video	dimensional/valence, arousal, liking
SEED-IV [37] bcmi.sjtu.edu.cn/~seed/seed-iv.html	EEG, eye tracking	15	video	discrete/positive, negative, neutral, fear
ENTERFACE'06 [38] www.enterface.net/results/	EEG, fNIRS, facial videos	5	IAPS	discrete/positive, negative, calm
MANHOB-HCI [39] mahnob-db.eu/hci-tagging/	EEG, GSR, ECG, RSP, ST, Eye-gaze, facial videos	27	video	dimensional/valence, arousal
AMIGOS [40] www.eecs.qmul.ac.uk/mmv/datasets/amigos/index.html	EEG, ECG, GSR	40	video	dimensional/valence, arousal, dominance, liking, familiarity; discrete/basic emotions
EMOEEG [41] www.tsi.telecom-paristech.fr/aao/en/2017/03/03/	EEG, EOG, EMG, ECG, skin conductance temperature	8	IAPS, video	dimensional/valence, arousal
ASCERTAIN [42] mhug.disi.unitn.it/index.php/datasets/ascertain/	EEG, ECG, GSR and visual	58	video	dimensional/valence, arousal
MPED [43]	EEG, ECG, RSP, GSR	23	video	discrete/joy, funny, anger, fear, disgust, disgust and neutrality

Sub.—number of subjects; EOG—electrooculogram; EMG—electromyogram; GSR—galvanic skin response; RSP—respiration; BVP—blood volume pressure; ST—skin temperature; ECG—electrocardiogram; IAPS—International affective picture system; Basic emotions represent the emotions of neutral, happiness, sadness, surprise, fear, anger and disgust.

Table 2. Research on the representativeness of multimodal emotion recognition based on open datasets.

Ref.	Database (Modality)	Feature Extraction	Results (Standard/#)	Innovation
[44]	SEED-IV (EEG + EYE) DEAP (EEG + PPS)	SEED-IV: EEG: PSD, DE in four bands. EYE: pupil diameter, fixation, blink duration, saccade, event statistics. DEAP: preprocessed data.	SEED-IV: 91.01% (avg./4) DEAP: 83.25% (avg. (valence/arousal/dominance/liking)/2)	Using BDAE to fuse EEG features and other features, this study shows that shared representation is a good feature for distinguishing different threads.
[45]	DEAP (EEG + PPS)	EEG + PPS: implicitly extract high-level temporal features.	92.87% (arousal/2) 92.30% (valence/2)	The MMResLSTM learns complex high-level features and the time correlation between two modalities through weight sharing.
[46]	SEED-IV (EEG + EYE) DEAP (EEG + PPS)	SEED-IV: EEG: DE in five bands. EYE: PSD and DE features of pupil diameters. DEAP: EEG: DE in four bands. PPS: statistical feature.	SEED-IV: 93.97% (avg./4) DEAP: 83.23% (arousal/2) 83.82% (valence/2)	The bimodal-LSTM model uses both temporal and frequency–domain information of features.
[21]	DEAP (EEG + PPS)	EEG: power differences, statistical PPS: statistical feature, frequency–domain feature.	83.00% (valence/2) 84.10% (arousal/2)	The parsimonious structure of the MESAE can be properly identified and lead to a higher generalization capability than other state-of-the-art deep-learning models.
[19]	MAHNOB-HCI (EEG + EYE)	EEG: PSD in five bands, spectral power asymmetry. EYE: pupil diameter, gaze distance, eye blinking.	76.40% (valence/3) 68.50% (arousal/3)	Using confidence summation fusion for decision-making fusion of EEG and eye movements can achieve good classification results.
[43]	MPED EEG, GSR, RSP, ECG	EEG: PSD in five bands, HOC, Hjorth, HHS, STFT; GSR: statistical feature; RSP + ECG: energy mean and SSE values.	71.57% (avg./3/positive-negative-neutral)	The novel attention-LSTM (A-LSTM) strengthens the effectiveness of useful sequences to extract more discriminative features.

Ref.—reference; EYE—eye movement; PPS—physiological signals in the DEAP dataset; PSD—power spatial density; DE—differential entropy; BDAE—deep belief autoencoders; LSTM—long short-term memory; MMResLSTM—multimodal residual LSTM; MESAE—multiple-fusion-layer ensemble stacked autoencoder; SSE—subband spectral entropy; HOC—high order crossing; HHS—Hilbert–Huang spectrum; STFT—short-time Fourier transform.

3. Combination of Behavior and Brain Signals

The core challenge of multimodal emotion recognition is to model the internal working of modalities and their interactions. Emotion is usually expressed through the interaction between neurophysiology and behavior; thus, it is crucial to capture the relationship between them accurately and make full use of the related information.

Basic emotion theory has shown that when emotions are aroused, a variety of human neurophysiological and external behavioral response systems are activated [47]. Therefore, theoretically, the combination of a subject's internal cognitive state and external subconscious behavior should greatly improve the recognition performance. Concomitantly, the development and promotion of neurophysiological and behavioral signal acquisition equipment has made emotion recognition using mixed multimodalities of human neurophysiological and behavioral performances a research hotspot in international emotional computing. Therefore, mixed modalities involving physiological and external behavior modalities have attracted more attention from emotion recognition researchers.

Among the major modalities of behavior, eye movement tracking signals and facial expressions are two modalities with content-aware information. Facial expression is the most direct method of emotional representation. By analyzing information from facial expressions and combining the results with a priori knowledge of emotional information (Figure 2a), we can infer a person's emotional state from facial information. Eye movement tracking signals can provide a variety of eye movement indicators and eye movement tracking signals can reflect user subconscious behaviors and provide important clues to the context of the subjects' current activity [48].

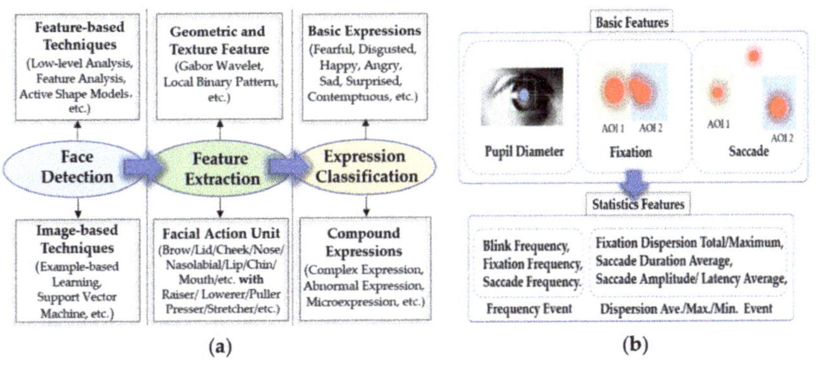

Figure 2. (**a**) Flowchart of emotion recognition based on expression. The facial expression recognition process includes three stages: face location recognition, feature extraction and expression classification. In the face location and recognition part, two technologies are usually adopted: feature-based and image-based [49]. The most commonly used emotion recognition methods for facial expressions are geometric and texture feature recognition and facial action unit recognition. Expressions are usually classified into seven basic expressions—fear, disgust, joy, anger, sadness, surprise and contempt—but people's emotional states are complex and can be further divided into a series of combined emotions, including complex expressions, abnormal expressions and microexpressions; (**b**) Overview of emotionally relevant features of eye movement (AOI 1: The first area of interest, AOI 2: The second area of interest). By collecting data regarding pupil diameter, gaze fixation and saccade, which are three basic eye movement characteristics, their characteristics can be analyzed and counted, including frequency events and special values of frequency event information (e.g., observing fixed frequency and collecting fixed dispersion total/maximum values).

3.1. EEG and Eye Movement

Eye-movement signals allow us to determine what is attracting a user's attention and observe their subconscious behaviors. Eye movements form important cues for a context-aware environment that contains complementary information for emotion recognition. Eye movement signals can provide a rich signal that reflects emotional characteristics, including three common basic features, pupil diameter, gaze information and saccade signals—as well as extended statistical features, including statistical frequency events and statistical deviation events. As shown in Figure 2b, the pupil refers to a resizable opening in the iris of the eye. Related studies [50,51] have shown that pupil size is related to cognition. When we are stimulated from a resting state to an emotional state, our pupils will change size accordingly. Fixation refers to a relatively stable position of the eyeball within a certain range of time and space offset thresholds. Saccade refers to rapid eye movement between two points of interest (or attention). Using these basic characteristics of eye movement signals, we can detect people's arousal and valence from the statistical values of fixation information and scan signals and then use them to evaluate people's inner activity states.

Soleymani [19] used two modalities, EEG signals and eye movement data. For EEG data, the unwanted artifacts, trend and noise were reduced prior to extracting the features from EEG data by preprocessing the signals. Drift and noise reduction were done by applying a 4–45 Hz band-pass filter. For eye movement data, a linear interpolation was used to replace the missing pupil diameter samples due to eye blinking. After removing the linear trend, the power spectrum of the pupil diameter variation was computed. In terms of modalities fusion, they applied two fusion strategies: feature-level fusion and decision-level fusion. Feature-level fusion did not improve the best experimental results of EEG and eye gaze data. However, the channel fusion strategy using decision-level fusion increased the optimal classification rates of arousal and valence to 76.4% and 68.5%, respectively. In feature level fusion, feature vectors from different modalities are combined to form a larger feature vector. Then, feature selection and classification methods are applied to the new feature set. Compared with feature-level fusion, the decision-level fusion strategy is more adaptive and scalable, and it allows modalities to be removed or added to the system without using decision-level fusion to retrain the classifier. A support vector machine (SVM) classifier with an RBF kernel is used in both modalities, and the classification results are fused to obtain multimodal fusion results. The authors drew lessons from the confidence and fusion mentioned in the study [8] to complete the fusion of the two modality classification results. The probability output of the classifier is used as a measure of confidence. For a given experiment, the sum rule is defined as follows:

$$g_a = \frac{\sum\limits_{q \in Q} P_q(\omega_a|x_i)}{\sum\limits_{a=1}^{K} \sum\limits_{q \in Q} P_q(\omega_a|x_i)} = \sum_{q \in Q} \frac{1}{|Q|} P_q(\omega_a|x_i) \tag{1}$$

where g_a is the summed confidence interval for an affected class ω_a. Q is the classifier ensemble selected for fusion, $|Q|$ is the number of classifiers, $P_q(\omega_a|x_i)$ is the posterior probability of having class ω_a and the sample is x_i according to classifier q. To obtain $P_q(\omega_a|x_i)$, the authors used the MATLAB libSVM implementation [52] of the Platt and Wu algorithms. The final choice was made by selecting the class ω_a with the highest g_a. Note that g_a can also be viewed as a confidence assessment on the class ω_a provided by the fusion of classifiers.

In [37], a multimodal framework called EmotionMeter was proposed to recognize human emotions using six EEG electrodes and eye-tracking glasses. The experiments in this study revealed the complementarity of EEG and eye movement in emotion recognition and a multimodal depth neural network was used to improve the recognition performance. For EEG data, in the preprocessing stage, a band-pass filter between 1 and 75 Hz was applied to filter the unrelated artifacts. Then they used the short-time Fourier transform without overlap in 4 s time window to extract the characteristic power spectral density (PSD) and differential entropy (DE) of five frequency bands of each channel. For eye movements, they extracted various features from different detailed parameters used in the literature, such as pupil diameter, fixation, saccade and blink. Among all the characteristics of eye movements, the pupil diameter is most directly related to the emotional state, but it is easily affected by the ambient brightness [53]. Therefore, it is particularly important to preprocess the influence of light and shadow removal on pupil diameter. Based on the observations that the changes in the pupil responses of different participants to the same stimuli have similar patterns, we applied a principal component analysis (PCA)-based method to estimate the pupillary light reflex. Suppose that $Y = A + B + C$ where Y is original sample data of pupil diameters, A is luminance influences that are prominent, B is emotional influences that we want and C is noise. They used PCA to decompose Y and computed the first principle component as the estimate of the light reflex. To enhance the recognition performance, they adopted a bimodal deep autoencoder (BDAE) to extract the shared representations of both EEG and eye movements. The authors construct two restricted Boltzmann machines (RBMs) for EEG and eye movement data, respectively. They connected the two hidden layers of the EEG-RBM and the eyes-RBM, trained the stacked RBMs and input their results into the BDAE, which then learned a shared representation of the two modalities from the RBMs. Finally, this new shared representation was used as the input to train a linear SVM. Their experiments show that compared with a single modality (eye movement: 67.82%, EEG: 70.33%), multimodal deep learning from combined EEG and eye movement features can significantly improve the accuracy of emotion recognition (85.11%).

Wu et al. [54] applied deep canonical correlation analysis (DCCA) to establish a multimodal emotion-recognition model in which the connecting functional features from EEG and those features from eye movements are fused. The architecture of the DCCA model includes three parts: stacked nonlinear layers to achieve nonlinear transformations for two modalities separately, followed by a canonical correlation analysis (CCA) calculation to maximize the correlation between the two transformed modalities. Finally, the two transformed features are fused by weighted average. An SVM is trained on the fused multimodal features to construct the affective model. Notably, the emotion-relevant critical subnetwork actually lies in the network topology. The three high-dimensional topological features, strength, clustering coefficient and eigenvector centrality, are extracted to represent the connected functional features of EEG. For the eye movement signals, the artifacts were eliminated using signals recorded from the electrooculogram (EOG) and FPz channels. Similar to [37], principal component analysis was adopted to eliminate the luminance reflex of the pupil and to preserve the emotion-relevant components. Next, the BeGaze2 [55] analysis software of SMI (SeoMotoric Itruments, Berlin, Germany) eye movement glasses was used to calculate the eye movement parameters, including pupil diameter, fixation time, blinking time, saccade time and event statistics. Then, the statistics of these parameters were derived as 33-dimensional eye movement features. The experimental results not only revealed the complementary representation characteristics between the EEG functional connection network and eye movement data, but also found that the brain functional connectivity networks based on the 18-channel EEG approach are comparable with that of 62-channel EEG under a multimodal pattern, which provided a solid theoretical basis for the use of portable BCI systems in real situations.

We believe that a highly robust emotion-recognition model can be achieved by combining internal physiological EEG signals and external eye movement behavioral signals. The strategies of the model include extracting discriminative EEG representations and eye movements for different emotions and then combining the EEG and eye movement signals through efficient model fusion methods.

3.2. EEG and Facial Expressions

Facial expressions are the most common emotional features. Facial expressions can usually be divided into basic expressions (such as happy and sad), complex expressions, abnormal expressions and microexpressions. The most commonly used emotion recognition methods for facial expressions are geometric and texture feature recognition and facial action unit (facial muscle action combination) recognition.

The texture operator has strong abilities for image-feature extraction. The extracted texture features are mainly used to describe the local gray changes in the image. The representative methods are the Gabor wavelet [56] and local binary pattern [57]. Geometric feature extraction is a classical emotional feature extraction method that typically locates the key points of the human face, measures the relative distances between the positioning points, and finally, defines the features according to the distances. In [58], the authors located eight key points in the eyebrows and the corners of the eyes and mouth. They calculated and obtained six normalized geometric feature vectors and used them in experiments to demonstrate the validity of the geometric feature extraction method.

According to anatomic principles, when a person's emotional state changes, the facial muscles will be subject to a certain degree of tension or relaxation. This process is dynamic, not static. Various (dynamic) facial expressions can be decomposed into combinations of facial action units (AU), which can be used to recognize complex expressions, abnormal expressions and micro expressions. Ekman et al. developed a facial action coding system (FACS) [59]. Facial expressions can be regarded as combinations of the different facial motion units defined by FACS.

Although emotion recognition methods based on expression are more direct and the facial modality data are easy to obtain, this approach lacks credibility. For example, people may show a smile, but it may be a wry smile. Moreover, it is difficult to detect emotional states through the facial expressions of patients with facial paralysis. Therefore, a combination of facial expression and EEG, which reflect the activities of the central nervous system, will undoubtedly detect changes in people's emotional states more objectively and accurately.

Huang et al. [60] proposed two multimodal fusion methods between the brain and peripheral signals for emotion recognition. Their approach achieved accuracy rates of 81.25% and 82.75% on four emotion-state categories (happiness, neutral, sadness and fear). Both models achieved accuracies higher than those of either facial expression (74.38%) or EEG detection (66.88%) alone. They applied principal component analysis (PCA) to analyze the facial expression data and extract high-level features and a fast Fourier transform to extract various PSD features from the raw EEG signals. Due to the limited data quantity, they proposed a method that can help prevent overfitting. From the modality fusion aspect, they adopted a decision strategy based on production rules. Such approaches are commonly found in simple expert systems in cognitive modeling and artificial intelligence fields.

However, their study proved that multimodal fusion detection achieves significant improvements compared with single-modality detection methods. Indeed, it may very well reflect how humans conduct emotion recognition: for example, an expression of weak happiness is typically answered with a neutral emotion, whereas a strong expression of sadness usually evokes fear.

In an extension of their work [22], they applied a pretrained, multitask convolutional neural network (CNN) model to automatically extract facial features and detect the valence and arousal values using a single-modal framework. For EEG, they first used the wavelet transform to capture the time-domain characteristics of the EEG when extracting PSD features; then, they used two different SVM models to recognize the values of valence and arousal. Finally, they obtained the decision-level fusion parameters based on training data for both fusion methods. In addition to implementing the widely used fusion method based on enumerating different weights between two models, they also explored a novel fusion method that requires a boosting technique. They employed both classifiers (facial expression and EEG) as subclassifiers of the AdaBoost algorithm to train the weights of the AdaBoost algorithm. The final results were calculated using Equations (2) and (3):

$$S_{\text{boost}} = 1/(1+\exp(-\sum_{j=1}^{n} w_j s_j)) \tag{2}$$

$$r_{\text{boost}} = \begin{cases} \text{high} & S_{\text{boost}} \geq 0.5 \\ \text{low} & S_{\text{boost}} < 0.5 \end{cases} \tag{3}$$

where S_{boost} stands for the score of AdaBoost score, and the scores of the two classifiers are fused by the AdaBoost method to obtain the final mood score. r_{boost} represents the prediction results (high or low) of the AdaBoost fusion classifier. $s_j \in \{-1,1\}(j = 1,2,\ldots,n)$ represents the corresponding output result of j-th sub-classifier. In this case, S_1 is the facial expression classifier and S_2 is the EEG classifier.

To obtain $w_j(j = 1, 2, \ldots, n)$ from a training set of size $m, s(x_i)_j \in \{-1, 1\}$ designates the output of the j-th classifier for the i-th sample and y_i denotes the true label of the i-th sample. They applied this method separately for the online experiment and achieved accuracies of approximately 68.00% for the valence space and 70.00% for the arousal space after fusion—both of which surpassed the highest-performing single-modality model.

To improve the classification accuracy and reduce noise, Sokolov et al. [61] proposed a combined classification method with decision-level fusion for automated estimation of emotion from EEG and facial expressions. In their study, different Hjorth parameters were adopted for different prime emotional quantities (e.g., arousal, valence and dominance) estimation tasks from a given EEG channel and frequency band. For face detection, to reduce the detection error and false alarm rate and speed up the image processing, a cascaded classifier and a monolithic classifier were combined into a two-level classifiers cascade. In the first level, the Haar-like feature cascade of the weak classifier was used to detect face-like objects, while the second level was used for face verification by a convolutional neural network. Then, the face feature was represented by PCA, which preserved the greatest amount of energy with the fewest principal components. They applied an SVM as a classifier for each modality. Finally, the two modalities were combined by the multi-sample–multi-source strategy [20], in which the final output is the average score from both modalities:

$$y_{\text{combined}} = \frac{1}{M}\sum_{j=1}^{M}\left[\frac{1}{N}\sum_{i=1}^{N}\left(y_{i,j}\right)\right] \tag{4}$$

where y_{combined} is the combined output score, M is the number of modalities used (EEG and face) and N is the number of samples for each biometric modality. $y_{i,j}$ is the output of the system for the i-th sample from j-th modality and $y_{i,j} \in [0, \ldots, 1]$.

Different from eye movement, facial expressions can be captured conveniently by a camera. Therefore, the application scenarios of EEG and facial expression modality fusion are more extensive. However, if subjects feign their facial expressions, they can always successfully "cheat" the machine. Therefore, how to use EEG as auxiliary information to avoid errors caused by subjects camouflaging their true emotions is an important research direction.

4. Various Hybrid Neurophysiology Modalities

Emotion usually refers to a state of mind that occurs spontaneously rather than consciously and is often accompanied by physiological changes in the central nervous system and the periphery, affecting EEG signals and heart rate. Many efforts have been made to reveal the relationships between explicit neurophysiology modalities and implicit psychological feelings.

4.1. EEG and Peripheral Physiology

In general, physiological reactions are the results of nonautonomic nerves. The physiological reactions and the corresponding signals are difficult to control when emotions are excited. Studies have used such physiological reactions to determine and classify different kinds of emotions [62]. A large number of studies [63,64] have shown that all kinds of physiological signals that change over time have various common characteristics. On one hand, their processing operations are very similar; on the other hand, they can be used to extract features from three dimensions (Figure 3a): the time, frequency and time–frequency domains.

Feature extraction is an important step in emotion evaluation because high-resolution features are critical for effective pattern recognition. The common time domain features include statistical features [65] and Hjorth features [66]. The common frequency domain features include PSD [67], DE [68] and rational asymmetric (RASM) [69] features. The common features in the time–frequency domain include wavelet [70], short time Fourier transform [71] and Hilbert–Huang transform [72] features.

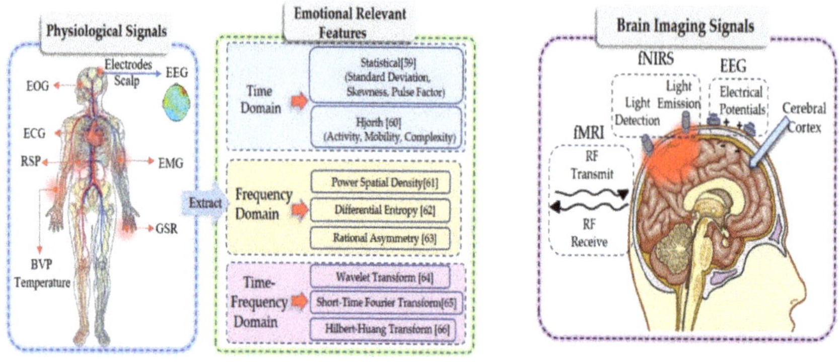

(a) (b)

Figure 3. (**a**) Relevant emotion features extracted from different physiological signals. Physiological features and where they were collected are listed, such as EEG, EOG, RSP, EMG, GSR and BVP temperature. We can extract emotionally relevant features from these physiological signals that change over time in three dimensions: the time, frequency and time-43frequency domains; (**b**) Measurement of brain activity by EEG, fNIRS and fMRI. Briefly, we introduced how these three kinds of brain imaging signals collected from the cerebral cortex work with fMRI based on radio frequency (RF) transmit and RF receive; fNIRS is based on light emission and light detection and EEG is based on electrical potentials.

From the aspect of emotion recognition based on various hybrid neurophysiology modalities, a method of emotion recognition of multimodal physiological signals based on a convolutional recurrent neural network is proposed [73]. In this method, a CNN was used to learn the fine spatial representation of multichannel EEG signals and an LSTM was used to learn the time representation of physiological signals. The two features were then combined to perform emotion recognition and classification and tested on the DEAP dataset. In the arousal emotion dimension, the average correct emotion recognition rate was 93.06%; in the valence emotion dimension, the average correct emotion recognition rate was 91.95%. To extract the spatial signals of EEG, this study develops a position mapping and uses "0" to represent the unused electrode channels in the DEAP dataset. The international 10–20 system is generalized with the test electrodes used in the DEAP dataset to a matrix (h × w), where h is the maximum number of vertical test points and w is the maximum number of horizontal test points. Through position mapping, a one-dimensional EEG data vector sequence is transformed into a two-dimensional EEG data matrix sequence. Finally, the two-dimensional matrix sequence is divided into several groups of two-dimensional matrix sequences. Each matrix sequence has a fixed dimension, and no overlap occurs between two consecutive matrix sequences. To extract the temporal feature of physiological modalities, the signals collected from 33–40 channels of the DEAP dataset are two EOG, two EMG, one GSR, one RSP, one BVP and one ST. Two stacked recurrent neural network (RNN) layers are built. Each layer of the RNN includes multiple LSTM units, and the output of the first RNN layer forms the input to the second RNN. At the fusion level, they use feature-level fusion to combine the extracted spatial features from the EEG signals with the temporal features extracted from the physiological signals. These fused features are input to a softmax layer to predict the emotional state. The final results are calculated using Equation (5):

$$P_j = \text{softmax}([V_S, V_T]), P_j \in R^2 \quad (5)$$

where V_S represents the spatial feature vector of EEG, V_T is the temporal feature vector of the physiological signals and P_j stands for the predicted emotional state.

Kwon et al. [74] proposed improving emotion classification accuracy and reducing model instabilities using a CNN model based on EEG and GSR data. First, a wavelet transform was applied to represent the EEG signal in the frequency domain. The EEG signal was collected from 32 electrodes and derived from a single stimulus. To learn the EEG features from all channels in the spectrogram image, this study adopted a multilayer 2D CNN instead of the one-layer, one-dimensional CNN applied in prior conventional research. In this way, the network was able to extract efficient temporal–spatial features for EEG. The GSR signals are preprocessed by using the short time zero-crossing rate (STZCR). After passing through the various layers of the CNN, a nonlinear activation function and a pooling layer, the EEG image is flattened and combined with the STZCR of the GSR. Based on these fused features, a fully connected layer and softmax were used to perform classification. The author applied data processing to denoise and design a reasonable network architecture to extract efficient features and combine features, and finally, was able to improve the classification performance significantly.

Currently, the advanced algorithms of multimodal emotion recognition based on EEG and physiological signals requires considerable training data to construct a high-quality machine learning model. This computational complexity limits the application of these advanced algorithms in portable devices and scenarios requiring timeliness.

Hyperdimensional (HD) computing [75] has demonstrated rapid learning ability on various biological signal processing tasks [76,77], each of which operates with a specific type of biological signal (see the overview in [78]). Chang et al. [79] extended single-task HD processing to multitask processing and applied it to physiological signals from multimodal sensors. The experimental results on the AMIGOS datasets show that the method achieved a balance between accurate and necessary training data to a certain extent; the proposed model's average classification accuracy was the highest, reaching 76.6%, and its learning speed was the fastest. They also proposed multimodal emotion recognition (HDC-MER) based on high-definition computing. HDC-MER uses random nonlinear functions to map real-valued features to binary HD vectors, further encodes them over time and fuses various patterns, including GSR, ECG and EEG. HDC-MER includes two stages: in the first stage, the original features are transformed into high-definition binary embedded features and in the second stage, multimodal fusion, learning and classification are performed. First, the spatial encoder bundles all the modality feature information at a given point in time by using most of the functions of the HD vector components. A time encoder is used to collect feature changes between videos to capture time-dependent mood swings. After spatial and time domain coding is completed, the next step is to fuse multimodal HD vectors. The fusion unit bundles the corresponding HD vectors into a fused d-bit HD vector. The output from the fusion unit is sent to the associative memory for training and inference. During the training phase, the fusion unit generated from the training data is bundled to its corresponding class prototype of the associative memory. That is, associative memory collects the fusion unit of the same class and bundles them to a prototype HD vector by the majority function. During the inference phase, they used the same encoding, but the label of the fusion unit is unknown; hence, they call it the query HD vector. To perform classification, the query HD vector is compared with all learned prototype HD vectors to identify its source class according to the Hamming distance (i.e., a measure of similarity), defined as the number of bits that differ between the two HD vectors. Finally, two emotional labels with the minimum distance are returned.

Based on the combination of peripheral physiological signals and central nerve signals, this approach can avoid recognition errors caused by emotional camouflage, and patients with dyskinesia can also be effectively processed.

4.2. EEG and Other Neuroimaging Modality

Although the arousal index of human emotional activity can be effectively detected to a certain extent by measuring the activity of the human peripheral nervous system, this approach cannot effectively measure the central nervous system of the human body. As a classic cognitive style, the generation of positive emotion mainly depends on related brain activities. To date, functional neuroimaging has become a more direct tool for exploring and explaining brain activity (Figure 3b). The low spatial resolution of EEG is one of its shortcomings in the study of emotional activity. In addition to EEG based on neural electrical activity, brain imaging techniques based on blood oxygen imaging, such as fNIRS and fMRI, have been widely used in neuroimaging research. Therefore, in the application of emotion recognition, integrating various brain imaging modality information can provide high-resolution spatiotemporal neural images that can help in further understanding the brain rules when emotional states occur. Then, related emotions can be identified.

Compared with EEG, the advantage of near-infrared technology is that it is not affected by widespread environmental electrical noise, and its sensitivity to EMG artifacts is much lower than that of EEG. Near-infrared light is absorbed when it penetrates biologic tissue; the measurement results of near-infrared spectroscopy are related to brain activity and are attributed to the effect of this interaction. The slow hemodynamic response showed that *Hb* increased slightly after the beginning of the neural activity, followed by a large, but delayed increase in HbO_2, which reached a peak at approximately 10 s [80,81] after activation, while *Hb* decreased correspondingly [82]. The changes in the concentration of oxygenated hemoglobin and deoxyhemoglobin can be calculated using the modified Beer-Lambert law (shown in Equation (6)) based on the detected changes in light intensity [83].

$$\begin{bmatrix} \Delta Hb \\ \Delta HbO_2 \end{bmatrix} = \begin{bmatrix} \alpha_{deaxy(\lambda 1)} & \alpha_{oxy(\lambda 1)} \\ \alpha_{deaxy(\lambda 2)} & \alpha_{axy(\lambda 2)} \end{bmatrix}^{-1} \cdot \begin{bmatrix} \Delta A_{(\lambda 1)} \\ \Delta A_{(\lambda 2)} \end{bmatrix} \cdot \mathrm{B} \quad (6)$$

where Δ represents the amount of change at a given time relative to an initial time, and α indicates the absorption rate of a certain hemoglobin (*oxy* or *deaxy*) to a certain wavelength of light ($\lambda 1$ or $\lambda 2$). *A* represents the light intensity of a certain wavelength detected. B indicates the length of the optical path, which is related to the distance between the emitters and receivers (usually 3 cm) and is a constant predetermined by the experiment. Thus, the sum of two unknowns (ΔHb and ΔHbO_2) can finally be calculated. However, the fNIRS system measures the hemodynamic response, which takes several seconds to develop. The delay in the hemodynamic response has been estimated by modeling simulations and computational methods [84,85]. More invasive methods also demonstrate delayed hemodynamic responses [86].

However, fNIRS technology has some problems; for example, the time resolution is insufficient and cannot directly reflect neural activity, which seriously affects the reliability of fNIRS in detecting brain function. However, fNIRS can determine the brain function signal source through channel localization. In contrast, EEG, which is a mature brain function detection technology, has high time resolution, but its disadvantage is that the detection signal cannot identify the brain region source. On the other hand, both fNIRS and EEG techniques have the advantages of small restrictions on the environment and subjects and can be used to detect the brain functions of subjects in a state of natural relaxation. Therefore, combining fNIRS and EEG technology into a bimodal detection technology capitalizes on their spatiotemporal resolution advantages and can help people better understand the neural mechanisms of brain activity in cognitive psychological tasks.

A multimodal method for the joint evaluation of fNIRS and EEG signals for emotional state detection was proposed in [87]. The emotional state was recorded from video capture of facial expressions, and the related neural activity was measured by wearable and portable neuroimaging systems: functional fNIRS and EEG, which can evaluate hemodynamic and electrophysiological responses, respectively. EmotivEPOC (Neurotech, San Francisco, CA, USA) headphones were used to collect EEG signals at a 128 Hz sampling rate, while fNIRS devices and sampling wireless fNIRS systems were used to monitor the prefrontal cortex of the receptors to avoid the problem of overlapping brain regions. The method included simultaneous detection and comparison of various emotional expressions through multimodalities and classification of spatiotemporal data with neural characteristics. The experimental results showed a strong correlation between spontaneous facial emotion expression and brain activity related to an emotional state. By comparing the recognition results of the system with the actual tags of the test images, the recognition accuracy of the system was approximately 74%. At the same time, the experimental results showed that the method using fNIRS and EEG achieved better performance than did the method using only fNIRS or EEG. Nevertheless, this study did not explain in detail the time synchronization method for the different time resolutions and measurement delays between fNIRS and EEG.

In practical applications of BCI systems, time synchronization may be a key problem because the information transfer rate is the most important factor in evaluating BCI systems. To address these problems, computational methods such as using prior information [88] or normalized features [89] were proposed to obtain better BCI performance than a single modality. Morioka et al. [88] used fNIRS features as prior information to estimate cortical currents in EEG, while Ahn et al. [89] combined EEG and fNIRS features by normalizing all features into the range [0,1] and applied the sum of the features. Although further optimization steps are still needed, these two novel approaches may become future solutions for overcoming the current limitations in integrating EEG-fNIRS features.

To the best of our knowledge, in the field of computer engineering, there are few studies on emotion recognition that integrate EEG-fNIRS, and most of them focus on the task of motion imagination. For example, in [90], the performance of a sensory motor rhythm-based BCI was significantly improved by simultaneously measuring EEG and NIRS [91]. Some studies [80,92] have shown that hemodynamic changes may be a promising indicator to overcome the limitations of command detection. It is expected that more researchers will conduct in-depth research on integrating EEG-fNIRS for emotion recognition in the future.

To monitor brain activity through fMRI, the principle is that the brain contains a large number of hydrogen protons in rich water, and the spins of hydrogen protons emit electromagnetic waves at a certain frequency under the action of an external main magnetic field (B0). If the proper radio frequency (RF) current is used to excite the protons from a direction perpendicular to the main magnetic field, the spin precession angle increases, and when the excitation current is removed, the proton will return to its original state and emit the same signal as the excitation frequency. To take advantage of this phenomenon, a coil is used to receive signals transmitted from the body in vitro for imaging (Figure 3b). Compared with EEG and fNIRS, the greatest advantage of monitoring brain activity with fMRI is that the spatial resolution is higher than fNIRS; nevertheless, like fNIRS, the time resolution is lower than that of EEG, which makes it difficult to achieve real-time data collection. Additionally, the current application environment of fMRI is relatively limited, which also limits its application scenarios. As far as we know, in the field of computer engineering, no research exists on using combined EEG-fMRI for emotion recognition; most of the existing studies focus on the neural mechanism.

5. Heterogeneous Sensory Stimuli

In the study of emotion recognition, to better simulate, detect and study emotions, researchers have employed use a variety of materials to induce emotions, such as pictures (visual), sounds (audio) and videos (audio-visual). Many studies [36,37] have shown that video-induced stimulation based on visual and auditory multisensory channels is effective because audio-visual integration enhances brain patterns and further improves the performance of brain–computer interfaces. Vision and audition, as the most commonly used sensory organs, can effectively provide objective stimulation to the brain, while the induction ability of other sensory channels, such as olfaction and tactile sensation, is still lacking. As the most primitive sense of human beings, olfaction plays an important role in brain development and the evolution of human survival. Therefore, in theory, it can provide more effective stimulation than can vision and audition.

5.1. Audio-Visual Emotion Recognition

Multisensory channel integration to induce subjects' emotions, especially video material that involves emotion recognition evoked by visual and auditory stimuli, will be a future trend. For audio-visual emotion recognition, a real-time BCI system to identify the emotions of patients with consciousness disorders was proposed [10]. Specifically, two classes of video clips were used to induce positive and negative emotions sequentially in the subjects, and the EEG data were collected and processed simultaneously. Finally, instant feedback was provided after each clip. Initially, they recruited ten healthy subjects to participate in the experiment, and their BCI system achieved a high average online accuracy of 91.5 ± 6.34%, which demonstrated that the subjects' emotions had been sufficiently evoked and efficiently recognized. Furthermore, they applied the system to patients with disorders of consciousness (DOC), who suffer from motor impairment and generally cannot provide adequate emotional expressions. Thus, using this BCI system, doctors can detect the potential emotional states of these patients. Eight DOC patients participated in the experiment and significant online accuracy achieved for three patients. These experimental results indicate that BCI systems based on audio-visual stimulation may be a promising tool for detecting the emotional states of patients with DOC.

5.2. Visual-Olfactory Emotion Recognition

Although the affective information from audio–visual stimuli has been extensively studied, for some patients with impaired visual and auditory abilities, such integration cannot play a role. If multisensory channels could be combined with odor to induce emotion stimulation, new discoveries and breakthroughs may be achieved in emotion recognition research, especially for those patients with normal olfactory function.

However, due to the volatile gases of odorant mixtures, the influences of peripheral organs, and the role of the brain, confusion can easily occur in these processes, and it is difficult to quantify. Therefore, research on odor-induced emotions is relatively rare. The representative example of multiple sensory emotion recognition related to olfactory activity is a single study that induced emotion in a patient with DOC [93]. During the experiment, the patient was asked to imagine an unpleasant odor or to 'relax' in response to either a downward pointing arrow or a cross appearing on a screen, respectively. The patients' electrophysiological responses to stimuli were investigated by means of EEG equipment and analyzed using a specific threshold algorithm. A significant result was observed and calculated, which shows that this paradigm may be useful for detecting covert signs of consciousness, especially when patients are precluded from carrying out more complex cognitive tasks.

6. Open Challenges and Opportunities

In this section, we discuss the important open issues, which may become popular in research on multimodal emotion recognition based on EEG in the future. In research of multimodal emotion recognition based on EEG, we found many technical challenges and opportunities (Figure 4). Here, we focus on some important research opportunities, which may also be obstacles to aBCI leaving the laboratory and moving to practical application.

6.1. Paradigm Design

For general BCI paradigms, the approaches of neurophysiology-informed affect sensing can be categorized in terms of their dependence on user volition and stimulation [3]. The user initiative means that the user sends instructions to the BCI system by actively thinking. The degree of stimulation depends on the users and essentially refers to whether the stimulation is specific (e.g., whether it is necessary to implement different stimuli for different users). This section introduces the latest emotion-related experimental paradigm according to the classification scheme presented in [94] and provides corresponding application suggestions.

6.1.1. Stimulus-Independent and Passive Paradigms

To explore emotions, researchers use general materials related to different emotions to design emotional paradigms, such as the international affective pictures (IAPS) [95], music, movie clips and videos. Pan [96] proposed an experimental paradigm based on open pictures. A facial expression was displayed in the center of the monitor. The emotional content of these images was measured by a self-assessment model (SAM) [97] that contained nine valence and arousal dimensions. The presentation time for each picture was eight seconds. During the presentation, the subjects were asked to focus on the smiling or crying faces. At the completion of the experiment, each subject was asked to mark each picture with the SAM. A music-induced method [98] can spontaneously lead subjects to a real emotional state. In [99], the researchers asked subjects to evoke emotions by recalling an unpleasant smell. Many studies [100,101] have shown that when people receive both auditory and visual sensory inputs, their brains may integrate the auditory and visual features of these stimuli, and audio–visual integration may be accompanied by increased brain activity and state. Huang et al. [22] developed a real-time BCI system based on audio-visual channels to identify emotions evoked by video clips. The researchers used video clips representing different emotional states to test and train subjects.

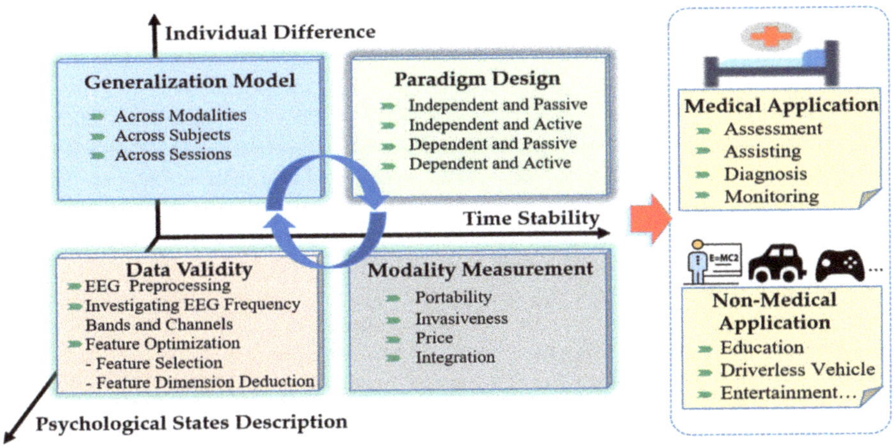

Figure 4. Open challenges and opportunities in multimodal emotion recognition for EEG-based brain–computer interfaces (BCI).

In this paradigm, the subjects generally self-report the emotional experience scale; thus, it is difficult to know whether the subjects truly received the passive stimulus during the experiment, but because this experimental design is relatively simple and does not require any elaborate laboratory settings, it is widely used.

6.1.2. Stimulus-Independent and Active Paradigms

In the design of this paradigm, some universal participatory materials can be used while simultaneously encouraging subjects to actively achieve a specific target state in some way during the experiment. The most common paradigm is to design emotions by having subjects participate in games. When players realize that their emotional state has an impact on the game parameters, they begin to actively induce their own state to manipulate the game environment according to their preferences [102]. Because the experimental material is universal and the task is completed actively by the user, this paradigm is both expansible and objective.

6.1.3. Stimulus-Dependent and Passive Paradigms

This paradigm is mainly customized based on the user's characteristics. Specifically, we can selectively provide or automatically play back media items that are known to induce a specific emotional state in certain users. Pan et al. [103] used this paradigm to identify the state of consciousness of patients with consciousness disturbances. In each experiment, the paradigm begins with an audio-visual description in Chinese: "focus on your own photo (or a stranger's photo) and count the number of frame flash lasting for eight seconds, indicating the target photo. Next, two photos appear, one of which has a flashing frame. The flashing frame is randomly selected and flashes five times. Ten seconds later, one of the two photos identified by the BCI algorithm appears in the center of the graphical user interface (GUI) as feedback. If the result is correct, a scale symbol, a positive audio feedback clip of applause and a detected photo are presented for four seconds to encourage the patient; otherwise, a question mark ('?') is presented. Patients are asked to selectively focus on the stimulus related to one of the two photos according to the audio–visual instructions (that is, a voice in the headset and sentences on the screen at the same time).

6.1.4. Stimulus-Dependent and Active Paradigms

Stimulus-dependent and active paradigms are relatively rarely used. Because this approach requires subjects to independently recall the past to stimulate their emotions, it is difficult to effectively control the changes in their emotional states. However, some studies [104,105] have shown that emotional self-induction techniques, such as relaxation, are feasible as control methods.

6.2. *Modality Measurement*

The most important thing for multimodal emotion identification is the measurement and collection of modality data. However, the portability, intrusiveness, cost and integration of the measuring equipment determine the key factors as to whether the multimodal emotion-recognition system can be widely used. The detection equipment for the behavior modality is relatively mature and has reached highly useful levels in terms of portability and the quality of the obtained signals. For face detection, a variety of high-fidelity cameras are very advanced options. For eye movement signal acquisition, conventional eye movement measurement methods include desktop-captured eye movements and glasses-type captured eye movements. Recently, it has been shown that CNNs can be used to extract relevant eye movement features from images captured by smart-phone cameras [106].

For brain imaging equipment, electrodes are directly implanted into the cerebral cortex by surgery, allowing high-quality neural signals to be obtained. However, these procedures pose safety risks and high costs, including wound healing difficulties and inflammatory reactions. In contrast, electroencephalograph leads attach to the scalp and fNIRS avoid expensive and dangerous operations. However, due to the attenuation effect of the skull on the brain signal, the signal strength and resolution obtained are weaker than those of the intrusive acquisition equipment. Although fMRI is noninvasive and has high temporal and spatial resolution, it is expensive and requires users to be in a relatively closed space; consequently, it is difficult to expand to wide use. A team of researchers [107] at the University of Nottingham in the UK has developed a magnetoencephalography system that can be worn like a helmet that allows the scanned person to move freely and naturally during the scanning process. This approach may lead to a new generation of lightweight, wearable neuroimaging tools in the near future, which in turn would promote practical applications of BCI based on brain magnetism.

For physiological signal acquisition, Chen et al. [108] designed "intelligent clothing" that facilitates the unnoticeable collection of various physiological indices of the human body. To provide pervasive intelligence for intelligent clothing systems, a mobile medical cloud platform was constructed by using mobile Internet, cloud computing and big data analysis technology. The signals collected by smart clothing can be used for emotion monitoring and emotion detection, emotional care, disease diagnosis and real-time tactile interaction.

Concerning multimodal integrated acquisition devices, the VR-capable headset LooxidVR produced by LooxidLabs (Daejeon, Korea) integrates head-mounted display (HMD) with built-in EEG sensors and eye tracking sensors. In addition, a phone can be attached to display virtual reality (VR) content [109]. This method can achieve direct synchronization and synchronous acquisition of eye movement tracking and matching EEG data, thus realizing high-fidelity synchronized eye-movement tracking and EEG data to augment VR experiences. The BCI research team [110] of the Technical University of Berlin has released a wireless modular hardware architecture that can simultaneously collect EEG and functional near-infrared brain functional images—as well as other conventional physiological parameters such as ECG, EMG and acceleration. A similar high-precision, portable and scalable hardware architecture for multiphysiological parameter acquisition is a prerequisite for engineering applications for multimodal emotion recognition research. In other words, the improvements in hardware for collecting modality signals will improve the signal quality, widen the user population and promote reform and innovation in the field of aBCI.

6.3. Data Validity

6.3.1. EEG Noise Reduction and Artifact Removal

EEG signals have been widely used in medical diagnosis, human-computer interaction, neural mechanism exploration and other research fields. However, EEG signals are extremely weak and easily polluted by unwanted noise, which leads to a variety of artifacts [111]. Artifacts are unwanted signals; these mainly occur stem from environmental noise, experimental errors and physiological artifacts [112]. Environmental artifacts and experimental errors from external factors are classified as external artifacts, while physiological factors from the body (such as blinking, muscle activity and heartbeat) can be classified as inherent artifacts [113,114]. To obtain high-quality EEG signals, in addition to the improvement and promotion of hardware acquisition equipment mentioned, effective preprocessing (noise reduction and artifact removal) of EEG signals is also very important.

For EEG processing, first of all, we should avoid artifacts from the source as much as possible and tell the subjects not to blink or do some actions that may cause artifacts before the start of EEG signal acquisition. Then for some unavoidable artifacts (EOG, EMG, ECG), we need to consider whether the EEG signal and the artifact signal overlap in frequency. If the frequencies do not overlap, we can try to remove the pseudo by linear filtering. For example, the frequency of the five frequency bands (delta: 1–3 Hz, theta: 4–7 Hz; alpha: 8–13 Hz; beta: 14–30 Hz; gamma 31–50 Hz) related to emotion of EEG is 1 ~50 Hz. Low-frequency filter is used to remove EMG artifacts with higher frequency and high-frequency filter is used to remove ocular artifacts with lower frequency. When the artifacts of electrophysiological signals such as frequency overlap, high amplitude and wide frequency band exist, the preprocessing of EEG signals needs to identify and separate the artifacts while retaining the EEG signals containing emotional information. Blind source separation (BSS) [115] techniques are commonly used to remove related artifacts, including canonical correlation analysis (CCA) [116] and independent component analysis (ICA) [117].

6.3.2. EEG Bands and Channels Selecting

The "emotional brain" theory [118] reveals that not every brain region is associated with emotional tasks. This inspires researchers to choose areas of the brain that are closely related to emotion for EEG measurement. At the same time, some studies [119] have shown that there is a close relationship between different EEG bands and different emotional states. By selecting the key frequency bands and channels and reducing the number of electrodes, not only can the computational costs be reduced, but the performance and robustness of the emotion-recognition model can be significantly improved, which is highly important for the development of wearable BCI devices.

Zheng et al. [120] proposed a novel critical channel and frequency band selection method through the weight distributions learned by deep belief networks. Four different configurations of 4, 6, 9 and 12 channels were selected in this experiment. The recognition accuracy of these four configurations is relatively stable, achieving a maximum accuracy of 86.65%—even better than that of the original 62 channels. They also compared the performances of DE characteristics in different frequency bands (delta, theta, alpha, beta and gamma) and found that the performance of the gamma and beta bands was better than that of other frequency bands. These results confirm that the β and γ oscillations of brain activity have a greater relationship with emotional processing than do other frequency oscillations.

6.3.3. Feature Optimization

Many studies [65,121] have found that different feature vectors have different effects on the accuracy of emotional state classification. Combining a variety of different features into high-dimensional feature vectors can also improve the classification accuracy. In addition, different subjects have different sensitivities to different features. Not all features carry important information about the emotional state. Irrelevant and redundant features not only increase the risk of overfitting, but also increase the difficulty of emotion recognition because of increasing the feature space.

Therefore, to eliminate the influence of feature irrelevance and redundancy, improve the real-time performance of the classification algorithm and improve the accuracy of multimodal emotion recognition, feature optimization is usually needed after feature extraction. Feature optimization can be divided into two types: feature selection and feature dimensionality reduction. We can assume that the feature set after feature extraction is $\{X_1, \ldots, X_n\}$, the features to be selected are X_i, the optimized features are Y_i, the number of features is n and m and the feature selection algorithm, which evaluates and selects the optimal feature subset with strong emotional representation ability from the original set of features is $f_s : \{X_1, \ldots, X_n\} \rightarrow \{X_1, \ldots, X_m\}(n \leq m)$. The feature dimensionality reduction algorithm is $f_d : \{X_1, \ldots, X_n\} \rightarrow \{Y_1, \ldots, Y_m\}(n \leq m)$, which maps the original feature set to a new feature set whose feature attributes are different than those of the original features.

- **Feature selection.** Selecting features with a strong ability to represent emotional state is highly important in emotion recognition tasks. Many algorithms exist that can reduce dimensionality by removing redundant or irrelevant features, such as particle swarm optimization (PSO) [122] and the genetic algorithm (GA) [123].
- **Feature dimension deduction.** The essence of feature dimension reduction is a mapping function that maps high-dimensional data to a low-dimensional space and creates new features through linear or nonlinear transformations of the original eigenvalues. The dimensionality reduction methods are divided into linear and nonlinear dimensionality reduction. Examples of linear dimensionality reduction include principal component analysis (PCA) [124] and independent component analysis (ICA) [125], etc. Nonlinear dimensionality reduction is divided into methods based on kernel functions and methods based on eigenvalues, such as kernel-PCA [126].

6.4. Generalization of Model

In practical applications, trained emotional models often need to remain stable for long periods; however, the physiological signals related to emotion often change substantially and data from different individuals will present differently in different time environments. In practical multimodal emotion identification, various problems often occur, such as modality data loss and incomplete modality data collection. Thus, whether we can conduct cross-modality emotion identification also involves system generalizability. However, there are natural differences in the data between different modalities. Generally, these problems limit the popularization and wide application of emotion-recognition systems. The important challenges in achieving a multimodal emotion-recognition system with strong generalizability lie in solving the problems of modality–modality, object–object and session–session variability. Currently, we can adopt the following three types of strategies to solve these problems:

(1) A general classifier is trained, but the traditional machine-learning algorithms are based on the assumption that the training data and the test data are independently and identically distributed. Therefore, when the general classifier encounters new domain data, its performance often degrades sharply.
(2) Look for effective and stable feature patterns related to emotion. The authors of [69] found that the lateral temporal areas activate more for positive emotions than for negative emotions in the beta and gamma bands, that the neural patterns of neutral emotions have higher alpha responses at parietal and occipital sites and that negative emotional patterns have significantly higher delta responses at parietal and occipital sites and higher gamma responses at prefrontal

sites. Their experimental results also indicate that the EEG patterns that remain stable across sessions exhibit consistency among repeated EEG measurements for same participant. However, more stable patterns still need to be explored.

(3) For the problem of differences in data distribution, the most mature and effective approach is to use transfer-learning to reduce the differences between different domains as much as possible. Assume that $D_s = \{X_S, Y_S\}$ and $D_t = \{X_t, Y_t\}$ represent the source domain and the target domain, respectively, where $X \in x, Y \in y$ is the sample data and the label. To overcome the three challenges, we need to find a feature transformation function f that makes the edge probability distribution and the conditional probability distribution satisfy $P(f(X_s)) = P(f(X_t))$ and $P(Y_s|f(X_s)) = P(Y_t|f(X_t))$, respectively.

- For the subject–subject problem, other objects are the source domain, and the new object is the target domain. Due to the large differences in EEG among different subjects, it is traditional to train a model for each subject, but this practice of user dependence is not in line with our original intention and cannot meet the model generalization requirements. In [127], the authors proposed a novel method for personalizing EEG-based affective models with transfer-learning techniques. The affective models are personalized and constructed for a new target subject without any labeled training information. The experimental results demonstrated that their transductive parameter transfer approach significantly outperforms other approaches in terms of accuracy. Transductive parameter transfer [128] can capture the similarity between data distributions by taking advantage of kernel functions and can learn a mapping from the data distributions to the classifier parameters using the regression framework.
- For the session–session problem, similar to the cross-subject problem, the previous session is the source domain, and the new session is the target domain. A novel domain adaptation method was proposed in [129] for EEG emotion recognition that showed superiority for both cross-session and cross-subject adaptation. It integrates task-invariant features and task-specific features in a unified framework and requires no labeled information in the target domain to accomplish joint distribution adaptation (JDA). The authors compared it with a series of conventional and recent transfer-learning algorithms, and the results demonstrated that the method significantly outperformed other approaches in terms of accuracy. The visualization analysis offers insights into the influence of JDA on the representations.
- For the modality–modality problem, the complete modality data are the source domain, and the missing modality data are the target domain. The goal is to achieve knowledge transfer between the different modality signals. The authors of [127] proposed a novel semisupervised multiview deep generative framework for multimodal emotion recognition with incomplete data. Under this framework, each modality of the emotional data is treated as one view, and the importance of each modality is inferred automatically by learning a nonuniformly weighted Gaussian mixture posterior approximation for the shared latent variable. The labeled-data-scarcity problem is naturally addressed within our framework by casting the semisupervised classification problem as a specialized missing data imputation task. The incomplete-data problem is elegantly circumvented by treating the missing views as latent variables and integrating them out. The results of experiments carried out on the multiphysiological signal dataset DEAP and the EEG eye-movement SEED-iv dataset confirm the superiority of this framework.

6.5. Application

Emotion recognition based on BCI has a wide range of applications that involve all aspects of our daily lives. This section introduce potential applications from two aspects: medical and nonmedical.

6.5.1. Medical Applications

In the medical field, emotion recognition based on BCI can provides a basis for the diagnosis and treatment of mental illnesses. The diagnosis of mental illness has remained at a subjective scale and lacks objective and quantitative indicators that can help clinicians diagnose medical treatments.

Computer-aided evaluation of the emotions of patients with consciousness disturbances can help doctors better diagnose the physical condition and consciousness of patients. The existing research on emotion recognition mainly involves offline analysis. For the first time, Huang et al. [10] applied an aBCI online system to the emotion recognition of patients with disorders of consciousness. Using this system, they were able to successfully induce and detect the emotional characteristics of some patients with consciousness disorders in real time. These experimental results showed that aBCI systems hold substantial promise for detecting emotions of patients with disorders of consciousness.

Depression is a serious mental health disease that has high social costs. Current clinical practice depends almost entirely on self-reporting and clinical opinions; consequently. There is a risk of a series of subjective biases. The authors of [130] used emotional sensing methods to develop diagnostic aids to support clinicians and patients during diagnosis and to help monitoring treatment progress in a timely and easily accessible manner. The experiment was conducted on an age- and sex-matched clinical dataset of 30 patients and 30 healthy controls. The results of experiments showed the effectiveness of this framework in the analysis of depression.

Mood disorders are not the only criteria for diagnosing autism spectrum disorders (ASD). However, clinicians have long relied on the emotional performances of patients as a basis for autism. The results of the study in [131] suggested that cognitive reassessment strategies may be useful for children and adolescents with ASD. Many studies have shown that emotion classification based on EEG signal processing can significantly improve the social integration abilities of patients with neurological diseases such as amyotrophic lateral sclerosis (ALS) or acute Alzheimer's disease [132].

6.5.2. Non-Medical Applications

In the field of education, students wore portable EEG devices with an emotion-recognition function, allowing teachers to monitor the students' emotional states during distance instruction. Elatlassi [133] proposed to model student engagement in online environments using real-time biometric measures and using acuity, performance and motivation as dimensions of student engagement. Real-time biometrics are used to model acuity, performance and motivation include EEG and eye-tracking measures. These biometrics have been measured in an experimental setting that simulates an online learning environment.

In the field of driverless vehicles, emotion recognition based on EEG adds an emotion-recognition system to the autopilot system, thus increasing the driving reliability of the automatic driving system [134]. At the same time, a human-machine hybrid intelligent automatic driving system in man's loop is built. To date, in the automatic driving system, because passengers do not know whether the driverless vehicle can correctly identify and assess the traffic condition or whether it can make the correct judgment and response in the process of driving, passengers are still very worried about the safety of pilotless driving. The brain computer interface technology can detect the passenger's emotion in real time and transmit the real feeling of the passenger in the driving process to the driverless system, which can adjust the driving mode according to the passenger's emotional feeling. In the whole system, the human being as a link of an automatic driving system is very good for man-machine cooperation.

In entertainment research and development, we can build a game assistant system for emotional feedback regulation based on EEG and physiological signals that provided players with a full sense of immersion and extremely interactive experiences. In the study of [135], EEG-based "serious" games for concentration training and emotion-enable applications including emotion-based music therapy on the web were proposed and implemented.

7. Conclusions

Achieving accurate, real-time detection of user emotional states is the main goal of the current aBCI research efforts. The rapidly expanding field of multimodal sentiment analysis shows great promise in accurately capturing the essence of expressed sentiments. This study provided a review of recent progress in multimodal aBCI research to illustrate how hBCI techniques may be implemented to address these challenges. The definition of multimodal aBCI was updated and extended, and three main types of aBCI were devised. The principles behind each type of multimodal aBCI were summarized, and several representative aBCI systems were highlighted by analyzing their paradigm designs, fusion methods and experimental results. Finally, the future prospects and research directions of multimodal aBCI were discussed. We hope that this survey will function as an academic reference for researchers who are interested in conducting multimodal emotion-recognition research based on combining EEG modalities with other modalities.

Author Contributions: Conceptualization, J.P. and Z.H.; Methodology, J.P., Z.H. and L.W.; Formal analysis, J.P., Z.H., F.Y. and Z.L.; Investigation, Z.H., C.Z. and J.P.; Resources, Z.H. and J.L.; Writing-original draft preparation, Z.H.; Writing-review and editing, J.P., Z.H., C.Z., J.L., L.W., and F.Y.; Visualization, Z.H. and J.P.; Supervision, J.P.; Project administration, J.P.; Funding acquisition, J.P. All authors have read and agreed to the published version of the manuscript.

Funding: This study was supported by the Key Realm R and D Program of Guangzhou under grant 202007030005, the Guangdong Natural Science Foundation under grant 2019A1515011375, the National Natural Science Foundation of China under grant 62076103, and the Special Funds for the Cultivation of Guangdong College Students' Scientific and Technological Innovation (pdjh2020a0145).

Conflicts of Interest: The authors declare that there are no conflicts of interest regarding the publication of this paper.

References

1. Wolpaw, J.R.; Birbaumer, N.; McFarland, D.J.; Pfurtscheller, G.; Vaughan, T.M. Brain–computer interfaces for communication and control. *Clin. Neurophysiol.* **2002**, *113*, 767–791. [CrossRef]
2. Mühl, C.; Nijholt, A.; Allison, B.; Dunne, S.; Heylen, D. Affective brain-computer interfaces (aBCI 2011). In Proceedings of the International Conference on Affective Computing and Intelligent Interaction, Memphis, TN, USA, 9–12 October 2011; p. 435.
3. Mühl, C.; Allison, B.; Nijholt, A.; Chanel, G. A survey of affective brain computer interfaces: Principles, state-of-the-art, and challenges. *Brain-Comput. Interfaces* **2014**, *1*, 66–84. [CrossRef]
4. Van den Broek, E.L. Affective computing: A reverence for a century of research. In *Cognitive Behavioural Systems*; Springer: Berlin/Heidelberg, Germany, 2012; pp. 434–448.
5. Ekman, P.E.; Davidson, R.J. *The Nature of Emotion: Fundamental Questions*; Oxford University Press: Oxford, UK, 1994.
6. Russell, J.A. A circumplex model of affect. *J. Personal. Soc. Psychol.* **1980**, *39*, 1161. [CrossRef]
7. Niemic, C. Studies of Emotion: A Theoretical and Empirical Review of Psychophysiological Studies of Emotion. *Psychophy* **2004**, *1*, 15–18.
8. Chanel, G.; Kierkels, J.J.; Soleymani, M.; Pun, T. Short-term emotion assessment in a recall paradigm. *Int. J. Hum.-Comput. Stud.* **2009**, *67*, 607–627. [CrossRef]
9. Li, Y.; Pan, J.; Long, J.; Yu, T.; Wang, F.; Yu, Z.; Wu, W. Multimodal BCIs: Target Detection, Multidimensional Control, and Awareness Evaluation in Patients With Disorder of Consciousness. *Proc. IEEE* **2016**, *104*, 332–352.
10. Huang, H.; Xie, Q.; Pan, J.; He, Y.; Wen, Z.; Yu, R.; Li, Y. An EEG-based brain computer interface for emotion recognition and its application in patients with Disorder of Consciousness. *IEEE Trans. Affect. Comput.* **2019**. [CrossRef]
11. Wang, F.; He, Y.; Qu, J.; Xie, Q.; Lin, Q.; Ni, X.; Chen, Y.; Pan, J.; Laureys, S.; Yu, R. Enhancing clinical communication assessments using an audiovisual BCI for patients with disorders of consciousness. *J. Neural Eng.* **2017**, *14*, 046024. [CrossRef] [PubMed]
12. D'mello, S.K.; Kory, J. A review and meta-analysis of multimodal affect detection systems. *ACM Comput. Surv. (CSUR)* **2015**, *47*, 1–36. [CrossRef]

13. Poria, S.; Cambria, E.; Bajpai, R.; Hussain, A. A review of affective computing: From unimodal analysis to multimodal fusion. *Inf. Fusion* **2017**, *37*, 98–125. [CrossRef]
14. Ebrahimi, T.; Vesin, J.; Garcia, G. Guest editorial braincomputer interface technology: A review of the second international meeting. *IEEE Signal Process. Mag.* **2003**, *20*, 14–24. [CrossRef]
15. Calvo, R.A.; D'Mello, S. Affect detection: An interdisciplinary review of models, methods, and their applications. *IEEE Trans. Affect. Comput.* **2010**, *1*, 18–37. [CrossRef]
16. Phan, A.H.; Cichocki, A. Tensor decompositions for feature extraction and classification of high dimensional datasets. *Nonlinear Theory Its Appl. IEICE* **2010**, *1*, 37–68. [CrossRef]
17. Congedo, M.; Barachant, A.; Bhatia, R. Riemannian geometry for EEG-based brain-computer interfaces; a primer and a review. *Brain-Comput. Interfaces* **2017**, *4*, 155–174. [CrossRef]
18. Zheng, W.-L.; Dong, B.-N.; Lu, B.-L. Multimodal emotion recognition using EEG and eye tracking data. In Proceedings of the 2014 36th Annual International Conference of the IEEE Engineering in Medicine and Biology Society, Chicago, IL, USA, 26–30 August 2014; pp. 5040–5043.
19. Soleymani, M.; Pantic, M.; Pun, T. Multimodal emotion recognition in response to videos. *IEEE Trans. Affect. Comput.* **2011**, *3*, 211–223. [CrossRef]
20. Liu, W.; Zheng, W.-L.; Lu, B.-L. Emotion recognition using multimodal deep learning. In Proceedings of the International Conference on Neural Information Processing, Kyoto, Japan, 16–21 October 2016; pp. 521–529.
21. Yin, Z.; Zhao, M.; Wang, Y.; Yang, J.; Zhang, J. Recognition of emotions using multimodal physiological signals and an ensemble deep learning model. *Comput. Methods Programs Biomed.* **2017**, *140*, 93–110. [CrossRef]
22. Huang, Y.; Yang, J.; Liu, S.; Pan, J. Combining Facial Expressions and Electroencephalography to Enhance Emotion Recognition. *Future Internet* **2019**, *11*, 105. [CrossRef]
23. Minotto, V.P.; Jung, C.R.; Lee, B. Multimodal multi-channel on-line speaker diarization using sensor fusion through SVM. *IEEE Trans. Multimed.* **2015**, *17*, 1694–1705. [CrossRef]
24. Poria, S.; Chaturvedi, I.; Cambria, E.; Hussain, A. Convolutional MKL based multimodal emotion recognition and sentiment analysis. In Proceedings of the 2016 IEEE 16th International Conference on Data Mining (ICDM), Barcelona, Spain, 12–15 December 2016; pp. 439–448.
25. Haghighat, M.; Abdel-Mottaleb, M.; Alhalabi, W. Discriminant correlation analysis: Real-time feature level fusion for multimodal biometric recognition. *IEEE Trans. Inf. Forensics Secur.* **2016**, *11*, 1984–1996. [CrossRef]
26. Zhalehpour, S.; Onder, O.; Akhtar, Z.; Erdem, C.E. BAUM-1: A spontaneous audio-visual face database of affective and mental states. *IEEE Trans. Affect. Comput.* **2016**, *8*, 300–313. [CrossRef]
27. Wu, P.; Liu, H.; Li, X.; Fan, T.; Zhang, X. A novel lip descriptor for audio-visual keyword spotting based on adaptive decision fusion. *IEEE Trans. Multimed.* **2016**, *18*, 326–338. [CrossRef]
28. Gunes, H.; Piccardi, M. Bi-modal emotion recognition from expressive face and body gestures. *J. Netw. Comput. Appl.* **2007**, *30*, 1334–1345. [CrossRef]
29. Koelstra, S.; Patras, I. Fusion of facial expressions and EEG for implicit affective tagging. *Image Vis. Comput.* **2013**, *31*, 164–174. [CrossRef]
30. Soleymani, M.; Asghari-Esfeden, S.; Pantic, M.; Fu, Y. Continuous emotion detection using EEG signals and facial expressions. In Proceedings of the 2014 IEEE International Conference on Multimedia and Expo (ICME), Chengdu, China, 14–18 July 2014; pp. 1–6.
31. Freund, Y.; Schapire, R.E. Experiments with a new boosting algorithm. In Proceedings of the ICML, Bari, Italy, 3–6 July 1996; pp. 148–156.
32. Ponti, M.P., Jr. Combining classifiers: From the creation of ensembles to the decision fusion. In Proceedings of the 2011 24th SIBGRAPI Conference on Graphics, Patterns, and Images Tutorials, Alagoas, Brazil, 28–30 August 2011; pp. 1–10.
33. Chang, Z.; Liao, X.; Liu, Y.; Wang, W. Research of decision fusion for multi-source remote-sensing satellite information based on SVMs and DS evidence theory. In Proceedings of the Fourth International Workshop on Advanced Computational Intelligence, Wuhan, China, 19–21 October 2011; pp. 416–420.
34. Nefian, A.V.; Liang, L.; Pi, X.; Liu, X.; Murphy, K. Dynamic Bayesian networks for audio-visual speech recognition. *EURASIP J. Adv. Signal Process.* **2002**, *2002*, 783042. [CrossRef]
35. Murofushi, T.; Sugeno, M. An interpretation of fuzzy measures and the Choquet integral as an integral with respect to a fuzzy measure. *Fuzzy Sets Syst.* **1989**, *29*, 201–227. [CrossRef]

36. Koelstra, S.; Muhl, C.; Soleymani, M.; Lee, J.-S.; Yazdani, A.; Ebrahimi, T.; Pun, T.; Nijholt, A.; Patras, I. Deap: A database for emotion analysis; using physiological signals. *IEEE Trans. Affect. Comput.* **2011**, *3*, 18–31. [CrossRef]
37. Zheng, W.-L.; Liu, W.; Lu, Y.; Lu, B.-L.; Cichocki, A. Emotionmeter: A multimodal framework for recognizing human emotions. *IEEE Trans. Cybern.* **2018**, *49*, 1110–1122. [CrossRef]
38. Savran, A.; Ciftci, K.; Chanel, G.; Mota, J.; Hong Viet, L.; Sankur, B.; Akarun, L.; Caplier, A.; Rombaut, M. Emotion detection in the loop from brain signals and facial images. In Proceedings of the eNTERFACE 2006 Workshop, Dubrovnik, Croatia, 17 July–11 August 2006.
39. Soleymani, M.; Lichtenauer, J.; Pun, T.; Pantic, M. A Multimodal Database for Affect Recognition and Implicit Tagging. *IEEE Trans. Affect. Comput.* **2012**, *3*, 42–55. [CrossRef]
40. Correa, J.A.M.; Abadi, M.K.; Sebe, N.; Patras, I. Amigos: A dataset for affect, personality and mood research on individuals and groups. *IEEE Trans. Affect. Comput.* **2018**. [CrossRef]
41. Conneau, A.-C.; Hajlaoui, A.; Chetouani, M.; Essid, S. EMOEEG: A new multimodal dataset for dynamic EEG-based emotion recognition with audiovisual elicitation. In Proceedings of the 2017 25th European Signal Processing Conference (EUSIPCO), Kos, Greece, 28 August–2 September 2017; pp. 738–742.
42. Subramanian, R.; Wache, J.; Abadi, M.K.; Vieriu, R.L.; Winkler, S.; Sebe, N. ASCERTAIN: Emotion and personality recognition using commercial sensors. *IEEE Trans. Affect. Comput.* **2016**, *9*, 147–160. [CrossRef]
43. Song, T.; Zheng, W.; Lu, C.; Zong, Y.; Zhang, X.; Cui, Z. MPED: A multi-modal physiological emotion database for discrete emotion recognition. *IEEE Access* **2019**, *7*, 12177–12191. [CrossRef]
44. Liu, W.; Zheng, W.-L.; Lu, B.-L. Multimodal emotion recognition using multimodal deep learning. *arXiv* **2016**, arXiv:1602.08225.
45. Ma, J.; Tang, H.; Zheng, W.-L.; Lu, B.-L. Emotion recognition using multimodal residual LSTM network. In Proceedings of the 27th ACM International Conference on Multimedia, Nice, France, 21–25 October 2019; pp. 176–183.
46. Tang, H.; Liu, W.; Zheng, W.-L.; Lu, B.-L. Multimodal emotion recognition using deep neural networks. In Proceedings of the International Conference on Neural Information Processing, Guangzhou, China, 14–18 November 2017; pp. 811–819.
47. Bulling, A.; Ward, J.A.; Gellersen, H.; Troster, G. Eye movement analysis for activity recognition using electrooculography. *IEEE Trans. Pattern Anal. Mach. Intell.* **2010**, *33*, 741–753. [CrossRef] [PubMed]
48. Ekman, P. An argument for basic emotions. *Cogn. Emot.* **1992**, *6*, 169–200. [CrossRef]
49. Bakshi, U.; Singhal, R. A survey on face detection methods and feature extraction techniques of face recognition. *Int. J. Emerg. Trends Technol. Comput. Sci.* **2014**, *3*, 233–237.
50. Võ, M.L.H.; Jacobs, A.M.; Kuchinke, L.; Hofmann, M.; Conrad, M.; Schacht, A.; Hutzler, F. The coupling of emotion and cognition in the eye: Introducing the pupil old/new effect. *Psychophysiology* **2008**, *45*, 130–140. [CrossRef] [PubMed]
51. Wang, C.-A.; Munoz, D.P. A circuit for pupil orienting responses: Implications for cognitive modulation of pupil size. *Curr. Opin. Neurobiol.* **2015**, *33*, 134–140. [CrossRef] [PubMed]
52. Chang, C.-C.; Lin, C.-J. LIBSVM: A library for support vector machines. *ACM Trans. Intell. Syst. Technol. (TIST)* **2011**, *2*, 1–27. [CrossRef]
53. Bradley, M.M.; Miccoli, L.; Escrig, M.A.; Lang, P.J. The pupil as a measure of emotional arousal and autonomic activation. *Psychophysiology* **2008**, *45*, 602–607. [CrossRef]
54. Wu, X.; Zheng, W.-L.; Lu, B.-L. Investigating EEG-Based Functional Connectivity Patterns for Multimodal Emotion Recognition. *arXiv* **2020**, arXiv:2004.01973.
55. SensoMotoric Instruments. *Begaze 2.2 Manual*; SensoMotoric Instruments: Teltow, Germany, 2009.
56. Xu, X.; Quan, C.; Ren, F. Facial expression recognition based on Gabor Wavelet transform and Histogram of Oriented Gradients. In Proceedings of the 2015 IEEE International Conference on Mechatronics and Automation (ICMA), Beijing, China, 2–5 August 2015; pp. 2117–2122.
57. Huang, X.; He, Q.; Hong, X.; Zhao, G.; Pietikainen, M. Improved spatiotemporal local monogenic binary pattern for emotion recognition in the wild. In Proceedings of the 16th International Conference on Multimodal Interaction, Istanbul, Turkey, 12–16 November 2014; pp. 514–520.
58. Saeed, A.; Al-Hamadi, A.; Niese, R. The effectiveness of using geometrical features for facial expression recognition. In Proceedings of the 2013 IEEE International Conference on Cybernetics (CYBCO), Lausanne, Switzerland, 13–15 June 2013; pp. 122–127.

59. Ekman, R. *What the Face Reveals: Basic and Applied Studies of Spontaneous Expression Using the Facial Action Coding System (FACS)*; Oxford University Press: New York, NY, USA, 1997.
60. Huang, Y.; Yang, J.; Liao, P.; Pan, J. Fusion of facial expressions and EEG for multimodal emotion recognition. *Comput. Intell. Neurosci.* **2017**, *2017*. [CrossRef] [PubMed]
61. Sokolov, S.; Velchev, Y.; Radeva, S.; Radev, D. Human Emotion Estimation from EEG and Face Using Statistical Features and SVM. In Proceedings of the Fourth International Conference on Computer Science and Information Technology, Geneva, Switzerland, 25–26 March 2017.
62. Chang, C.Y.; Tsai, J.S.; Wang, C.J.; Chung, P.C. Emotion recognition with consideration of facial expression and physiological signals. In Proceedings of the IEEE Conference on Computational Intelligence in Bioinformatics & Computational Biology, Nashville, TN, USA, 30 March–2 April 2009.
63. Chunawale, A.; Bedekar, D. Human Emotion Recognition using Physiological Signals: A Survey. In Proceedings of the 2nd International Conference on Communication & Information Processing (ICCIP), Tokyo, Japan, 20 April 2020.
64. Vijayakumar, S.; Flynn, R.; Murray, N. A comparative study of machine learning techniques for emotion recognition from peripheral physiological signals. In Proceedings of the ISSC 2020 31st Irish Signals and System Conference, Letterkenny, Ireland, 11–12 June 2020.
65. Liu, Y.; Sourina, O. Real-Time Subject-Dependent EEG-Based Emotion Recognition Algorithm. In *Transactions on Computational Science XXIII*; Springer: Berlin/Heidelberg, Germany, 2014; pp. 199–223.
66. Bo, H. EEG analysis based on time domain properties. *Electroencephalogr. Clin. Neurophysiol.* **1970**, *29*, 306–310.
67. Thammasan, N.; Moriyama, K.; Fukui, K.I.; Numao, M. Continuous Music-Emotion Recognition Based on Electroencephalogram. *IEICE Trans. Inf. Syst.* **2016**, *99*, 1234–1241. [CrossRef]
68. Shi, L.C.; Jiao, Y.Y.; Lu, B.L. Differential entropy feature for EEG-based vigilance estimation. In Proceedings of the 2013 35th Annual International Conference of the IEEE Engineering in Medicine and Biology Society (EMBC), Osaka, Japan, 3–7 July 2013; pp. 6627–6630.
69. Zheng, W.-L.; Zhu, J.-Y.; Lu, B.-L. Identifying stable patterns over time for emotion recognition from EEG. *IEEE Trans. Affect. Comput.* **2017**, *10*, 417–429. [CrossRef]
70. Akin, M. Comparison of Wavelet Transform and FFT Methods in the Analysis of EEG Signals. *J. Med. Syst.* **2002**, *26*, 241–247. [CrossRef] [PubMed]
71. Kıymık, M.K.; Güler, N.; Dizibüyük, A.; Akın, M. Comparison of STFT and wavelet transform methods in determining epileptic seizure activity in EEG signals for real-time application. *Comput. Biol. Med.* **2005**, *35*, 603–616. [CrossRef] [PubMed]
72. Hadjidimitriou, S.K.; Hadjileontiadis, L.J. Toward an EEG-Based Recognition of Music Liking Using Time-Frequency Analysis. *IEEE Trans. Biomed. Eng.* **2012**, *59*, 3498–3510. [CrossRef]
73. Liao, J.; Zhong, Q.; Zhu, Y.; Cai, D. Multimodal Physiological Signal Emotion Recognition Based on Convolutional Recurrent Neural Network. *IOP Conf. Ser. Mater. Sci. Eng.* **2020**, *782*, 032005. [CrossRef]
74. Yea-Hoon, K.; Sae-Byuk, S.; Shin-Dug, K. Electroencephalography Based Fusion Two-Dimensional (2D)-Convolution Neural Networks (CNN) Model for Emotion Recognition System. *Sensors* **2018**, *18*, 1383.
75. Rahimi, A.; Datta, S.; Kleyko, D.; Frady, E.P.; Olshausen, B.; Kanerva, P.; Rabaey, J.M. High-Dimensional Computing as a Nanoscalable Paradigm. *IEEE Trans. Circuits Syst. I Regul. Pap.* **2017**, *64*, 2508–2521. [CrossRef]
76. Montagna, F.; Rahimi, A.; Benatti, S.; Rossi, D.; Benini, L. PULP-HD: Accelerating Brain-Inspired High-Dimensional Computing on a Parallel Ultra-Low Power Platform. In Proceedings of the 2018 55th ACM/ESDA/IEEE Design Automation Conference (DAC), San Francisco, CA, USA, 24–28 June 2018.
77. Rahimi, A.; Kanerva, P.; Millán, J.D.R.; Rabaey, J.M. Hyperdimensional Computing for Noninvasive Brain–Computer Interfaces: Blind and One-Shot Classification of EEG Error-Related Potentials. In Proceedings of the 10th EAI International Conference on Bio-Inspired Information and Communications Technologies (Formerly BIONETICS), Hoboken, NJ, USA, 15–17 March 2017.
78. Rahimi, A.; Kanerva, P.; Benini, L.; Rabaey, J.M. Efficient Biosignal Processing Using Hyperdimensional Computing: Network Templates for Combined Learning and Classification of ExG Signals. *Proc. IEEE* **2019**, *107*, 123–143. [CrossRef]

79. Chang, E.-J.; Rahimi, A.; Benini, L.; Wu, A.-Y.A. Hyperdimensional Computing-based Multimodality Emotion Recognition with Physiological Signals. In Proceedings of the 2019 IEEE International Conference on Artificial Intelligence Circuits and Systems (AICAS), Hsinchu, Taiwan, 18–20 March 2019.
80. Huppert, T.J.; Hoge, R.D.; Diamond, S.G.; Franceschini, M.A.; Boas, D.A. A temporal comparison of BOLD, ASL, and NIRS hemodynamic responses to motor stimuli in adult humans. *Neuroimage* **2006**, *29*, 368–382. [CrossRef] [PubMed]
81. Jasdzewski, G.; Strangman, G.; Wagner, J.; Kwong, K.K.; Poldrack, R.A.; Boas, D.A. Differences in the hemodynamic response to event-related motor and visual paradigms as measured by near-infrared spectroscopy. *Neuroimage* **2003**, *20*, 479–488. [CrossRef]
82. Malonek, D.; Grinvald, A. Interactions between electrical activity and cortical microcirculation revealed by imaging spectroscopy: Implications for functional brain mapping. *Science* **1996**, *272*, 551–554. [CrossRef] [PubMed]
83. Ayaz, H.; Shewokis, P.A.; Curtin, A.; Izzetoglu, M.; Izzetoglu, K.; Onaral, B. Using MazeSuite and functional near infrared spectroscopy to study learning in spatial navigation. *J. Vis. Exp.* **2011**, *56*, e3443. [CrossRef]
84. Liao, C.H.; Worsley, K.J.; Poline, J.-B.; Aston, J.A.; Duncan, G.H.; Evans, A.C. Estimating the delay of the fMRI response. *NeuroImage* **2002**, *16*, 593–606. [CrossRef]
85. Buxton, R.B.; Uludağ, K.; Dubowitz, D.J.; Liu, T.T. Modeling the hemodynamic response to brain activation. *Neuroimage* **2004**, *23*, S220–S233. [CrossRef]
86. Duckett, S.G.; Ginks, M.; Shetty, A.K.; Bostock, J.; Gill, J.S.; Hamid, S.; Kapetanakis, S.; Cunliffe, E.; Razavi, R.; Carr-White, G. Invasive acute hemodynamic response to guide left ventricular lead implantation predicts chronic remodeling in patients undergoing cardiac resynchronization therapy. *J. Am. Coll. Cardiol.* **2011**, *58*, 1128–1136. [CrossRef]
87. Sun, Y.; Ayaz, H.; Akansu, A.N. Neural correlates of affective context in facial expression analysis: A simultaneous EEG-fNIRS study. In Proceedings of the 2015 IEEE Global Conference on Signal and Information Processing (GlobalSIP), Orlando, FL, USA, 14–16 December 2015; pp. 820–824.
88. Morioka, H.; Kanemura, A.; Morimoto, S.; Yoshioka, T.; Oba, S.; Kawanabe, M.; Ishii, S. Decoding spatial attention by using cortical currents estimated from electroencephalography with near-infrared spectroscopy prior information. *Neuroimage* **2014**, *90*, 128–139. [CrossRef]
89. Ahn, S.; Nguyen, T.; Jang, H.; Kim, J.G.; Jun, S.C. Exploring neuro-physiological correlates of drivers' mental fatigue caused by sleep deprivation using simultaneous EEG, ECG, and fNIRS data. *Front. Hum. Neurosci.* **2016**, *10*, 219. [CrossRef]
90. Fazli, S.; Mehnert, J.; Steinbrink, J.; Curio, G.; Villringer, A.; Müller, K.-R.; Blankertz, B. Enhanced performance by a hybrid NIRS–EEG brain computer interface. *Neuroimage* **2012**, *59*, 519–529. [CrossRef]
91. Tomita, Y.; Vialatte, F.-B.; Dreyfus, G.; Mitsukura, Y.; Bakardjian, H.; Cichocki, A. Bimodal BCI using simultaneously NIRS and EEG. *IEEE Trans. Biomed. Eng.* **2014**, *61*, 1274–1284. [CrossRef] [PubMed]
92. Liu, Z.; Rios, C.; Zhang, N.; Yang, L.; Chen, W.; He, B. Linear and nonlinear relationships between visual stimuli, EEG and BOLD fMRI signals. *Neuroimage* **2010**, *50*, 1054–1066. [CrossRef] [PubMed]
93. Pistoia, F.; Carolei, A.; Iacoviello, D.; Petracca, A.; Sarà, M.; Spezialetti, M.; Placidi, G. EEG-detected olfactory imagery to reveal covert consciousness in minimally conscious state. *Brain Inj.* **2015**, *29*, 1729–1735. [CrossRef]
94. Zander, T.O.; Kothe, C. Towards passive brain–computer interfaces: Applying brain–computer interface technology to human–machine systems in general. *J. Neural Eng.* **2011**, *8*, 025005. [CrossRef] [PubMed]
95. Lang, P.J.; Bradley, M.M.; Cuthbert, B.N. International affective picture system (IAPS): Technical manual and affective ratings. *NIMH Center Study Emot. Atten.* **1997**, *1*, 39–58.
96. Pan, J.; Li, Y.; Wang, J. An EEG-based brain-computer interface for emotion recognition. In Proceedings of the 2016 International Joint Conference on Neural Networks (IJCNN), Vancouver, BC, Canada, 24–29 July 2016; pp. 2063–2067.
97. Morris, J.D. Observations: SAM: The Self-Assessment Manikin; an efficient cross-cultural measurement of emotional response. *J. Advert. Res.* **1995**, *35*, 63–68.
98. Kim, J.; André, E. Emotion recognition based on physiological changes in music listening. *IEEE Trans. Pattern Anal. Mach. Intell.* **2008**, *30*, 2067–2083. [CrossRef]
99. Iacoviello, D.; Petracca, A.; Spezialetti, M.; Placidi, G. A real-time classification algorithm for EEG-based BCI driven by self-induced emotions. *Comput. Methods Programs Biomed.* **2015**, *122*, 293–303. [CrossRef]

100. An, X.; Höhne, J.; Ming, D.; Blankertz, B. Exploring combinations of auditory and visual stimuli for gaze-independent brain-computer interfaces. *PLoS ONE* **2014**, *9*, e111070. [CrossRef]
101. Wang, F.; He, Y.; Pan, J.; Xie, Q.; Yu, R.; Zhang, R.; Li, Y. A novel audiovisual brain-computer interface and its application in awareness detection. *Sci. Rep.* **2015**, *5*, 1–12.
102. Gilleade, K.; Dix, A.; Allanson, J. Affective videogames and modes of affective gaming: Assist me, challenge me, emote me. In Proceedings of the International Conference on Changing Views, Vancouver, BC, Canada, 16–20 June 2005.
103. Pan, J.; Xie, Q.; Qin, P.; Chen, Y.; He, Y.; Huang, H.; Wang, F.; Ni, X.; Cichocki, A.; Yu, R. Prognosis for patients with cognitive motor dissociation identified by brain-computer interface. *Brain* **2020**, *143*, 1177–1189. [CrossRef]
104. George, L.; Lotte, F.; Abad, R.V.; Lécuyer, A. Using scalp electrical biosignals to control an object by concentration and relaxation tasks: Design and evaluation. In Proceedings of the 2011 Annual International Conference of the IEEE Engineering in Medicine and Biology Society, Boston, MA, USA, 30'August–3 September 2011; pp. 6299–6302.
105. Hjelm, S.I. Research+ Design: The Making of Brainball. *Interactions* **2003**, *10*, 26–34. [CrossRef]
106. Brousseau, B.; Rose, J.; Eizenman, M. Hybrid Eye-Tracking on a Smartphone with CNN Feature Extraction and an Infrared 3D Model. *Sensors* **2020**, *20*, 543. [CrossRef]
107. Boto, E.; Holmes, N.; Leggett, J.; Roberts, G.; Shah, V.; Meyer, S.S.; Muñoz, L.D.; Mullinger, K.J.; Tierney, T.M.; Bestmann, S. Moving magnetoencephalography towards real-world applications with a wearable system. *Nature* **2018**, *555*, 657–661. [CrossRef] [PubMed]
108. Chen, M.; Ma, Y.; Song, J.; Lai, C.-F.; Hu, B. Smart clothing: Connecting human with clouds and big data for sustainable health monitoring. *Mob. Netw. Appl.* **2016**, *21*, 825–845. [CrossRef]
109. Lim, J.Z.; Mountstephens, J.; Teo, J. Emotion Recognition Using Eye-Tracking: Taxonomy, Review and Current Challenges. *Sensors* **2020**, *20*, 2384. [CrossRef]
110. Von Lühmann, A.; Wabnitz, H.; Sander, T.; Müller, K.-R. M3BA: A mobile, modular, multimodal biosignal acquisition architecture for miniaturized EEG-NIRS-based hybrid BCI and monitoring. *IEEE Trans. Biomed. Eng.* **2016**, *64*, 1199–1210. [CrossRef]
111. Radüntz, T.; Scouten, J.; Hochmuth, O.; Meffert, B. Automated EEG artifact elimination by applying machine learning algorithms to ICA-based features. *J. Neural Eng.* **2017**, *14*, 046004. [CrossRef] [PubMed]
112. Du, X.; Li, Y.; Zhu, Y.; Ren, Q.; Zhao, L. Removal of artifacts from EEG signal. *Sheng Wu Yi Xue Gong Cheng Xue Za Zhi J. Biomed. Eng. Shengwu Yixue Gongchengxue Zazhi* **2008**, *25*, 464–467, 471.
113. Urigüen, J.A.; Garcia-Zapirain, B. EEG artifact removal—State-of-the-art and guidelines. *J. Neural Eng.* **2015**, *12*, 031001. [CrossRef] [PubMed]
114. Islam, M.K.; Rastegarnia, A.; Yang, Z. Methods for artifact detection and removal from scalp EEG: A review. *Neurophysiol. Clin. Clin. Neurophysiol.* **2016**, *46*, 287–305. [CrossRef] [PubMed]
115. Jung, T.P.; Makeig, S.; Humphries, C.; Lee, T.W.; Mckeown, M.J.; Iragui, V.; Sejnowski, T.J. Removing electroencephalographic artifacts by blind source separation. *Psychophysiology* **2000**, *37*, 163–178. [CrossRef] [PubMed]
116. Dong, L.; Zhang, Y.; Zhang, R.; Zhang, X.; Gong, D.; Valdes-Sosa, P.A.; Xu, P.; Luo, C.; Yao, D. Characterizing nonlinear relationships in functional imaging data using eigenspace maximal information canonical correlation analysis (emiCCA). *Neuroimage* **2015**, *109*, 388–401. [CrossRef]
117. Makeig, S.; Bell, A.J.; Jung, T.-P.; Sejnowski, T.J. Independent component analysis of electroencephalographic data. In Proceedings of the Advances in Neural Information Processing Systems, Denver, CO, USA, 2–5 December 1996; pp. 145–151.
118. LeDoux, J. *The Emotional Brain: The Mysterious Underpinnings of Emotional Life*; Simon and Schuster: New York, NY, USA, 1998.
119. Li, M.; Lu, B.-L. Emotion classification based on gamma-band EEG. In Proceedings of the 2009 Annual International Conference of the IEEE Engineering in Medicine and Biology Society, Minneapolis, MN, USA, 2–6 September 2009; pp. 1223–1226.
120. Zheng, W.-L.; Lu, B.-L. Investigating critical frequency bands and channels for EEG-based emotion recognition with deep neural networks. *IEEE Trans. Auton. Ment. Dev.* **2015**, *7*, 162–175. [CrossRef]

121. Samara, A.; Menezes, M.L.R.; Galway, L. Feature extraction for emotion recognition and modelling using neurophysiological data. In Proceedings of the 2016 15th International Conference on Ubiquitous Computing and Communications and 2016 International Symposium on Cyberspace and Security (IUCC-CSS), Granada, Spain, 14–16 December 2016; pp. 138–144.
122. Li, Z.; Qiu, L.; Li, R.; He, Z.; Xiao, J.; Liang, Y.; Wang, F.; Pan, J. Enhancing BCI-Based Emotion Recognition Using an Improved Particle Swarm Optimization for Feature Selection. *Sensors* **2020**, *20*, 3028. [CrossRef]
123. Gharavian, D.; Sheikhan, M.; Nazerieh, A.; Garoucy, S. Speech emotion recognition using FCBF feature selection method and GA-optimized fuzzy ARTMAP neural network. *Neural Comput. Appl.* **2012**, *21*, 2115–2126. [CrossRef]
124. Nawaz, R.; Cheah, K.H.; Nisar, H.; Voon, Y.V. Comparison of different feature extraction methods for EEG-based emotion recognition. *Biocybern. Biomed. Eng.* **2020**, *40*, 910–926. [CrossRef]
125. Kang, J.-S.; Kavuri, S.; Lee, M. ICA-evolution based data augmentation with ensemble deep neural networks using time and frequency kernels for emotion recognition from EEG-data. *IEEE Trans. Affect. Comput.* **2019**. [CrossRef]
126. Aithal, M.B.; Sahare, S.L. Emotion Detection from Distorted Speech Signal using PCA-Based Technique. *Emotion* **2015**, *2*, 14–19.
127. Du, C.; Du, C.; Wang, H.; Li, J.; Zheng, W.L.; Lu, B.L.; He, H. Semi-supervised Deep Generative Modelling of Incomplete Multi-Modality Emotional Data. In Proceedings of the ACM Multimedia Conference, Seoul, Korea, 22–26 October 2018.
128. Sangineto, E.; Zen, G.; Ricci, E.; Sebe, N. We are not all equal: Personalizing models for facial expression analysis with transductive parameter transfer. In Proceedings of the 22nd ACM International Conference on Multimedia, Orlando, FL, USA, 3–7 November 2014; pp. 357–366.
129. Li, J.; Qiu, S.; Du, C.; Wang, Y.; He, H. Domain Adaptation for EEG Emotion Recognition Based on Latent Representation Similarity. *IEEE Trans. Cogn. Dev. Syst.* **2020**, *12*, 344–353. [CrossRef]
130. Joshi, J.; Goecke, R.; Alghowinem, S.; Dhall, A.; Wagner, M.; Epps, J.; Parker, G.; Breakspear, M. Multimodal assistive technologies for depression diagnosis and monitoring. *J. Multimodal User Interfaces* **2013**, *7*, 217–228. [CrossRef]
131. Samson, A.C.; Hardan, A.Y.; Podell, R.W.; Phillips, J.M.; Gross, J.J. Emotion regulation in children and adolescents with autism spectrum disorder. *Autism Res.* **2015**, *8*, 9–18. [CrossRef] [PubMed]
132. Gonzalez, H.A.; Yoo, J.; Elfadel, I.A.M. EEG-based Emotion Detection Using Unsupervised Transfer Learning. In Proceedings of the 2019 41st Annual International Conference of the IEEE Engineering in Medicine and Biology Society (EMBC), Berlin, Germany, 23–27 July 2019; pp. 694–697.
133. Elatlassi, R. Modeling Student Engagement in Online Learning Environments Using Real-Time Biometric Measures: Electroencephalography (EEG) and Eye-Tracking. Master's Thesis, Oregon State University, Corvallis, OR, USA, 2018.
134. Park, C.; Shahrdar, S.; Nojoumian, M. EEG-based classification of emotional state using an autonomous vehicle simulator. In Proceedings of the 2018 IEEE 10th Sensor Array and Multichannel Signal Processing Workshop (SAM), Sheffield, UK, 8–11 July 2018; pp. 297–300.
135. Sourina, O.; Wang, Q.; Liu, Y.; Nguyen, M.K. A Real-time Fractal-based Brain State Recognition from EEG and its Applications. In Proceedings of the BIOSIGNALS 2011—The International Conference on Bio-Inspired Systems and Signal Processing, Rome, Italy, 26–29 January 2011.

brain sciences

MDPI

Article

An Emotion Assessment of Stroke Patients by Using Bispectrum Features of EEG Signals

Choong Wen Yean [1], Wan Khairunizam Wan Ahmad [2,*], Wan Azani Mustafa [2], Murugappan Murugappan [3], Yuvaraj Rajamanickam [4], Abdul Hamid Adom [2], Mohammad Iqbal Omar [1], Bong Siao Zheng [1], Ahmad Kadri Junoh [5], Zuradzman Mohamad Razlan [6] and Shahriman Abu Bakar [6]

1 Faculty of Electronic Engineering Technology, Universiti Malaysia Perlis (UniMAP), Arau 02600, Perlis, Malaysia; wenyean0412@gmail.com (C.W.Y.); iqbalomar@unimap.edu.my (M.I.O.); wendy880806@gmail.com (B.S.Z.)
2 Faculty of Electrical Engineering Technology, Universiti Malaysia Perlis (UniMAP), Arau 02600, Perlis, Malaysia; wanazani@unimap.edu.my (W.A.M.); abdhamid@unimap.edu.my (A.H.A.)
3 Department of Electronics and Communication Engineering, Kuwait College of Science and Technology, Doha Area, 7th Ring Road, Kuwait City 13133, Kuwait; m.murugappan@gmail.com
4 School of Electrical and Electronic Engineering, Nanyang Technological University (NTU), 50 Nanyang Avenue, Singapore 639798, Singapore; yuva2257@gmail.com
5 Institute of Engineering Mathematics, Universiti Malaysia Perlis, Arau 02600, Perlis, Malaysia; kadri@unimap.edu.my
6 Faculty of Mechanical Engineering Technology, Universiti Malaysia Perlis (UniMAP), Arau 02600, Perlis, Malaysia; zuradzman@unimap.edu.my (Z.M.R.); shahriman@unimap.edu.my (S.A.B.)
* Correspondence: khairunizam@unimap.edu.my

Received: 9 August 2020; Accepted: 22 September 2020; Published: 25 September 2020

Abstract: Emotion assessment in stroke patients gives meaningful information to physiotherapists to identify the appropriate method for treatment. This study was aimed to classify the emotions of stroke patients by applying bispectrum features in electroencephalogram (EEG) signals. EEG signals from three groups of subjects, namely stroke patients with left brain damage (LBD), right brain damage (RBD), and normal control (NC), were analyzed for six different emotional states. The estimated bispectrum mapped in the contour plots show the different appearance of nonlinearity in the EEG signals for different emotional states. Bispectrum features were extracted from the alpha (8–13) Hz, beta (13–30) Hz and gamma (30–49) Hz bands, respectively. The k-nearest neighbor (KNN) and probabilistic neural network (PNN) classifiers were used to classify the six emotions in LBD, RBD and NC. The bispectrum features showed statistical significance for all three groups. The beta frequency band was the best performing EEG frequency-sub band for emotion classification. The combination of alpha to gamma bands provides the highest classification accuracy in both KNN and PNN classifiers. Sadness emotion records the highest classification, which was 65.37% in LBD, 71.48% in RBD and 75.56% in NC groups.

Keywords: emotion; stroke; electroencephalogram (EEG); bispectrum

---

1. Introduction

Stroke is one of the highest causes of death in Malaysia, with more than 40,000 survivors are managing their health today [1]. Globally, there were 6.2 million deaths caused by stroke in 2017, where the highest rates of stroke mortality countries were reported in Eastern Europe, Africa, and Central Asia [2]. Stroke is caused by the insufficient supply of oxygen to the brain, damaging damage brain cells. This is turn will definitely affect some brain functions which results in stroke survivors to have difficulties in daily living, such as mobility, communication and expressing their thoughts. Also, stroke patients often suffer from emotional and behavioral changes due to their dissatisfaction with the current conditions.

Past studies have been carried out to investigate emotional changes in stroke patients as the influence of their physiological phenomenon [3–5]. These studies revealed that emotions and thoughts are seen as interactive reactions and are intimately related to the health and physiological problems. This leads to the increase risk of a second or recurrent stroke with persistent depression. Therefore, emotion recognition of stroke patients is very helpful in the diagnosis of their psychological and physiological conditions.

The assessment of the emotional conditions and mood of stroke patients is required during rehabilitation to identify the presence of mental health problems such as persistent depression and mood disorders. This also assists in identifying the severity of associated functional impairment of the patients.

Conventionally, emotion assessment can be done through interviews with patients [3,6], an observation on patients' behaviors [6] as well as using standardized measures such as the Hospital Depression and Anxiety Scale (HADS) [6] and Beck Depression Inventory (BDI) [7]. These standardized measures determine the emotional states of the patient by scoring. However, the conventional approaches could be cheated by patients and information that is acquired then will be not accurate. Consequently, researchers tried other approaches to understand the emotional states of patients. Recent studies have stated that emotion assessment can be performed using physiological signals [8], such as skin conductance (SC) [9], respiration signal [10], electrocardiogram (ECG) [11], and electroencephalogram (EEG) [12].

This paper is organized as follows: Section 1, the problem and the context of the study in emotion assessment in stroke patients is discussed. Then, Section 2 reviews the literature on EEG analysis and non-linear features. This section also discusses the use of bispectrum features in EEG analysis. Section 3 focuses on the materials and methods used in this study, including the description of the EEG data, preprocessing, feature extraction, statistical analysis and classification methods. The next section presents the results and their discussions. Lastly, the summary of this paper is briefly discussed.

2. Related Works

EEG is the brain signal that can be measured from placing electrode sensors along the scalp to record the electrical activity of the brain that happens near the surface of the scalp [13]. EEG signal can be used for diagnostic purposes and any abnormalities detected from it connotes that there is brain disorder in that person.

From previous research, the brain has been reported as having higher responsibility and involvement in emotional activities [14]. The brain as the center of emotions is responsible to give responses when it perceives a stimulus. Hence, brain signals are able to provide emotional information of a stroke patient. With this concept, most recent studies of emotion assessment for stroke patients have utilized brain signals. Adamaszek et al. studied the emotional impairment using the event-related potentials (ERP) of a stroke patient [15], Doruk et al. studied the emotional impairment in stroke patients by comparing the emotional score in the Stroke Impact Scale (SIS) with the EEG features, the EEG power asymmetry and coherence [16]. Bong et al. assessed the emotions of stroke patients by using EEG signals in the time-frequency domain [12]. In this study, the electroencephalogram (EEG)-based emotion recognition algorithm is proposed to study the emotional states of stroke patients.

According to previous studies, stroke patients suffer from emotional impairment and consequently, hence their emotional experiences are less significant compared to normal people [15,17–19]. In another related study by Bong et al. [12], left brain damage (LBD) stroke patients were most dominant in perceiving sadness emotion and RBD stroke patients were most dominant in anger emotion. In addition, the authors' dominant frequency band was the beta band by using wavelet packet transform (WPT) with Hurst exponent feature. The highest accuracy obtained was 76.04% in the happiness emotion for the normal control (NC) group using the features from beta to gamma band.

Previous emotional classification studies by Yuvaraj et al. [20] have also shown that the accuracy of the feature extracted from the single frequency band was higher in the beta and gamma bands. Also, the highest accuracy was obtained when all frequency bands from delta to gamma were combined. The author obtained an average accuracy of 66.80% in NC using the combinations of the five frequency bands. In addition, they obtained an average accuracy of 64.73% with the beta band and 65.80% with the gamma band of NC. These results were optimized with the application of the feature selection technique.

The brain is a chaotic dynamical system [21–23], where EEG signals are generated by nonlinear deterministic processes. This is also referred to as deterministic chaos theory with nonlinear coupling interactions between neuronal populations [24,25]. In contrast with linear analysis, nonlinear analysis methods will give more meaningful information about the emotional state changes of stroke patients. Over the last few years, a number of research works have been reported on analyzing EEG signals by using non-linear methods [25–27]. For example, a recurrence measure was applied to study the seizure EEG signals [25]. Zappasodi et al. used fractal dimension (FD) to study the neuronal impairment in stroke patients [26]. In addition, Acharya et al. studied sleep stage detection in EEG signals by using different nonlinear dynamic methods, higher order spectra (HOS) features and recurrence quantification analysis (RQA) features [28]. In their study, HOS was used to extract momentous information which helped with the diagnosis of neurological disorders.

HOS has been claimed as an effective method for analyzing EEG signals. HOS feature has been the most commonly used nonlinear feature. It is the frequency domain or spectral representation of higher order cumulants of a random process. HOS only includes cumulants with third order and above. HOS gains its advantage with the elimination of Gaussian noise and provides a high signal to noise ratio (SNR) [29,30]. HOS provides the ability to extract information deviation from Gaussian and preserves the phase information of signals. Thus, HOS is able to estimate the phase of the non-Gaussian parametric signals. In addition, HOS detects and characterizes nonlinearities in signals. In contrast, the second order measure is power spectrum, which can only reveal linear and Gaussian information of signals.

The third order HOS is bispectrum and is able to preserve phase information of EEG signals. Bispectrum is the easiest HOS to be worked out [31]. Bispectrum has been utilized in the emotional study in EEG signals. Yuvaraj et al. applied bispectrum to study the difference between Parkinson's disease patients and normal people in six discrete emotions (happiness, sadness, fear, anger, surprise, and disgust) [27,32]. Hosseini applied bispectrum to classify the two emotional states (calm and negatives states) of normal subjects [33].

However, the emotional states of stroke patients are yet to be analyzed using the bispectrum features. Hence, in this work, the bispectrum feature is used to classify stroke patients' EEG signals in different emotional states.

Bispectrum is proven in its ability to detect quadratic phase coupling (QPC), a phenomenon of nonlinearity interaction in EEG signals. QPC is the sum of phases at two frequency variables given by $f_1 + f_2$ [34,35]. Bispectrum can be estimated through two approaches: direct and indirect methods. For a stationary, discrete time, random process $x(k)$, the direct method is estimated by taking the 1D-Fourier transform of the discrete series given by:

$$Bi(f_1, f_2) = E[X(f_1)X(f_2)X^*(f_1 + f_2)], \quad (1)$$

where Bi is the bispectrum magnitude, E [ ] denotes statistical expectation operation, $X(f)$ is the Fourier transform (1-D FFT) of the time series, $x(k)$ and * denote the complex conjugate.

For the indirect method, bispectrum is estimated by first estimating the third order cumulants of the random process $x(k)$. Then the nth-order moment is equal to the expectation over the process multiplied by the $(n-1)$ lagged version of itself. Therefore, the third order moment, m_{3x} is:

$$m_{3x}(\tau_1, \tau_2) = E[X(k)X(k+\tau_1)X(k+\tau_2)], \quad (2)$$

where $E[\,]$ denotes statistical expectation operation, τ_1 and τ_2 are lags of the moment sequence.

The third order cumulant sequence, $C_{3x}(\tau_1, \tau_2)$, is identical to its third order moment sequence. It can be calculated by taking an expectation over the process multiplied by 2 lagged versions given by:

$$C_{3x}(\tau_1, \tau_2) = E[X(k)X(k+\tau_1)X(k+\tau_2)]. \quad (3)$$

The bispectrum, $B(f_1, f_2)$, is the 2D-Fourier transform of the third order cumulant function is given by:

$$B(f_1, f_2) = \sum_{\tau_1=-\infty}^{\infty} \sum_{\tau_2=-\infty}^{\infty} C_{3x}(\tau_1, \tau_2) \exp[-j(f_1\tau_1 + f_2\tau_2)], \quad (4)$$

for $|f_1| \leq \pi$, $|f_2| \leq \pi$, and $|f_1 + f_2| \leq \pi$.

Bispectrum is a symmetric function as shown in Figure 1. The shaded area is the non-redundant region of computation of the bispectrum, where $f_2 \geq 0$, $f_2 \geq f_1$, $f_1 + f_2 \leq \pi$, which is sufficient to describe the whole bispectrum [36].

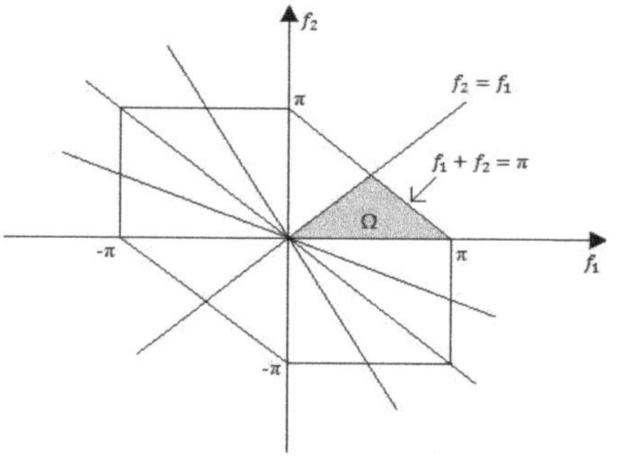

Figure 1. Symmetry regions and non-redundant region (Ω) of bispectrum.

3. Materials and Methods

3.1. EEG Data

The EEG database used in this study was collected from stroke patients, with left brain damage (LBD), right brain damage (RBD) and normal control (NC) at the Hospital Canselor Tuanku Muhriz (HCTM), Kuala Lumpur. (formal approval obtained from UKM Medical Center and Ethics committee for human research, reference no.: UKM 1.5.3.5/244/FF-354-2012). The EEG raw signals of 15 subjects each from every group (LBD, RBD, and NC) were used for the analysis. The background and neurophysiological characteristics of the subjects in the three groups are described in Table 1. The subjects passed the Mini-Mental State Examination (MMSE) with scores of more than 24 over a total of 30 points which was conducted to exclude dementia. The subjects also passed the Beck Depression Inventory (BDI) with scores of less than 18 points, to exclude subjects with psychological problems. The Edinburg Handedness Inventory (EHI) was used to determine the handedness of the subjects, and measured in a scale from −1 to 1. The scales were interpreted as pure left hander for a score of −1, mixed left hander for a score of −0.5, neutral for a score of 0, mixed right hander for a score of 0.5 and pure right hander for a score of 1. From Table 1, the scores show that all subjects were right handers. All subjects were self-reported to have normal vision or corrected to normal vision (with spectacles or contact lenses) to ensure better effect of perceiving emotions from audio–visual stimuli.

Table 1. Background and neurophysiological characteristics (mean ± std) of left brain damage (LBD), right brain damage (RBD), and normal control (NC) subjects.

Variables	LBD	RBD	NC	*p*-Value
Sample size, *N*	15	15	15	NA
Age (year)	56.73 ± 6.15	55.87 ± 6.21	51.87 ± 4.19	0.05979
Female/male	5/10	5/10	12/3	NA
MMSE score (range: 0–30)	26.93 ± 1.77	27.2 ± 1.87	28.87 ± 0.81	0.00392
BDI scale (range: 0–21)	7.07 ± 2.91	6.20 ± 1.90	5.47 ± 1.20	0.14936
EHI (range: −1 to 1)	0.85 ± 0.50	0.85 ± 0.47	0.89 ± 0.40	0.96493
Duration of disease (year)	1.74 ± 1.47	2.24 ± 1.97	NA	NA

The EEG data were collected using a 14-channel wireless EEG device, Emotiv EPOC headset, with built in digital 5th order Sinc filter. The electrode placement was based on the international standard 10–20 system as shown in Figure 2. The EEG data were collected at sampling frequency of 128 Hz. One of the limitations of the EEG is that it has poor spatial resolution as compared to high resolution brain imaging devices, such as functional magnetic resonance imaging (fMRI) and positron emission tomography (PET) scans [37]. However, the Emotiv EPOC device has 14 electrodes with 2 references providing appropriate spatial resolution as well as practical in terms of time and money for this study. Moreover, the EEG device provides high temporal resolution data that record the neural activity changes in milliseconds, which is impossible for fMRI and PET scans.

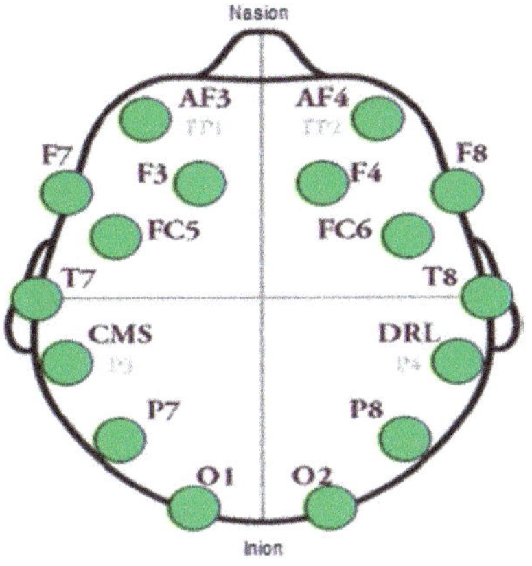

Figure 2. Electrodes placement of Emotiv EPOC according to 10–20 system.

To collect the emotional EEG data, an emotional elicitation protocol was designed to stimulate the emotional states of subjects. The data collection protocol is shown in Figure 3. The stimuli used to evoke the emotions in subjects were audio–visual in the form of video clips edited from International Affective Picture System (IAPS) and International Affective Digital Sound (IADS). Six emotional content video clips were presented to stimulate six discrete emotions, namely anger (A), disgust (D), fear (F), happiness (H), sadness (S) and surprise (SU) [12].

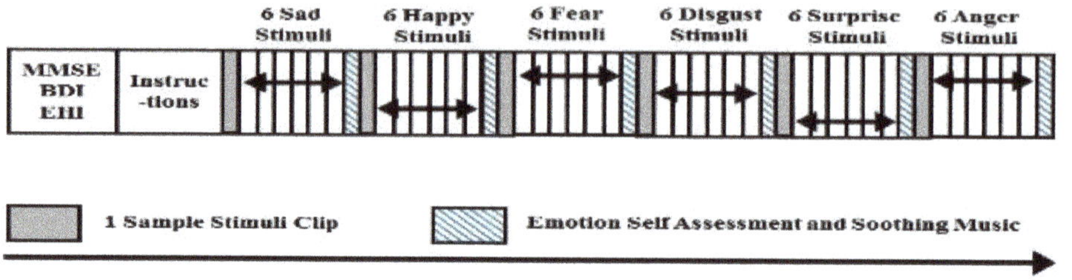

Figure 3. Data collection protocol.

Prior to the experiment, the subjects were asked to complete the MMSE, BDI, and EHI tests and informed consent was given to them. Then, instruction about the experimental procedure was given to the subjects. The experiment started with a sample video clip, followed by six trials of video clips which were displayed continuously. Emotional EEG signals were recorded during the six trials video clips display. After that, the EEG recording was stopped for self-assessment, where the subjects were asked about the emotions they felt or perceived from the video clips. The self-assessment time was at least 1 min and it was subject-dependent. During this period, subjects were asked to relax and get ready for the next video. This was to avoid stimulus order effects. Then the experiment began with the sadness emotion. The same experimental procedures were repeated for happiness (H), fear (F), disgust (D), surprise (SU) and anger (A) emotions. There were a total of 42 video clips, including those of the sample video clips. The duration of each video clip was 46 s to 1 min, therefore, the total duration of the data collection was between 90 to 120 min.

3.2. Preprocessing

There were a total of 36 trials of EEG signals collected from each subject in all groups (LBD, RBD and NC). The collected EEG signals were preprocessed to remove the effects of noises and artifacts that caused interference to the raw signals. The preprocessing of the EEG signals was performed using MATLAB.

The artifacts due to eye blinks were filtered using thresholding method, where the potentials higher than 80 μV and lower than −80 μV were offset from each EEG raw signal [32]. A 6th order Butterworth bandpass filter was used to filter the EEG signals with cut-off frequencies from 0.5 to 49 Hz to extract the delta to gamma frequency bands [32].

3.3. Feature Extraction

The indirect method was used in this study to estimate bispectrum using the *bispeci* function in the MATLAB Higher Order Statistics Toolbox. The number of points used to form each fast Fourier transform (NFFT) was 1024. The bispectrum features were extracted from data by using 50% overlap with Hanning window. The preprocessed time domain EEG data were segmented into six seconds length for every channel. Each data segment is also known as an epoch, and contains 768 data. Three types of EEG frequency sub-bands were used for analysis, namely the alpha (8–13) Hz, beta (13–30) Hz and gamma (30–49) Hz bands.

Bispectrum features were computed from the non-redundant region (Ω) of bispectrum The features extracted from each epoch were variance (v), sum of logarithmic of bispectrum ($H1$), sum of logarithmic of diagonal elements in the bispectrum ($H2$), first moment of diagonal elements in the bispectrum ($H3$), second moment of diagonal elements in the bispectrum ($H4$) and moment of bispectrum ($H5$).

The variance, v of the bispectrum was computed as:

$$v = \frac{1}{N-1}\sum_{i=1}^{N}\left|B_i - \mu\right|^2, \tag{5}$$

where N is the total number of bispectrum in Ω, μ is the mean of bispectrum in Ω, B_i is the bispectrum series for $i = 1, 2, 3, \ldots, N$.

Sum of logarithmic amplitudes of bispectrum ($H1$):

$$H1 = \sum_{\Omega} \log\left(\left|B(f_1, f_2)\right|\right), \quad (6)$$

where Ω is the non-redundant region of bispectrum, f_1 and f_2 are frequency variables of bispectrum and $B(f_1, f_2)$ is the bispectrum feature of f_1 and f_2 in Ω.

The sum of logarithmic amplitudes of diagonal elements in the bispectrum ($H2$):

$$H2 = \sum_{\Omega} \log\left(\left|B(f_m, f_m)\right|\right), \quad (7)$$

where Ω is the non-redundant region of bispectrum and $B(f_m, f_m)$ is the diagonal element of bispectrum feature in Ω.

The first-order spectral moment of amplitudes of diagonal elements in the bispectrum ($H3$):

$$H3 = \sum_{m=1}^{N} m \cdot \log\left(\left|B(f_m, f_m)\right|\right), \quad (8)$$

where $B(f_m, f_m)$ is the diagonal element of bispectrum feature in Ω, N is the total number diagonal elements of bispectrum in Ω, and $m = 1, 2, 3, \ldots, N$.

The second-order spectral moment of the amplitudes of diagonal elements in the bispectrum ($H4$):

$$H4 = \sum_{m=1}^{N} (m - H3)^2 \cdot \log\left(\left|B(f_m, f_m)\right|\right), \quad (9)$$

where $B(f_m, f_m)$ is the diagonal element of bispectrum feature in Ω, N is the total number diagonal elements of bispectrum in Ω, and $m = 1, 2, 3, \ldots, N$.

The moment of bispectrum ($H5$):

$$H5 = \left(\sqrt{f_1^2 + f_2^2}\right) \cdot \left|B(f_1, f_2)\right|, \quad (10)$$

where f_1 and f_2 are frequency variables of bispectrum and $B(f_1, f_2)$ is the bispectrum feature of f_1 and f_2 in Ω.

3.4. Statistical Analysis

One-way analysis of variance (ANOVA) was used to test the significant difference of the bispectrum features among the six emotions classes for LBD, RBD and NC respectively. The use of ANOVA was to statistically analyze the bispectrum features for whether there were differences among the class means of the six emotions. The use of ANOVA requires the assumption that the observations from the feature were approximately normally distributed, the observations were independent and the variances of the classes were equal. The null hypothesis was: "All the emotions of the extracted feature have equal mean". The null hypothesis was rejected and the bispectrum features were validated as statistically significant among the six emotional states if the p-value is less than or equal to 0.05. When the null hypothesis was not rejected, it implies that all the emotions of the extracted feature have equal mean, thus the feature that failed to reject the null hypothesis was not suitable to be used for emotion classification.

3.5. Classification

Each feature used for classification has a total of 90 trials (6 trials × 15 subjects) with 84 feature vectors (14 channels × 6 windows) for each emotion. The *k*-nearest neighbor (KNN) and probabilistic neural network (PNN) classifiers were used to classify the six emotions in the three groups (LBD, RBD and NC). The KNN is one of the most widely applied classifier due to it lower complexity and fast decision making. The KNN searches for the nearest distance or to examine for the most likeliness between the unknown sample and the training dataset. The distance of the unknown sample and the training dataset is determined by the distance metric. In this study, the Cityblock distance metric was implemented in the KNN classification [38].

The PNN uses the Parzen window for nonparametric approximation of the probability distribution function (PDF) of each class and applies Bayes' rule to allocate the new input data to the class with the highest probability by using the PDF of each class [39]. The classifier parameter is the spread value and is proportional to the standard deviation of the Parzen window in PNN. A small spread value gives narrow PDF, whereas a large spread value gives wide PDF and the classifier becomes less selective [40,41].

In this work, the k values of 1 to 15 were tested in KNN and the spread values of 0.1 to 1.5 with an increment of 0.1 were used in PNN to classify the features. The performance of the classifiers was validated through 10-fold cross validation, where 90% of the data were used for training and 10% of the data were used for testing.

4. Results and Discussions

Bispectrum features were extracted from the EEG signals in three groups of subjects (LBD, RBD, and NC) for the analysis of six emotions, namely anger (A), disgust (D), fear (F), happiness (H), sadness (S), and surprise (SU). The contour plots of the estimated bispectrum using the anger emotion of one subject from the LBD group was plotted for the alpha, beta and gamma bands as shown in Figure 4. The plots of the bispectrum magnitude show the relationship between the two bispectrum frequency variables, f_1 and f_2, of the anger emotion. In Figure 4, the f_1 (x-axis) and f_2 (y-axis) are phased coupled. Frequency variables that are phase coupled indicate the presence of quadratic phase coupling (QPC) [31], where the QPC represents the underlying neuronal interaction of the emotional state at the frequencies (f_1 and f_2). The higher magnitude indicates stronger QPC between the frequencies. The red color represents the greatest increase in the magnitude of bispectrum, while the blue color represents the greatest decrease in the magnitude of bispectrum.

The distribution of the bispectrum over the (f_1, f_2) plane differs in each frequency band. The alpha band in Figure 4a shows more bispectrum distribution at lower phase coupled frequencies, which is between (0.04, 0.04) Hz and (0.1, 0.1) Hz in the non-redundant region and other symmetry regions. Whereas the beta band in Figure 4b and gamma band in Figure 4c show the bispectrum distribution at higher phase coupled frequencies. These are between (0.1, 0.1) Hz and (0.2, 0.2) Hz in the beta band and between (0.3, 0.3) Hz and (0.4, 0.4) Hz in the gamma band. Moreover, the maximum magnitude of the bispectrum in the alpha band is the lowest among the three frequency bands. The beta band has larger maximum bispectrum magnitude than the alpha band, while the gamma band has the largest maximum bispectrum magnitude among the frequency bands.

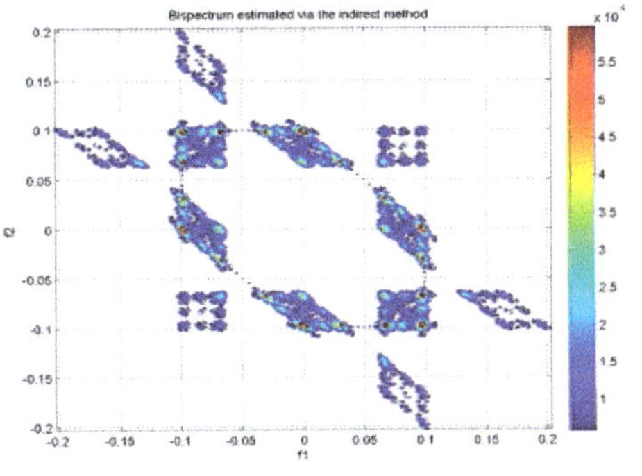

(a)

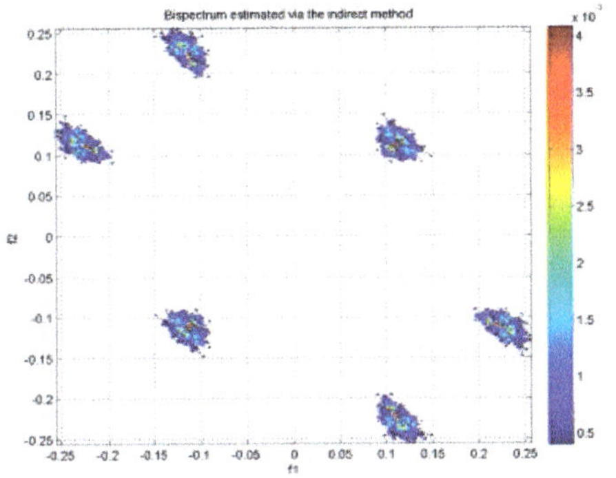

(b)

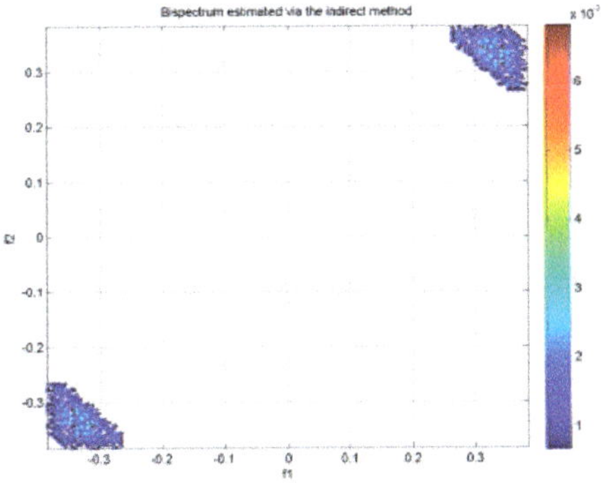

(c)

Figure 4. Bispectrum contour plot of LBD anger emotion in (**a**) alpha band, (**b**) beta band, and (**c**) gamma band.

Figures 5–7 show the bispectrum plots in the non-redundant region and one symmetry region of the six emotions of Subjects #1 from NC, LBD and RBD groups, respectively. From these figures, the different emotional states have different bispectrum distribution over the plane with different phased coupled peaks and maximum magnitude for each. In the past studies, bispectrum has been claimed as a useful signal classification method as it is able to show distinctive distribution in different conditions, such as the left-hand motor imagery and the right-hand motor imagery [42]. The bispectrum provides an EEG feature that is able to recognize these two conditions. Another study has shown that the bispectrum feature is different before meditation and during meditation [43]. This study revealed that the bispectrum exhibit more phase-coupled distribution during meditation than the state before meditation. In addition, the maximum bispectrum magnitude increased during meditation. For the non-human experiment, the "induced" ischemic stroke in rat showed the difference bispectrum distribution in different states of ischemia [44]. In this study, the bispectrum distribution decreased as the rat turns from normal state to ischemic state. Consequently, the distinctive bispectrum pattern of the six emotional states presented in this study implies that the emotional states of each group were distinguishable by applying bispectrum analysis. The significant difference of the emotional states using the bispectrum feature is further validated by the statistical analysis using ANOVA as shown in Table 2.

Table 2. Statistical validation results of LBD, RBD, and NC by using ANOVA (statistically significant at $p \leq 0.05$).

Group	Features	Alpha		Beta		Gamma	
		F Value	*p*-Value	F Value	*p*-Value	F Value	*p*-Value
LBD	v	11.403	<0.001	8.081	<0.001	28.332	<0.001
	$H1$	49.542	<0.001	37.080	<0.001	36.839	<0.001
	$H2$	35.788	<0.001	48.353	<0.001	78.123	<0.001
	$H3$	35.993	<0.001	50.731	<0.001	78.527	<0.001
	$H4$	1.716	0.127	1.347	0.241	1.595	0.158
	$H5$	27.171	<0.001	31.501	<0.001	41.921	<0.001
RBD	v	3.091	0.009	18.464	<0.001	9.743	<0.001
	$H1$	11.070	<0.001	4.255	0.001	10.508	<0.001
	$H2$	18.778	<0.001	14.958	<0.001	28.436	<0.001
	$H3$	18.529	<0.001	15.113	<0.001	26.585	<0.001
	$H4$	1.785	0.112	8.005	<0.001	2.676	0.020
	$H5$	7.429	<0.001	27.299	<0.001	25.434	<0.001
NC	v	6.256	<0.001	14.068	<0.001	8.138	<0.001
	$H1$	2.993	0.011	6.004	<0.001	10.874	<0.001
	$H2$	4.887	<0.001	20.415	<0.001	38.428	<0.001
	$H3$	4.903	<0.001	20.139	<0.001	36.136	<0.001
	$H4$	2.335	0.040	0.442	0.820	1.550	0.171
	$H5$	6.704	<0.001	11.123	<0.001	13.184	<0.001

From the experiment, six types of bispectrum features were extracted from preprocessed EEG data of LBD, RBD and NC. The statistical test using ANOVA was performed on the extracted features and the degrees of freedom were 45,354. The results are shown in Table 2 in three different frequency bands for LBD, RBD and NC respectively. For a *p*-value less than or equal to 0.05, this indicates that the differences between some of the means of the emotional states are statistically significant. The significant bispectrum features imply that there is an interaction of neuronal subcomponents at different frequencies in different emotional states. The shaded *p*-values show the feature which are statistically not significant between the means of emotion classes as they are larger than 0.05. All the bispectrum features were statistically significant in LBD, RBD and NC except the second moment of the diagonal elements in bispectrum ($H4$), thus, $H4$ was discarded in classification. Moreover, from Table 2, the F values are higher in $H1$ and $H3$ for LBD, $H2$ and $H5$ in RBD and v, $H5$, and $H2$ in NC. The highest overall F values are in the LBD group, while NC has comparably smaller values compared to both LBD and RBD groups.

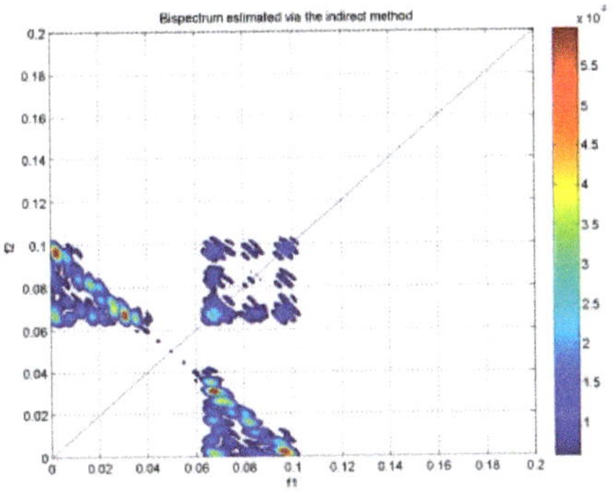

(**a**) anger

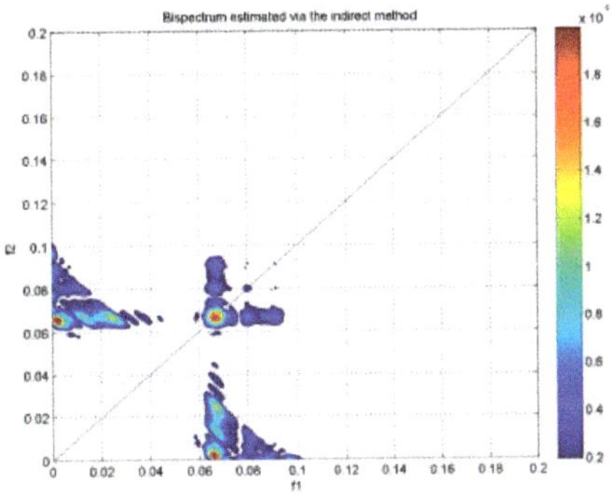

(**b**) disgust

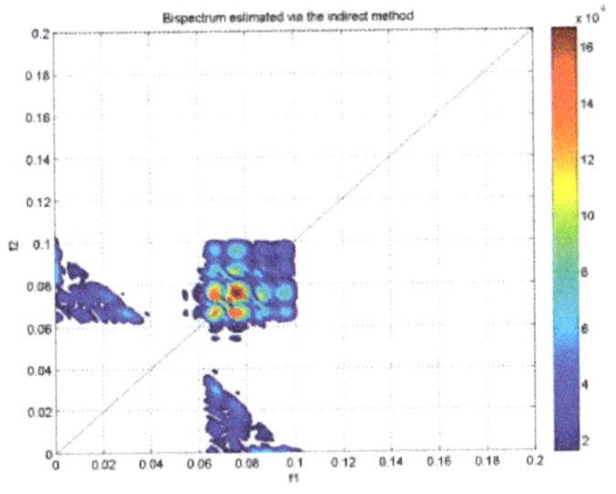

(**c**) fear

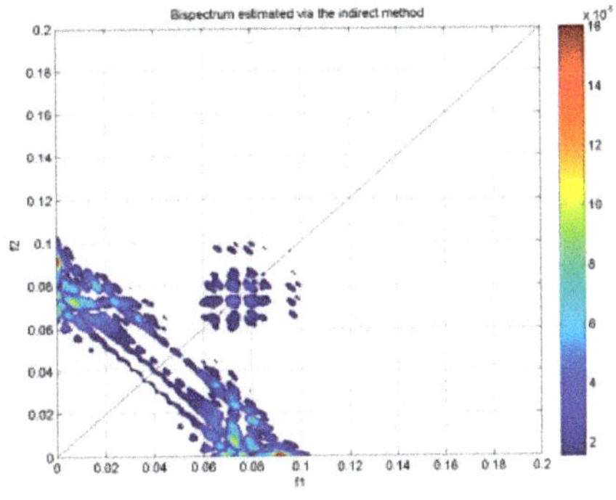

(**d**) happiness

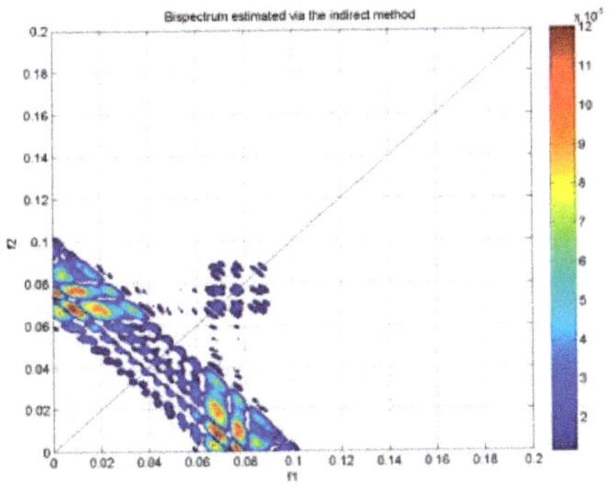

(**e**) sadness

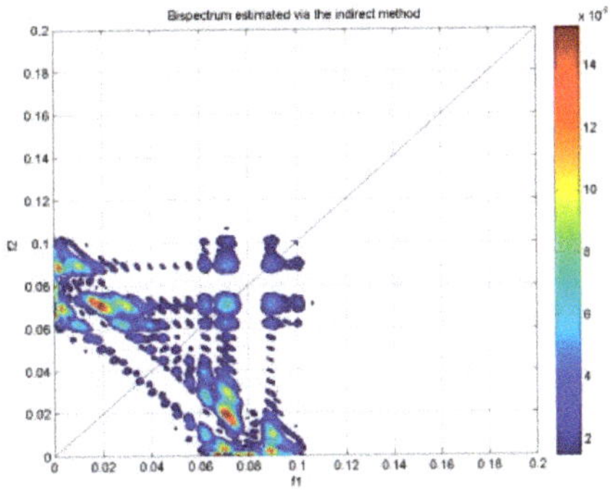

(**f**) surprise

Figure 5. The bispectrum contour plot of the non-redundant region and one symmetry region in the alpha band of subject #1 NC group.

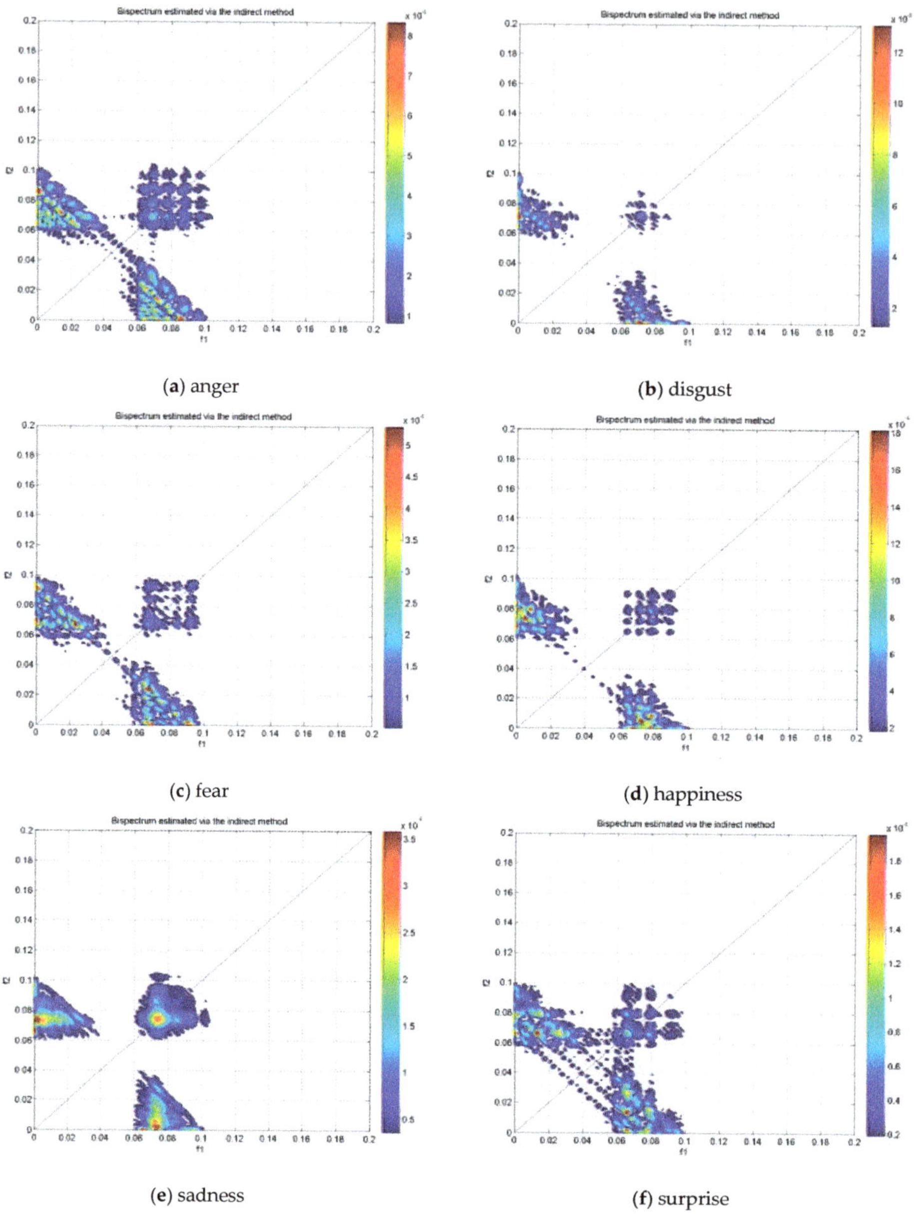

(**a**) anger (**b**) disgust (**c**) fear (**d**) happiness (**e**) sadness (**f**) surprise

Figure 6. The bispectrum contour plot of the non-redundant region and one symmetry region in the alpha band of subject #1 LBD group.

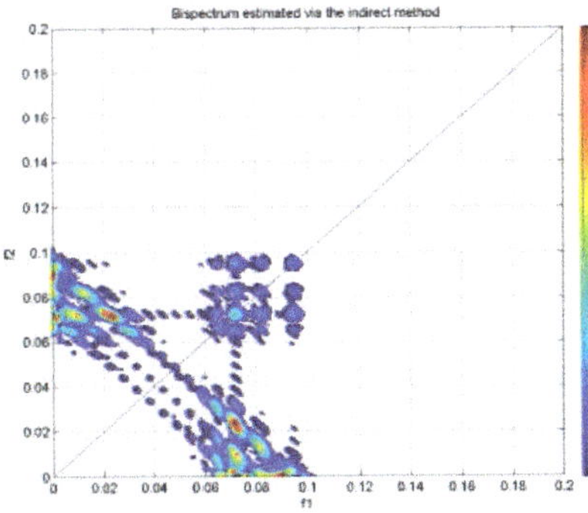

(**a**) anger

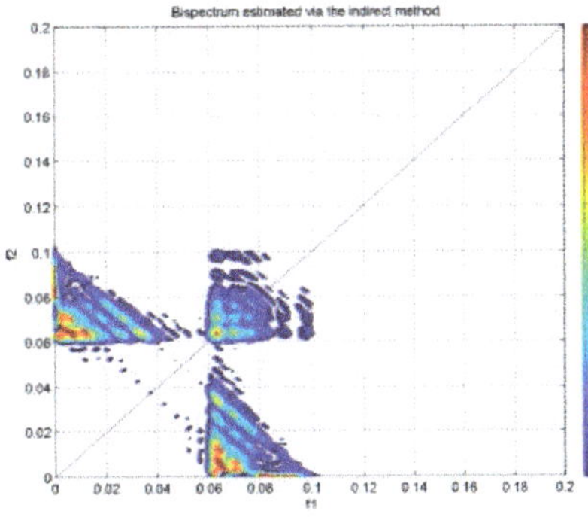

(**b**) disgust

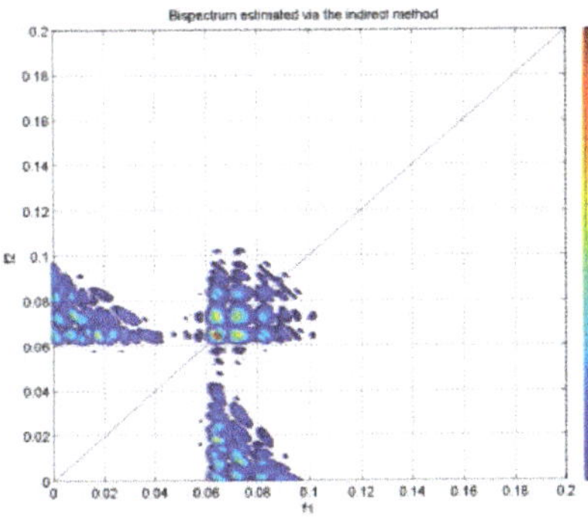

(**c**) fear

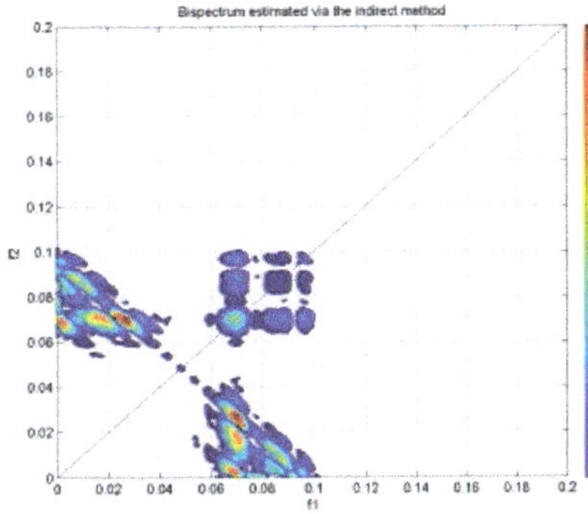

(**d**) happiness

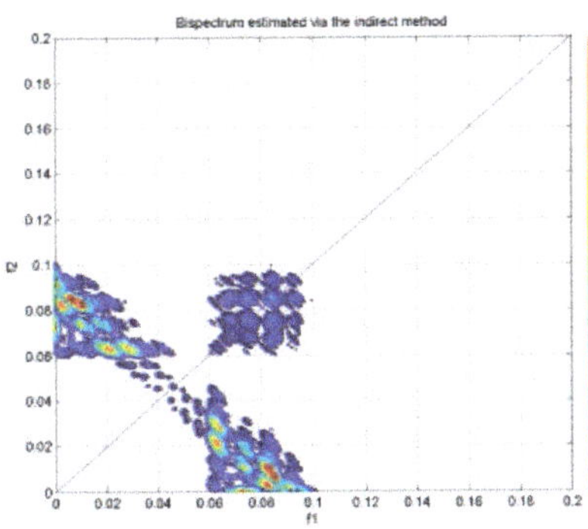

(**e**) sadness

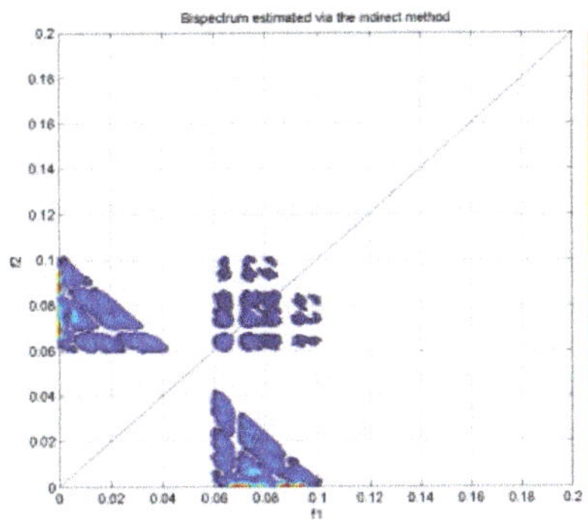

(**f**) surprise

Figure 7. The bispectrum contour plot of the non-redundant region and one symmetry region in the alpha band of subject #1 RBD group.

In emotion classification, the features were trained with varying k values for KNN and spread values for PNN. The classifiers were tested for all groups and frequency bands. Figures 8–10 show the classification performance of varying *k* values in three individual EEG frequency sub-bands (alpha, beta, and gamma) and the combination of the three bands using Cityblock KNN classifier. From the figures, the average accuracy of the bispectrum features was similar across all *k* values tested for alpha, beta, and gamma bands. However, the *k* value of 1 achieved the highest average accuracy when using the features from the combination of the alpha to gamma band. Moreover, the combination of the alpha to gamma band significantly performs better than other frequency bands for all *k* values as shown in Figures 8–10. The beta band, on the other hand, is the single band that performs best among the three EEG sub-bands.

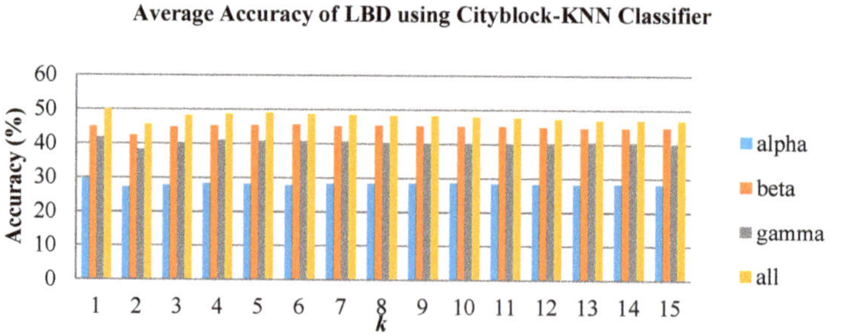

Figure 8. Average classification performance of bispectrum features by varying *k* values for the LBD group using *k*-nearest neighbor (KNN).

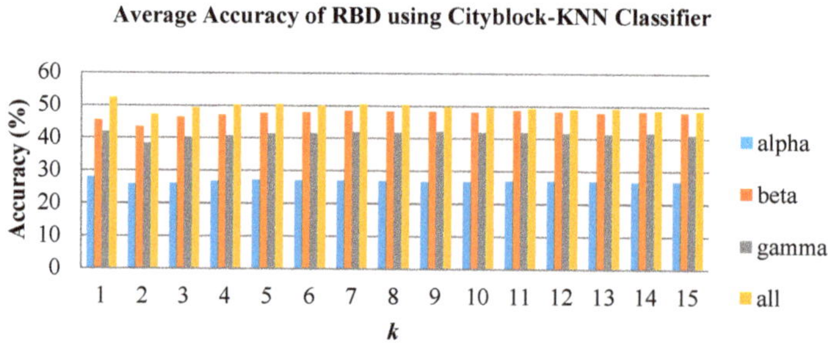

Figure 9. Average classification performance of bispectrum features by varying *k* values for the RBD group using KNN.

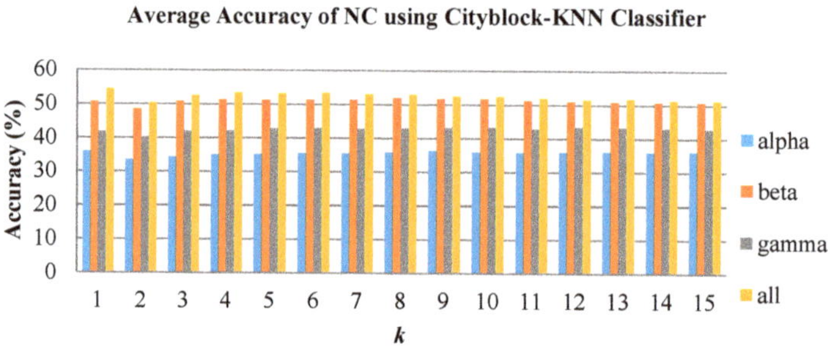

Figure 10. Average classification performance of bispectrum features by varying *k* values for the NC group using KNN.

In Figures 11–13, the average accuracy of the emotion classification of varying spread values using PNN classifier are plotted for LBD, RBD and NC, respectively. For most of the features, the accuracies are consistent at the spread value between 0.1 and 0.6. Then the accuracy is observed to gradually drop when spread value is larger than 0.6 and further declines when spread value increases. The spread value of 0.4 was chosen to classify the six emotional states as it has achieved the optimum accuracy for most of the features. Similarly, the combination of frequency bands has the highest average accuracy for all spread values. The beta frequency band is the best performance individual frequency band among the three frequency sub-bands in all groups.

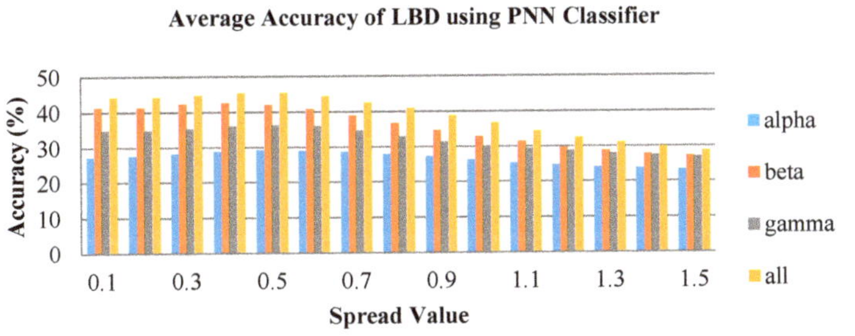

Figure 11. Average classification performance of bispectrum features by varying spread values for the LBD group using probabilistic neural network (PNN).

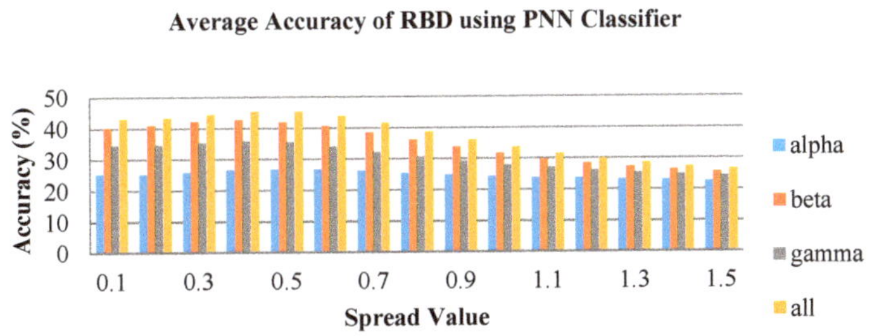

Figure 12. Average classification performance of bispectrum features by varying spread values for the RBD group using PNN.

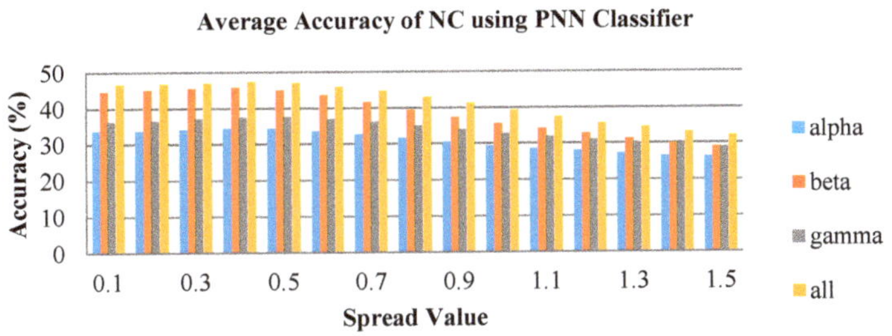

Figure 13. Average classification performance of bispectrum features by varying spread values for the NC group using PNN.

Table 3 shows the average accuracy of all emotional states of the bispectrum features from the combination of all bands from alpha to gamma using KNN and PNN classifiers. For both classifiers, the optimum parameters for LBD, RBD and NC are found to be the same. The optimum k value in KNN classification for all three groups is 1, and the optimum spread values in PNN classification is 0.4. In Table 3, the KNN is observed to have higher average accuracy than the PNN classifier for all three groups. Notably, the $H3$ feature is seen to have the highest average accuracy feature in all three groups using KNN, whereas the $H3$ feature achieves the highest accuracy in the LBD group using PNN. Meanwhile, the $H1$ feature obtains highest average accuracy in RBD and NC using PNN. According to the results obtained, the top three features are $H3$, $H1$, and $H2$ for all the groups, whereas the worst performing bispectrum feature is the variance. The highest average classification accuracy is 65.40% in the NC group using KNN. Hence the *H3* feature is considered the most effective bispectrum feature in this study.

Table 3. Summary of average accuracy of all emotions of different bispectrum features using the combination of alpha to gamma bands.

Classifier		**KNN**			**PNN**	
Group	**LBD**	**RBD**	**NC**	**LBD**	**RBD**	**NC**
k/Spread	1	1	1	0.4	0.4	0.4
v	31.02	30.28	32.72	28.43	28.30	28.70
H1	58.27	61.79	63.67	53.24	**55.06**	**57.41**
H2	55.59	60.06	62.90	49.88	49.72	55.25
H3	**58.67**	**62.22**	**65.40**	**54.57**	52.84	56.11
H5	46.54	47.38	47.10	40.46	40.31	38.83

The confusion matrix of the *H3* feature in KNN emotion classification is presented in Tables 4–6 for LBD, RBD and NC, respectively. From Table 4, the highest predicted class is happiness in LBD. In Table 5, the RBD group has the highest predicted value in sadness and surprise emotions, whereas the NC group has the highest predicted value in sadness emotion in Table 6. For PNN classification, the confusion matrix is presented in Tables 7–9 for each subject group. Likewise, the PNN classification predicted the happiness emotion correctly in the LBD group, as shown in Table 7. In addition, the sadness emotion has the highest classification accuracy in RBD and NC groups as shown in Tables 8 and 9.

Table 4. Confusion matrix of the LBD group using the *H3* feature in KNN classification.

		Actual					
		A	**D**	**F**	**H**	**S**	**SU**
Predicted	A	35	8	4	3	2	8
	D	4	31	6	3	5	5
	F	5	5	31	3	2	2
	H	3	2	7	41	7	3
	S	3	3	5	4	35	5
	SU	4	5	1	0	3	31

Table 5. Confusion matrix of the RBD group using the *H3* feature in KNN classification.

		Actual					
		A	**D**	**F**	**H**	**S**	**SU**
Predicted	A	36	3	5	3	0	3
	D	2	35	4	3	2	4
	F	4	10	32	3	6	3
	H	3	4	9	36	5	4
	S	1	1	2	6	38	2
	SU	8	1	2	3	3	38

Table 6. Confusion matrix of the NC group using the *H3* feature in KNN classification.

		Actual					
		A	**D**	**F**	**H**	**S**	**SU**
Predicted	A	39	4	1	4	1	6
	D	2	40	3	0	3	9
	F	1	4	34	4	3	4
	H	2	3	6	38	5	0
	S	2	1	6	6	41	1
	SU	8	2	4	2	1	34

Table 7. Confusion matrix of the LBD group using the *H*3 feature in PNN classification.

		Actual					
		A	**D**	**F**	**H**	**S**	**SU**
Predicted	A	32	6	3	4	1	7
	D	8	32	7	3	4	1
	F	5	5	30	3	4	2
	H	5	4	5	37	7	7
	S	3	2	6	5	35	3
	SU	1	5	3	2	3	34

Table 8. Confusion matrix of the RBD group using *H*1 feature in PNN classification.

		Actual					
		A	**D**	**F**	**H**	**S**	**SU**
Predicted	A	27	4	0	1	1	6
	D	5	35	5	2	4	5
	F	7	3	32	8	4	1
	H	4	2	6	34	2	5
	S	1	2	6	6	41	2
	SU	10	8	5	3	2	35

Table 9. Confusion matrix of the NC group using the *H*1 feature in PNN classification.

		Actual					
		A	**D**	**F**	**H**	**S**	**SU**
Predicted	A	32	3	2	2	1	8
	D	5	35	10	4	6	8
	F	5	3	33	2	4	3
	H	4	5	5	35	3	2
	S	3	2	3	9	40	3
	SU	5	6	1	2	0	30

The classification rates using the KNN classifier for individual emotions are show in Figure 14. From the figure, the emotion with highest accuracy in all groups was sadness, where the LBD group achieved 65.37%, RBD group achieved 71.48% and NC group achieved 75.56%. Meanwhile, the fear emotion recorded the lowest accuracy in all the three groups, which was 53.52%, 57.96% and 60.74% for LBD, RBD and NC respectively.

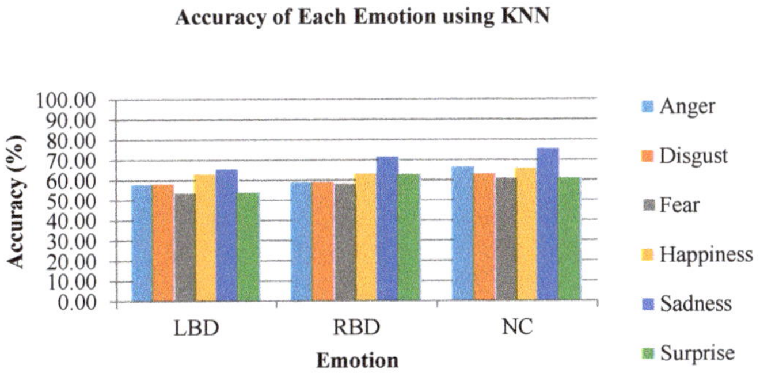

Figure 14. The accuracy of each emotional state using the KNN classifier.

The accuracy of the individual emotional states classified using the PNN classifier is shown in Figure 15. The PNN classifier has the same highest accuracy emotion with KNN, which was the sadness emotion. The LBD group has 57.41%, RBD has 62.59% and NC has 65.19% classification accuracy for sadness emotion using PNN. In Figure 15, the lowest classification accuracy for LBD and NC groups is the surprise emotion, which is 50.93% and 47.22%, respectively. In the RBD group, on the other hand, disgust emotion recorded the lowest classification accuracy of only 50.00%.

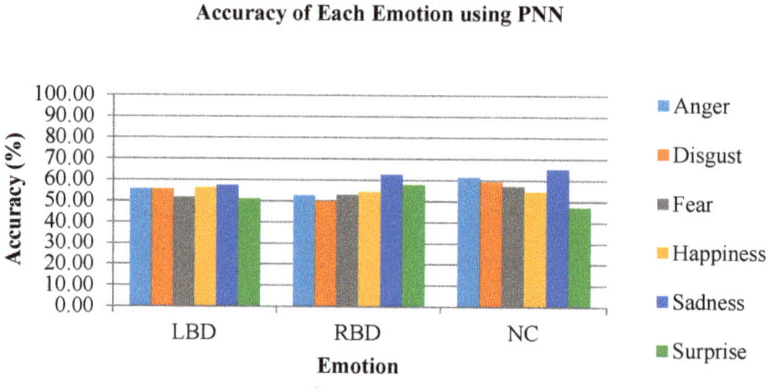

Figure 15. The accuracy of each emotional state using the PNN classifier.

In this work, the surprise and fear achieved lower recognition rates compared to other emotions. The happiness was the most accurately recognized emotion, as well as the facial expressions for anger, sadness and disgust [45,46]. According to past studies, there is no convincing evidence for the surprise and fear emotions to be accurately recognized [47–49].

The emotional state that shows highest classification accuracy in each group (LBD, RBD and NC) indicates that the emotion is more significant compared to other emotional states in the respective groups. From this current result, all of the LBD, RBD and NC groups show highest classification accuracy for sadness. Meanwhile, NC group exhibits the highest average accuracy for both classifiers, followed by RBD with LBD trailing behind.

As a result, in this study, the LBD and RBD stroke patients have recorded a lower classification accuracy compared to the NC. This suggests that the emotional states of NC are more significant than the stroke patients. In order to validate the significant differences among the three groups, ANOVA was used to test the statistical difference among the average accuracy obtained from the KNN classifier and the resultant p-value was less than 0.05. Hence, the emotion classification accuracy for LBD, RBD and NC were statistically significant. This signifies the significant difference among the three groups, which implies that there are differences in the emotional experiences between LBD, RBD and NC groups. From this work, the NC group was observed to have the highest emotion classification accuracy, followed by the RBD group and the LBD group performed worst. Therefore, the NC group has the highest efficiency in EEG emotional classification with the use of machine learning, while the LBD group the lowest.

This work is significant to those past studies in which only second order measures of statistics, such as the power spectrum [50,51], which is a linear feature, was used. The power spectrum can only reveal the amplitude information about the EEG signals, the phase information, such as the phase coupling in the signal, cannot be observed by applying the power spectrum. Furthermore, the use of linear approaches has ignored the nonlinear characteristics of the EEG signals, thus, bispectrum was implemented in this study to detect and characterize the nonlinearities of EEG signals. Also, this current study using the bispectrum was able to provide distinctive information for different emotional states which was useful for emotion classification by achieving the highest accuracy of 75.56% using the $H3$. bispectrum feature.

5. Conclusions

The importance of emotion assessment of stroke patients stems from the need to seek information on the severity of emotional impairment symptoms. Therefore, an accurate emotion assessment approach is required to identify the symptoms of mood disorders in stroke patients. This work proposed the use of the bispectrum feature to classify the discrete emotions (anger, disgust, fear, happiness, sadness and surprise) of stroke patients and normal people. This study aims to develop an accurate emotion identification method, which can be used to recognize the current emotional state of strokes patient during diagnosis.

In this work, the bispectrum reveals the presence of QPC in the EEG signals and exhibits different QPC relations in each emotional state. This difference in the harmonic components and peaks were shown in the bispectrum contour plots arising from the nonlinear interactions between neuronal populations in each emotional state. In this study, the proposed method of emotion classification by using the bispectrum feature and KNN classifier has shown its effectiveness in the combination of alpha to gamma frequency bands. In addition, the bispectrum feature, *H3*, was able to provide an accuracy of 75.56% in the NC group. Moreover, the proposed method gave a comparable result with some current studies in emotion classification, However, there were only six types of bispectrum features implemented in this study and there are more to be explored. Also, future works could also focus on the optimization of the classification accuracy.

To conclude, bispectrum-based features are effective to analyze the nonlinearity EEG signals, and therefore is a useful feature for emotion assessment. Bispectrum feature was able to provide the emotional information of stroke patients and hence can be used as the substitute for conventional observation-based or scoring methods.

Author Contributions: Conceptualization, M.I.O., C.W.Y. and W.K.W.A.; methodology, M.I.O., C.W.Y. and W.K.W.A.; software, C.W.Y. and S.A.B.; validation, M.M., Y.R. and W.A.M.; formal analysis, A.H.A.; investigation, C.W.Y. and W.K.W.A.; resources, B.S.Z. and M.M.; data curation, A.K.J.; writing—original draft preparation, C.W.Y. and W.K.W.A.; writing—review and editing, C.W.Y. and A.H.A.; visualization, Z.M.R.; supervision, W.K.W.A.; project administration, W.K.W.A.; funding acquisition, W.K.W.A. and Z.M.R. All authors have read and agreed to the published version of the manuscript.

Funding: The author would like to acknowledge the support from the Fundamental Research Grant Scheme (FRGS) under a grant number of FRGS/1/2019/ICT04/UNIMAP/02/1 from the Ministry of Education Malaysia.

Acknowledgments: The author would like to thank Medyna Rehab and Services for allowing us to conduct data collection.

Conflicts of Interest: The authors declare no conflict of interest.

References

1. Lee, Y.; Shafie, A.; Sidek, N.; Aziz, Z. Economic burden of stroke in Malaysia: Results from national neurology registry. *J. Neurol. Sci.* **2017**, *381*, 167–168. [CrossRef]
2. American Heart Association. High Blood Cholesterol and Other Lipids. In *2019 Heart Disease & Stroke Statistical Update Fact Sheet Blacks & Cardiovascular Diseases*; American Heart Association: Dallas, TX, USA, 2019; pp. 2012–2015.
3. Li, J.; Oakley, L.D.; Brown, R.L.; Li, Y.; Ye, M.; Luo, Y. Early symptom measurement of Post-Stroke Depression (PSD). *J. Affect. Disord.* **2016**, *197*, 215–222. [CrossRef] [PubMed]
4. Mayor, S. Persistent depression doubles stroke risk despite treatment, study finds. *Stroke Vasc. Neurol.* **2015**, *350*, h2611. [CrossRef] [PubMed]
5. Chriki, L.S.; Stern, T.A.; Bullian, S.S. The Recognition and Management of Psychological Reactions to Stroke: A Case Discussion. *Prim. Care Companion J. Clin. Psychiatry* **2006**, *8*, 234–240. [CrossRef]
6. Improvement.nhs.uk. "Psychological Care after Stroke," *NHS Improvement—Stroke.* 2011. Available online: https://www.england.nhs.uk/improvement-hub/publication/psychological-care-after-stroke-improving-stroke-services-for-people-with-cognitive-and-mood-disorders/ (accessed on 24 September 2020).
7. Berg, A.; Kaste, M.; Lönnqvist, J.; Palomäki, H. Assessment of Depression after Stroke. *Stroke* **2009**, *40*, 523–529. [CrossRef]

8. Jerritta, S.; Murugappan, M.; Nagarajan, R.; Wan, K. Physiological signals based human emotion Recognition: A review. In Proceedings of the 2011 IEEE 7th International Colloquium on Signal Processing and Its Applications, Penang, Malaysia, 4 March 2011; pp. 410–415. [CrossRef]
9. Nava, E.; Romano, D.; Grassi, M.; Turati, C. Skin conductance reveals the early development of the unconscious processing of emotions. *Cortex* **2016**, *84*, 124–131. [CrossRef]
10. Zhang, Q.; Chen, X.; Zhan, Q.; Yang, T.; Xia, S. Respiration-based emotion recognition with deep learning. *Comput. Ind.* **2017**, *92*, 84–90. [CrossRef]
11. Selvaraj, J.; Murugappan, M.; Wan, K.; Yaacob, S. Electrocardiogram-based emotion recognition system using empirical mode decomposition and discrete Fourier transform. *Expert Syst.* **2013**, *31*, 110–120. [CrossRef]
12. Bong, S.Z.; Wan, K.; Murugappan, M.; Ibrahim, N.M.; Rajamanickam, Y.; Mohamad, K. Implementation of wavelet packet transform and non linear analysis for emotion classification in stroke patient using brain signals. *Biomed. Signal Process. Control.* **2017**, *36*, 102–112. [CrossRef]
13. Schalk, G.; Mellinger, J. Brain Sensors and Signals. In *A Practical Guide to Brain—Computer Interfacing with BCI2000*; Springer: London, UK, 2010; pp. 9–35.
14. Lindquist, K.A.; Wager, T.D.; Kober, H.; Bliss-Moreau, E.; Barrett, L.F. The brain basis of emotion: A meta-analytic review. *Behav. Brain Sci.* **2012**, *35*, 121–143. [CrossRef]
15. Adamaszek, M.; Olbrich, S.; Kirkby, K.; Woldag, H.; Willert, C.; Heinrich, A. Event-related potentials indicating impaired emotional attention in cerebellar stroke—A case study. *Neurosci. Lett.* **2013**, *548*, 206–211. [CrossRef] [PubMed]
16. Doruk, D.; Simis, M.; Imamura, M.; Brunoni, A.R.; Morales-Quezada, L.; Anghinah, R.; Fregni, F.; Battistella, L.R. Neurophysiologic Correlates of Post-stroke Mood and Emotional Control. *Front. Hum. Neurosci.* **2016**, *10*. [CrossRef] [PubMed]
17. Yuvaraj, R.; Murugappan, M.; Sundaraj, K.; Khairiyah, M.; Norlinah, M. Review of Emotion Recognition in Stroke Patients. *Dement. Geriatr. Cogn. Disord.* **2013**, *36*, 179–196. [CrossRef]
18. Yeh, Z.-T.; Tsai, C.-F. Impairment on theory of mind and empathy in patients with stroke. *Psychiatry Clin. Neurosci.* **2014**, *68*, 612–620. [CrossRef]
19. Aben, H.P.; Reijmer, Y.D.; Visser-Meily, J.M.A.; Spikman, J.M.; Biessels, G.J.; De Kort, P.L.M.; PROCRAS Study Group. Impaired Emotion Recognition after Left Hemispheric Stroke: A Case Report and Brief Review of the Literature. *Case Rep. Neurol. Med.* **2017**, *2017*, 1045039. [CrossRef]
20. Yuvaraj, R.; Murugappan, M.; Acharrya, U.R.; Adeli, H.; Ibrahim, N.M.; Mesquita, E. Brain functional connectivity patterns for emotional state classification in Parkinson's disease patients without dementia. *Behav. Brain Res.* **2016**, *298*, 248–260. [CrossRef]
21. Klonowski, W. Everything you wanted to ask about EEG but were afraid to get the right answer. *Nonlinear Biomed. Phys.* **2009**, *3*, 2. [CrossRef] [PubMed]
22. Tsuda, I. Toward an interpretation of dynamic neural activity in terms of chaotic dynamical systems. *Behav. Brain Sci.* **2001**, *24*, 793–810. [CrossRef] [PubMed]
23. Huang, G.; Zhang, D.; Meng, J.; Zhu, X. Interactions between two neural populations: A mechanism of chaos and oscillation in neural mass model. *Neurocomputing* **2011**, *74*, 1026–1034. [CrossRef]
24. Lee, Y.-J.; Zhu, Y.-S.; Xu, Y.-H.; Shen, M.-F.; Zhang, H.-X.; Thakor, N.V. Detection of non-linearity in the EEG of schizophrenic patients. *Clin. Neurophysiol.* **2001**, *112*, 1288–1294. [CrossRef]
25. Rangaprakash, D.; Pradhan, N. Study of phase synchronization in multichannel seizure EEG using nonlinear recurrence measure. *Biomed. Signal Process. Control.* **2014**, *11*, 114–122. [CrossRef]
26. Zappasodi, F.; Olejarczyk, E.; Marzetti, L.; Assenza, G.; Pizzella, V.; Tecchio, F. Fractal Dimension of EEG Activity Senses Neuronal Impairment in Acute Stroke. *PLoS ONE* **2014**, *9*, e100199. [CrossRef] [PubMed]
27. Yuvaraj, R.; Murugappan, M.; Ibrahim, N.M.; Sundaraj, K.; Omar, M.I.; Mohamad, K.; Palaniappan, R.; Omar, M.I. Detection of emotions in Parkinson's disease using higher order spectral features from brain's electrical activity. *Biomed. Signal Process. Control.* **2014**, *14*, 108–116. [CrossRef]
28. Acharrya, U.R.; Bhat, S.; Faust, O.; Adeli, H.; Chua, E.C.-P.; Lim, W.J.E.; Koh, J.E.W. Nonlinear Dynamics Measures for Automated EEG-Based Sleep Stage Detection. *Eur. Neurol.* **2015**, *74*, 268–287. [CrossRef]
29. Nikias, C.L. Higher-order spectral analysis. In Proceedings of the 15th Annual International Conference of the IEEE Engineering in Medicine and Biology Societ, San Diego, CA, USA, 28 October 1993. [CrossRef]
30. Nikias, C.L.; Raghuveer, M.R. Bispectrum estimation: A digital signal processing framework. *Proc. IEEE* **1987**, *75*, 869–891. [CrossRef]

31. Nikias, C.; Mendel, J. Signal processing with higher-order spectra. *IEEE Signal Process. Mag.* **1993**, *10*, 10–37. [CrossRef]
32. Yuvaraj, R.; Murugappan, M.; Ibrahim, N.M.; Sundaraj, K.; Omar, M.I.; Mohamad, K.; Palaniappan, R. Optimal set of EEG features for emotional state classification and trajectory visualization in Parkinson's disease. *Int. J. Psychophysiol.* **2014**, *94*, 482–495. [CrossRef] [PubMed]
33. Hosseini, S.A. Classification of Brain Activity in Emotional States Using HOS Analysis. *Int. J. Image Graph. Signal Process.* **2012**, *4*, 21–27. [CrossRef]
34. Venkatakrishnan, P.; Sukanesh, R.; Sangeetha, S. Detection of quadratic phase coupling from human EEG signals using higher order statistics and spectra. *Signal Image Video Process.* **2010**, *5*, 217–229. [CrossRef]
35. Kiciński, W.; Szczepański, A. Quadratic Phase Coupling Phenomenon and Its Properties. *Hydroacoustics* **2004**, *7*, 97–106.
36. Chua, K.C.; Chandran, V.; Acharrya, U.R.; Lim, C.M. Application of higher order statistics/spectra in biomedical signals—A review. *Med. Eng. Phys.* **2010**, *32*, 679–689. [CrossRef] [PubMed]
37. Burle, B.; Spieser, L.; Roger, C.; Casini, L.; Hasbroucq, T.; Vidal, F. Spatial and temporal resolutions of EEG: Is it really black and white? A scalp current density view. *Int. J. Psychophysiol.* **2015**, *97*, 210–220. [CrossRef]
38. Choong, W.Y. Analysis of the Distance Metrics of KNN Classifier for EEG Signal in Stroke Patients. In Proceedings of the 2018 International Conference on Computational Approach in Smart Systems Design and Applications (ICASSDA), Kuching, Malaysia, 15–17 August 2018. [CrossRef]
39. Specht, D.F. Probabilistic neural networks. *Neural Netw.* **1990**, *3*, 109–118. [CrossRef]
40. Farrokhrooz, M.; Karimi, M.; Rafiei, A. A new method for spread value estimation in multi-spread PNN and its application in ship noise classification. In Proceedings of the 2007 9th International Symposium on Signal Processing and Its Applications, Sharjah, UAE, 12–15 February 2007; pp. 1–4. [CrossRef]
41. Pastell, M.; Kujala, M. A Probabilistic Neural Network Model for Lameness Detection. *J. Dairy Sci.* **2007**, *90*, 2283–2292. [CrossRef] [PubMed]
42. Zhou, S.-M.; Gan, Q.; Sepulveda, F. Classifying mental tasks based on features of higher-order statistics from EEG signals in brain–computer interface. *Inf. Sci.* **2008**, *178*, 1629–1640. [CrossRef]
43. Goshvarpour, A.; Goshvarpour, A.; Rahati, S.; Saadatian, V. Bispectrum Estimation of Electroencephalogram Signals during Meditation. *Iran. J. Psychiatry Behav. Sci.* **2012**, *6*, 48–54.
44. Zhang, J.-W.; Zheng, C.-X.; Xie, A. Bispectrum analysis of focal ischemic cerebral EEG signal using third-order recursion method. *IEEE Trans. Biomed. Eng.* **2000**, *47*, 352–359. [CrossRef]
45. Elfenbein, H.A.; Ambady, N. On the universality and cultural specificity of emotion recognition: A meta-analysis. *Psychol. Bull.* **2002**, *128*, 203–235. [CrossRef]
46. Mancini, G.; Biolcati, R.; Agnoli, S.; Andrei, F.; Trombini, E. Recognition of Facial Emotional Expressions among Italian Pre-adolescents, and Their Affective Reactions. *Front. Psychol.* **2018**, *9*, 1303. [CrossRef]
47. Reisenzein, R.; Horstmann, G.; Schützwohl, A. The Cognitive-Evolutionary Model of Surprise: A Review of the Evidence. *Top. Cogn. Sci.* **2017**, *11*, 50–74. [CrossRef]
48. Delicato, L.S. A robust method for measuring an individual's sensitivity to facial expressions. *Atten. Percept. Psychophys.* **2020**, *82*, 2924–2936. [CrossRef] [PubMed]
49. Crivelli, C.; Russell, J.A.; Jarillo, S.; Fernández-Dols, J.-M. The fear gasping face as a threat display in a Melanesian society. *Proc. Natl. Acad. Sci. USA* **2016**, *113*, 12403–12407. [CrossRef] [PubMed]
50. Yuvaraj, R.; Murugappan, M.; Ibrahim, N.M.; Omar, M.I.; Sundaraj, K.; Mohamad, K.; Palaniappan, R.; Mesquita, E.; Satiyan, M. On the analysis of EEG power, frequency and asymmetry in Parkinson's disease during emotion processing. *Behav. Brain Funct.* **2014**, *10*, 12. [CrossRef] [PubMed]
51. Jadhav, N.; Manthalkar, R.; Joshi, Y.V. Effect of meditation on emotional response: An EEG-based study. *Biomed. Signal Process. Control.* **2017**, *34*, 101–113. [CrossRef]

brain sciences

MDPI

Article

Peak Detection with Online Electroencephalography (EEG) Artifact Removal for Brain–Computer Interface (BCI) Purposes

Mihaly Benda and **Ivan Volosyak** *

Faculty of Technology and Bionics, Rhine-Waal University of Applied Sciences, 47533 Kleve, Germany
* Correspondence: ivan.volosyak@hochschule-rhein-waal.de

Received: 23 October 2019; Accepted: 25 November 2019; Published: 29 November 2019

Abstract: Brain–computer interfaces (BCIs) measure brain activity and translate it to control computer programs or external devices. However, the activity generated by the BCI makes measurements for objective fatigue evaluation very difficult, and the situation is further complicated due to different movement artefacts. The BCI performance could be increased if an online method existed to measure the fatigue objectively and accurately. While BCI-users are moving, a novel automatic online artefact removal technique is used to filter out these movement artefacts. The effects of this filter on BCI performance and mainly on peak frequency detection during BCI use were investigated in this paper. A successful peak alpha frequency measurement can lead to more accurately determining objective user fatigue. Fifteen subjects performed various imaginary and actual movements in separate tasks, while fourteen electroencephalography (EEG) electrodes were used. Afterwards, a steady-state visual evoked potential (SSVEP)-based BCI speller was used, and the users were instructed to perform various movements. An offline curve fitting method was used for alpha peak detection to assess the effect of the artefact filtering. Peak detection was improved by the filter, by finding 10.91% and 9.68% more alpha peaks during simple EEG recordings and BCI use, respectively. As expected, BCI performance deteriorated from movements, and also from artefact removal. Average information transfer rates (ITRs) were 20.27 bit/min, 16.96 bit/min, and 14.14 bit/min for the (1) movement-free, (2) the moving and unfiltered, and (3) the moving and filtered scenarios, respectively.

Keywords: Brain-Computer Interface (BCI); Steady-State Visual Evoked Potential (SSVEP); artefact removal; Individual Alpha Peak; movement artefact; Electroencephalography (EEG)

---

1. Introduction

Electroencephalography (EEG) recordings of brain activity are used for multiple purposes, from medical diagnostics to brain–computer interfaces (BCIs) [1,2]. The recorded activity is analysed with various methods according to the end goal, and one or several features are extracted and interpreted.

BCIs evaluate specific components of brain activity and try to classify them according to criteria set previously, in order to execute a corresponding command when such a component is detected. By providing multiple types of commands, the control of a BCI system can be handled by the users' brain activity alone (interpreted by the BCI) without the need for muscle movements. Steady-state visual evoked potentials (SSVEPs) are one of the specific brain activities which BCIs can utilise. They are generated when the user is looking at a source of light that flickers with a constant frequency (for example, by changing colour or luminance). BCI performance can be easily influenced by the recording environment. The lighting conditions in the room, movements of the users, or even the attention and fatigue levels significantly alter the speed of the BCI.

User fatigue could be partially or even totally countered by changing the parameters of the BCI. For this, a measure of the subjects' fatigue is necessary. Although there are subjective methods for acquiring fatigue levels from the users, for example, questionnaires, there are two main drawbacks to these methods. The subjectivity can cause mistakes in the following parameter changes, possibly not improving the BCI performance at all, or even detrimentally affecting it. Secondly, these methods require the users to stop using the BCI and, for example, fill out a questionnaire. As BCIs are online systems taking breaks during their use does not make sense. Therefore an online and objective measure is required for optimal use with BCIs.

EEG recordings are also commonly utilised in the research of brain activity and functions [3,4]. For example alpha activity can be associated with attention [5]. Alpha peaks and mean powers of different frequency bands have been proposed to indicate user attention or tiredness during BCI use [6–9]. The reported results of these investigations vary and are sometimes contradicting.

Moreover, there are findings in the field of neurosciences, which were not considered by the previously mentioned researches for measuring fatigue associated with BCIs. Namely, the inter-individual differences, how these affect the bandwidths, already discussed in [10], and the methods for determining the peak frequency in a band [11]. The traditional band limits may be inappropriate, as there are differences between the subjects to such an extent that their peak alpha frequency, for example, may fall entirely out of the traditional alpha range. Although this will not affect finding the peak in most cases, as it is still likely within the range, the mean power or any ratio calculated from it will be affected, however. To determine the individual peaks, a robust and accurate method is required, which can handle the common pitfalls of peak detection, such as split peaks.

There are several different techniques, with benefits and drawbacks, that have been applied for determining peak frequencies. They include simple and complicated methods alike [11]. One of the most common methods is specifying the frequency band, by extracting data from the fast Fourier transform (FFT), which is limited by traditional, personalised, or in some way generalised frequency borders (e.g., 8–13 Hz for alpha band), and finding the local maximum. Determining the peak alpha frequency in a condition where the eyes are closed is usually straightforward; however, with open eyes this task can become quite challenging. If there are no obvious peaks in the range, or there is a split peak, the estimation can become biased and incorrect [11]. Since visual BCIs require open eyes, this method is not suitable for peak detection during SSVEP-based BCI use.

An alternative method of determining the highest peak in a frequency band was developed originally by [12]. The estimation is done by calculating a weighted average of the power contained in the frequency band that is sensitive to the spectral distribution. This method can yield results even if a clear peak is not detectable. However, it requires a clear definition of the boundaries of the band. Since brain activity has a high inter-subject variance, the boundaries cannot be defined in a generalised way without somehow biasing the estimation. The behaviour of the frequency components of the recorded brain activity can also be profoundly different. This makes the estimation of the peak frequency challenging to automate, even when utilising data recorded with different conditions (e.g., eyes open and closed) [11].

A less commonly used method is curve fitting, which can alleviate several of the previous issues [13,14]. The problems split peaks have caused can be alleviated, for example, and the boundaries play a lesser role in finding the peak frequency. A curve fitting method for finding peak alpha frequencies was introduced by [13] and was improved later to account for split peaks [15].

A promising and already implemented approach with curve fitting is provided by [11], who utilises a Savitzky–Golay filter for the smoothing of the FFT, which can ease peak detection. It also includes calculating the derivatives of the FFT spectrum and finding inflexion points before applying curve fitting based on the least-squares approach. Savitzky–Golay filters have the important property of not altering the properties of the peaks. In this experiment this method is used for individual alpha frequency (IAF) detection during simple EEG recordings and SSVEP-based BCI tasks.

With the individual alpha frequency (IAF), the individual alpha ranges can be defined, and phase information can be calculated, which seem to be promising approaches to measuring attention or fatigue. They can show whether the target brain area is receiving external information from the stimuli, or if the information gathering is blocked by the alpha activity [5,16].

There is another issue to consider when using BCIs and neural activity measurements, which is the artefacts present in the recorded EEG data. All previously mentioned peak detection methods can suffer from ocular or muscular artefacts, which can easily occur during a recording. With all different methods of peak estimation, it is crucial to have data with a high signal to noise ratio (SNR), or preferably, without any noise. Most of the studies handling EEG data, to minimise noise, require the subjects to sit in a comfortable position and move as little as possible, or even physically fix the position of the head by using head-mounts.

However, BCIs aim to develop solutions for people with disabilities or for use in everyday scenarios, and as such they have to consider head movements and blinking, which are unavoidable for any prolonged use of the system. This is especially true with mobile systems, as more movements are expected if the wires do not restrict the users. Commonly offline analysis is used after rejecting all noisy data from further calculations, however, this cannot be done with BCI systems. BCIs require online and therefore (semi-)automatic artefact removal and analysis. Optimally BCI systems require an artefact correction (and not rejection) method, in order to always be able to process the users' EEG activity. The exact choice of artefact removal algorithm is not simple. These usually remove one or both of the most common EEG artefacts, eye movements, and muscle movements.

The authors in [17] presented a method based on correlation index and the feature of power distribution to automatically detect eye blink components, using extended infomax ICA. Ref. [18] presented a way of removing ocular artefacts by using blind source separation on the raw EEG recording.

Regarding muscular artefacts, Ref. [19] demonstrated muscular artefact cancellation in single-channel EEG recordings with a combination of ensemble empirical mode decomposition and joint blind source separation. They successfully removed muscular artefacts without altering the underlying EEG activity.

More recently, Ref. [20] introduced the source-estimate-utilizing noise-discarding (SOUND) algorithm. It uses Wiener estimators and employs anatomical information to identify and suppress noise and artefacts in EEG and MEG. Also recently, Ref. [21] developed a generic EEG artefact removal algorithm, which allows the annotation of artefact segments and clear segments. With this information the algorithm based on the multi-channel Wiener filter (MWF) can remove a wide variety of artefacts from EEG data. The result was a high-performance semi-automatic artefact removal algorithm able to remove both muscular and ocular artefacts. This algorithm requires only a short time to do computations and handles both common EEG artefact types—ocular and muscular—therefore, it is optimal for use with BCIs. Authors in [21] tested their algorithm performance using both hybrid and real EEG recordings. However, the calculations were offline, and the selection of the artefact segments is made manually by the experimenter. For this experiments' purpose the calculations had to be done online. Moreover, the effect of such a filter on the measurement of peak frequencies from an FFT transformed signal needed to be investigated.

In this experiment, we wished to create a scenario that could easily occur when using a mobile BCI system. Therefore, the experiment necessitated movements which would occur in everyday scenarios, such as chewing, speaking, and head gestures, freely selected and even combined by the users. We then used the automatised version of the presented artefact removal algorithm in online EEG recordings, and BCI experiments to filter out these common movements, and used the recorded EEG data to determine the IAFs using curve fitting methods.

By checking the effect of online artefact removal on peak detection, we can grasp how effective is it to measure attention and fatigue-related EEG parameters while the users are mobile. For BCIs whose target user group is healthy people, mobility or movements are expected and indeed necessary to account for. Although the exact parameters or combination of them for describing objective user fatigue or attention is not clear yet, IAFs can be used as a base for many parameter estimations. Once determined, the negative effects of fatigue could be countered by altering BCI parameters. For both artefact removal and peak detection we utilised novel methods and algorithms. In our study we used IAF measurement methods as an indicator, or starting step for determining objective fatigue. However, it is out of the scope of this paper to make measurements or assumptions measuring either fatigue or attention during BCI use. Additionally we measured the effect of the artefact removal on BCI performance. However, the main goal remains the evaluation of the artefact removal combined with peak detection during BCI use. Even if BCI performance is worse using these methods, it can be easily amended by simply not filtering the data for BCI classification.

First, the materials are described, followed by the description of the implementation and changes to the artefact removal method, followed by the peak detection method and finally the experimental protocol including the used BCI system. The results of the simple EEG recordings and the BCI use are detailed separately and discussed in the respective sections of the paper.

2. Materials and Methods

2.1. Participants

Fifteen healthy users (eight female) participated. All of them were students of the Rhine-Waal University of Applied Sciences. The average age (SD) was 23.8 (2.9) years. After discussing the experimental protocol with each subject, they signed a consent form according to the Declaration of Helsinki. The experiment was approved by the ethical committee of the Medical Faculty of the University Duisburg-Essen. Subjects were paid a small fee to participate in the experiment.

2.2. Hardware

For recording EEG, a biosignal amplifier, g.USBamp (Guger Technologies, Graz, Austria) was utilised. Passive Ag/AgCl electrodes were used to measure EEG signals, fourteen of them were placed at the following positions: P_Z, PO_3, PO_4, O_1, PO_Z, O_2, O_9, O_{10}, P_3, C_Z, P_4, F_1, F_Z, and F_2 according to the international 10-5 electrode placement system. AF_Z was used as a ground, and the left earlobe was used for reference. Before the experiment, all electrodes were prepared with an electrolytic gel to lower impedances below 5 kΩ.

Data were recorded at a sampling rate of 256 Hz. A bandpass filter between 2 Hz and 60 Hz, as well as a notch filter between 45 Hz and 55 Hz to remove power line noise were applied. These filters were applied before utilising the artefact removal method, specified in Section 2.4. Data were sent to be processed in blocks of 64 samples (250 ms long recordings).

The BCI program, including the graphical user interface (GUI) and all calculations, ran on a laptop (MSI GE72MVR 7RG Apache Pro (17.3 inches), resolution: 1920 × 1080 pixels, vertical refresh rate: 120 Hz, Intel(R) Core(TM) i7-7700HQ CPU @ 2.80 GHz, operating on Microsoft Windows 10 Education).

2.3. Experimental Protocol

The experiment was divided into three phases, each with its subsequent tasks. After signing the consent form, subjects were prepared for recording. Electrode gel was applied at all recording sites. This was followed by the first phase, setting up the artefact removal filter (Section 2.4).

In the filter setup phase users had to follow the instructions on screen, altogether six of them, while keeping their gaze as much as possible in the middle of the screen, marked by a cross. Between the tasks they could take short breaks as needed, during which no EEG data were saved. Each task required a specific activity for ten s, and they were the following: blink, move your head, do face movements/gesticulation and remain as still as possible (for three times in total). The order of the tasks was randomised. The data recorded during these tasks was used to create the multi-channel Wiener filter. For further details on this phase please see Section 2.4.

After the filter has been created, in the second phase of the experiment, users had to do ten specific tasks. The tasks were in a randomised order, presented by the GUI. During this phase there was no stimulation presented to the users; simply EEG was recorded. The tasks were the combination of three distinct settings, eyes open or closed, filter on or off, and relaxing/imagining movements/doing movements. The relaxing conditions with both eyes open and closed were only measured without the filter being on, as there was nothing to filter out and consequently precise results were expected even with less data, thus resulting in $2 \times 2 \times 3 - 2 = 10$ tasks. The GUI did not show any information about the filter, only whether to keep eyes closed/open and what activity to do. Subjects were instructed to do any combination of the movements they had done during the first phase, but not any new type of movement. Each user could freely select any combination of the movements done previously, however during the recording they were monitored by the experimenter to assure they kept moving/still during the whole recording as per instructed. If not all conditions were fulfilled (e.g., a subject opened his or her eyes, did not keep still, or did not move according to the specific task) the task was repeated. Each task had to be maintained for 45 s, during which EEG was recorded.

For the third phase of the experiment, users had to use an SSVEP-based BCI speller to write a word selected by them (approximately 5–6 characters long, or 15–18 selections with the BCI, respectively, but otherwise not specified). Due to its robustness in previous experiments, a three step speller was used (see Section 2.5.2). The same word had to be written thrice while executing one of the tasks: keeping as still as possible, moving according to the movements in phase one of the experiment, and the same movements, but with the filter active. For the keeping still task, no filter was used. However, during the later offline analysis the filtered data was calculated from the corresponding unfiltered data. The state of the filter was, again, not shown to users, and they were instructed when necessary by the experimenter not to stop moving, similarly as in phase two. These three tasks were randomised as well. The experiment was finished if the user has written the preferred word thrice, or if after a prolonged time no progress was made towards finishing the spelling task. In the latter case the condition was deemed unsuccessful for spelling with the BCI.

The whole experiment lasted approximately one hour, with possibilities for short breaks between the tasks (when needed by the users) For an overview of the phases of the experiment, please see Figure 1.

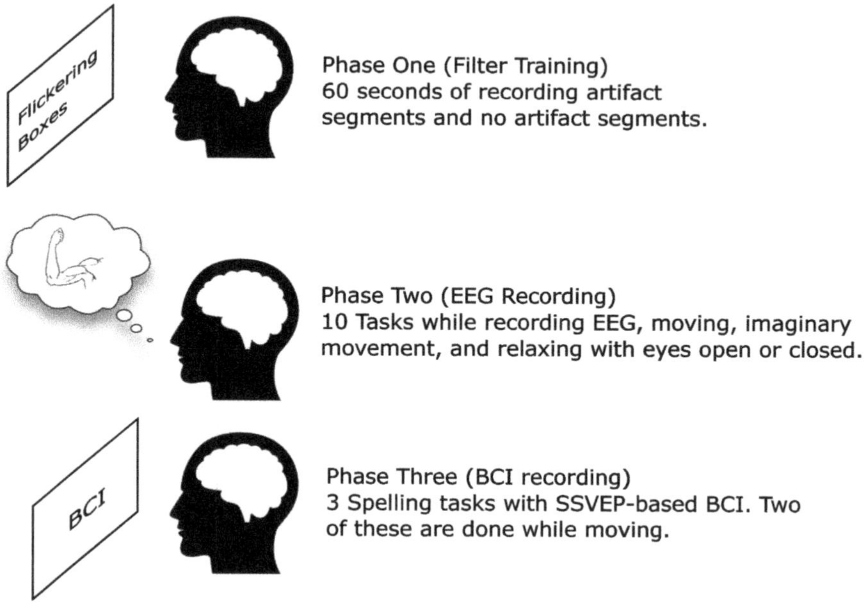

Figure 1. Three phases of the online experiment. Electroencephalography (EEG), brain–computer interface (BCI), steady-state visual evoked potential (SSVEP).

2.4. Artefact Removal

The artefact removal algorithm presented by [21] was adopted for this experiment. As a summary of their method: The algorithm calculates an estimate of the multi-channel artefact signal by linearly combining the channels of observations. The input data, as mentioned before, is labelled as artefact segments and artefact-free segments, which are used in acquiring an optimal filter solution using only covariance matrix estimates. The neural responses can be obtained by subtracting this estimated artefact from the data.

Furthermore the spectral properties of the data (different effects on different electrode locations) are also considered, and the algorithm can be extended by performing a finite impulse response filtering in each channel, which acts as a per-channel spectral filter. This way, the algorithm can optimally remove the pre-defined artefact types while at the same time minimises the removal of actual EEG components. For a detailed description of methods and calculation please refer to [21].

This algorithm was applied in our custom made BCI program (Section 2.5.2), which was also handling EEG recordings. For this, the algorithm was made automatic and online, calculations being done after each block of recorded EEG data (every 250 ms) to remove possible artefacts before being processed by the BCI classification. For the automation a training phase was added, where the generic marking of artefact segments was done.

The experiment started with this training phase for creating the filter. Users were asked to follow instructions presented in the GUI, which told them to remain as still as possible for several seconds or to do movements. Six tasks were listed in a randomised order, requiring blinking, head movements, face movements/gesticulation and remaining as still as possible (three times in total), for ten seconds each. The instructions were closely monitored by the experimenter, and if any deviation from them was noted, the whole phase was repeated. There were no limitations on the movement types, e.g., for head movements nodding or shaking of the head could be done as well as any other head movement, however subjects were instructed to remember the movements they made in this phase and replicate them in the later phases. By specifying whole data segments of this phase as artefact segments or clean segments, the manual marking was omitted, making the artefact removal automatic. This, however, could have influenced the performance of the removal process. In a practical application the users are not in the presence of experts, and since their knowledge of EEG artefacts can be minimal or even non-existent, they cannot be asked to mark these artefacts segments themselves.

During this training phase, four targets were flickering, precisely as in the spelling task later, with the same frequencies. This was done to mitigate the effect of the filter on the signal the BCI was searching for. Although there was flickering, no interaction was possible for the users (no selection, no feedback, no classification). Users were instructed to do the movements while looking at the middle of the screen, marked by a cross. Thus the four flickering targets were in their visual field, but the users were not looking directly at them. The tasks where users had to remain still were marked as artefact-free data, while all other recordings were marked as artefacts.

The filter was created with a delay of four samples. This means that time-lagged versions of each channel (up to $\pm$four samples, or $\sim$16 ms) are stacked to the observation matrix, which is used to calculate the multichannel Wiener filter. This delay was selected considering the temporal and spatial effects (e.g., blink artefacts can have large autocorrelation coefficients after tens of milliseconds) of artefacts on EEG. For details please refer to [21]. The resulting filter was a 126 $\times$ 126 matrix, 9 (from -4 to +4 sample time lags) $\times$ 14 (electrodes). This was applied to each incoming block (14 electrodes $\times$ 64 samples) of data when the filter was active. First, the time-lagged versions of the incoming data were calculated with zero-padding to match the original dimensions and the dimension of the filter. Then the artefact estimate was calculated for the original (not time-lagged) channels using the filter. The artefact estimate was then removed from the EEG to get the filtered data as described in [21].

2.5. *Offline Analysis*

After the experiment, an offline analysis was conducted to determine peak frequencies in the theta, alpha, and beta ranges. The program recorded EEG data after the notch filtering at 50 Hz and the bandpass filtering between 2 Hz and 60 Hz in every case (referred to as unfiltered from here on), and additionally when the artefact removal filter was operational, it recorded the data after the removal process as well (referred to as filtered from here on). The offline analysis was done differently for the data recorded in phases two and three of the experiment.

In phase two, after the training phase for the artefact removal, the users had to do different movement-related tasks or imaginary movements while EEG data were being recorded. In the cases where the artefact removal was not applied online during the recording, the filtered data was calculated offline from the corresponding unfiltered data, this way providing more data for the statistical analysis, providing more robust results. Altogether ten different tasks were required from the users, and for both the unfiltered and the filtered data the peak detection algorithm from [11] was applied to find IAFs.

First, the FFT was normalised, then a smoothing filter (Savitzky–Golay filter) was applied. Potential alpha peaks were determined by finding zero crossings in the first derivative of the smoothed normalised FFT. If there were multiple crossings, the highest peak was used. If the peak was higher than the next highest peak by a predefined threshold, it became a peak frequency. Inflexion points were determined from the second derivative of the FFT, and the area under the curve (Q) between the two inflexion points around the peak was calculated.

The EEG data were separated into three sets, according to the spatial position of the recording electrodes. The occipital area had seven recording electrodes: PO_3, PO_4, O_1, PO_Z, O_2, O_9, and O_{10} the centro-parietal area consisted of P_Z, PO_3, PO_4, P_3, C_Z, and P_4, while the frontal area encompassed only F_1, F_Z, and F_2. This was done, so the results are easier to present here.

2.5.1. Center of Gravity

Center of Gravity (CoG) calculation is a more global method of peak frequency detection, as information is given about the shape of the peak as well, and even not so pronounced peaks can be detected. First, the FFT of the epoch has to be calculated, and a frequency range specified for the calculations. Originally, as proposed by Klimesh et al. [22], this was done by visually inspecting the signal, and finding the beginning of the "ascent" and the end of the "descent" of the alpha peak. The peak frequency is calculated using the following formula:

$$IAF = \sum(a(f)xf) / \sum a(f), \tag{1}$$

where IAF is the individual peak frequency, and $a(f)$ is the power spectral estimate from the FFT at frequency f. The frequency range for this equation was the previously determined start of "ascent" and end of "descent".

Corcoran et al. [11], used the centre of gravity calculation with an automatic search for the frequency range. After finding the alpha peak as described above, for the CoG calculation the first derivative of the FFT was searched for local minima or near horizontal functions prior and after the peak. If there were multiple minima before/after the peak, the closest ones to the peak were used.

2.5.2. BCI

Classification was done only during the third phase of the experiment when the users had to write a word using BCI. In the other phases the EEG data was only processed using the method described in Section 2.4 and offline.

Minimum energy combination (MEC) was used to classify the recorded EEG data, similarly to [23]. MEC combines the data from the least noisy channels. The amount of noise in the data recorded by each channel is calculated by removing the target signals and assessing the rest. The combination is executed for each target frequency, resulting in comparable SNR measures for all targets. After normalization, the result of the classifier is given in percentages for each investigated frequency. For more details please see [23].

In our case, not a single classifier, but four of them were analysing data simultaneously. The only difference between them was the amount of data to analyse, which was 3, 4, 5, and 6 s respectively. The calculations of a classifier started only if enough data were available (for example the 5-second classifier started after 5 s of recording). However, once started they would analyse after each block of incoming data, by shuffling out the oldest block of data and appending the new block. If more than six seconds of recording were available, all four classifiers were calculating simultaneously. The results were combined by weighted averaging, by assigning the highest weights to the longest classifiers. For more details please see [24].

After selecting a target, the flickering stopped for two seconds, and the data recording for the classifiers was started from the beginning (3, 4, 5, 6, or more seconds were needed again for the respective classifiers to start calculating). This gaze shifting time was implemented to allow users to find the next target and to allow the dissipation of the SSVEPs generated by the previous flickering.

In phase four flickering targets were utilised, however, to reduce the occurrence of false positives, three additional frequencies were involved in the calculations of the classifier, without being presented to the users as flickering stimuli. If one of the additional stimuli was classified, no output was produced. The four target frequencies were: 14.0 Hz,14.2 Hz,14.4 Hz, and 14.6 Hz, while the additional three (not displayed) were: 14.13 Hz,14.33 Hz, and 14.53 Hz. This makes measuring activities in the different wavebands easier as there is minimal overlap. The range 14–15 Hz is above the traditional alpha range and the expected peak alpha frequency. Conversely, the range is below the expected peak beta frequency and as such the SSVEPs should have little or no effect on finding these peak values.

2.5.3. Graphical User Interface

The GUI was presented to the users throughout the entire experiment. However, the users could not interact with it during the first two phases. No selection was possible there, and in phase two even the flickering effect was not present. For the third phase (BCI spelling task) it had full functionality.

This speller was a three-step speller; three selections were necessary to write any letter, similar to [24]. Twenty-seven characters (letters of the English alphabet and '_' for space) were organised into three flickering targets in the initial layout, and an additional target enabled the users to delete the last written character (Figure 2). Each selection narrowed down the presented characters to the ones contained in the selected target, e.g., selecting the first target from the initial layout resulted in the first nine characters of the English alphabet to be distributed among three targets. If a target was selected that only contained a single letter, that letter was written. At each layout other than the initial, the option to go back to the previous layout was provided to the users (replacing the delete option). For more details on the spelling logic please see for example [25].

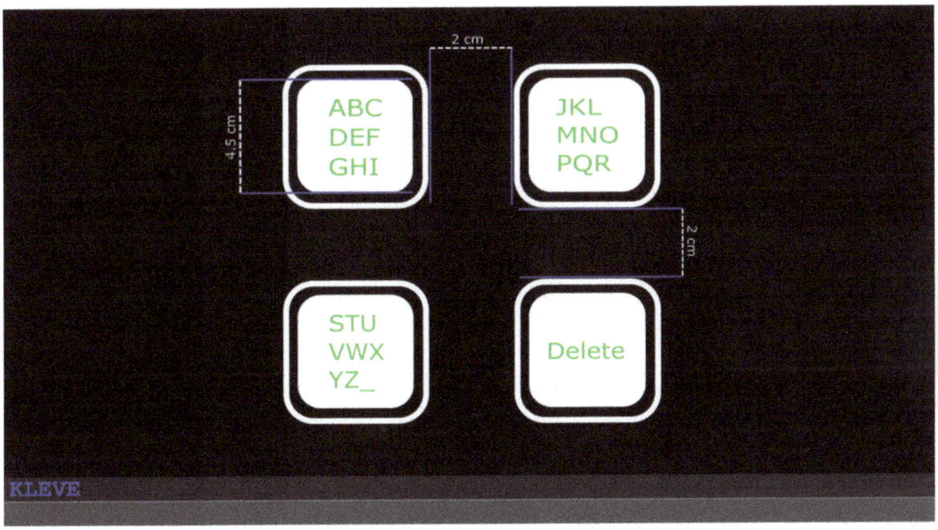

Figure 2. An image of the GUI, with the size of the stimuli and the distances between them. Users were looking at it from approximately 80 cm distance. The stimuli are the smaller squares, surrounded by non-flickering frames, and the length of their sides are equal.

3. Results

3.1. Peak Detection

With the methods mentioned in Section 2.5, an alpha peak was determined for each subject and each electrode with each task. To provide more compact, comprehensible results, the electrodes have been grouped according to their areas into three groups, occipital, centro-parietal, and frontal. Between the first two groups there was a small overlap, PO_3, and PO_4 are a part of both groups.

The parameters for the offline analysis, according to [11] were as described above (e.g., the sampling rate was 256 Hz, 45 s of EEG data was used for 14 recording electrodes). Additionally, alpha peaks were expected in the range of 7–14 Hz, with the Savitzky–Golay filter of frame width 15 and ninth polynomial order. In the case of competing peaks 20% peak height difference was set as the threshold, and the minimum number of channel estimates to resolve for calculating average CoG and peak alpha frequency estimates were 4, 3, and 2 for the occipital, centro-parietal, and frontal areas, respectively.

A few examples of the FFT from electrode O_Z from the occipital area, after the Savitzky–Golay smoothing filter was applied, are shown in Figures 3–5.

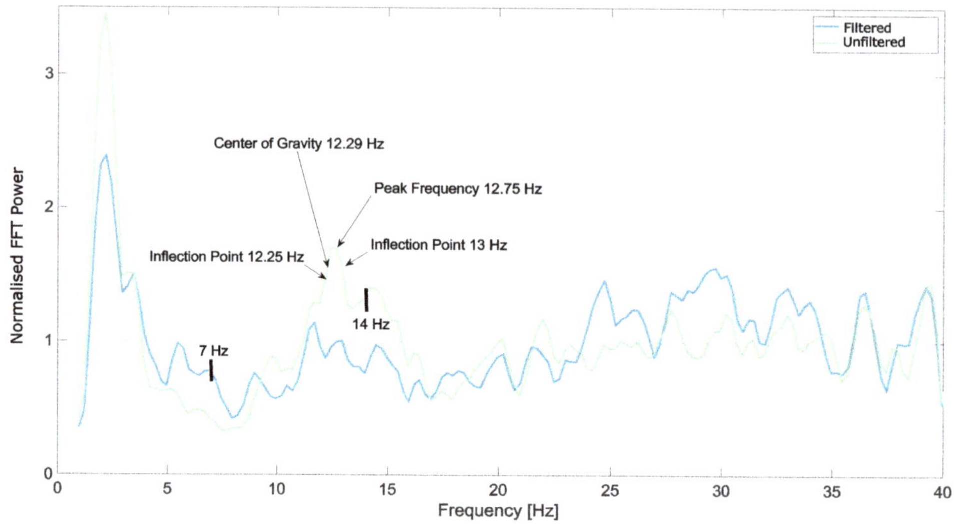

Figure 3. Smoothed fast Fourier transform (FFT) from Subject 1, electrode O_Z, eyes open, executing movements. The artefact removal in this case did not result in better peak detection. The borders of the automatic detection range, 7 Hz and 14 Hz are marked on the plot as well.

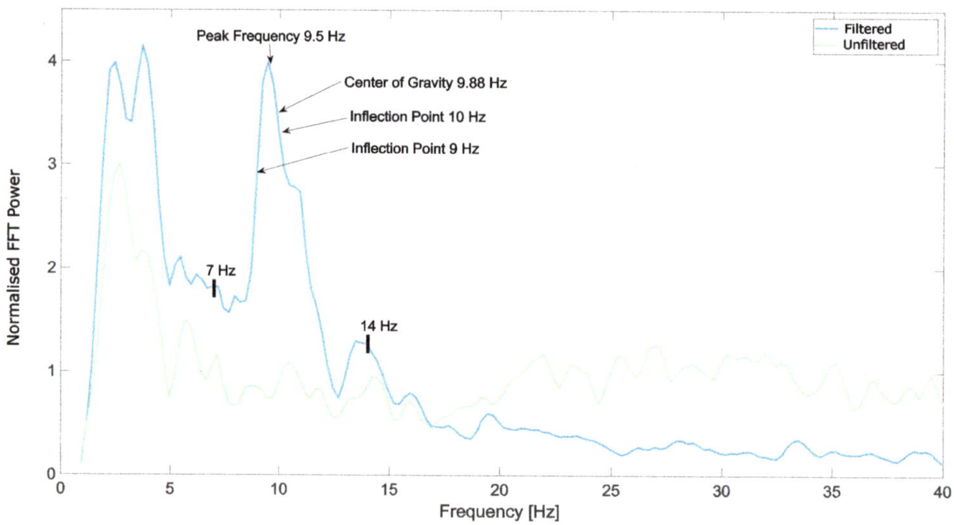

Figure 4. Smoothed FFT from Subject 3, electrode O_Z, eyes open, relaxing. The artefact removal in this case resulted in better peak detection. The borders of the automatic detection range, 7 Hz and 14 Hz are marked on the plot as well.

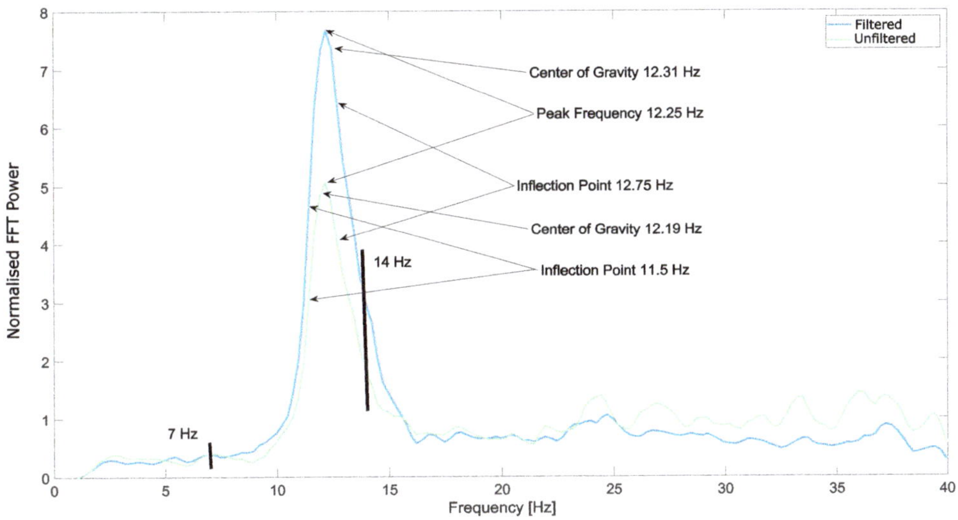

Figure 5. Smoothed FFT from Subject 5, electrode O_Z, eyes open, imagining movements. In this case, both the unfiltered and the filtered data could be used to find a clear peak. The borders of the automatic detection range, 7 Hz and 14 Hz are marked on the plot as well.

For each area specified, a mean and standard deviation were calculated. Peaks of individual channel estimates were weighted by Q_f, which is calculated by dividing Q (area under the curve between the inflexion points) by the bandwidth of this range (the number of frequency bins between the inflexion points). Q_f aims to quantify the relative strength of each channel peak, as described by [11]. As an example, the results of Subject 6 are shown in Table 1.

Table 1. Examples of the calculated peak alpha frequencies with the curve fitting and Center of Gravity (CoG) methods for Subject 6. The results are presented by task, with "Mov." indicating movements during the recording and "Imag." indicating imaginary movements done by the subject. The column "Ch." lists the number of channels that were used to calculate the Peak and SD values. If a channel could not be used for detecting a peak, it was excluded from the average calculation. For the Occipital, Centro-Parietal and Frontal areas 4, 3, and 2 electrodes were the minimum to calculate the average peaks, respectively.

		Occipital											
		Curve Fitting						Center of Gravity					
Eyes	**State**	Unfiltered			Filtered			Unfiltered			Filtered		
		Peak (Hz)	**SD**	**Ch.**	**Peak (Hz)**	**SD**	**Ch.**	**Peak (Hz)**	**SD**	**Ch.**	**Peak (Hz)**	**SD**	**Ch.**
Closed	**Relax**	9.43	0.12	7	9.47	0.09	7	9.48	0.02	7	9.51	0.04	7
Open	**Relax**	10.80	0.17	7	10.79	0.09	7	10.66	0.05	7	10.70	0.03	7
Closed	**Mov.**	9.88	0.13	7	9.96	0.09	7	9.77	0.03	7	10.04	0.03	7
Closed	**Mov.**	9.75	0.00	7	9.78	0.09	7	9.74	0.05	7	9.81	0.03	7
Closed	**Imag.**	9.53	0.09	7	9.71	0.09	7	9.67	0.04	7	9.84	0.04	7
Closed	**Imag.**	9.64	0.13	7	9.75	0.00	7	9.69	0.03	7	9.76	0.02	7
Open	**Mov.**	-	-	0	-	-	0	-	-	0	-	-	1
Open	**Mov.**	-	-	3	-	-	0	-	-	3	-	-	0
Open	**Imag.**	10.50	0.00	7	10.50	0.00	7	9.85	0.06	7	10.05	0.02	7
Open	**Imag.**	10.50	0.00	7	10.50	0.00	7	10.11	0.06	7	10.25	0.01	7

Table 1. *Cont.*

		Centro-Parietal											
Eyes	**State**	**Curve Fitting**						**Center of Gravity**					
		Unfiltered			**Filtered**			**Unfiltered**			**Filtered**		
		Peak (Hz)	**SD**	**Ch.**	**Peak (Hz)**	**SD**	**Ch.**	**Peak (Hz)**	**SD**	**Ch.**	**Peak (Hz)**	**SD**	**Ch.**
Closed	**Relax**	9.50	0.00	6	9.50	0.00	6	9.50	0.04	6	9.57	0.03	6
Open	**Relax**	10.85	0.13	6	10.85	0.13	6	10.70	0.08	6	10.67	0.06	6
Closed	**Mov.**	9.71	0.10	6	9.82	0.13	6	9.76	0.06	6	10.05	0.08	6
Closed	**Mov.**	9.75	0.00	6	9.87	0.14	6	9.83	0.05	6	9.84	0.03	6
Closed	**Imag.**	9.70	0.10	6	9.75	0.00	6	9.78	0.06	6	9.90	0.02	6
Closed	**Imag.**	9.67	0.13	6	9.75	0.00	6	9.71	0.05	6	9.72	0.04	6
Open	**Mov.**	-	-	0	-	-	0	-	-	0	-	-	2
Open	**Mov.**	-	-	0	-	-	0	-	-	0	-	-	0
Open	**Imag.**	10.52	0.16	6	10.46	0.10	6	9.69	0.18	6	9.93	0.07	6
Open	**Imag.**	10.40	0.21	6	10.39	0.21	6	10.14	0.14	6	10.21	0.08	6
		Frontal											
		Curve Fitting						**Center of Gravity**					
		Unfiltered			**Filtered**			**Unfiltered**			**Filtered**		
		Peak (Hz)	**SD**	**Ch.**	**Peak (Hz)**	**SD**	**Ch.**	**Peak (Hz)**	**SD**	**Ch.**	**Peak (Hz)**	**SD**	**Ch.**
Closed	**Relax**	9.25	0.00	3	9.50	0.00	3	9.37	0.01	3	9.47	0.01	3
Open	**Relax**	10.50	0.00	3	10.75	0.00	3	9.24	0.03	3	10.06	0.01	3
Closed	**Mov.**	9.75	0.00	3	9.75	0.00	3	9.59	0.01	3	9.78	0.00	3
Closed	**Mov.**	9.75	0.00	3	9.75	0.00	3	9.77	0.00	3	9.83	0.01	3
Closed	**Imag.**	9.50	0.00	3	9.75	0.00	3	9.70	0.01	3	9.69	0.00	3
Closed	**Imag.**	9.50	0.00	3	9.75	0.00	3	9.66	0.00	3	9.59	0.01	3
Open	**Mov.**	-	-	0	-	-	0	-	-	0	-	-	0
Open	**Mov.**	-	-	0	-	-	0	-	-	0	-	-	0
Open	**Imag.**	10.58	0.14	3	10.00	0.00	3	9.47	0.01	3	9.61	0.01	3
Open	**Imag.**	10.42	0.14	3	10.00	0.00	3	9.97	0.01	3	9.89	0.00	3

The measured peaks were manually inspected to check the results provided by the algorithm. This was done for each electrode separately. The previously used areas are not used here. The results of the manual inspection are shown in Table 2.

Table 2. Manual inspection of peaks from phase two of the experiment. Values in parenthesis mark cases when the automatic and manual inspections both found peaks, however the peaks were more than 0.5 Hz apart, so they are considered wrong. The not parenthesized numbers in the same cells include these cases.

Manual Inspection		**Manual Peaks**			
		Unfiltered		**Filtered**	
		Peak Found	**No Peak**	**Peak Found**	**No Peak**
Automatic Peaks	**Peak Found**	1266	70 (10)	1447	41 (6)
	No Peak	113	651	189	423

Using this confusion matrix, the accuracy of the automatic peak measurement can be assessed by dividing the number of true negative and true positive cases by the number of all cases. An online tool for accuracy calculation can be found at https://bci-lab.hochschule-rhein-waal.de/en/acc.html. It was found to be 89.69% accurate if manual inspection is considered ground truth. The true correct peaks divided by all cases can be used to compare the efficacy of the algorithm in finding peaks in different scenarios. The comparisons with these values are solely used here for grasping the difficulty of finding alpha peaks in different scenarios. The tasks were inspected individually, each with its confusion matrix, and the summary of these results is shown in Figure 6, with the accuracy and the previously mentioned efficacy.

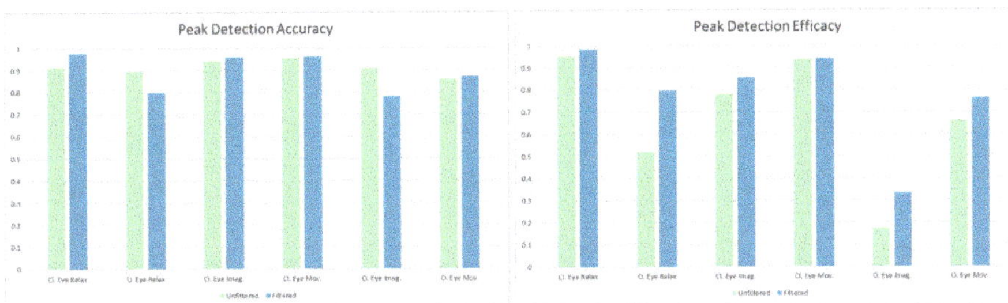

Figure 6. The accuracy and efficacy (true positive divided by the total) of the second phase of the experiment, shown individually for each task the users had to do during the recordings. "Cl." notes tasks with closed eyes, "O." is for open eyes, "Imag." notes imaginary movement, and "Mov." stands for actual movements. The results of the same task from the online recordings were averaged, e.g., "Cl. Eye Mov." shows the combined accuracy and efficacy of two tasks. As mentioned in Section 2.3 the relaxation tasks were only done once, every other case contains twice the amount of data.

The accuracy results from Figure 6 are mixed; in some cases the unfiltered data is more accurate; in other cases the artefact removal increases accuracy. The average difference is 2.18%, with the unfiltered data being more accurate. However, the efficacy, or how often a true peak was found in the different tasks, is always higher for the filtered data (Figure 6). In some cases there is not much difference, e.g., with closed eyes relaxing there is only a 3.22% increase, but in the most pronounced case, with eyes open and relaxing, 27.51% more alpha peaks were found when the artefact removal was applied.

To statistically evaluate the effectiveness of peak detection with and without artefact removal, the cases when the peak was successfully determined were compared. For each subject, each electrode and each task the results of the peak detection were deemed unsuccessful if no peak could be determined with the above-mentioned settings, or successful if a peak was found. This way 2100 (15 Subjects, 14 Electrodes, and 10 Tasks) data points were gathered for both the filtered and unfiltered conditions. The comparison was done by using McNemar's test, for both the automatic detection method (without changing false positive and negative findings) and the manually corrected results. The automatic results showed a significant difference ($p < 0.0001$), with an average successful detection rate of 65% for the unfiltered condition and 72% for the filtered condition, while the manual results also showed a significant difference ($p < 0.0001$), with detection rates of 67% and 78% respectively. By examining the tasks separately (merging data from separate recordings with the same task), McNemar tests show significant differences for the eyes closed relaxing task, $p = 0.011$ and $p = 0.004$ for the automatic and manual results respectively and for eyes closed moving, eyes open relaxing, eyes open imaginary movement, and eyes open moving conditions, $p < 0.0001$ in every case for both automatic and manual results. The only not significantly different condition was with eyes closed and imaginary movement, $p = 0.70$ and $p = 0.286$ for the automatic and manual results respectively. For all cases which were significantly different, the filtered data provided a better rate of finding peaks.

The results were also compared task-wise to see if different alpha peaks were detected using the filtered/unfiltered data. For this comparison, the grouped data was used, with a separate condition for each group. For the occipital group at least four out of the seven electrodes needed a determined peak to calculate an average, for the centro-parietal area this was three out of six, and for the frontal area, two out of three. As in some cases no peak was detected, the number of samples for which this comparison could be done was varied and limited. The measured average values were compared for each task separately with a repeated measures two factor ANOVA, as this enabled more samples for some of the comparisons, and the data were checked with regard to filtering (movement artefacts filtered out in the specified way or not), and the peak detection method (curve fitting or center of gravity). The results are shown in Table 3.

Table 3. The results of the comparison (repeated measures two factor ANOVA) of the detected peaks for all tasks. The values are *p* values, the significant results (under 0.05) are marked with an '*'. Methods are CoG and curve fitting, Filtering notes the presence/absence of the artefact removal.

ANOVA Results	Area	Method	Filtering	Method*Filtering
Closed Eyes Relax	Occipital	0.112	0.084	0.830
	Parietal	0.025 *	0.989	0.831
	Frontal	0.057	0.061	0.831
Open Eyes Relax	Occipital	0.933	0.109	0.377
	Parietal	0.332	0.297	0.139
	Frontal	0.382	0.540	0.268
Closed Eyes Move 1	Occipital	0.104	0.049 *	0.090
	Parietal	0.104	0.525	0.301
	Frontal	0.146	0.588	0.320
Closed Eyes Move 2	Occipital	0.313	0.882	0.853
	Parietal	0.047 *	0.397	0.252
	Frontal	0.059	0.133	0.077
Closed Eyes Imaginary 1	Occipital	0.026 *	0.050 *	0.707
	Parietal	0.078	0.587	0.491
	Frontal	0.012 *	0.088	0.940
Closed Eyes Imaginary 2	Occipital	0.634	0.002 *	0.580
	Parietal	0.919	0.260	0.222
	Frontal	0.024 *	0.253	0.818
Open Eyes Move 1	Occipital	-	-	-
	Parietal	-	-	-
	Frontal	-	-	-
Open Eyes Move 2	Occipital	-	-	-
	Parietal	-	-	-
	Frontal	-	-	-
Open Eyes Imaginary 1	Occipital	0.191	0.924	0.070
	Parietal	0.013 *	0.372	0.580
	Frontal	0.821	0.168	0.070
Open Eyes Imaginary 2	Occipital	0.189	0.236	0.423
	Parietal	0.002 *	0.956	0.728
	Frontal	0.235	0.162	0.891

As can be seen from the table, the majority of the detected peaks were not significantly different. More details about the significant differences are shown in Table 4. The largest difference in means when the filtering is concerned is 0.141 Hz. Regarding the selected algorithm, the difference of means can be as high as 0.353 Hz. If more precise peak detection is necessary in the future, the parameters of the artefact removal and peak detection methods likely have to be adjusted.

Table 4. The significantly different cases from Table 3. Most differences arose from the used peak determination method, but there are examples of the filtering-out of artefacts causing differences.

Significant		Cl. Eyes Relax		Cl. Eyes Move		Cl. Eyes Imag.		Cl. Eyes Imag.	
		Parietal		**Parietal**		**Occipital**		**Frontal**	
		Mean	*SD*	*Mean*	*SD*	*Mean*	*SD*	*Mean*	*SD*
Method	*Curve Fitting*	9.950	0.250	100.003	0.357	100.094	0.324	90.670	0.267
	CoG	90.780	0.222	90.904	0.359	90.985	0.305	90.473	0.247
		Cl0. Eyes Imag0.		**O0. Eyes Imag0.**		**O0. Eyes Imag0.**			
		Frontal		**Parietal**		**Parietal**			
		Mean	*SD*	*Mean*	*SD*	*Mean*	*SD*		
Method	*Curve Fitting*	90.716	0.328	100.325	0.328	100.457	0.385		
	CoG	90.505	0.269	90.972	0.325	100.210	0.402		
		Cl0. Eyes Move		**Cl0. Eyes Imag0.**		**Cl0. Eyes Imag0.**			
		Occipital		**Occipital**		**Occipital**			
		Mean	*SD*	*Mean*	*SD*	*Mean*	*SD*		
Filtering	*Unfiltered*	100.448	0.405	100.015	0.317	90.948	0.244		
	Filtered	100.307	0.413	100.064	0.311	100.042	0.246		

3.2. Peak Detection During BCI Phase

The analysis of IAF during BCI use was done as it would be for fatigue or attention level analysis. This means the EEG data was separated into flicker-free and flickering segments. These segments were then further subdivided into different time segments of the recording. This way, peak detection could be done for different time segments of the experiment, which could be used to track the properties of the IAF throughout the recording. For all these segments the manual inspections proved to be more complicated than the previous phase due to the frequent lack of clear peaks, and even when peaks were found they were mostly flat or distorted. The analysis of the flicker-free and flickering segments was done on an electrode basis (not grouped into areas) and is discussed separately in the next sections.

3.2.1. Flicker-Free Segments

After every selection, a two-second gaze shifting time was implemented in the BCI, for the users to have enough time to find the next target letter. During this gaze shifting time the flickering of the stimuli was turned off. These segments were merged and divided into eight-second long segments (or 4096 samples with the sampling rate 256 Hz). These segments were separately checked for peaks in the alpha range with the curve fitting method described above. This was followed by manual inspection, and the results of this are shown in Table 5. The accuracy of the automatic detection is 85.12% if the manually detected peaks are considered ground truth. The accuracy and efficacy (as described above) values calculated for the two cases are shown in Figure 7, together with the same results from the flickering segments, which are described in the next section.

Table 5. Manual inspection of peaks from the BCI recordings (phase three of the experiment), when the stimuli were not flickering. Values in parenthesis mark cases when both the automatic and manual inspections found peaks, however, the peaks were more than 0.5 Hz apart, so they were considered wrong. The not parenthesized numbers in the same cells include these cases.

Manual Inspection		Manual Peaks			
		Unfiltered		Filtered	
		Peak Found	No Peak	Peak Found	No Peak
Automatic Peaks	Peak Found	594	86 (16)	781	43 (11)
	No Peak	243	939	182	856

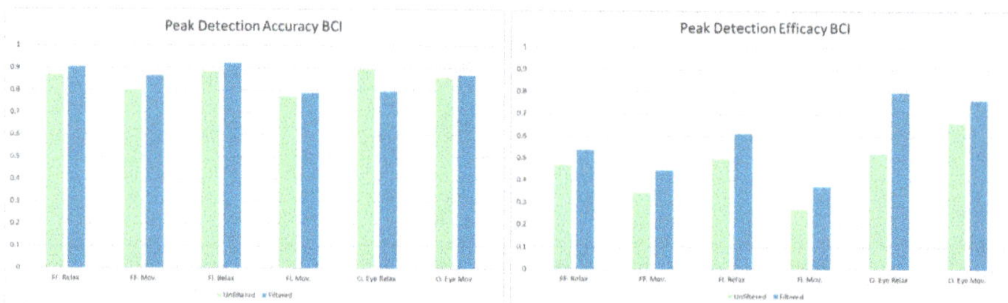

Figure 7. The accuracy and efficacy (true positive divided by the total) of the third phase of the experiment, shown for using the BCI while relaxing/moving, as well as open eyes while relaxing/moving from phase two.

3.2.2. Flickering Segments

The rest of the recordings during BCI use (when the stimuli were flickering), were merged and divided into 15 second long segments for this analysis. Since the recording time was different for each subject, the available data was also varied. The length of the segments (15 s) was chosen to provide at least three segments from each participants' data. For this analysis, all subjects' EEG data was used, regardless of whether they could finish the BCI spelling task or not. The peak detection method was slightly altered to avoid mistakes from the SSVEPs. The boundaries for the search were altered, to 8–13 Hz (this way the ~14 Hz SSVEP and ~7 Hz subharmonic were both excluded from the range). The following manual inspection results are shown in Table 6 and Figure 7.

Table 6. Manual inspection of peaks from the BCI recordings (phase three of the experiment), when the stimuli were flickering. Values in parenthesis mark cases when both the automatic and manual inspections found peaks, however, the peaks were more than 0.5 Hz apart, so they were considered wrong. The not parenthesized numbers in the same cells include these cases.

Manual Inspection		Manual Peaks			
		Unfiltered		Filtered	
		Peak Found	No Peak	Peak Found	No Peak
Automatic Peaks	Peak Found	893	183 (12)	1206	60 (8)
	No Peak	528	1882	600	1620

3.3. BCI Performance

The accuracy, the total time and the Information Transfer Rate (ITR) of the spelling tasks were used to evaluate the BCI performance of the three different scenarios, relaxing, moving without applying artefact removal, and moving while applying artefact removal. An online tool for ITR calculation can be found at https://bci-lab.hochschule-rhein-waal.de/en/itr.html. These measures are shown in Table 7 together with the mean and SD for the scenarios. The cases when users could not finish the spelling tasks are excluded, and not used in the statistical evaluation. The scenarios were compared with one factor repeated measures ANOVA, and the respective results are $p = 0.036$, $p = 0.001$ and $p = 0.011$ (with Greenhouse-Geisser correction) for the accuracy, ITR and spelling time respectively. All three parameters show significant difference.

Further investigations were done by pairwise tests (paired t-tests). For brevity, the relaxing scenario is marked RE, the moving without filter MW, and the moving while filtering MF, from here on. The pairwise accuracy results are: $p = 0.556$, $p = 0.024$, and $p = 0.085$ for RE-MW, RE-MF, and MW-MF, respectively. For ITR: $p = 0.048$, $p = 0.003$, and $p = 0.014$ for RE-MW, RE-MF, and MW-MF, respectively. Finally, for spelling time: $p = 0.020$, $p = 0.012$, and $p = 0.049$ for RE-MW, RE-MF, and MW-MF, respectively. This translates into the MW and MF scenarios performing significantly worse than the movement-free scenario in every aspect, except accuracy, which is not different significantly between the MW and RE scenarios.

Table 7. Performance results of the online BCI tasks. The top row indicates the scenario.

	Relaxing			**Move & No Filter**			**Move & Filter**		
	Acc (%)	**ITR (bpm)**	**Time (s)**	**Acc (%)**	**ITR (bpm)**	**Time (s)**	**Acc (%)**	**ITR (bpm)**	**Time (s)**
S1	92.3	17.2	67.3	100.0	19.2	75.0	92.3	11.0	105.0
S2	100.0	24.5	73.5	100.0	19.6	91.8	94.1	15.8	102.0
S3	100.0	22.9	78.5	-	-	-	89.5	7.9	194.0
S4	100.0	24.0	120.0	100.0	23.2	124.0	93.3	16.3	170.0
S5	95.0	11.6	169.0	87.5	7.0	258.0	95.5	8.8	249.0
S6	100.0	23.8	90.8	-	-	-	-	-	-
S7	100.0	24.6	73.3	94.1	9.9	163.0	90.5	6.4	275.0
S8	100.0	13.2	136.0	94.7	15.0	123.0	93.8	12.5	120.0
S9	100.0	24.5	103.0	100.0	23.8	106.0	100.0	24.0	105.0
S10	94.1	17.5	92.5	100.0	22.4	80.3	100.0	21.9	82.3
S11	100.0	18.0	102.0	94.0	11.0	142.0	86.0	7.0	202.0
S12	94.1	16.2	99.8	100.0	13.8	130.0	80.0	5.4	267.0
S13	100.0	24.2	74.3	100.0	22.8	78.8	100.0	22.6	79.8
S14	100.0	23.8	75.5	94.1	12.4	130.0	94.1	14.8	109.0
S15	100.0	24.2	74.3	100.0	20.3	88.5	100.0	17.3	104.0
Mean	**98.37**	**20.68**	**95.32**	**97.26**	**16.96**	**122.34**	**93.51**	**13.69**	**154.58**
SD	**20.68**	**4.57**	**28.22**	**4.00**	**5.71**	**49.00**	**5.81**	**6.27**	**70.40**

Additionally two subjects could not finish the spelling task with the MW scenario, and one could not finish the task with the MF scenario. Furthermore, the MF scenarios' performance is worse than the MW scenarios' regarding ITR and spelling time. The potential causes of this are examined in the Discussion section.

4. Discussion

The online automatic artefact removal method applied proved to improve IAF detection. For simple EEG recordings the method from [21] proved to result in data significantly better for determining alpha peaks using the described curve fitting method from [11]. The detection rate increased from 64.87% to 71.52%. After manual inspection and correction the increase is from 66.57%

to 78.48%. The increase was even more pronounced in some cases, especially while the users were relaxing with open eyes.

Generally, movements did not affect alpha peak detection, which is likely the combined result of several effects. Movement control is associated with the central brain area, which in this experiment was measured by a single electrode. The effect of these potentials in the central area did not influence the occipital area, where most recording electrodes were located. Furthermore the movements did not require any visualisation or precision, and thus while the movements were executed by the users likely the visual cortex pertained a high alpha activity, possibly even higher than in a relaxing condition.

As opposed to movement-related artefacts not influencing the alpha peak detection, imaginary movement tasks resulted in a more considerable decrease in the amount of found peaks. Without artefact removal, this decrease was 17.61% and 35.00% of the total for the closed and open-eyed conditions, respectively. With artefact removal it changed to 13.23% and 46.18% of the total, respectively. This effect is likely the result of users not trained for executing imaginary movement tasks; thus they were likely visualising the movements. This, in turn, decreases alpha activity in the occipital area, and a peak is harder to detect. In these cases the artefact removal algorithm made the peak detection substantially more effective.

The most substantial effect of filtering, however, was for the eyes open and relaxing condition. The reason for this is hard to pinpoint and requires further investigation. One reason could be that users were inspecting their surroundings during this task, which would then reduce alpha activity in the occipital area.

When the SSVEP-based BCI was used by subjects while relaxing, compared to the open eyes relaxing condition from phase two, there was no substantial decrease in efficacy (5.33% and 2.84% of the total for the flicker-free and the flickering conditions, respectively), when checking the unfiltered results. With artefact removal, the differences increased to 25.96% and 18.61% of the total. These differences confirm the degradation of peak detection efficacy when our SSVEP-based BCI is used. The substantial change in efficacy after artefact removal is due to the substantial improvement of peak detection in phase two for the eyes open and relaxing condition.

When users were moving during BCI use, the decrease was 31.61% and 38.94% of the total for the flicker-free and the flickering conditions with the unfiltered data, respectively. With artefact removal, these differences remained high, 38.94% and 39.05% of the total, respectively. This result shows that BCI use while the users are moving effects the detectable peaks substantially.

Although the BCI use, especially with the users moving degraded peak detection by a large amount, the artefact removal provided an improvement in every condition, the efficacy (true positive rate) increased on average by 9.68% of the total (combining flicker-free and flickering conditions, as well as relaxing and moving scenarios) if the filtering is applied.

The performance of the BCI decreased for the scenarios when users were moving as expected. However, the filtering had no positive effect. Instead the opposite occurred, performance was worse than without filtering. There can be several reasons for this, the most obvious one being the filter affecting the prevalence of the SSVEPs generated by the flickering. This could be the result of setting up the filter, and defining the coefficients for filtering. If the SSVEP during this phase (phase one of this experiment) is not comparable in strength to the one during the experiment, the filter can decrease the power of the frequency component during the online task to the levels of the training phase, which decreases BCI performance. As shown by [26], attention affects the properties of the generated activity, and, as in our experiment, users were instructed to look at the middle of the screen in the training phase, not directly at the stimuli, the decrease in performance can very well be a consequence. To investigate this and other potential causes, further studies are necessary.

Another important detail of note is the classification method, MEC, which selects the least noise-ridden electrodes data for classification. As in our case, eight electrodes were providing data for the classifier; if half of them were influenced by artefacts, the four remaining could still be used to classify without too much difficulty. This can be another factor in the performance difference between the filtered and unfiltered BCI tasks. As the classification method is robust against noise, and the artefacts in this experiment did not cause enough noise to necessitate the artefact removal, the only effect of the filter was the attenuation of SSVEP responses, which resulted in slower classification. The use of fewer electrodes to necessitate the use of slightly noisy electrode channels or the use of a different classification algorithm can be used to investigate this effect further.

Although the detection rate can be improved, during BCI use a considerably lower number of peaks was found. This can be the result of a less boring task (BCI use), or change in mental fatigue, or just from the difficulty of finding peaks during BCI use. However, the investigation of this is not in the scope of this paper. Peak alpha frequency determined during the eyes open condition for example can be measured with the filtering method (providing an improvement), which could then be used to calculate the individual alpha range and provide a list of other parameters based on the alpha range (area under the curve, power in the lower alpha range/higher alpha range etc.).

5. Conclusions

The measurement of objective user fatigue can provide a way to minimize its negative effects on BCI performance, by adjusting parameters of the BCI accordingly. Methods which help to measure user fatigue objectively, accurately, and online are therefore highly beneficial for BCIs that are planned to be used for a prolonged time. As mentioned previously, BCIs in the future are expected to be used in everyday, practical scenarios. In these cases, movements can cause artefacts in EEG recordings, this was also observed in this experiment as well. Therefore, some movements have to be anticipated and handled accordingly. The measurement of fatigue or attention with EEG has the same difficulties regarding movement artefacts, as the cases where fatigue measurements are needed are always related to some activity, e.g., after prolonged driving phases. The presented online automatic artefact removal showed an average 9.68% of the total increase in the number of peaks found during an SSVEP-based BCI use, where the users were moving to generate artefacts. When no BCI was used, the increase was on average 10.91% of the total.

This means that the used techniques are beneficial for detecting the peak alpha frequency from the EEG recordings, even during BCI use under noisy conditions. Utilising artefact removal and curve fitting for peak alpha frequency measurements, the basis for determining objective fatigue accurately was greatly improved. These results were achieved without restrictions on the specific movements. Furthermore, the artefact removal was trained in a generic way without a specific artefact detection algorithm. Refining the parameters of both the removal method and the peak detection algorithm can lead to even better results, as can the implementation of an online artefact detection algorithm.

Our experiment employed movements which would occur in everyday scenarios, such as talking or chewing gum. The next step regarding mobility will be testing in a noisy environment using a mobile amplifier.

Regarding objective fatigue and attention measurement, increasing the number of measured parameters is planned, e.g., by determining theta peaks, extracting phase information for alpha peaks, as well as assessing the spatial information, to find a reliable way to measure fatigue and at the final end e.g., the level of attention of BCI users.

To conclude, the presented system provided, on average, a nearly 10% (of the total) increase in the amount of detected alpha peak frequencies. Even when users were moving or executing imaginary movement tasks it provided a better peak finding rate. With small adjustments, further improvements can be expected, providing a promising way towards extracting information from EEG in practical, everyday, mobile scenarios.

Author Contributions: Conceptualization, M.B.; Data curation, M.B.; Formal analysis, M.B.; Funding acquisition, I.V.; Investigation, M.B.; Methodology, M.B.; Project administration, I.V.; Resources, I.V.; Software, M.B. and I.V.; Supervision, I.V.; Validation, M.B.; Visualization, M.B.; Writing—original draft, M.B.; Writing—review & editing, M.B. and I.V.

Funding: This research was supported by the European Fund for Regional Development (EFRD or EFRE in German) under the Grant IT-1-2-001.

Conflicts of Interest: The authors declare no conflict of interest.

References

1. Teplan, M. Fundamentals of EEG measurement. *Meas. Sci. Rev.* **2002**, *2*, 1–11.
2. Wolpaw, J.R.; Birbaumer, N.; McFarland, D.J.; Pfurtscheller, G.; Vaughan, T.M. Brain–Computer Interfaces for Communication and Control. *Clin. Neurophysiol.* **2002**, *113*, 767–791, doi:10.1016/S1388-2457(02)00057-3. [CrossRef]
3. Jung, T.P.; Makeig, S.; Stensmo, M.; Sejnowski, T.J. Estimating alertness from the EEG power spectrum. *IEEE Trans. Biomed. Eng.* **1997**, *44*, 60–69. [CrossRef] [PubMed]
4. Klimesch, W. EEG alpha and theta oscillations reflect cognitive and memory performance: A review and analysis. *Brain Res. Rev.* **1999**, *29*, 169–195. [CrossRef]
5. Klimesch, W. Alpha-band oscillations, attention, and controlled access to stored information. *Trends Cogn. Sci.* **2012**, *16*, 606–617. [CrossRef]
6. Cao, T.; Wan, F.; Wong, C.M.; da Cruz, J.N.; Hu, Y. Objective evaluation of fatigue by EEG spectral analysis in steady-state visual evoked potential-based brain-computer interfaces. *Biomed. Eng. Online* **2014**, *13*, 28. [CrossRef]
7. Xie, J.; Xu, G.; Wang, J.; Li, M.; Han, C.; Jia, Y. Effects of mental load and fatigue on steady-state evoked potential based brain computer interface tasks: A comparison of periodic flickering and motion-reversal based visual attention. *PLoS ONE* **2016**, *11*, e0163426. [CrossRef]
8. Xie, J.; Xu, G.; Luo, A.; Li, M.; Zhang, S.; Han, C.; Yan, W. The role of visual noise in influencing mental load and fatigue in a steady-state motion visual evoked potential-based brain-computer interface. *Sensors* **2017**, *17*, 1873. [CrossRef]
9. Benda, M.; Stawicki, P.; Gembler, F.; Rezeika, A.; Saboor, A.; Volosyak, I. SSVEP-Based BCI Performance and Objective Fatigue Under Different Background Conditions. In Proceedings of the 2018 IEEE International Conference on Systems, Man, and Cybernetics (SMC), Miyazaki, Japan, 7–10 October 2018; IEEE: Piscataway, NJ, USA, 2018; pp. 1116–1121.
10. Klimesch, W.; Doppelmayr, M.; Roehm, D.; Pöllhuber, D.; Stadler, W. Simultaneous desynchronization and synchronization of different alpha responses in the human electroencephalograph: A neglected paradox? *Neurosci. Lett.* **2000**, *284*, 97–100. [CrossRef]
11. Corcoran, A.W.; Alday, P.M.; Schlesewsky, M.; Bornkessel-Schlesewsky, I. Toward a reliable, automated method of individual alpha frequency (IAF) quantification. *Psychophysiology* **2018**, *55*, e13064. [CrossRef]
12. Klimesch, W.; Schimke, H.; Ladurner, G.; Pfurtscheller, G. Alpha frequency and memory performance. *J. Psychophysiol.* **1990**.
13. Chiang, A.; Rennie, C.; Robinson, P.; Roberts, J.; Rigozzi, M.; Whitehouse, R.; Hamilton, R.; Gordon, E. Automated characterization of multiple alpha peaks in multi-site electroencephalograms. *J. Neurosci. Methods* **2008**, *168*, 396–411. [CrossRef] [PubMed]
14. Van Albada, S.; Kerr, C.; Chiang, A.; Rennie, C.; Robinson, P. Neurophysiological changes with age probed by inverse modeling of EEG spectra. *Clin. Neurophysiol.* **2010**, *121*, 21–38. [CrossRef] [PubMed]
15. Chiang, A.; Rennie, C.; Robinson, P.; Van Albada, S.; Kerr, C. Age trends and sex differences of alpha rhythms including split alpha peaks. *Clin. Neurophysiol.* **2011**, *122*, 1505–1517. [CrossRef] [PubMed]
16. Fries, P. Rhythms for cognition: communication through coherence. *Neuron* **2015**, *88*, 220–235. [CrossRef]
17. Kong, W.; Zhou, Z.; Hu, S.; Zhang, J.; Babiloni, F.; Dai, G. Automatic and direct identification of blink components from scalp EEG. *Sensors* **2013**, *13*, 10783–10801. [CrossRef]
18. Zeng, H.; Song, A.; Yan, R.; Qin, H. EOG artifact correction from EEG recording using stationary subspace analysis and empirical mode decomposition. *Sensors* **2013**, *13*, 14839–14859. [CrossRef]

19. Chen, X.; Liu, A.; Peng, H.; Ward, R. A preliminary study of muscular artifact cancellation in single-channel EEG. *Sensors* **2014**, *14*, 18370–18389. [CrossRef]
20. Mutanen, T.P.; Metsomaa, J.; Liljander, S.; Ilmoniemi, R.J. Automatic and robust noise suppression in EEG and MEG: The SOUND algorithm. *Neuroimage* **2018**, *166*, 135–151. [CrossRef]
21. Somers, B.; Francart, T.; Bertrand, A. A generic EEG artifact removal algorithm based on the multi-channel Wiener filter. *J. Neural Eng.* **2018**, *15*, 036007. [CrossRef]
22. Klimesch, W. EEG-alpha rhythms and memory processes. *Int. J. Psychophysiol.* **1997**, *26*, 319–340. [CrossRef]
23. Volosyak, I. SSVEP-based Bremen–BCI interface—Boosting information transfer rates. *J. Neural Eng.* **2011**, *8*, 036020. [CrossRef] [PubMed]
24. Benda, M.; Stawicki, P.; Gembler, F.; Grichnik, R.; Rezeika, A.; Saboor, A.; Volosyak, I. Different Feedback Methods For An SSVEP-Based BCI. In Proceedings of the 2018 40th Annual International Conference of the IEEE Engineering in Medicine and Biology Society (EMBC), Honolulu, HI, USA, 17–21 July 2018; IEEE: Piscataway, NJ, USA, 2018; pp. 1939–1943.
25. Rezeika, A.; Benda, M.; Stawicki, P.; Gembler, F.; Saboor, A.; Volosyak, I. Surface Electromyographic Control of a Three-Steps Speller Interface. In Proceedings of the 2018 IEEE International Conference on Systems, Man, and Cybernetics (SMC), Miyazaki, Japan, 7–10 October 2018; IEEE: Piscataway, NJ, USA, 2018; pp. 147–152.
26. Kelly, S.P.; Lalor, E.C.; Finucane, C.; McDarby, G.; Reilly, R.B. Visual spatial attention control in an independent brain-computer interface. *IEEE Trans. Biomed. Eng.* **2005**, *52*, 1588–1596. [CrossRef] [PubMed]

brain sciences

MDPI

Article

In-Ear EEG Based Attention State Classification Using Echo State Network

Dong-Hwa Jeong [1] and Jaeseung Jeong [1,2,*]

1 Department of Bio and Brain Engineering, College of Engineering, Korea Advanced Institute of Science and Technology (KAIST), Daejeon 34141, Korea; donghwa@kaist.ac.kr
2 Program of Brain and Cognitive Engineering, Korea Advanced Institute of Science and Technology (KAIST), Daejeon 34141, Korea
* Correspondence: jsjeong@kaist.ac.kr

Received: 24 March 2020; Accepted: 24 May 2020; Published: 26 May 2020

Abstract: It is important to maintain attention when carrying out significant daily-life tasks that require high levels of safety and efficiency. Since degradation of attention can sometimes have dire consequences, various brain activity measurement devices such as electroencephalography (EEG) systems have been used to monitor attention states in individuals. However, conventional EEG instruments have limited utility in daily life because they are uncomfortable to wear. Thus, this study was designed to investigate the possibility of discriminating between the attentive and resting states using in-ear EEG signals for potential application via portable, convenient earphone-shaped EEG instruments. We recorded both on-scalp and in-ear EEG signals from 6 subjects in a state of attentiveness during the performance of a visual vigilance task. We have designed and developed in-ear EEG electrodes customized by modelling both the left and right ear canals of the subjects. We use an echo state network (ESN), a powerful type of machine learning algorithm, to discriminate attention states on the basis of in-ear EEGs. We have found that the maximum average accuracy of the ESN method in discriminating between attentive and resting states is approximately 81.16% with optimal network parameters. This study suggests that portable in-ear EEG devices and an ESN can be used to monitor attention states during significant tasks to enhance safety and efficiency.

Keywords: In-ear EEG; echo state network (ESN); attention monitoring; vigilance task

1. Introduction

Humans are placed in many situations where it is necessary to sustain attention, such as working, studying, driving, and exercising. However, it is difficult to maintain rigorous attention for a long time. For instance, when subjects were placed in a laboratory setting, their level of attention immediately dropped within 30 min and gradually decreased further over time [1]. The decrease in attention was accelerated as the workload—and, thus, the cognitive demand—increased [2,3]. Degradation of attention sometimes results in dire consequences, for instance, at construction sites, in cars, at hospitals, or on battlefields. Loss of attention has been reported to have severe consequences such as failure to learn or work [4], medical malpractice [5], and traffic accidents [6]. Thus, it is important to monitor attention states during significant tasks requiring high levels of safety and efficiency, and if the level of attention is reduced during such tasks, it is important to take appropriate actions aimed at preventing critical mistakes and improving performance.

There has been a large body of studies on monitoring attention states through techniques that measure brain activity. Electroencephalography (EEG), which records the summed electrical potential from a large ensemble of neurons beneath electrodes, is the most common method used for attention monitoring because it is more portable and cost-effective than other neuroimaging techniques. The theta

(4–8 Hz) and alpha (8–11 Hz) bands within EEG signals are known to be associated with the level of attention during a task [7]. In addition, gamma (>30 Hz) oscillations are regarded as an EEG correlate of sustained attention and high cognitive performance [8]. Measuring these electrophysiological features using portable EEG devices has been used to detect attention states during the performance of tasks. However, conventional headsets or cap-shaped EEG devices are uncomfortable to wear in daily life. On the other hand, as mobile phones have advanced to provide multimedia services, earphones are now an essential accessory for smartphone users. Thus, a novel earphone-shaped instrument measuring EEG signal in the ear canal and around the ears has emerged as a strong candidate among attention-measuring devices.

Since the in-ear EEG concept was first introduced [9], a few groups have reported in-ear EEG device prototypes and their signal-detecting properties [10–16]. In-ear EEG signals show alpha attenuation, defined as the suppression of alpha activity (at approximately 10 Hz) when subjects open their eyes. In-ear EEG signals are highly correlated with on-scalp EEG signals recorded from electrodes near the temporal regions. EEG characteristics, such as auditory steady-state responses (ASSRs) [9,10,12,13,15,16], event-related potentials (ERPs) [9–12], steady-state visual evoked potentials (SSVEPs) [9,16,17], and sleep-related EEG signals [18–20] have been detected and identified from in-ear EEG signals.

There has been a small body of work using in-ear EEG signals to classify brain states using brain–computer interface (BCI) techniques. Most previous studies using in-ear signals and BCI paradigms are synchronous or reactive systems that use external cues, such as ERPs [11,21,22], ASSRs [23], and SSVEPs [17]. The P300 ERP component, which is elicited by target stimuli, is detected with approximately 85% accuracy [11]. When two different sound stimuli are delivered to the right and left ears, the attended stream can be identified from P300 components with approximately 77% accuracy [12]. SSVEPs, which are elicited by visual stimulation at specific frequencies, can be classified with 79.9% accuracy [17]. Since these paradigms are dependent on external visual or auditory stimuli, they cannot be used to detect mental states that require constant monitoring independent of external stimuli. To our knowledge, only a few studies have reported the use of an asynchronous or active BCI that detects mental states in individuals. One study has reported that drowsiness during driving simulations can be recognized from in-ear EEG signals with approximately 85% accuracy over 10 s epochs and 98.5% over 230 s epochs [24]. A similar study to measure day time drowsiness reported that in-ear EEG signals during 30 s epochs of drowsiness were discriminated from 30 s epochs of wakefulness with 80% accuracy [25]. Another study reported that mental workload and motor action during a visuomotor tracking task were detected using a two-channel in-ear EEG system with 68.55% accuracy in 5 s windows and 78.51% accuracy when a moving average filter was applied over five such windows [26]. One study has reported that in-ear EEG signals could be distinguished when subjects viewed emotional pictures for 30 s [27]. In binary classification tasks, positive valence and negative valence could be discriminated with 71.07% accuracy and high and low arousal could be discriminated with 72.89% accuracy. A four-way classification task using all combinations of high or low valence and high or low arousal group was performed with 54.89% accuracy. These studies successfully detected mental states such as drowsiness, mental workload, and emotional states, but long time windows were required for successful classification. A reduced time window and increased classification performance are necessary for asynchronous BCI systems that monitor mental states for the prevention of attention lapses.

The aim of this study is to examine the possibility of discrimination between the attentive state and the resting state using in-ear EEG signals for the potential development of portable, convenient earphone-shaped EEG instruments for attention monitoring. In this study, we recorded both in-ear and on-scalp EEG signals in the attentive state from 6 subjects during the performance of the visual vigilance task. We have designed and developed in-ear EEG electrodes customized by impressions of both the left and right ear canals of the subjects.

In this study, more importantly, we have used an echo state network (ESN), a branch of reservoir computing which is one of the powerful algorithms in machine learning techniques, to discriminate attention states using in-ear EEG. The recurrent property of reservoirs (internal units) in an ESN has been used to provide powerful prediction of nonlinear time series data [28–31]. Since EEG signals are highly nonlinear and nonstationary, an ESN has been used for EEG prediction, such as monitoring epileptic seizures [32], distinguishing ERP signals elicited by emotional stimuli [33,34], and decoding the intention to move in different directions [35]. These studies have demonstrated that an ESN is more effective than other EEG feature extraction methods. Additionally, ESNs have distinguished human mental states with higher performance than other machine learning classifiers. Therefore, we hypothesize that ESNs are potentially useful for detecting attention states using in-ear EEG signals.

2. Materials and Methods

2.1. Data Acquisition

In this study, we used moldable plastic beads (InstaMorph, Happy Wire Dog, LLC. USA) and conductive silver paste (ELCOAT P-100, CANS, Japan) to develop in-ear EEG electrodes to place in the ear canal. Ear canal impressions were taken with InstaMorph and connected to electric leads. Then, conductive silver paste was painted on the impressions for electrical conductivity (Figure 1). An in-ear EEG electrodes was placed in each ear. Flat silver disks were produced to place the on-scalp electrodes on the forehead (right and left). Ag/AgCl foam electrodes with conductive adhesive hydrogel (Kendall®, Coviden, USA) were used for the ground and reference channels. Lead wires attached to each electrode were connected to an OpenBCI Cyton Board (32 bits, 250 Hz sampling rate). The validity of biosignal acquisition using the developed electrodes was tested and identified by measuring electrocardiography (EKG) signals. The right mastoid process (behind the ear) was selected as the reference site, and the left mastoid process was selected as the ground site. In addition, on-scalp EEG was performed on the forehead (Fp1 and Fp2) under the same conditions as the in-ear EEG to compare the two types of signals.

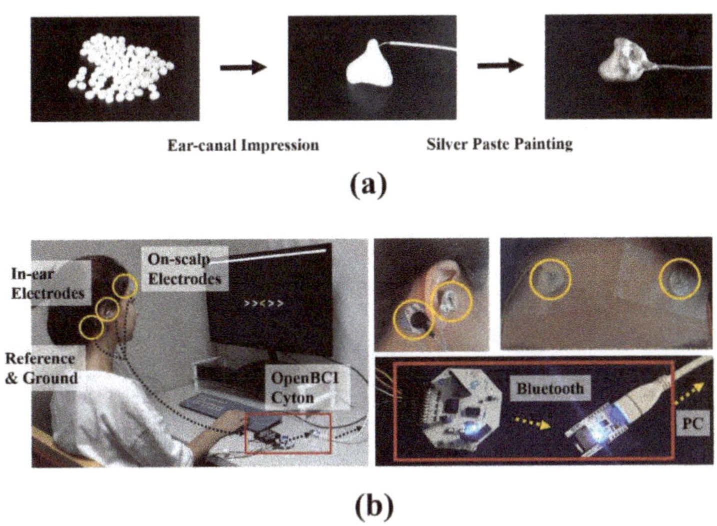

Figure 1. The design of the in-ear electroencephalography (EEG) electrodes. (**a**) Impressions were taken of the ear canal using moldable plastic beads, and conductive silver paste was painted on the impressions for electrical conductivity. (**b**) The participants wore in-ear EEG electrodes on both ears and an on-scalp electrode on either side of the forehead. The mastoid processes were used for the reference and ground channels. Each electrode was connected to an OpenBCI Cyton Board, and then EEG signals were transmitted to a computer (PC) via Bluetooth technology.

2.2. Participants

Six right-handed participants between 25 and 30 years old were recruited (mean age = 28.17 ± 2.32 years, 4 males) for this study. All participants had normal or corrected vision and no history of neuropsychiatric disease or ear-related problems. We took impressions of participants' ear canals three days before the experiment. The participants were asked to sleep a sufficient amount and abstain from smoking, alcohol, and caffeine for at least 24 h before the experiment.

Signed consent forms for the experiment were obtained from all participants after the nature of the experiment and the associated precautions had been explained to them. Participants received financial compensation for participating in this experiment, and additional rewards were given based on their task performance. Participants could quit the experiment whenever they felt too tired to maintain their attention. The study and all experimental processes were approved by the institutional review board (IRB) of KAIST.

2.3. Experimental Stimuli and Protocol

To verify the in-ear EEG acquisition, we obtained eyes-closed and eyes-open resting-state signals to identify alpha attenuation after cleaning the ear canals with ethanol (the results are shown in Appendix A). Then, attention states were elicited by a visual vigilance task, which was modified from a psychomotor vigilance task (PVT) [36] and the Eriksen flanker task [37]. PVTs are widely used for identifying sustained attention and behavioral alertness by measuring a subject's reaction time to a specific visual stimulus [38,39]. In general, subjects are asked to press a button as fast as possible when a red dot appears on a monitor. Response-stimulus intervals vary randomly from 2 to 10 s. The Eriksen flanker task is also a widely used task to measure selective attention and executive functions [40,41]. Subjects are asked to press a button corresponding to the target stimulus presented at the center of the screen as quickly as possible, regardless of the flanker stimuli surrounding the target.

Since those two tasks are often used for measuring a subject's attention state, a visual vigilance task combining the two could effectively induce users to maintain their attention with minimal movement during the EEG recording (Figure 2). The participants in this study were asked to focus on a fixation cross centered on a monitor and to press the right or left arrow key when stimuli were presented. The stimuli consisted of five successive arrows pointing in two opposite directions (left or right); one yellow target arrow was positioned at the center, and four white flankers were positioned to the left and right of the target arrow. Two types of flanker arrays were presented: Congruent and incongruent. The congruent flankers pointed in the same direction as the target, and the incongruent flankers pointed the opposite direction from the target. The two flanker types were equal in number and randomly permuted. The time interval from the presentation of the fixation cross to the stimulus in each trial was $6 \pm \alpha$ seconds, where α is a random number less than 2. EEG data collected during this period, when participants were paying attention while expecting to see the stimuli, were regarded as the signal of an attentive state. Moreover, the EEG signal taken during this time would not be corrupted by motion artifacts from keystrokes. If the participants responded before a certain threshold time, they received additional rewards. The threshold time was initially set to 0.4 s in the practice session but was adjusted for each run depending on each participant's performance to encourage them. Each run consisted of 8 self-paced trials. After one run, the participants rested for 48 s while trying not to move. The resting period of 48 s was set to obtain a dataset of a similar total length to that of the attention state.

There were a total of ten runs, but the participants could quit the experiment if they felt too exhausted to maintain attention. Therefore, the total numbers of runs and trials were different for each subject. On average, each subject performed 8.17 ± 1.72 runs (min = 6 runs, max = 10 runs). The average duration of vigilance trials for each subject was 387.10 ± 83.27 s, and the average resting time was 416.2 ± 89.80 s.

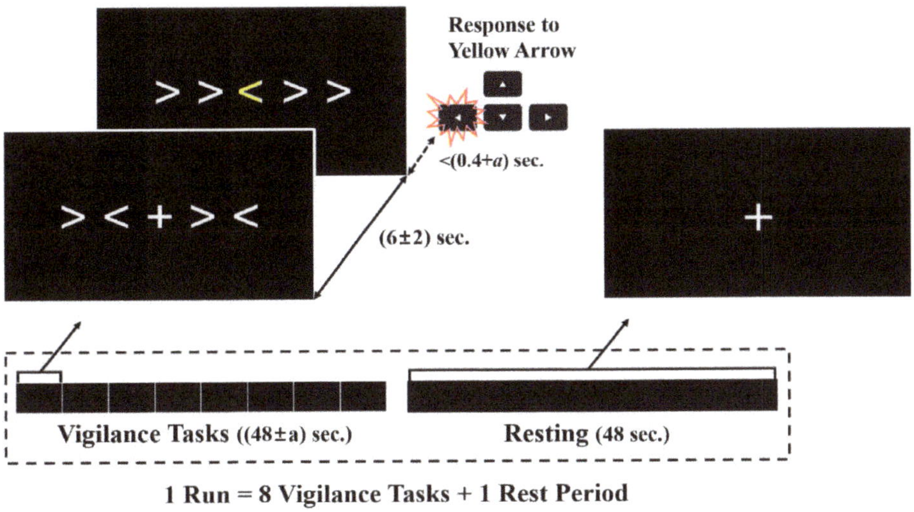

Figure 2. The task for eliciting the attention and resting states. The upper left inset shows the paradigms of the visual vigilance tasks; the target cue centered on the monitor (yellow arrow) was randomly presented with congruent or incongruent flankers. Participants were to press the arrow key corresponding to the target cue as quickly as possible, regardless of the flankers. After 8 trials of vigilance tasks, the participants rested for 48 s while trying not to move.

2.4. EEG Preprocessing and Feature Extraction

The EEG signals were segmented into windows of 0.5 s (125 points) each and bandpass filtered at 1–50 Hz with a 6th-order Butterworth filter to reduce artifacts. Then, spectral and temporal features were extracted from the filtered signals in epochs of 0.5 s. First, the short-time Fourier transform (STFT) was used to estimate the power spectral densities (PSDs) using an interval of 0.5 s. The square root of the spectral power was subdivided into five EEG frequency bands (*delta*: 1–4 Hz, *theta*: 4–8 Hz, *alpha*: 8–13 Hz, *beta*: 13–30 Hz, and *gamma*: 30–50 Hz). Second, five temporal features for EEG signals corresponding to five EEG frequency bands were also extracted. The EEG signals were filtered with five bandpass filters according to EEG frequency bands (i.e., *delta*, 1–4 Hz; *theta*, 4–8 Hz; *alpha*, 8–13 Hz; *beta*, 13–30 Hz; and *gamma*, 30–50 Hz). The mean amplitude, standard deviation, peak-to-peak amplitude, skewness, and kurtosis were calculated for 0.5 s windows for each frequency band. In total, 10 spectral features (5 frequency bands × 2 channels (right and left)) and 50 temporal features (5 measurements × 5 frequency bands × 2 channels) were collected (Table 1).

All input features were standardized using the following equation:

$$\overline{\mathrm{F_{ch}}} = \frac{F_{ch} - mean(F_{ch})}{std(F_{ch})} \tag{1}$$

where F_{ch} denotes the original value of an input feature from each channel. Standardized features $\overline{\mathrm{F_{ch}}}$ were also rescaled to a range of −1 to 1, and used as inputs for the classification of resting versus attentive states. The preprocessing and feature extraction were performed with MATLAB Signal Processing Toolbox.

Table 1. Description of extracted features.

EEG Bands	Freq. Range	Spectral Feature	Temporal Features				
Delta	1–4 Hz	*Delta* power	Mean amplitude	Standard Deviation	Peak to Peak	Skewness	Kurtosis
Theta	4–8 Hz	*Theta* power	Mean amplitude	Standard Deviation	Peak to Peak	Skewness	Kurtosis
Alpha	8–13 Hz	*Alpha* power	Mean amplitude	Standard Deviation	Peak to Peak	Skewness	Kurtosis
Beta	13–30 Hz	*Beta* power	Mean amplitude	Standard Deviation	Peak to Peak	Skewness	Kurtosis
Gamma	30–50 Hz	*Gamma* power	Mean amplitude	Standard Deviation	Peak to Peak	Skewness	Kurtosis
Total number of features (in single channel)		5			25		

2.5. Echo State Network (ESN)

The discrimination of the attentive and resting states using in-ear and on-scalp EEGs was performed using an ESN. An ESN, which is a type of recurrent neural network (RNN) with a sparsely connected internal unit layer (hidden layer), is recognized as a powerful tool to learn chaotic systems using the recurrent property of biological neural networks [42]. In this study, as presented in Figure 3, the ESN consisted of an input layer, an internal unit layer (also called a reservoir), and a readout layer (also called an output layer). The weights of the neurons in the internal unit layer were initially set to have sparse and random connectivity. The weights of all connections to the readout (output) layer could be tuned to generate specific temporal patterns.

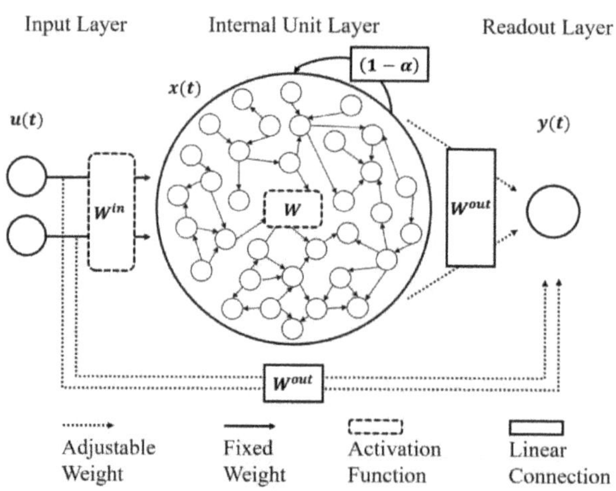

Figure 3. The structure of the echo state network (ESN). The ESN consisted of an input layer (2 input units in this study), an internal unit layer and a readout layer (1 readout). The units of the input layer were connected to the internal units with fixed weights. These internal units were recursively connected to each other with fixed weights. The units of the readout layer were linearly connected from the units of the input and the internal layers with adjustable weights (the figure was modified from [35]).

RNNs, including ESNs, have the fading or short-term memory due to the recurrent properties of the internal unit layer. The state of the internal unit, $x(t)$, is described by the following equation:

$$x(t) = (1-\alpha)\cdot x(t-1) + \alpha\cdot f\left(W^{in}\cdot u(t) + W\cdot x(t-1)\right), \quad (2)$$

where $u(t)$ is an input vector at time step t with W^{in}, the weight matrices between the input and internal units. Vector $x(t-1)$ was the previous state of the internal unit with W, the weight matrices within internal units. The most distinctive characteristics of ESNs compared to conventional RNNs is that W is randomly generated and fixed during learning. Function f is the activation function, and α is the leaking rate of the reservoir. The hyperbolic tangent (*tanh*) function was used as the activation function in this study. The units of the readout layer $y(t)$ were updated according to the following equation:

$$y(t) = W^{out}(u(t), x(t)), \quad (3)$$

where $(u(t),x(t))$ is the concatenation of input and internal units. The feedback from the previous output $y(t)$ can be delivered to the next internal state $x(t+1)$ and output $y(t+1)$ but it was not used for this study (for details, see [35]). The echo state, the current state of the internal unit layer, was continuously updated by input streams. The most recent input had the most influence on the echo state, and the influence of any given input decayed over time [43]. Due to this recurrent property of the "reservoir", ESNs are particularly useful for the prediction of nonlinear, complex time series.

Another characteristic feature of ESNs is that they use simpler learning methods than conventional RNNs. The input layer of an ESN is linearly connected to the internal units ($W^{in} \cdot u(t)$) and the readout layer ($W^{out} \cdot u(t)$). The internal units have recursive connections ($W \cdot x(t-1)$) and are linearly connected to the readout layers ($W^{out} \cdot x(t)$). Any linear learning rules can be applied to the ESN because the weights of the input and internal units (W^{in} and W) are randomly selected at the initialization of the network and remain unchanged. Only the weights of the readouts (W^{out}) were adjusted during linear supervised learning. Despite using a simpler learning rule, ESNs can solve complex problems. Since an ESN has a sufficient number of internal units, the information from the inputs can be expanded to a higher dimension to produce the best solution [44–46]. Thus, ESNs have been used in EEG signal analysis [32–35], brain modeling [47–49], and various engineering fields [28–31].

The selection of parameters is highly significant in constructing an ESN. Many studies on ESNs reported that the spectral radius of the internal weight matrix (λ) [50], the leaking rate (α) [51,52], the scaling of input weights (σ) [53], the size of the internal unit layer (N) [44], and the connectivity (c) [45] prominently affected the performance of the those networks. The optimal values of these parameters could vary according to the data.

In this study, the leaking rate and spectral radius were optimized using the grid search method, which created a "grid" of all possible parameters specified by the settings, and calculated the sum of squared errors (SSE) at each one to find the best possible fit. The leaking rate α controlled the speed of the reservoir update dynamics. A smaller α, which induced the slow dynamics of the reservoir, increased the duration of short-term memory in the ESN [51]. The spectral radius λ is the most important feature determining the characteristics of a reservoir. The spectral radius was rescaled to have one as the largest eigenvalue of the internal weight matrix. In theory, a λ smaller than one ($|\lambda_{max}| < 1$) was important in the ESN for maintaining the echo state property, i.e., the fading influence of the previous input over time in the reservoir [50]. In practice, however, the spectral radius could be slightly greater than 1, but close to 1 [51,54]. Therefore, in this study, α was optimized in the range of (0, 1] and λ was optimized in the range of (0, 2]. The step length of the grid search for each parameter was set to 0.1. In total, 200 (10×20) ESNs were generated and evaluated for parameter optimization. The ESN with each parameter set was evaluated 10 times. The performances obtained from 10 iterations of grid search were averaged, and the parameters that had the best average performance on average were selected. After the optimization of α and λ with 100 internal units, the size of the internal unit layer N and the connectivity c (sparsity of internal units) were also examined. Although a large reservoir resulted in good performance via regularization to prevent overfitting, it incurred considerable computational costs. Therefore, it was important to find the optimal N. The connectivity c was strongly associated with N because it determined the sparsity of the interconnectivity of internal units. Although ESNs were initially designed for sparsely connected reservoirs (1% interconnectivity) to have echo state properties [42], they were reported to work well with fully connected reservoirs [32,52,55]. In this study, the performance of 110 ESNs was evaluated when the number of internal units was 0.1, 0.2, 0.3, ... , 1.0, and the connectivity was 0.01, 0.1, 0.2, 0.3, ... , 1.0. In addition, 20 ESNs with sparse connectivity ($c = 0.01, 0.1$) were generated for a large reservoir (N = 100, 200, ... , 1000).

For the supervised learning of the output weight matrix, Tikhonov regularization (ridge regression) methods were used instead of linear regression, which often leads to numerical instabilities [56]. The regularization parameter was set to a very small value ($\beta = 10^{-8}$) so that the properties would be similar to those of linear regression. Finally, the classification accuracy was obtained with the test set from the optimized and trained ESN. In this study, only one readout was used for the ESN output because there were two classes (resting and attentive states) to distinguish. The attentive states were assigned a value of 1, and the resting states were assigned a value of −1. The predicted states were determined from the values of the readout: the state was classified as an attentive state if the readout returned a positive value or a resting state if the readout returned a negative value.

2.6. Data Separation and Evaluation

In order to train and evaluate the attention state classifiers, three cross-validation schemes were used. The first cross-validation was within-subject validation, which was designed to evaluate individual classifiers for each subject. The EEG signals were divided into training and test sets based on the total number of runs. When the dataset consisted of K runs, $K-1$ runs were used to train the classifier, and the remaining run was used to evaluate the trained classifier. The same process was repeated K times by changing the training and test sets as shown Figure 4a. Therefore, classification performances was obtained for each individual subject. Next, cross-subject validation was performed (Figure 4b). The EEG features from one subject were used for testing, and those from the remaining 5 subjects were used for training classifier. This process was repeated for each of 6 subjects. Finally, 10-fold cross-validation was performed to evaluate generic classifiers for all subjects. As presented in Figure 4c, all the data were combined and randomly split into training and test set. For each validation, 90% of data were used for training the classifier, and 10% of data were used for evaluating the trained classifier. This process was repeated 10 times, with a different training and test set each time. In all three cross-validation schemes, attention epochs whose response times were too short (false start < 100 ms) or long (lapse > mean(RT) + 3 × std(RT)) were not regarded as "attended trials" and were excluded.

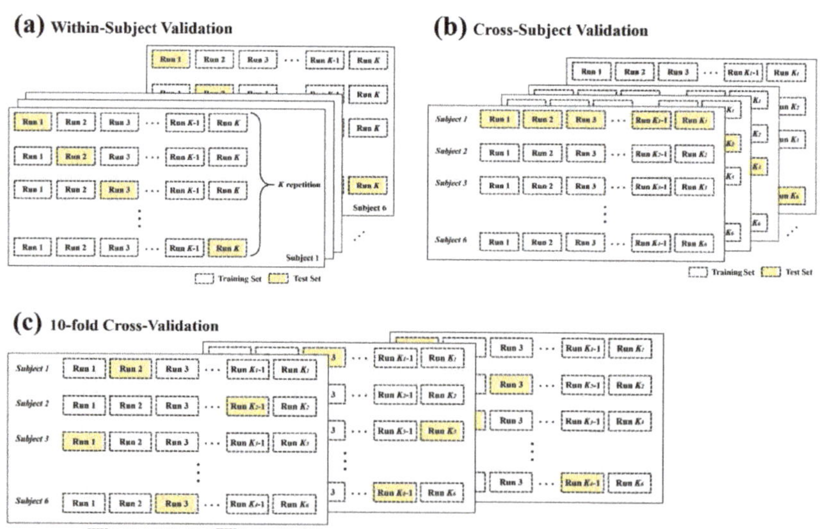

Figure 4. Data separation. (**a**) Within-subject validation was used to train and evaluate the individual classifiers on the attentive and resting states. One run was used for the test set, and the remaining runs

were used for the training set. This process was repeated K times, and the test set was switched every time. The accuracy was averaged over K repetitions. (**b**) Cross-subject testing was performed. The data from one subject were used as a training set, and the data from the other 5 subjects were used as a test set. This process was repeated for each of subjects. (**c**) A generic classifier was evaluated using 10-fold cross-validation. The complete dataset from all subjects was collected and randomly split into a test set (10%) and a training set (90%). This process was repeated 10 times, with a different training set and a different test set each time. The accuracy was averaged over 10 repetitions.

3. Results

3.1. Classification Results

The ESN had a single readout that indicated whether the subject was in an attentive state or a resting state. Because the attentive state was labeled 1 and the resting state was labeled −1, positive readout values were classified as an attentive state, and negative values were classified as a resting state. The classification performance was evaluated using three cross-validation schemes: Within-subject validation, cross-subject validation, and 10-fold cross-validation. Parameter optimization was performed by averaging accuracies obtained from 10 iterations of the grid search. First, individually trained ESN for each subject was evaluated using the within-subject validation. The within-subject validation provided a K number of performances if the total number of runs was K for each individual. The results of all runs were averaged for each subject. The maximum training accuracy resulting from the grid search was 92.62% on average (Table 2) when in-ear EEG signals were used. The test accuracy using the test set was 81.16%. The results were not much different from those of the on-scalp EEG (82.44%).

Table 2. The maximum training accuracy and test accuracy for each subject in the within-subject validation.

	In-Ear EEG		On-Scalp EEG	
Subject #	**Training Accuracy (%)**	**Test Accuracy (%)**	**Training Accuracy (%)**	**Test Accuracy (%)**
1 (M)	92.77 ± 2.14	81.42 ± 4.18	98.14 ± 0.54	91.23 ± 2.13
2 (M)	91.59 ± 1.49	75.89 ± 2.91	88.25 ± 2.26	78.52 ± 2.84
3 (M)	94.11 ± 1.34	83.28 ± 2.88	92.06 ± 1.64	80.64 ± 2.79
4 (M)	93.97 ± 1.76	79.34 ± 3.39	96.25 ± 0.67	85.73 ± 3.82
5 (F)	91.25 ± 3.47	79.46 ± 5.01	92.24 ± 1.07	83.05 ± 4.47
6 (F)	92.00 ± 2.09	87.59 ± 3.25	90.74 ± 1.45	75.46 ± 3.40
Avg.	92.62 ± 0.45	81.16 ± 2.20	92.95 ± 2.19	82.44 ± 2.24

Next, the cross-subject validation and the 10-fold cross-validation were used for evaluating a generic classifier. Table 3 and Figure 5 demonstrated the classification results obtained from two validations. In the 10-fold cross-validation, in which all data were combined and split, the classification accuracy was 74.15% on average when in-ear EEG signals were used (73.73% on average when on-scalp EEG signals were used). These results were slightly lower than those obtained from the within-subject validation, which individually trained and tested for each subject. In addition, cross-subject validation, in which data from one subject were used for test set and data from the other 5 subjects were used for training set, resulted in much lower classification performance (64% for in-ear EEG and 65.7% for on-scalp EEG) than the other two validation schemes.

Table 3. The maximum training accuracy and test accuracy in the cross-subject validation and 10-fold cross-validation.

		In-Ear EEG		On-Scalp EEG	
Validation Method	Subject #	Training Accuracy (%)	Test Accuracy (%)	Training Accuracy (%)	Test Accuracy (%)
Cross-Subject Validation	1 (M)	73.46	62.65	77.17	79.54
	2 (M)	63.55	58.36	74.56	60.12
	3 (M)	66.00	54.59	61.46	55.31
	4 (M)	81.16	65.39	83.33	76.35
	5 (F)	83.55	69.52	72.88	58.63
	6 (F)	85.08	73.47	78.73	64.24
	Avg.	75.46 ± 3.44	64.00 ± 2.60	74.69 ± 2.77	65.70 ± 3.71
10-fold Cross-Validation	Avg.	80.89 ± 1.93	74.15 ± 2.20	78.42 ± 2.19	73.73 ± 2.24

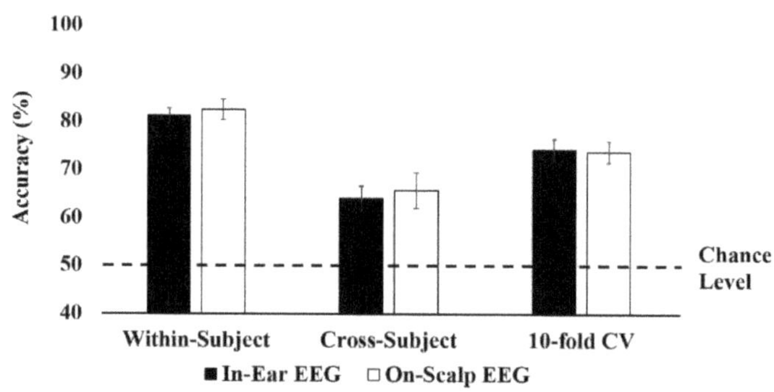

Figure 5. The test accuracy for three cross-validation schemes: within-subject validation, cross-subject validation, and 10-fold cross-validation (CV).

3.2. Smoothing

The ESN identified the attentive or resting state in epochs of 0.5 s. The ESN outputs can greatly fluctuate due to the influence of external artifacts or internal states. As seen from the black dotted lines in Figure 6a, the readouts fluctuated with a large amplitude, which leads to rapid fluctuation of predictions (blue lines in Figure 6a).

In order to overcome this problem, the readout values were smoothed using a moving average filter. The current output was the average of itself and n previous outputs when the window size was n as shown below:

$$y(t) = \sum_{t-n+1}^{t} y(t), \tag{4}$$

where $y(t)$ was the current output and n was the window size. If there were fewer previous outputs than the window size, the outputs were averaged with every available previous output. The window size was set between 1 and 12 windows (0.5 to 6 s). In Figure 6b, the red lines were outputs smoothed with 6 s windows. The smoothed outputs provided higher classification accuracy than that of the original outputs by reducing fluctuations of readouts (Figure 6c). The average accuracy for the in-ear EEG classification was increased by 2.45% for the within-subject validation, 1.26% for the 10-fold cross validation, and 1.86% for the cross-subject validation (1.03% for the within-subject validation, 0.73% for the 10-fold cross validation, and −0.26% for the cross-subject validation in the on-scalp EEG classification with a 6 s smoothing window). This result indicates that smoothing the readout values successfully reduces their fluctuation and improves the classification performance (Table 4).

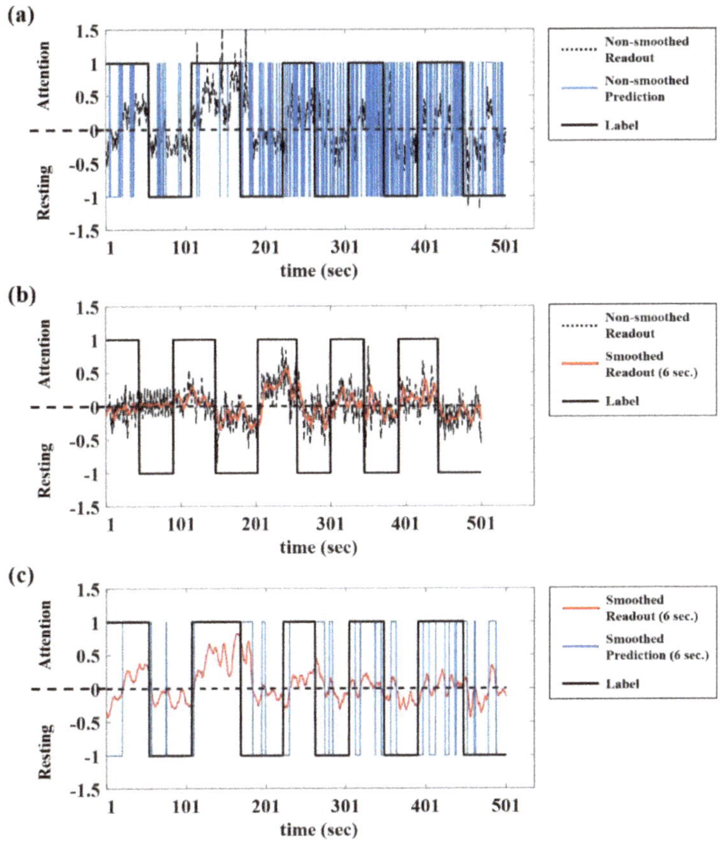

Figure 6. The smoothing of the readout in the ESN. (**a**) The classification results obtained from the original values of the readout fluctuated (black dotted lines: original values of readouts, blue lines: prediction results using original readouts). (**b**) Averaging with previous 6 s outputs corrected the fluctuation (red lines: smoothed readouts using 6 s window). (**c**) The smoothing resulted in improved classification results (blue lines: prediction results using smoothed readouts).

Table 4. The performances according to smoothing window.

	Within-Subject		Cross-Subject		10-fold CV	
Smoothing Window (second)	**In-Ear EEG (%)**	**On-Scalp EEG (%)**	**In-Ear EEG (%)**	**On-Scalp EEG (%)**	**In-Ear EEG (%)**	**On-Scalp EEG (%)**
Non (0.5 s)	81.16	82.44	64.00	65.70	74.15	73.73
2 (1 s)	81.32	82.73	64.64	65.78	74.75	73.63
4 (2 s)	82.33	83.56	65.86	65.73	75.07	73.89
6 (3 s)	82.90	83.74	65.84	65.64	75.32	74.01
8 (4 s)	83.24	83.81	66.09	65.36	75.36	74.22
10 (5 s)	83.24	83.70	65.97	65.73	75.34	74.54
12 (6 s)	83.62	83.47	65.85	65.44	75.41	74.46

3.3. Comparison with Conventional Machine Learning Methods

In order to evaluate the discrimination performance of the ESN, various machine learning methods commonly used in EEG classification were also investigated to compare for the in-ear and on-scalp EEG signals. The following 7 machine learning methods were used: (1) Regularized linear discriminant analysis (R-LDA), (2) decision tree (DT), (3) random forest (RF), (4) naïve Bayesian algorithm (NB), (5) k-nearest neighbor algorithm (k-NN), (6) support vector machine (SVM) with linear kernels, and (7) SVM with Gaussian kernels. A detailed explanation of each machine learning methods can be found in Appendix B. The same features used in ESN classification were used for these conventional machine learning methods. The hyperparameters for each classifier were optimized during training. All processes were performed in MATLAB using Statistics and Machine Learning Toolbox. The accuracies obtained from each validation for each conventional machine learning method were compared with those obtained from ESN using Student's t-test and the multiple comparison problem was corrected using Bonferroni correction.

When within-subject validation was conducted (Figure 4a), we found that the ESN resulted in 81.16% for the in-ear EEG (82.44% for on-scalp EEG) classification accuracy without smoothing and 83.62% (83.47% for on-scalp EEG) accuracy after smoothing with a 6 s window. These results significantly outperformed those of the 11 machine learning methods, as shown in Figure 7.

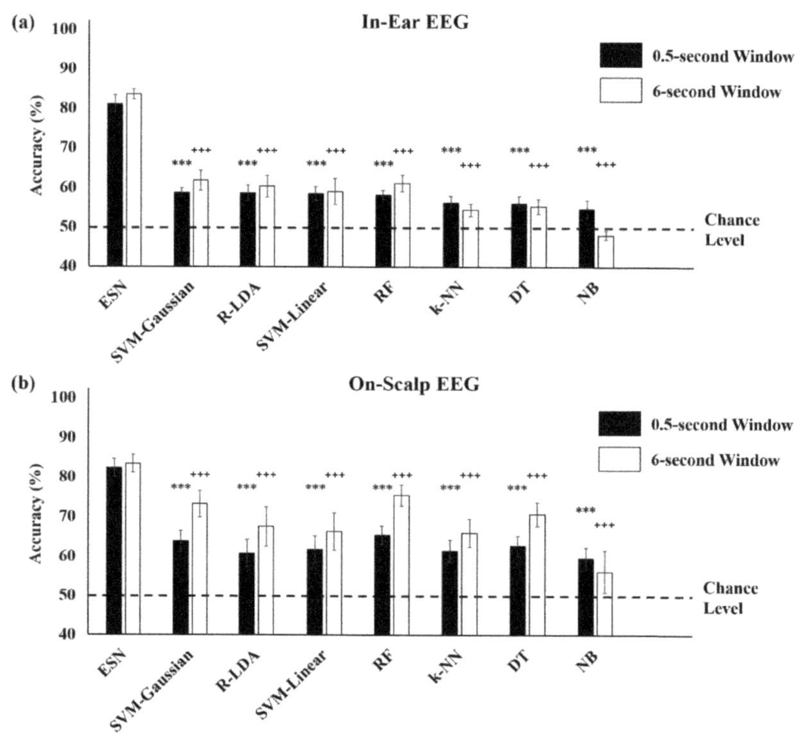

Figure 7. Comparison of classification accuracy between the echo state network (ESN) and conventional machine learning methods and smoothing obtained from the within-subject validation. The ESN classification highly outperformed other conventional machine learning methods in both (**a**) in-ear and (**b**) on-scalp EEGs. The results were sorted in descending order based on the accuracy of nonsmoothed prediction. The dotted line denoted the chancel level (50%). ESN: echo state network, SVM-Gaussian: support vector machine (SVM) with Gaussian kernels, R-LDA: regularized linear discriminant analysis (LDA), SVM-Linear: SVM with linear kernels, RF: random forest, k-NN: k-nearest neighbor algorithm, DT: decision tree, and NB: naïve Bayesian algorithm (*** denotes $p < 0.001$ when comparing original predicted results without smoothing (0.5 s window) of the ESN and other methods, $^{+++}$ denotes $p < 0.001$ when comparing smoothed results using 6 s window of the ESN and other methods, Bonferroni corrected).

The classification results obtained from 10-fold cross validation and cross-subject validation were also higher with an ESN compared to other machine learning methods (Figure 8). The smoothing of classification results with 6 s window led to greater increases in performance in conventional machine learning methods compared to ESN. In the 10-fold cross-validation, the classification accuracies using smoothing classification results obtained from RF and SVM with Gaussian kernels were not significantly different from those that were obtained using the ESN. In the cross-subject validation, SVM with linear kernels, regularized LDA, and SVM with Gaussian kernels provided performances that were statistically not different from those of the ESN. However, the ESN still outperformed these methods for all validations.

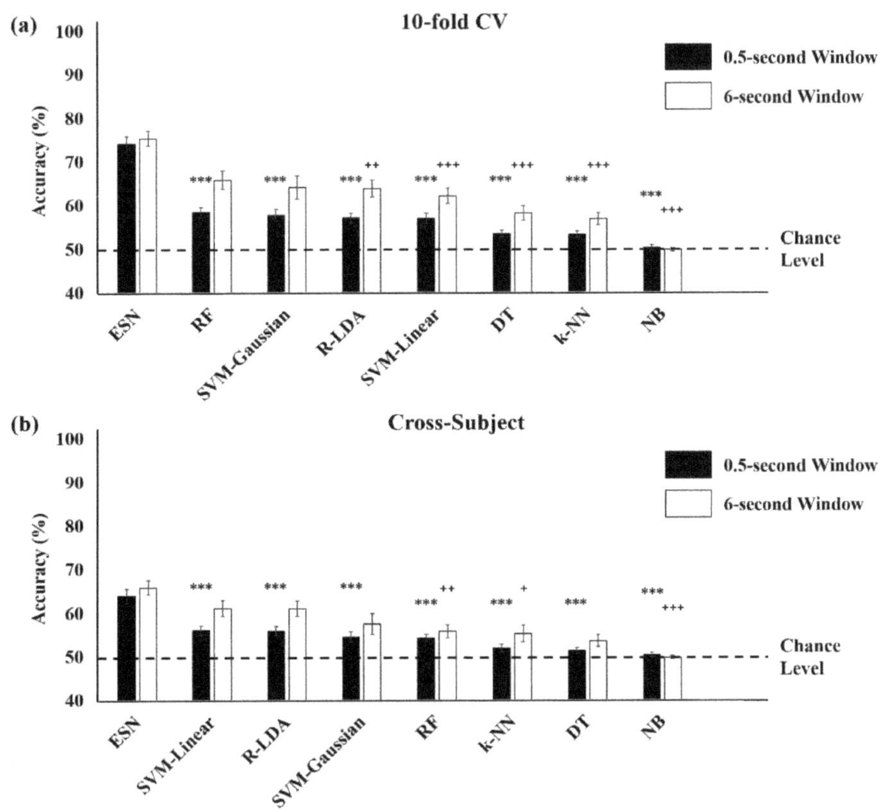

Figure 8. Comparison of classification accuracy between the echo state network (ESN) and conventional machine learning methods obtained from the (**a**) 10-fold cross-validation (CV) and (**b**) cross-subject validation using in-ear EEG signals. The results were sorted in descending order based on the accuracy of nonsmoothed prediction. The dotted denotes the chance level (50%). (*** $p < 0.001$, ** $p < 0.01$, * $p < 0.05$ for comparisons of original predicted results without smoothing (0.5 s window), $^{+++}$ $p < 0.001$, $^{+++}$ $p < 0.01$, $^{+}$ $p < 0.05$ for comparisons of smoothed results using 6 s window, Bonferroni corrected).

4. Discussion

It is sometimes critical to maintain attention when carrying out tasks requiring high levels of safety and efficiency in daily life [7,8]. During these tasks, attention monitoring may be helpful for preventing mistakes and improving performance by providing proper solutions, such as neurofeedback or brain stimulation. In this study, we have demonstrated that the ESN classification of in-ear EEG signals is a potentially powerful method to discriminate the attention state from the resting state compared with other conventional machine learning techniques and even with on-scalp EEGs. In addition, we have shown that parameter optimization procedure is important for producing better performance and have suggested the range of optimal parameters in ESN for in-ear EEGs for the highest results.

Based on these results, we suggest that this approach can be applied to the prediction of sleep deprivation and of highly stressful states, as vigilance degradation is associated with lack of sleep [36] and with high levels of anxiety and stress [3,37]. Furthermore, attention monitoring using in-ear EEG and ESNs could potentially aid in the diagnosis of attention-related diseases such as attention deficit hyperactivity disorder (ADHD) [57,58] or Alzheimer's disease [59,60].

Due to the inconvenience of conventional cap-type or headset-type EEG devices, even though extensive research has been performed, BCI techniques for attention state monitoring have not been widely used in daily life. We suggest that earphone-shaped EEG devices using in-ear EEG signals would be a strong candidate for potential BCI devices in future, which can monitor human mental states including attention states even when the users are listening to music or watching the movies. Since the first research on the "in-the-ear recording concept" was published in 2012 [9], the BCI application of in-ear EEG signals has been investigated using the external stimuli such as visual or auditory cues [11,17,21–23] or independently of external stimuli [24,25]. Compared with the performance of the previous studies on the BCI application of in-ear EEG signals to mental state monitoring, our performance using the ESN technique is higher than theirs: Previous studies successfully have detected drowsiness [24,25], mental workload during visuomotor tracking task [26], and emotional states [27] but have required long time window (more than 10 s) to achieve high classification accuracy (Table 5). In this study, we suggest that the attention monitoring system using in-ear EEG and the ESN is much faster to classify mental states than previous studies, within every 0.5 s with high accuracy of 81.16% when using one run as the test set and remaining runs as the training set within each subject. We have demonstrated that the classification accuracy increased to 83.62% after smoothing the classification results with a 6-s window, which is much higher than those of conventional machine learning methods used for EEG classification compared in this study (Figure 7). The classification accuracy was lowered to 74.15% in the 10-fold cross validation, which was performed by combining all features from all subjects and splitting into training and test set, and 64% in the cross-subject validation, which was performed by using data from one subject as test set and data from remaining 5 subjects as training set. However, these results were still outperformed conventional machine learning methods (Figure 8).

The decreased accuracy in the cross-subject validation compared to those in the within-subject model might be resulted from intersubject variability of EEG signals. Because the parameters of ESN greatly affect classification performance, it is important to apply parameter optimization. The optimized parameters obtained from the grid search were varied for each validation. Therefore, in the cross-subject validation, the ESN could not find optimal parameters and thus could not learn distinguishing features for the classification due to the difference of EEG properties for each individual. The spectral radius λ and the leaking rate α were optimized using the grid-search. The leaking rate, which determines how fast the dynamics of the reservoir are updated, was optimized in the range of (0, 1]. The spectral radius, which determines characteristics of reservoir (short-term or long-term), was optimized in the range of (0, 2]. In theoretical, a λ smaller than one was suggested for the echo state property but a λ larger than one (but close to 1) can be employed in practice [51,54]. We found that a λ larger than one was selected in many cases. Determining the proper size of the reservoir is also important in the performance of ESN. When internal units were sparsely connected to each other, insufficient number of internal units could not extract nonlinear features. Too many internal units resulted in decreased accuracy as well as high computational cost. Although the denser connectivity required higher computational cost, it did not ensure higher accuracy. Therefore, it is important to find the optimal reservoir size and sparsity. The additional discussions about parameter optimization were attached in Appendix C.

Table 5. Comparison with previous studies on asynchronous brain–computer interface (BCI) using in-ear EEG signals (CV denotes cross-validation).

Authors	Mental States (Classes)	Window (Seconds)	Methods	Validation	Accuracy
Hong et al. (2018) [24]	Drowsiness (5 levels)	10	RF	5-fold CV	0.780 (kappa value)
Nakamura et al. (2018) [25]	Drowsiness (Wake vs. N1)	30	SVM	Leave-one trial-out (all subjects)	80%
				10-fold CV (all subjects)	82.9%
Kuatsjah et al. (2019) [26]	Mental workload (Visuomotor task vs. Rest)	5	The best among various ML approaches	Across-trial for each subject	68% (approx.)
		25			79.30%
		5	NN	5-fold CV for each subject	71.50%
Athavipach et al. (2019) [27]	Emotion (Valence)	30	SVM	10-fold CV for each subject	73.01%
	Emotion (Arousal)				75.70%
	Emotion (Valence+Arousal)				59.23%
This Study	**Attention (Vigilance task vs. Rest)**	**0.5**	**ESN**	**Across-trial for each subject**	**81.16%**
				10-fold CV (all subjects)	**74.15%**
				Cross-subject	**64.00%**

The bold types were used for discriminating our results from others'.

Real time prediction of test sets in in-ear EEGs for attention state monitoring may be possible, once the training process is accomplished. However, it is also necessary to train in real time to reduce the computational cost. We should address that the supervised learning method in this study has incurred a high computational cost, even if the size of the dataset is not too large. To monitor mental state continuously in real time, the network needs to be adaptive to new data constantly. Therefore, we will modify and improve the training method suitable for real-time monitoring in future studies.

In this study, we have designed and developed the in-ear EEG electrodes by customizing each subject's ear canals. It is difficult to develop a generic earpiece that suits all users because the shape and length of both left and right ear canals in each user are different [61]. Therefore, we suggest that generic and more comfortable in-ear electrodes, which can be made flexible with carbon nanotube polydimethylsiloxane (CNT/PDMS) [10] or memory foam substrate [13], are required for the production of earphone-shaped EEG devices suitable for individuals to achieve better measurement performance.

In this study, we have identified only binary mental states: Attention and resting states. The attention states will be further divided into various types of attention states and levels beyond binary classification for our future investigation. In addition, we suggest that this methodology can be potentially expanded to apply to monitoring of other mental states, such as stressfulness, drowsiness and sleepiness, or emotion (positive/negative valence). We also suggest that the ESN and other machine learning techniques are likely useful for analysis of the in-ear EEG signals for mental state monitoring systems. Furthermore, we speculate that earphone-shaped mental state monitoring system using in-ear EEG signals can be a strong candidate device for massive commercial services of BCI.

5. Conclusions

This study suggests that the attention state can be detected with high accuracy using the ESN and in-ear EEG signals. The attention states can be discriminated from the resting state for every 0.5 s with 81.16% accuracy when ESN was trained and tested using in-ear EEG signals within each subject. We suggest that this method can be likely applied to asynchronous or active BCIs, which can detect mental states without external stimuli. Unlike synchronous or passive BCIs which use external stimuli, asynchronous or active BCIs are potentially useful in daily life. The smoothing of ESN readouts will be useful for stable BCI systems because large fluctuations of classification results can cause negative effects in practice such as excessive feedback to users. The application of this technology using earphone-shaped EEG devices and the ESN may pave the way for comfortable mental monitoring devices in the near future.

Author Contributions: Conceptualization, J.J.; methodology, D.-H.J.; software, D.-H.J.; validation, J.J.; formal analysis, D.-H.J.; investigation, D.-H.J. and J.J.; resources, D.-H.J.; data curation, D.-H.J.; writing—original draft preparation, D.-H.J.; writing—review and editing, J.J.; visualization, D.-H.J.; supervision, J.J.; project administration, J.J.; funding acquisition, J.J.; All authors have read and agreed to the published version of the manuscript.

Funding: This research was funded by National Research Foundation of Korea Grant funded by the Ministry of Science, ICT & Future Planning, grant number NRF-2015-R1D1A1A02062365& 2016M3C7A1904988l; This research was supported by the Brain Research Program through the National Research Foundation of Korea (NRF) funded by the Ministry of Science, ICT & Future Planning [2016M3C7A1904988]; This paper is based on a research which has been conducted as part of the KAIST-funded Global Singularity Research Program for 2020.

Conflicts of Interest: The authors declare no conflict of interest.

Appendix A

To verify the in-ear and on-scalp EEG acquisition, the alpha attenuation tests were performed prior to the visual vigilance task. It is known that the *alpha* wave shows dominant peak approximately 10 Hz when eyes are closed but decreases when eyes are opened. This phenomenon is widely used to assess EEG signals. The STFT was used to estimate the PSD using a 1-s (250 data points) window with a 50% overlap. The PSDs of each state were averaged and compared for each channel. The alpha attenuation effect was observed both from in-ear and on-scalp EEG signals but the effect was diminished for in-ear EEG signals (Figure A1).

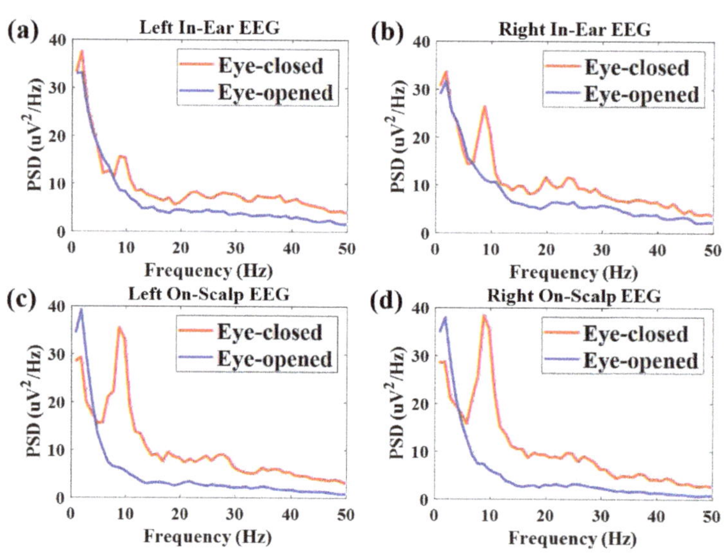

Figure A1. Alpha attenuation effect. Red lines denote averaged power spectral densities (PSDs) during eyes-closed resting state and blue lines are averaged PSDs during eyes-open resting state from (**a**) left in-ear EEG channel, (**b**) right in-ear EEG channel, (**c**) left on-scalp EEG channel, and (**d**) right on-scalp EEG channel.

Appendix B

The classification accuracy of ESN was compared with conventional machine learning methods in Section 3.3. Total 60 features, which is the same feature set used in ESNs (Table 1), were used as features for 7 conventional machine learning methods: (1) R-LDA, (2) DT, (3) RF, (4) NB, (5) k-NN, (6) SVM with linear kernels, and (7) SVM with Gaussian kernels.

Discriminant analysis (DA) is the most widely used classification method, which finds optimal boundaries to separate two or more classes using multivariate observations [62,63]. LDA assumes that observations in all classes have normal distributions with identical covariance. When the covariance matrix is regularized from the observations, it is called (1) regularized LDA (R-LDA). (2) DT learning constructs a predictive model (decision tree) for rule-based classification by splitting multiple binary nodes with input features and pruning trees with labeled outputs [63]. (3) RF constructs multiple DTs in training and classifies the class using multiple outputs from trained trees [64–66]. Using multiple DTs reduces overfitting and noise in every tree. (4) NB is a simple probabilistic classifier based on Bayes' theorem, which infers posterior probability (class) from prior probability, likelihood, and evidence (current observation, i.e., input) [62]. (5) k-NN classifies input observations based on their closeness calculated by Euclidean distance [62]. The classification of new observation (test data) is performed based on the k closest neighbors (training data). The 5-NN was used to avoid overfitting in this study. SVM is a classifier used to find the optimal hyperplane using the largest margin (support vectors) between the two classes [62]. The method for computation of hyperplane is called kernel function. (6) SVM with linear kernel is an originally proposed method for SVM construction, which uses simple inner (dot) products. In the case of nonlinear classification, (7) Gaussian function (SVM with Gaussian kernel) can be used instead of inner products.

Appendix C

The influence of each parameter was compared using the training results. The optimized parameters (leaking rate α, spectral radius λ, reservoir size N, and the sparsity of interconnectivity c) were varied for each validation. Figure A2a shows the average training accuracy in the 10-fold cross validation when each of the two parameters (α, λ) was changed. In most cases, the selected λ values were larger than 1 or close to 1. The selected α values were varied in the rage of 0.3 to 1.

The influences of the reservoir size and connectivity of the internal unit layer were also examined. An insufficient number of internal units ($N < 40$) resulted in poor classification accuracy, but the accuracy increased as the size increased (Figure A2b,d). ESNs with large reservoir sizes (N = 100, 200, … , 1000) were also generated with sparse connectivity (c = 0.01, 0.1). Although the optimal sizes and connectivity were different for each subject, the maximum accuracy was obtained from 200 internal units and 0.01 connectivity. The larger reservoir size had lower classification accuracy in both in-ear and on-scalp EEG. The accuracy was not influenced by sparsity of internal units if the size was large enough. The calculation durations in training ESN were also compared. The calculation time increased linearly as a function of the reservoir size (Figure A2d). We found that the reservoir with lower density (c = 0.01) was more computationally effective while maintaining the accuracy compared to the reservoir with higher density (c = 0.1). Larger reservoir size increased the gap of computational cost between reservoirs of two different degrees of sparsity.

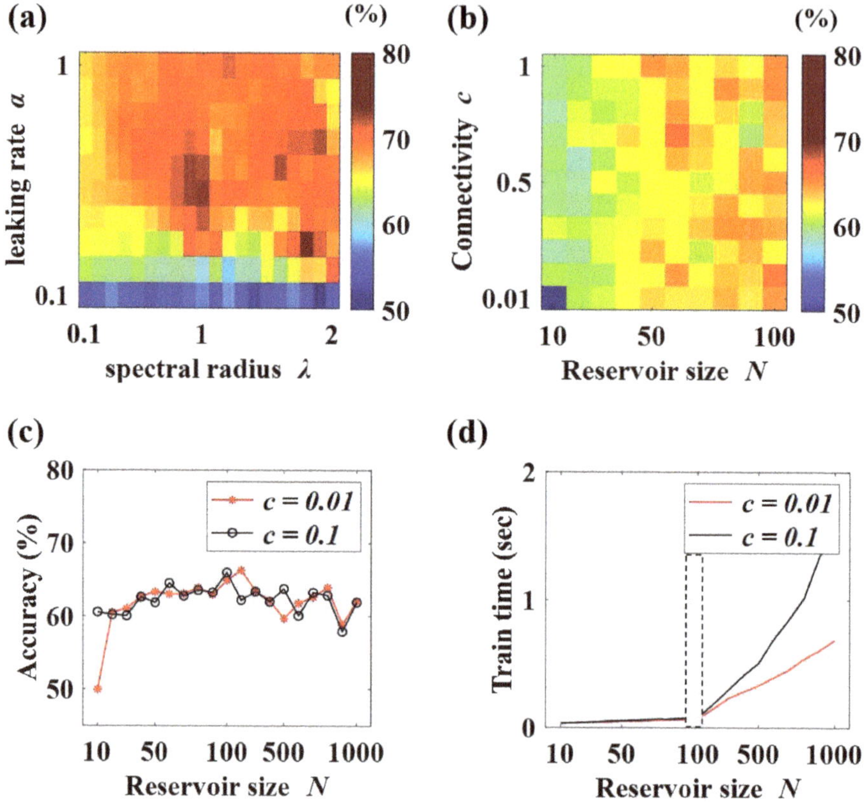

Figure A2. The influences of the parameters in the echo state network (ESN) in the 10-fold cross-validation. (**a**) The average accuracy according to spectral radius λ and leaking rate α. (**b**) The average accuracy according to the number of internal units (N = 10, 20, ... , 100) and interconnectivity (c = 0.1, 0.2, ... , 1). (**c**) Accuracy according to the number of internal units (N = 100, 200, ... , 1000) with sparse interconnectivity (c = 0.1, 0.01). (**d**) The computational cost of the training ESN according to the number of internal units. The computational cost linearly increased as the size increased. The sparser reservoir (c = 0.01) had less computational cost compared with the denser reservoir (c = 0.1), which became more evident as the reservoir size increased. The dotted box was inserted when the reservoir size was 100 because the N increases in steps of 10 between 10 and 100, and in steps of 100 between 100 and 1000.

References

1. Mackworth, N.H. The breakdown of vigilance during prolonged visual search. *Q. J. Exp. Psychol.* **1948**, *1*, 6–21. [CrossRef]
2. Helton, W.S.; Hollander, T.D.; Warm, J.S.; Tripp, L.D.; Parsons, K.; Matthews, G.; Dember, W.N.; Parasuraman, R.; Hancock, P.A. The abbreviated vigilance task and cerebral hemodynamics. *J. Clin. Exp. Neuropsychol.* **2007**, *29*, 545–552. [CrossRef] [PubMed]
3. Warm, J.S.; Matthews, G.; Finomore, V.S., Jr. Vigilance, Workload, and Stress. In *Performance Under Stress*; CRC Press: Boca Raton, FL, USA, 2008.
4. Young, M.S.; Robinson, S.; Alberts, P. Students pay attention!: Combating the vigilance decrement to improve learning during lectures. *Act. Learn. High. Educ.* **2009**, *10*, 41–55. [CrossRef]

5. Taylor-Phillips, S.; Elze, M.C.; Krupinski, E.A.; Dennick, K.; Gale, A.G.; Clarke, A.; Mello-Thoms, C. Retrospective Review of the Drop in Observer Detection Performance Over Time in Lesion-enriched Experimental Studies. *J. Digit. Imaging* **2014**, *28*, 32–40. [CrossRef] [PubMed]
6. Atchley, P.; Chan, M. Potential benefits and costs of concurrent task engagement to maintain vigilance: A driving simulator investigation. *Hum. Factors* **2011**, *53*, 3–12. [CrossRef]
7. Kamzanova, A.T.; Kustubayeva, A.M.; Matthews, G. Use of EEG workload indices for diagnostic monitoring of vigilance decrement. *Hum. Factors* **2014**, *56*, 1136–1149. [CrossRef]
8. Clayton, M.S.; Yeung, N.; Cohen Kadosh, R. The roles of cortical oscillations in sustained attention. *Trends Cogn. Sci.* **2015**, *19*, 188–195. [CrossRef]
9. Looney, B.D.; Kidmose, P.; Park, C.; Ungstrup, M.; Rank, M.L.; Rosenkranz, K. The in-the-ear recording concept: User-centered and wearable brain monitoring. *IEEE Pulse* **2012**, *3*, 32–42. [CrossRef]
10. Hoon Lee, J.; Min Lee, S.; Jin Byeon, H.; Sook Hong, J.; Suk Park, K.; Lee, S.-H. CNT/PDMS-based canal-typed ear electrodes for inconspicuous EEG recording. *J. Neural Eng.* **2014**, *11*, 046014. [CrossRef]
11. Bleichner, M.G.; Lundbeck, M.; Selisky, M.; Minow, F.; Jäger, M.; Emkes, R.; Debener, S.; De Vos, M. Exploring miniaturized EEG electrodes for brain–computer interfaces. An EEG you do not see? *Physiol. Rep.* **2015**, *3*, 1–9. [CrossRef]
12. Mikkelsen, K.B.; Kappel, S.L.; Mandic, D.P.; Kidmose, P. EEG recorded from the ear: Characterizing the Ear-EEG Method. *Front. Neurosci.* **2015**, *9*, 1–8. [CrossRef] [PubMed]
13. Goverdovsky, V.; Looney, D.; Kidmose, P.; Mandic, D.P. In-Ear EEG from Viscoelastic Generic Earpieces: Robust and Unobtrusive 24/7 Monitoring. *IEEE Sens. J.* **2016**, *16*, 271–277. [CrossRef]
14. Mikkelsen, K.B.; Kidmose, P.; Hansen, L.K. On the Keyhole Hypothesis: High Mutual Information between Ear and Scalp EEG. *Front. Hum. Neurosci.* **2017**, *11*, 1–9. [CrossRef] [PubMed]
15. Kappel, S.L.; Looney, D.; Mandic, D.P.; Kidmose, P. Physiological artifacts in scalp EEG and ear-EEG. *Biomed. Eng. Online* **2017**, *16*, 103. [CrossRef] [PubMed]
16. Kappel, S.L.; Rank, M.L.; Toft, H.O.; Andersen, M.; Kidmose, P. Dry-Contact Electrode Ear-EEG. *IEEE Trans. Biomed. Eng.* **2019**, *66*, 150–158. [CrossRef] [PubMed]
17. Ahn, J.W.; Ku, Y.; Kim, D.Y.; Sohn, J.; Kim, J.-H.; Kim, H.C. Wearable in-the-ear EEG system for SSVEP-based brain–computer interface. *Electron. Lett.* **2018**, *54*, 413–414. [CrossRef]
18. Zibrandtsen, I.; Kidmose, P.; Otto, M.; Ibsen, J.; Kjaer, T.W. Case comparison of sleep features from ear-EEG and scalp-EEG. *Sleep Sci.* **2016**, 1–4. [CrossRef]
19. Mikkelsen, K.B.; Villadsen, D.B.; Otto, M.; Kidmose, P. Automatic sleep staging using ear-EEG. *Biomed. Eng. Online* **2017**, *16*, 1–15. [CrossRef]
20. Nakamura, T.; Goverdovsky, V.; Morrell, M.J.; Mandic, D.P.; Mandic, D.P. Point-of-Care Technologies Automatic Sleep Monitoring Using Ear-EEG. *IEEE J. Transl. Eng. Health Med.* **2017**, *5*, 1–8. [CrossRef]
21. Fiedler, L.; Wöstmann, M.; Graversen, C.; Brandmeyer, A.; Lunner, T.; Obleser, J. Single-channel in-ear-EEG detects the focus of auditory attention to concurrent tone streams and mixed speech. *J. Neural Eng.* **2017**, *14*, 036020. [CrossRef]
22. Denk, F.; Grzybowski, M.; Ernst, S.M.A.; Kollmeier, B.; Debener, S.; Bleichner, M.G. Event-Related Potentials Measured From In and Around the Ear Electrodes Integrated in a Live Hearing Device for Monitoring Sound Perception. *Trends Hear.* **2018**, *22*, 1–14. [CrossRef] [PubMed]
23. Christensen, C.B.; Kappel, S.L.; Kidmose, P. Auditory Steady-State Responses across Chirp Repetition Rates for Ear-EEG and Scalp EEG. In Proceedings of the 2018 40th Annual International Conference of the IEEE Engineering in Medicine and Biology Society (EMBC), Honolulu, HI, USA, 18–21 July 2018; pp. 1376–1379.
24. Hong, S.; Kwon, H.; Choi, S.H.; Park, K.S. Intelligent system for drowsiness recognition based on ear canal electroencephalography with photoplethysmography and electrocardiography. *Inf. Sci.* **2018**, *453*, 302–322. [CrossRef]
25. Nakamura, T.; Alqurashi, Y.D.; Morrell, M.J.; Mandic, D.P. Automatic detection of drowsiness using in-ear EEG. In Proceedings of the 2018 International Joint Conference on Neural Networks (IJCNN), Rio de Janeiro, Brazil, 8–13 July 2018; pp. 1–6.
26. Kuatsjah, E.; Zhang, X.; Khoshnam, M.; Menon, C. Two-channel in-ear EEG system for detection of visuomotor tracking state: A preliminary study. *Med. Eng. Phys.* **2019**, *68*, 25–34. [CrossRef] [PubMed]
27. Athavipach, C.; Pan-Ngum, S.; Israsena, P. A wearable in-ear EEG device for emotion monitoring. *Sensors* **2019**, *19*, 1–16. [CrossRef]

28. Prater, A. Spatiotemporal signal classification via principal components of reservoir states. *Neural Netw.* **2017**, *91*, 66–75. [CrossRef]
29. Gong, C.; Tao, D.; Chang, X.; Yang, J. Ensemble Teaching for Hybrid Label Propagation. *IEEE Trans. Cybern.* **2019**, *49*, 388–402. [CrossRef]
30. Lacy, S.E.; Smith, S.L.; Lones, M.A. Using echo state networks for classification: A case study in Parkinson's disease diagnosis. *Artif. Intell. Med.* **2018**, *86*, 53–59. [CrossRef]
31. Yang, C.; Qiao, J.; Han, H.; Wang, L. Design of polynomial echo state networks for time series prediction. *Neurocomputing* **2018**, *290*, 148–160. [CrossRef]
32. Sun, L.; Jin, B.; Yang, H.; Tong, J.; Liu, C.; Xiong, H. Unsupervised EEG feature extraction based on echo state network. *Inf. Sci.* **2019**, *475*, 1–17. [CrossRef]
33. Bozhkov, L.; Koprinkova-Hristova, P.; Georgieva, P. Learning to decode human emotions with Echo State Networks. *Neural Netw.* **2016**, *78*, 112–119. [CrossRef] [PubMed]
34. Bozhkov, L.; Koprinkova-Hristova, P.; Georgieva, P. Reservoir computing for emotion valence discrimination from EEG signals. *Neurocomputing* **2017**, *231*, 28–40. [CrossRef]
35. Kim, H.H.; Jeong, J. Decoding electroencephalographic signals for direction in brain–computer interface using echo state network and Gaussian readouts. *Comput. Biol. Med.* **2019**, *110*, 254–264. [CrossRef]
36. Dinges, D.F.; Powell, J.W. Microcomputer analyses of performance on sustained operations. *Behav. Res. Methods* **1985**, *17*, 652–655. [CrossRef]
37. Eriksen, B.A.; Eriksen, C.W. Effects of noise letters upon the identification of a target letter in a nonsearch task. *Percep. Psychophys.* **1974**, *16*, 143–149. [CrossRef]
38. Basner, M.; Dinges, D.F. Maximizing sensitivity of the Psychomotor Vigilance Test (PVT) to sleep loss. *Sleep* **2011**, *34*, 581–591. [CrossRef]
39. Sprajcer, M.; Jay, S.M.; Vincent, G.E.; Vakulin, A.; Lack, L.; Ferguson, S.A. How the chance of missing the alarm during an on-call shift affects pre-bed anxiety, sleep and next day cognitive performance. *Biol. Psychol.* **2018**, *137*, 133–139. [CrossRef]
40. Hedge, C.; Powell, G.; Sumner, P. The reliability paradox: Why robust cognitive tasks do not produce reliable individual differences. *Behav. Res. Methods* **2018**, *50*, 1166–1186. [CrossRef]
41. Beaton, L.E.; Azma, S.; Marinkovic, K. When the brain changes its mind: Oscillatory dynamics of conflict processing and response switching in a flanker task during alcohol challenge. *PLoS ONE* **2018**, *13*, 1–24. [CrossRef]
42. Jaeger, H.; Haas, H. Harnessing Nonlinearity: Predicting Chaotic Systems and Saving Energy in Wireless Communication. *Science* **2004**, *304*, 78–80. [CrossRef] [PubMed]
43. Farkaš, I.; Bosák, R.; Gergeľ, P. Computational analysis of memory capacity in echo state networks. *Neural Netw.* **2016**, *83*, 109–120. [CrossRef] [PubMed]
44. Oztuik, M.C.; Xu, D.; Principe, J.C. Analysis and design of echo state networks. *Neural Comput.* **2007**, *19*, 111–138. [CrossRef] [PubMed]
45. Cui, H.; Liu, X.; Li, L. The architecture of dynamic reservoir in the echo state network. *Chaos* **2012**, 22. [CrossRef] [PubMed]
46. Inubushi, M.; Yoshimura, K. Reservoir Computing beyond Memory-Nonlinearity Trade-off. *Sci. Rep.* **2017**, *7*, 1–10. [CrossRef] [PubMed]
47. Dominey, P.F. Biological Cybernetics on recurrent state representation and reinforcement learning. *J. Comp. Neurol.* **1995**, *274*, 265–274.
48. Dominey, P.F.; Hoen, M.; Blanc, J.M.; Lelekov-Boissard, T. Neurological basis of language and sequential cognition: Evidence from simulation, aphasia, and ERP studies. *Brain Lang.* **2003**, *86*, 207–225. [CrossRef]
49. Dominey, P.F.; Hoen, M.; Inui, T. A neurolinguistic model of grammatical construction processing. *J. Cogn. Neurosci.* **2006**, *18*, 2088–2107. [CrossRef]
50. Jaeger, H. *The "Echo State" Approach to Analysing and Training Recurrent Neural Networks, GMD Report*; GMD—German National Research Institute for Computer Science: Darmstadt, Germany, 2001; Volume 148.
51. Jaeger, H.; Lukoševičius, M.; Popovici, D.; Siewert, U. Optimization and applications of echo state networks with leaky- integrator neurons. *Neural Netw.* **2007**, *20*, 335–352. [CrossRef]
52. Lukoševičius, M.; Jaeger, H. Reservoir computing approaches to recurrent neural network training. *Comput. Sci. Rev.* **2009**, *3*, 127–149. [CrossRef]

53. Hermans, M.; Schrauwen, B. Memory in Reservoirs for High Dimensional Input. In Proceedings of the 2010 International Joint Conference on Neural Networks (IJCNN), Barcelona, Spain, 18–23 July 2010; pp. 1–7.
54. Verstraeten, D.; Schrauwen, B.; D'Haene, M.; Stroobandt, D. An experimental unification of reservoir computing methods. *Neural Netw.* **2007**, *20*, 391–403. [CrossRef] [PubMed]
55. Gallicchio, C.; Micheli, A.; Pedrelli, L. Deep reservoir computing: A critical experimental analysis. *Neurocomputing* **2017**, *268*, 87–99. [CrossRef]
56. Tikhonov, A.N.; Arsenin, V.Y. *Solutions of Ill-Posed Problems*; Winston and Sons: Washington, DC, USA, 1977.
57. Monastra, V.J.; Lynn, S.; Linden, M.; Lubar, J.F.; Gruzelier, J.; La Vaque, T.J. Electroencephalographic biofeedback in the treatment of attention-deficit/hyperactivity disorder. *J. Neurother.* **2006**, *9*, 5–34. [CrossRef]
58. Schmeling, A.; Olze, A.; Reisinger, W.; König, M.; Geserick, G. Statistical analysis and verification of forensic age estimation of living persons in the Institute of Legal Medicine of the Berlin University Hospital Charité. *Proces. Leng. Nat.* **2003**, *2*, 3–5.
59. Duchek, J.M.; Hunt, L.; Ball, K.; Buckles, V.; Morris, J.C. Attention and Driving Performance in Alzheimer's Disease. *J. Gerontol. Ser. B Psychol. Sci. Soc. Sci.* **1998**, *53*, 130–141. [CrossRef]
60. Rapp, M.A.; Reischies, F.M. Attention and executive control predict Alzheimer disease in late life: Results from the Berlin Aging Study (BASE). *Am. J. Geriatr. Psychiatry* **2005**, *13*, 134–141. [CrossRef]
61. Pirzanski, C.; Berge, B. Ear canal dynamics: Facts versus perception. *Hear. J.* **2005**, *58*, 50–58. [CrossRef]
62. Hastie, T.; Tibshirani, R.; Friedman, J. *The Elements of Statistical Learning*; Springer: New York, NY, USA, 2001.
63. Guo, Y.; Hastie, T.; Tibshirani, R. Regularized linear discriminant analysis and its application in microarrays. *Biostatistics* **2007**, *8*, 86–100. [CrossRef]
64. Ho, T.K. The random subspace method for constructing decision forests. *IEEE Trans. Pattern Anal. Mach. Intell.* **1998**, *20*, 832–844.
65. Skurichina, M.; Duin, R. Bagging, Boosting and the Random Subspace Method for Linear Classifiers. *Pattern Anal. Appl.* **2002**, *5*, 121–135. [CrossRef]
66. Breiman, L. Random Forests. *Mach. Learn.* **2001**, *45*, 5–32. [CrossRef]

brain sciences

MDPI

Article

Exploring Shopper's Browsing Behavior and Attention Level with an EEG Biosensor Cap

Dong-Her Shih [1,*], Kuan-Chu Lu [1] and Po-Yuan Shih [2]

1 Department of Information Management, National Yunlin University of Science and Technology, Douliou, Yunlin 64002, Taiwan; qq1214x@yahoo.com.tw
2 Department of Finance, National Yunlin University of Science and Technology, Douliou, Yunlin 64002, Taiwan; D10424003@yuntech.edu.tw
* Correspondence: shihdh@yuntech.edu.tw; Tel.: +886-932-690178

Received: 12 October 2019; Accepted: 29 October 2019; Published: 31 October 2019

Abstract: The online shopping market is developing rapidly, meaning that it is important for retailers and manufacturers to understand how consumers behave online compared to when in brick-and-mortar stores. Retailers want consumers to spend time shopping, browsing, and searching for products in the hope a purchase is made. On the other hand, consumers may want to restrict their duration of stay on websites due to perceived risk of loss of time or convenience. This phenomenon underlies the need to reduce the duration of consumer stay (namely, time pressure) on websites. In this paper, the browsing behavior and attention span of shoppers engaging in online shopping under time pressure were investigated. The attention and meditation level are measured by an electroencephalogram (EEG) biosensor cap. The results indicated that when under time pressure shoppers engaging in online shopping are less attentive. Thus, marketers may need to find strategies to increase a shopper's attention. Shoppers unfamiliar with product catalogs on shopping websites are less attentive, therefore marketers should adopt an interesting style for product catalogs to hold a shopper's attention. We discuss our findings and outline their business implications.

Keywords: consumer behavior; electroencephalogram (EEG) biosensor; attention and meditation; brain computer interface

1. Introduction

E-commerce, which has grown exponentially because of Internet technology, has induced changes at the market, industry, and economic levels, and has profoundly altered life, politics, and society [1]. Online network platforms are used globally to undertake various online services, and such platforms provide a robust means for generating income and, for an immeasurable number of consumers from around the world, to shop online [2]. Shopping websites display numerous products organized by category; despite being produced by different firms, and many of these products share similar features. However, these products, along with their information, are too great in number to be processed by the human brain because of a human's limited cognitive capacity, thus causing the consumer confusion and low satisfaction [3–5]. In addition, shopping is a series of decision-making processes aimed at satisfying consumer needs. The focus of academic attention should be shifted to online shopping behavior because of the mismatch between excessive stimuli and limited brain capacity [6]. According to Drucker [7], "the objective of a business is to create and retain customers". Information about customers largely concerns their consumption behavior, which involves the processing and selection of product information.

Generally, retailers want consumers to spend more time shopping, browsing, and searching for products in the hope that they make a purchase. On the other hand, consumers may want to restrict their duration of stay on websites due to a perceived risk of loss of time or convenience [8]. Previous research discussing the purchasing decision process has assumed that shoppers face time pressure. For example, Lin and Wu [9] found that time pressure will increase the proportion of consumers unable to make a judgment or a choice. Vermeir and Kenhove [10] suggested that consumers under high time pressure search less for coupons and products with a promotion. Rieskamp and Hoffrage [11] demonstrate that compared to those under low time pressure, individuals under high time pressure accelerate the search for information, using less information, and staying focused on the most important features. Liu et al. [12] indicate that when shopping online under time pressure, participants' observation length and count for browsing products with high brand awareness were respectively longer and higher than those for browsing products with low brand awareness. However, when they shopped online without time pressure, no difference between products with high and low brand awareness levels was observed.

Time pressure is an essential variable of consumer behavior; it prompts a decision to be made within a limited time [13]. Moon and Lee [14] perceived time-pressure purchases as a consumption decision made within time constraints specified by the consumer, suggesting that time pressure indicates a sense of psychological urgency. Moreover, consumers typically base their purchasing decisions more on limited knowledge than on careful deliberation and comparison; such decisions tend to be made in a matter of seconds [15–17]. Pieters and Warlop [18] showed that time pressure affects visual attention in ways such that consumers skip certain brand elements to optimize their decision-making. Moreover, both the cue utilization model proposed by Olson and Jacoby [19] and the theory of planned behavior proposed by Ajzen [20] assume that consumers are aware of their purchase motives and can distinguish products and brands they intend to purchase. Thus, some consumers have selection criteria that form a basis for evaluating product brands and selecting the top-ranked ones.

Shoppers behavior online has been reported in many studies, and the browsing behavior and attention span of shoppers engaging in online shopping under time pressure were investigated in the present study. The remainder of this paper is structured as follows. Section 2 reviews relevant literature and describes hypotheses about online shopping behavior. Section 3 introduces the method of this study. The findings are presented in Section 4 and their implications and suggestions are discussed in Section 5. Finally, Section 6 concludes this study and outlines this paper's contributions.

2. Background and Hypotheses

Time pressure is an influential factor in consumer behavior [21]; it can have a marked influence on decision-making and restrict information-processing ability [22]. Its effects on people's decision making intensify in the face of information overload [23]. Moreover, Payne et al. [24] found that people progress through a hierarchy of responses as time pressure intensifies. Specifically, shoppers under moderate time pressure become faster and slightly more selective at information processing, whereas those under heavy pressure tend to skim through information superficially without examining every single detail. However, some studies have suggested that time pressure typically prompts decision makers to make decisions and execute decision-making strategies through simple means [25,26], and that people under time constraints can turn to other strategies to facilitate their information processing [27]. In addition, Levy [28] showed that when people were in a hurry, they hastened their decision making. Pieters and Warlop [18] argued that consumers under time pressure will filter some information, accelerate information acquisition, and adjust their information acquisition strategies.

Generally, time pressure reduces visual attention [29]. Although products with newly designed packaging can attract visual attention [30], such products can be neglected by people who perceive their packaging to be overly novel [31], leading to financial loss and even the removal of some products from the shelf [32].

Clement et al. [6] noted that consumers under time pressure tend to focus on certain products and brands, as well as their characteristics. Studies conducted in brick-and-mortar stores have found that the timing of purchases made under time pressure is similar to those made when not under time pressure. This indicates that consumers do not select certain products due to time pressure; they either make decisions in a matter of seconds when they need to identify familiar information quickly from a pool of information [33], or adjust their search strategies to concentrate on the design features of brands [18]. Accordingly, this study argues that shoppers under time pressure focus on fewer products to facilitate their product search on shopping websites, and that they adjust their search strategies to identify the salient design features of products; this information-processing strategy reflects the stimulation of the brain in a top-down fashion. Based on the aforementioned argument, Hypotheses 1 and 2 were formulated as follows:

Hypotheses (H1). *Shoppers view fewer products when shopping under time pressure than they would when shopping not under time pressure.*

Hypotheses (H2). *Shoppers focus more on renowned brands when shopping under time pressure than they would when shopping under no time pressure.*

Our ability to focus on the task at hand is a key element in efficient information processing and our attention is easily distracted by novel events or changes in the stimulus environment [34]. Bettman et al. [35] maintained that attention changes occur because of reflexive reactions to threats such as time pressure. In a study by Ordonez and Benson [27], subjects dealing with decisions under time pressure adopted different decision-making strategies to accelerate their information-processing speed. Zur and Breznitz [36] also argued that decision makers typically spend less time viewing information when they are under time pressure, indicating that under such circumstances they may change their decision-making strategies and thereby change their level of attention. Therefore, Hypothesis 3 was formulated as follows:

Hypotheses (H3). *Under time pressure, shoppers engaging in online shopping are less attentive than those not under time pressure.*

In the United Kingdom, approximately 70% of consumers who enter grocery stores have incomplete purchase intentions [37]. Previous research [38] has shown that 85% of consumers do not handle commodity items while shopping and 90% of consumers view only the covers of commodity items. Furthermore, consumers tend to purchase products they like after simply viewing them; such actions occur most frequently during online shopping [39]. Brands with sophisticated designs and noticeable visual elements (e.g., product names, logos, layouts, and slogans) can make a deep impression on consumers [40–42].

From a cognitive neuropsychological perspective, visual attention can be expressed in terms of orientation-attention and discover-attention. Orientation-attention is a parallel and non-selective pre-attentive search process that enables a considerable amount of information to be processed efficiently and simultaneously. Discover-attention is a serial search process of sequentially searching for information details on the packaging of a product (e.g., textual content and caution labels). In the view of Perkins [43], orientation-attention is the primitive stage of attention, whereas discover-attention enables the complete understanding of a commodity. Neither cognitive system can be distinguished easily in real-world contexts other than shopping [44]. Generally, consumers depend on slow, serial search processes [45]. The presence of branded products and previous online shopping experiences can facilitate their search. Thus, when they have to make purchase decisions in a short time frame or if they intend to purchase renowned products, they tend to simplify their search on shopping websites. Clement et al. [6] assumed that a comprehensive understanding of product catalogs and experiences of shopping at physical stores can expedite product searches, although their findings showed that consumer product searches in brick-and-mortar contexts were facilitated not by their familiarity with product catalogs, but by their understanding of the way products were displayed in-store. However, this study argues that product catalogs on shopping websites differ from those of physical stores; hence, they might facilitate online product searches. Accordingly, Hypotheses 4 and 5 were formulated as follows:

Hypotheses (H4). *Familiarity with product catalogs on shopping websites can reduce product search time during shopping.*

Hypotheses (H5). *Experience using other shopping websites can reduce product search time during shopping.*

3. Methods

We aimed to understand the effect of time pressure on consumer browsing behavior and attention level with an EEG (electroencephalogram) biosensor cap with regard to branded products on online shopping website. To verify our hypotheses, we conducted a laboratory study on a real-world website. Participants were recruited and assigned to two time-pressure levels (the presence or absence of time-pressure situations). They were assigned a purchasing task and instructed to browse on Taobao (a famous Chinese shopping website). We used an EEG biosensor cap to track the attention level of the participants as they browsed products on the webpage. Upon completion of the experiment, the participants were given a $20 gift card as our token of appreciation for their time and effort.

3.1. Electroencephalogram (EEG) Technique

According to the traditional model of control, physiological systems self-regulate their activity to preserve steadiness by reducing fluctuations around a homeostatic equilibrium point. By contrast with this view, a wide bulk of evidence has recently been provided that several physiological time signals exhibit intrinsic fractal fluctuations. Indeed, heartbeat, respiration, gait rhythm, dynamics of neurotransmitter release, electromyography, and brain activity reveal similar temporal patterns over multiple time scales [46]. In an active postsynaptic neuron, a negative voltage between neural dendrites and other locations along the neuron is generated. Within a small brain compartment in which dendritic structure are parallel and follow a main direction, such a situation can be modelled as a current dipole generating an electromagnetic field. Both electrical potentials and magnetic fields, generated from the dipole in this compartment, can be measured non-invasively by sensors located on or close to the scalp. The technology that measures electrical potentials is called electroencephalography [47].

In this study, a light NeuroSky EEG biosensor cap (i.e., MindWave Mobile as shown in Figure 1) was used for measuring the attention and meditation levels of shoppers. The MindWave Mobile is a portable, wireless hardware cap developed by NeuroSky Company (Taipei, Taiwan). Crowley et al. [48] have evaluated a similar NeuroSky EEG biosensor cap (i.e., Mindset) to measure the attention and meditation levels of a subject in practice. MindWave Mobile outputs 12 bit raw-brainwaves (3–100 Hz) with a sampling rate of 512 Hz and EEG power spectra (alpha, beta, etc.). The detected waves were interpreted by eSense™ (NeuroSky's proprietary algorithm for characterizing mental states, Windows version v1.2.3) to indicate each subject's mental state when they were shopping online. For each different mental state (i.e., attention, meditation), the meter value from eSense™ is reported on a relative scale of 1 to 100. On this scale, a value between 40 and 60 at any given moment in time is considered "neutral". A value from 60 to 80 is considered "slightly elevated", and may be interpreted as levels being possibly higher than normal. Values from 80 to 100 are considered "elevated". Similarly, a value between 20 and 40 indicates "reduced", while a value between 1 and 20 indicates a "strongly lowered" level of each different mental state.

In addition, meditation is considered as a promising technique for body and mind regulation. Meditation plays an important role at physical, mental, and spiritual levels. EEG measures the brain activity useful to recognize the emotional states. EEG has excellent resolution at the millisecond scale, and is superior to positron emission tomography (PET) and functional magnetic resonance imaging (fMRI) [49]. Crowley et al. [48] have evaluated the use of NeuroSky's Mindset headset to measure the attention and meditation levels of a subject in practice. Thus, analyzing shoppers' attention and meditation level when shopping under time pressure or not is straightforward.

Figure 1. MindWave Mobile, NeuroSky.

3.2. Subjects and Tasks

To address the research questions, a sample of 30 participants who had online shopping experience was recruited via convenience sampling. While wearing an EEG cap, the subjects performed tasks of product purchases on Taobao. They used the catalogs, listed recommendations, and keywords provided by the website and purchased products of their preference. The experiment was conducted in a quiet laboratory with a laptop computer to ensure that the subjects would not be disturbed. The EEG biosensor cap was connected with Bluetooth to a laptop to record subjects' brainwaves and obtain experimental data.

3.3. Experimental Procedure

An Institutional Review Board (IRB) proof was conducted (Approval No.: NCKU-HREC-E-104-101-2) before this experiment. All subjects were asked to complete a questionnaire regarding their mental and physical states and whether they had ever shopped on any shopping websites, and to sign an informed consent form.

To reduce any discomfort from wearing the cap, which would affect the experimental results, the subjects were given some time (approximately 3 min) at the beginning of the experiment to accustom themselves to the cap. During the experiment, each subject purchased 10 specific items in odd and even number from the 20 best-selling products sold on Taobao (Figure 2) while under time pressure (10 min) and not under time pressure (unlimited time) conditions. The sample size was comparable with in-store studies of shopper navigation and the number of purchases was also comparable with that used in past in-store work. Table 1 presents the top 20 products on Taobao shopping website at the time of the experiment and their respective item numbers. This experiment was aimed at investigating whether the subjects focused on certain products or renowned brands when under time pressure. The renowned brands were defined according to the American Marketing Association, World Brand Lab and other related websites. The shopper's choices, durations, visual attention and site navigation were recorded using our own designed program. After the experiment, each subject completed a questionnaire regarding the number of years of experience they had in using shopping websites. Data collected from the questionnaire were analyzed to determine whether familiarity with shopping website product catalogs and experience using shopping websites facilitated the subjects' purchase behavior in online shopping.

Figure 2. Taobao home page.

Table 1. Top 20 products on Taobao and assigned items.

Condition	Under Time Pressure	Not Under Time Pressure
Item1	Sweater coat	Dress
Item2	Women's footwear	Mobile phone
Item3	Shirt	Sweater
Item4	Windbreaker	Children's apparel
Item5	Wallpaper	iPhone
Item6	Wall sticker	Purse
Item7	Men's footwear	Cotton-padded clothing
Item8	Thermos	Dr. Martens boots
Item9	Spring and autumn dresses	Spring and autumn women's bottoming shirt
Item10	Watch	Tablet computer

4. Results

To test the proposed hypotheses, the experimental data on the subjects' online shopping behavior were analyzed through the paired t-test to compare the test outcomes between different test conditions and attention types. Descriptive statistics and paired *t*-test results are shown below.

4.1. Demographic Data

The demographic data in Table 2 show that the sample comprised 15 men and 15 women who had experience using shopping websites. The subjects were 21–30 years old and all held a bachelor's degree. Most of the subjects had extensive experience using the Internet (>10 years, 83.4%; 5–10 years, 13.3%; <1 year, 3.3%) and reported that they had used Ruten (86.7%), Yahoo! (80%), PChome (53.3%), Taobao (26.7%), and Amazon (10%) for online shopping. Regarding the frequency with which they used online shopping websites, 46.8% reported that they used them 1–5 times per year, 26.6% reported using them 5–10 times per year, and 26.6% used them >10 times per year. For the number of years of experience using online shopping websites, 50% had 1–5 years of experience, 33.3% had 5–10 years of experience, and 16.7% had >10 years of experience.

4.2. T-Test Results

4.2.1. Shoppers Viewed Fewer Products under Time Pressure

The mean of products viewed by all 30 subjects was 28.78 (standard deviation (SD): ±11.986), and the mean time spent on purchasing the 10 assigned product items was 9.097 min (SD: ±3.9072). An independent t-test revealed a non-significant gender difference in the number of products viewed, as shown in Table 3, where SD stands for standard deviation and SE stands for standard error. The F-value was non-significant at $0.958 > 0.05$ for the under time-pressure condition and at $0.960 > 0.05$ for the not under time-pressure condition. Thus, an equal-variances test was conducted for the under time-pressure condition ($t = 0.323$, $p = 0.749 > 0.05$) and the not under time-pressure condition ($t = -0.643$, $p = 0.525 > 0.05$). No significant difference was observed between the numbers of products viewed by the male and female participants, regardless of the condition. Accordingly, the data were subjected to further analysis.

Table 4 tabulates the descriptive statistics for the number of products viewed under both conditions, and Table 5 presents the paired *t*-test results. The p value was 0.001 indicates a significant difference in the number of products viewed between two conditions; specifically, the subjects under time-pressure condition viewed more products.

Table 2. Demographic statistics.

Item	Variable	N	%
Sex	M	15	50
	F	15	50
Age	21–31	30	100
Highest level of education	Graduate	30	100
How many years of experience do you have using the Internet?	<1 year	1	3.3
	5–10 years	4	13.3
	>10 years	25	83.4
Have you shopped online before?	Yes	30	100
Which of these online shopping website(s) have you purchased items from before?	Ruten	26	86.7
	PChome	16	53.3
	Yahoo	24	80
	Taobao	8	26.7
	Amazon	3	10
How frequently do you use shopping websites each year?	1–5 times	14	46.8
	5–10 times	8	26.6
	>10 times	8	26.6
How many years of experience do you have using shopping websites?	1–5 times	15	50
	5–10 times	10	33.3
	>10 times	5	16.7

Table 3. Independent *t*-test results for gender differences in the number of products viewed.

Independent Variable	*n*	Mean	SD	SE	*df*	*t*	*p*-Value
Under time pressure (male)	15	23.867	4.580	1.182	28	0.323	0.749
Under time pressure (female)	15	23.333	4.466	1.153			
Not under time pressure (male)	15	32.200	14.178	3.660	28	−0.643	0.525
Not under time pressure (female)	15	35.733	15.867	4.097			

Table 4. Descriptive statistics for the number of products viewed.

Condition	*n*	Mean	Median	Min	Max	SD
Under time pressure	30	23.600	29	14	37	4.453
Not under time pressure	30	33.967	22	18	84	14.893

Table 5. Paired *t*-test results for the number of products viewed between two conditions.

Independent Variable	*n*	Mean	SD	SE	*p*-Value
Under time pressure—Not under time pressure	30	−10.366	15.082	2.753	0.001 ***

*** $p < 0.001$.

In addition, regarding the EEG analysis, a paired *t*-test was conducted on the attention and meditation levels of the subjects when shopping under time pressure and not under time pressure conditions; the corresponding descriptive statistics and paired t-test results are presented in Tables 6 and 7, respectively. The *p*-value for the difference between the attention levels was 0.008 and the difference between the meditation levels was 0.572 (Table 7). These results indicate that under time-pressure and not under time-pressure conditions, the subjects differed significantly in attention but not in meditation. Their attention during online shopping was weaker while under time pressure.

Table 6. Descriptive statistics for attention and meditation levels.

Condition	*n*	Mean	Median	Min	Max	SD
Under time pressure (attention)	30	46.941	52.38	33.85	60.48	6.216
Not under time pressure (attention)	30	50.615	53.49	37.93	64.7	6.931
Under time pressure (meditation)	30	56.127	58.26	46.71	64.74	4.453
Not under time pressure (meditation)	30	55.702	56.94	49.2	69.04	14.893

Table 7. Paired *t*-test results for attention and meditation levels.

Independent Variable	*n*	Mean	SD	SE	*p*-Value
Under time pressure—Not under time pressure (attention)	30	−3.673	7.097	1.295	0.008 **
Under time pressure—Not under time pressure (meditation)	30	0.424	4.060	0.741	0.572

** $p < 0.01$.

4.2.2. Shoppers Focused more on Renowned Brands while under Time Pressure

This section discusses whether shoppers focus more on renowned brands when under time pressure. Of the 10 assigned product items to be purchased, 1.31 products were from renowned brands on average (SD: ±0.8658). An independent *t*-test revealed a no significant gender difference in the number of branded products purchased (Table 8). The *F*-value was not significant at 0.806 > 0.05 for the under time-pressure condition and at 0.259 > 0.05 for the not shopping under time-pressure condition. Thus, an equal-variances test was conducted for under the time-pressure condition ($t = 0.638$, $p = 0.529 < 0.05$) and not shopping under time-pressure condition ($t = -0.475$, $p = 0.638 > 0.05$). No significant difference was observed between the numbers of branded products purchased by the male and female subjects, regardless of the condition.

Table 8. Independent *t*-test results for gender differences in the number of renowned brands.

Independent Variable	*n*	Mean	SD	SE	*df*	*t*	*p*-Value
Under time pressure (male)	15	1.067	0.883	0.228	28	0.638	0.529
Under time pressure (female)	15	0.867	0.833	0.215			
Not under time pressure (male)	15	1.600	0.632	0.163	28	−0.475	0.638
Not under time pressure (female)	15	1.733	0.883	0.228			

A paired *t*-test was conducted to examine whether deducting the number of renowned brand products purchased with the under time-pressure condition from those purchased with the not under time-pressure condition would yield a result greater than zero. Descriptive statistics and the paired *t*-test results are shown in Tables 9 and 10, respectively. The *p*-value was 0.001 (Table 10), which indicates a significant difference in the number of renowned brand products purchased between the two conditions; specifically, fewer products were purchased under time pressure.

Table 9. Descriptive statistics for renowned brand products purchased.

Condition	n	Mean	Median	Min	Max	SD
Under time pressure	30	0.967	1	0	3	0.850
Not under time pressure	30	1.667	1	0	3	0.758

Table 10. Paired t-test results for the number of products purchased.

Independent Variable	n	Mean	SD	SE	p-Value
Under time pressure—Not under time pressure	30	−0.7	0.987	0.180	0.001 ***

*** $p < 0.001$.

4.2.3. Familiarity with Product Catalogs on Shopping Websites Facilitated Product Searches during Shopping

When shopping with the not under time-pressure condition, the subjects were asked to purchase five products under the condition that the subjects were unfamiliar with the product catalogs, and five others under the condition that the subjects were familiar with the product catalogs. The products are shown in Table 11. The amount of time that the male (ID a, b, c, ... with symbol ●) and female (ID A, B, C, ... with symbol ▲) subjects spent on product searches is depicted by Figure 3, in which the **x**-axis denotes the amount of time spent searching for products in catalogs that the subjects were familiar with, and the y-axis represents the amount of time they spent searching for products in catalogs that they were unfamiliar with.

Table 11. Taobao's best-selling products purchased not under time pressure.

Condition	Catalog Unfamiliarity	Catalog Familiarity
1	Dress	Purse
2	Mobile phone	Cotton-padded clothing
3	Sweater	Dr. Martens boots
4	Children's apparel	Spring and autumn women's bottoming shirt
5	iPhone	Tablet computer

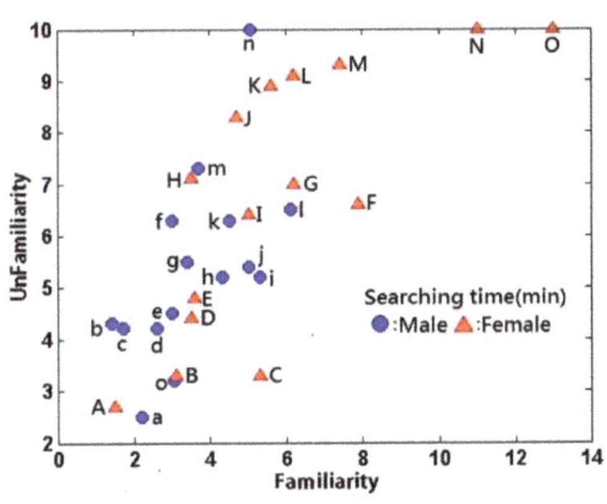

Figure 3. Product search time in minutes.

An independent t-test was conducted to determine the significance level of the gender difference in the product search times (Table 12). The F-value was not significant at 0.057 > 0.05 for catalog familiarity and at 0.075 > 0.05 for catalog unfamiliarity. Thus, an equal-variances test was conducted for the catalog familiarity condition ($t = -2.550$, $p = 0.017 < 0.05$) and the catalog unfamiliarity condition ($t = -1.745$, $p = 0.092 > 0.05$). A significant gender difference was observed in the product search times under the catalog familiarity condition but not under the catalog unfamiliarity condition. Accordingly, the data were subjected to further analysis.

Table 12. Independent *t*-test results for gender differences in the product search times.

Independent Variable	*n*	Mean	SD	SE	*df*	*t*	*p*-Value
Familiarity (male)	15	3.649	1.386	0.357	28	−2.550	0.017
Familiarity (female)	15	5.901	3.127	0.807			
Unfamiliarity (male)	15	5.415	1.796	0.463	28	−1.745	0.092
Unfamiliarity (female)	15	6.847	2.620	0.676			

A paired *t*-test was conducted to examine whether deducting the product search time under the catalog unfamiliarity condition from that under the catalog familiarity condition would yield a result greater than 0. Descriptive statistics and the paired *t*-test results for the product search times are presented in Tables 13 and 14, respectively. The *p*-value was 0.000 (Table 14), which indicates a significant difference in the product search times between the catalog familiarity and unfamiliarity conditions; specifically, longer search times were observed under the catalog unfamiliarity condition as expected.

Table 13. Descriptive statistics for the product search times.

Condition	*n*	Mean	Median	Min	Max	SD
Unfamiliarity	30	6.331	5.50	2.59	10.66	2.295
Familiarity	30	4.998	3.10	1.44	13.53	2.819

Table 14. Paired *t*-test results for the product search times (familiarity vs. unfamiliarity).

Independent Variable	*n*	Mean	SD	SE	*p*-Value
Unfamiliarity—Familiarity	30	1.356	1.789	0.326	0.000 ***

*** $p < 0.001$.

Moreover, the number of product web pages surfed under the catalog familiarity condition was compared with that under the catalog unfamiliarity condition (Figure 4). An independent *t*-test was used to determine the significance level of the gender difference in the number of product web pages surfed (Table 15). The F-value was non-significant at 0.733 > 0.05 under the catalog familiarity condition and at 0.511 > 0.05 under the catalog unfamiliarity condition. Thus, an equal-variances test was conducted for the catalog familiarity condition ($t = 0.173$, $p = 0.864 > 0.05$) and catalog unfamiliarity condition ($t = -1.434$, $p = 0.163 > 0.05$). No significant gender difference was observed in the number of product web pages surfed between the male and female subjects, regardless of the catalog familiarity or unfamiliarity condition. Accordingly, the data were subjected to further analysis.

Table 15. Independent *t*-test results for gender in the number of web page surfed.

Independent Variable	*n*	Mean	SD	SE	*df*	*t*	*p*-Value
Familiarity (male)	15	15.467	8.854	2.286	28	0.173	0.864
Familiarity (female)	15	15.000	5.567	1.437			
Unfamiliarity (male)	15	16.733	8.655	2.234	28	−1.434	0.163
Unfamiliarity (female)	15	21.400	9.155	2.364			

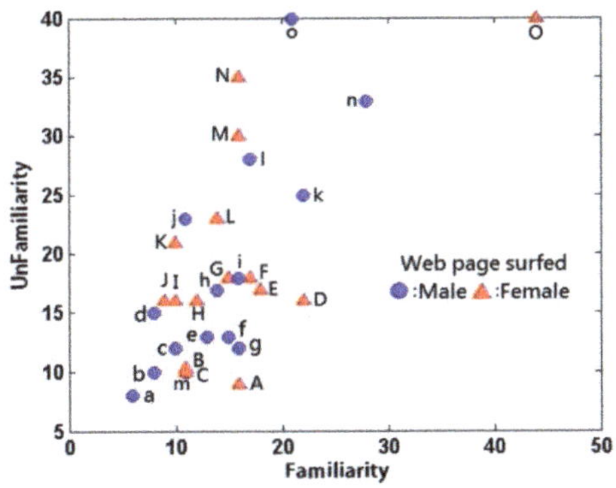

Figure 4. Number of product web pages surfed (familiarity vs. unfamiliarity).

The number of product web pages surfed was compared between the catalog familiarity and unfamiliarity conditions. The descriptive statistics and paired *t*-test results are presented in Tables 16 and 17, respectively. The *p*-value was 0.004, which indicates a significant difference in the number of product web pages surfed between the two conditions; specifically, more pages were surfed under the catalog unfamiliarity condition as expected.

Table 16. Descriptive statistics for the number of product web page surfed.

Condition	*n*	Mean	Median	Min	Max	SD
Unfamiliarity	30	19.067	9.50	8	40	9.070
Familiarity	30	15.233	13.50	6	44	7.271

Table 17. Paired *t*-test results for the number of web page surfed.

Independent Variable	*n*	Mean	SD	SE	*p*-Value
Unfamiliarity—Familiarity	30	−3.833	6.664	1.216	0.004 **

** $p < 0.01$.

Testing for significant differences in attention and meditation levels between the catalog familiarity and unfamiliarity conditions was undertaken. The descriptive statistics and paired *t*-test results are presented in Tables 18 and 19, respectively. The *p*-value for attention was 0.007 and the *p*-value for meditation was 0.946 (in Table 19). These results indicate a significant difference between the catalog familiarity and unfamiliarity conditions in the attention levels of the subjects but not in their meditation levels. Notably, the subjects with catalog unfamiliarity demonstrated weaker attention during product searches than those with catalog familiarity.

Table 18. Descriptive statistics for attention and meditation.

Condition	*n*	Mean	Median	Min	Max	SD
Familiarity (attention)	30	52.914	55.44	41.71	71.63	8.741
Unfamiliarity (attention)	30	48.797	51.30	32.94	58.9	6.464
Familiarity (meditation)	30	56.169	55.44	48.01	72.28	5.143
Unfamiliarity (meditation)	30	56.241	58.82	49.16	66.44	4.885

Table 19. Paired t-test results for attention and meditation levels.

Independent Variable	n	Mean	SD	SE	p-Value
Unfamiliarity—Familiarity (attention)	30	4.117	7.820	1.427	0.007 **
Unfamiliarity—Familiarity (meditation)	30	−0.072	5.791	1.057	0.946

** $p < 0.01$.

4.2.4. More Experience Using Shopping Websites Facilitated Product Search

Before the experiment, all the subjects were asked to complete a questionnaire that included items about their number of years of experience using shopping websites. A survey of Taiwanese online shoppers conducted by Foreseeing Innovative New Digiservices (which operates under the Institute for Information Industry, a non-governmental organization promoting the development of Taiwan's information industry) revealed that most shoppers have more than 5 years of online shopping experience. Accordingly, in this study, those with more than 5 years of experience were defined as "more experienced online shoppers," and those with less than 5 years of experience were defined as "less experienced online shoppers." In this survey of our participants, the more experienced online shoppers spent an average of 9.93 min (SD: ±4.2937), compared with their less experienced counterparts, who spent an average of 11.75 min (SD: ±4.8990) in purchases. Therefore, the null hypothesis is "There is no significant difference in the product search times between more experienced and less experienced online shoppers." Table 20 presents the independent t-test results for the product search times between the more experienced and less experienced online shoppers. The test statistic was $t = 1.073$ and $p = 0.293 > 0.05$. Therefore, the difference in product search times between the more experienced and less experienced online shoppers was not significant.

Table 20. Independent t-test results for the product search times.

Independent Variable	n	Mean	SD	SE	df	t	p-Value
Less experienced shoppers	16	11.754	4.899	1.224	28	1.073	0.293
More experienced shoppers	14	9.937	4.293	1.147			

5. Discussion and Implications

After experiment and hypothesis testing, the findings of this study and their implications are summarized as follows.

5.1. Under Time Pressure, Shoppers Focus on Fewer Products during Online Shopping

This finding corresponds with previous studies that have shown that shoppers under time pressure tend to hasten their product selection [50,51], expedite their information searches to reduce time spent processing information [25,36], or concentrate on specific brands and desired product attributes when making purchase decisions [18]. Therefore, comparing the results of the previous studies revealed that online shopping behavior under time pressure has not changed much despite the rapid development of the Internet and growing use of online shopping services over the past decade.

Moreover, Iyer [22] showed that customers with sufficient time for shopping but without shopping lists are inclined to make more purchases. Dhar and Nowlis [50] noted that online stores typically offer discounts for rush purchases. Ahituv et al. [13] suggested that under time pressure, decision makers tend to make decisions and execute decision-making strategies through simple means. Discounts promote consumption and, under time constraints, they can prompt quick purchase decisions. Most shopping website operators offer limited-edition products that can only be purchased by applying for a membership within certain periods. Such promotional campaigns, which feature a limited number of products, can prompt shoppers to hasten their product searches and make quick purchase decisions.

Shopping website operators can launch similar campaigns to encourage consumers shopping under time pressure, such as promotions and special offers, to boost sales and reduce the server load.

5.2. Shoppers Engaging in Online Shopping Focus More on Renowned Brand Products When Not under Time Pressure

When shopping under time pressure, specific characteristics of products typically draw the attention of consumers [26,36,52]. New characteristics added to a product often become essential factors that affect consumers' purchase decisions [53,54]. Distinctiveness exerts stronger effects on product purchase decisions when consumers are under time pressure [50]. Contrary to these previous studies, this study found that subjects did not pay more attention to renowned brand products when they were under time pressure. The result indicated that the renowned brands characteristic of a product are not equivalent to product distinctiveness or novelty, which attract consumer attention under time pressure. In other words, only when a consumer is not under time pressure do they have adequate time to select renowned brand products. This can be attributed to renowned brand products typically being high-priced, prompting consumers to give more consideration prior to making a purchase than they would give on non-renowned brand products. Moreover, Mitchell and Greatorex [55] found that consumers tend to shop at reputable stores to reduce the risk of purchasing low-quality products. Huang et al. [56] showed that brand awareness is crucial for reducing purchase risk. Accordingly, shoppers tend to pay more attention to searching for renowned brand products when not under time pressure to reduce this risk. According to the aforementioned arguments, shopping website operators can sell more renowned brand products during non-promotional periods to encourage consumption and improve customer trust. They can also offer their own-brand products during their time-limited promotions to boost their profits.

5.3. Under Time Pressure, Shoppers Engaging in Online Shopping are Less Attentive

The EEG measurement results of this study in Section 4.2.1 reveal that shoppers engaging in online shopping are more attentive when not under time pressure, probably because they adopt the depth strategy under this condition, enabling them to focus on the content and depth of products they view [57]. Thus, shopping website operators are suggested to improve the content and depth of their products during non-promotional periods to enhance consumer trust and approval indirectly. They can also encourage changes in consumer behavior through promotional activities, which can prompt shoppers to process information more quickly [27].

5.4. Catalog Familiarity Reduces Product Search Times

Hoque and Lohse [58] found that user-friendly user interfaces can facilitate product searches. Sharpe and Staelin [59] observed that people typically prefer spending less time on familiarizing themselves with the layout of a website. This study showed that consumers familiar with product catalogs of a website spend less time on product searches; this finding accords with those of previous studies in a brick-and-mortar store. Mccarthy and Aronson [60] suggested that browsing functionality on webpages should be designed in a manner that renders the pages easy to navigate. Elliott and Speck [61] remarked that convenient browsing, simple interfaces, and well-organized frameworks of websites can enhance operation ease of use and improve user experience. Other authors have identified that consumers may leave a website quickly if they felt the information was useless [62] or had to complete a hard task online [63]. To avoid this unwanted outcome, shopping website operators should avoid making substantial changes to their user interfaces; such changes can confuse consumers, lengthening their product search times. If the operators intend to refine their websites while reducing the likelihood of deterring customers, they should consider hosting online scavenger hunt-type games so that participants can accustom themselves to the product catalogs on the websites.

5.5. Shoppers Unfamiliar with Product Catalogs on Shopping Websites are Less Attentive

Numerous people base their decisions on their past actions [64,65] and inevitably repeat those actions. In psychology, this type of behavior is known as "familiarity" [66]. Soderlund [67] and Payne et al. [68] have argued that familiarity with the shopping environment affects purchase intention; specifically, shoppers with higher familiarity with the environment are more likely to make purchases [69,70] and choose products [71,72]. In familiar shopping environments, shoppers depend on their long-term memory; by contrast, in unfamiliar environments, they rely largely on external messages such as visual stimuli [73]. Moreover, stimuli in unfamiliar environments can attract attention [74], and shoppers at brick-and-mortar stores they are unfamiliar with are highly attentive during shopping [75]. However, the EEG measurement results of this study indicate that shoppers familiar with product catalogs on shopping websites are more attentive during shopping, which is different from Garling et al. [73] and Ashby et al. [76]. Shopping on websites is different from in brick-and-mortar stores. Thus, how consumer attention is affected during online shopping necessitates further research. According to these findings, shopping website operators can retain the original layout of their product catalogs to focus consumer attention ontheir products, which can subsequently facilitate more immediate purchases.

5.6. Product Search Times are Not Significantly Shorter for More Experienced Shoppers

Whereas Clement et al. [6] showed that shoppers with more brick-and-mortar shopping experience are more efficient at product searches, this study found no notable reduction in product search times among the more experienced online shoppers. These findings are perhaps due to the differences between the physical and virtual shopping environments. Furthermore, Daly [77] noted that positive attitudes and satisfaction strongly affect online shopping intentions. Swaminathan et al. [78], Deighton [79], and Lepkowska-White et al. [80] have maintained that significant browsing convenience can make information searches easier on websites and improve their popularity. Jin and Park [81] found that less experienced online shoppers have higher perceived risks of shopping websites, whereas their more experienced counterparts tend to focus on the services offered by the websites. They also asserted that service quality becomes increasingly critical for consumers as their transaction relationships with sellers mature. Thus, website operators can improve the security and service quality of their websites (instead of investigating whether their customers have shopped elsewhere online) to strengthen their customer relations and attract new business.

6. Conclusions

This study investigated the behavior of consumers shopping online under time pressure, hypothesizing that (1) shoppers under time pressure focus on renowned brand products and are attentive, (2) shoppers with more online shopping experience are more efficient at shopping, and (3) familiarity with product catalogs facilitates product searches. However, the results show that shoppers under time pressure view fewer products and those not under time pressure focus on renowned brand products. In addition, shoppers are less attentive when under time pressure. Moreover, more online shopping experience does not significantly reduce product search times, indicating that the presence of renowned brand products on online shopping websites can lower shoppers' perceived product risks. Shoppers unfamiliar with product catalogs on shopping websites are less attentive. Furthermore, shoppers under time pressure tend to hasten their purchase decisions and browse fewer product pages. The findings and implications of this study may contribute to relevant academic research and online shopping businesses.

Author Contributions: Conceptualization, D.-H.S.; Formal analysis, K.-C.L.; Investigation, K.-C.L.; Methodology, D.-H.S.; Project administration, D.-H.S.; Validation, K.-C.L. and P.-Y.S.; Writing, review and editing, P.-Y.S.

Acknowledgments: IRB protocol approval number of this study is NCKU HREC-E-104-101-2 (5/7/2015) at Taiwan. (IRB stands for Institutional Review Board. IRBs review and monitor how a research study will be conducted to ensure the study does not cause unreasonable risks to participants.)

Conflicts of Interest: The authors declare no conflict of interest.

References

1. Drucker, P. *Managing in the Next Society*; Truman Talley Books; St. Martin's Press: New York, NY, USA, 2002.
2. Chatterjee, D.; Grewal, R.; Sambamurthy, V. Shaping up for e-commerce: Institutional enablers of the organizational assimilation of web technologies. *MIS Q.* **2002**, *26*, 65–89. [CrossRef]
3. Miller, G.A. The magical number seven plus or minus two. *Psychol. Rev.* **1956**, *63*, 81–97. [CrossRef] [PubMed]
4. Petty, R.E.; Cacioppo, J.T.; Schumann, D. Central and peripheral routes to advertising effectiveness: The moderating role of involvement. *J. Consum. Res.* **1983**, *10*, 135–146. [CrossRef]
5. Schwartz, B. The tyranny of choice. *Sci. Am. Am. Ed.* **2004**, *290*, 70–75. [CrossRef] [PubMed]
6. Clement, J.; Kristensen, T.; Gronhaug, K. Understanding consumers' in-store visual perception: The influence of package design features on visual attention. *J. Retail. Consum. Serv.* **2013**, *20*, 234–239. [CrossRef]
7. Drucker, P.F. *Management: Tasks, Responsibilities, Practices*; HarperCollins: New York, NY, USA, 1973.
8. Forsythe, S.M.; Shi, B. Consumer patronage and risk perceptions in Internet shopping. *J. Bus. Res.* **2003**, *56*, 867–875. [CrossRef]
9. Lin, C.H.; Wu, P.H. How to deal with conflicts? The effect of consumer's subjective time pressure on product attitude judgment and choice. *J. Am. Acad. Bus.* **2005**, *6*, 219–224.
10. Vermeir, I.; Kenhove, P.V. The influence of need for closure and perceived time pressure on search effort for price and promotional information in a grocery shopping context. *Psychol. Mark.* **2005**, *22*, 71–95. [CrossRef]
11. Rieskamp, J.; Hoffrage, U. Inferences under time pressure: How opportunity costs affect strategy selection. *Acta Psychol.* **2008**, *127*, 258–276. [CrossRef]
12. Liu, C.W.; Hsieh, A.Y.; Lo, S.K.; Hwang, Y. What Consumers See when Time Is Running Out: Consumers' Browsing Behaviors on Online Shopping Websites when under Time Pressure. *Comput. Hum. Behav.* **2017**, *70*, 391–397. [CrossRef]
13. Ahituv, N.; Igbaria, M.; Sella, A.V. The effects of time pressure and completeness of information on decision-making. *J. Manag. Inf. Syst.* **1998**, *15*, 153–172. [CrossRef]
14. Moon, J.; Lee, K. Influence of time pressure on the purchase decision making process in apparel shopping. *Res. J. Costume Cult.* **2013**, *21*, 117–128. [CrossRef]
15. Dickson, P.R.; Sawyer, A.G. The price knowledge and search of supermarket shoppers. *J. Mark.* **1990**, *54*, 42–53. [CrossRef]
16. Hoyer, W.D. An examination of consumer decision making for a common repeat purchase product. *J. Consum. Res.* **1984**, *11*, 822–829. [CrossRef]
17. Shiv, B.; Fedorikhin, A. Heart and mind in conflict: The interplay of affect and cognition in consumer decision making. *J. Consum. Res.* **1999**, *26*, 278–292. [CrossRef]
18. Pieters, R.; Warlop, L. Visual attention during brand choice: The impact of time pressure and task motivation. *Int. J. Res. Mark.* **1999**, *16*, 1–16. [CrossRef]
19. Olson, J.C.; Jacoby, J. Cue utilization in the quality perception process. In Proceedings of the Third Annual Conference of the Association for Consumer Research, Chicago, IL, USA, 3–5 November 1972; pp. 167–179.
20. Ajzen, I. The theory of planned behavior. *Organ. Behav. Hum. Process.* **1991**, *50*, 179–211. [CrossRef]
21. Howard, J.A.S.; Jagdish, N. The theory of buyer behavior (No. 658.834 H6). *J. Am. Stat. Inf.* **1969**. [CrossRef]
22. Iyer, E.S. Unplanned purchasing: Knowledge of shopping environment and time pressure. *J. Retail.* **1989**, *65*, 40–57.
23. Davidson, D. A Coherence Theory of Truth and Knowledge. In *Truth and Interpretation. Perspectives on the Philosophy of Donald Davidson*; LePore, E., Ed.; Blackwell: Oxford, UK, 1986; pp. 307–319.
24. Payne, J.W.; Bettman, J.R.; Johnson, E.J. Adaptive strategy selection in decision making. *J. Exp. Psychol. Learn. Mem. Cogn.* **1988**, *14*, 534. [CrossRef]
25. Edland, A.; Svenson, O. Judgment and decision making under time pressure. In *Time Pressure and Stress in Human Judgment and Decision Making*; Springer: Berlin/Heidelberg, Germany, 1993; pp. 27–40.

26. Harris, J.; Blair, E. Consumer preference for product bundles: The role of reduced search costs. *J. Acad. Mark. Sci.* **2006**, *34*, 506–513. [CrossRef]
27. Ordonez, L.; Benson, L. Decisions under time pressure: How time constraint affects risky decision making. *Organ. Behav. Hum. Decis. Process.* **1997**, *71*, 121–140. [CrossRef]
28. Levy, S.A. Flexible and/or rigid control of oculomotor scanning behavior. In *Eye Movements: Cognition and Visual Perception*; Fisher, D.F., Monty, R.A., Senders, J.W., Eds.; Erlbaum: Hillsdale, NJ, USA, 1981; pp. 299–316.
29. Rosbergen, E.; Pieters, F.G.M.; Wedel, M. *Undirected Visual Attention to Advertising: A Segment-Level Analysis*; University of Groningen: Groningen, The Netherlands, 1995.
30. Sherwood, M. Winning the shelf wars. *Glob. Cosmet. Ind.* **1999**, *164*, 64–67.
31. Schoormans, J.P.; Robben, H.S. The effect of new package design on product attention, categorization and evaluation. *J. Econ. Psychol.* **1997**, *18*, 271–287. [CrossRef]
32. Lee, J.Y.; Gao, Z.; Brown, M.G. A study of the impact of package changes on orange juice demand. *J. Retail. Consum. Serv.* **2010**, *17*, 487–491. [CrossRef]
33. Fasolo, B.; Carmeci, F.A.; Misuraca, R. The effect of choice complexity on perception of time spent choosing: When choice takes longer but feels shorter. *Psychol. Mark.* **2009**, *26*, 213–228. [CrossRef]
34. Salo, E.; Salmela, V.; Salmi, J.; Numminen, J.; Alho, K. Brain activity associated with selective attention, divided attention and distraction. *Brain Res.* **2017**, *1664*, 25–36. [CrossRef]
35. Bettman, J.R.; Luce, M.F.; Payne, J.W. Constructive consumer choice processes. *J. Consum. Res.* **1998**, *25*, 187–217. [CrossRef]
36. Zur, H.B.; Breznitz, S.J. The effect of time pressure on risky choice behavior. *Acta Psychol.* **1981**, *47*, 89–104.
37. Rettie, R.; Brewer, C. The verbal and visual components of package design. *J. Prod. Brand Manag.* **2000**, *9*, 56–70. [CrossRef]
38. Urbany, J.E.; Dickson, P.R.; Kalapurakal, R. Price search in the retail grocery market. *J. Mark.* **1996**, *60*, 91–104. [CrossRef]
39. Nordfalt, J. Improving the attention-capturing ability of special displays with the combination effect and the design effect. *J. Retail. Consum. Serv.* **2011**, *18*, 169–173. [CrossRef]
40. Keller, K.L. Conceptualizing, measuring, and managing customer-based brand equity. *J. Mark.* **1993**, *5*, 1–22. [CrossRef]
41. Keller, K.L. Brand synthesis: The multidimensionality of brand knowledge. *J. Consum. Res.* **2003**, *29*, 595–600. [CrossRef]
42. Underwood, R.L.; Klein, N.M. Packaging as brand communication: Effects of product pictures on consumer responses to the package and brand. *J. Mark. Theory Pract.* **2002**, *10*, 58–68. [CrossRef]
43. Perkins, D.N. *Why Smart People Can be So Stupid*; Yale University Press: New Haven, CT, USA, 2002; pp. 64–85.
44. Duncan, J.; Humphreys, G.W. Visual search and stimulus similarity. *Psychol. Rev.* **1989**, *96*, 433–458. [CrossRef] [PubMed]
45. Posner, M.I.; Snyder, C.R.; Davidson, B.J. Attention and the detection of signals. *J. Exp. Psychol. Gen.* **1980**, *109*, 160–174. [CrossRef]
46. Croce, P.; Quercia, A.; Costa, S.; Zappasodi, F. Circadian Rhythms in Fractal Features of EEG Signals. *Front. Physiol.* **2018**, *9*, 1567. [CrossRef]
47. Croce, P.; Zappasodi, F.; Marzetti, L.; Merla, A.; Pizzela, V.; Chiarelli, A. Deep Convolutional Neural Networks for feature-less automatic classification of Independent Components in multi-channel electrophysiological brain recordings. *IEEE Trans. Biomed. Eng.* **2018**, *1*. [CrossRef]
48. Crowley, K.; Sliney, A.; Pitt, I.; Murphy, D. Evaluating a Brain-Computer Interface to Categories Human Emotional Response. In Proceedings of the 10th IEEE International Conference on Advanced Learning Technologies, Sousse, Tunisia, 12 April 2010; pp. 276–278.
49. Jadhav, N.; Manthalkar, R.; Joshi, Y. Effect of meditation on emotional response: An EEG-based study. *Biomed. Signal Process. Control* **2017**, *34*, 101–113. [CrossRef]
50. Dhar, R.; Nowlis, S.M. The effect of time pressure on consumer choice deferral. *J. Consum. Res.* **1999**, *25*, 369–384. [CrossRef]
51. Bell, D.; Corsten, D.; Knox, G. From Point of Purchase to Path to Purchase: How Pre-Shopping Factors Drive Unplanned Buying. *J. Mark.* **2011**, *75*, 31–45. [CrossRef]
52. Svenson, O.; Edland, A. Change of Preferences under Time Pressure: Choices and Judgments. *Scand. J. Psychol.* **1987**, *28*, 322–330. [CrossRef]

53. Nowlis, S.M. The effect of time pressure on the choice between brands that differ in quality, price, and product features. *Mark. Lett.* **1995**, *6*, 287–295. [CrossRef]
54. Nowlis, S.M.; Simonson, I. The effect of new product features on brand choice. *J. Market. Res.* **1996**, *33*, 36–46. [CrossRef]
55. Mitchell, V.W.; Greatorex, M. Risk perception and reduction in the purchase of consumer services. *Serv. Ind. J.* **1993**, *13*, 179–200. [CrossRef]
56. Huang, W.Y.; Schrank, H.; Dubinsky, A.J. Effect of brand name on consumers' risk perceptions of online shopping. *J. Consum. Behav.* **2004**, *4*, 40–50. [CrossRef]
57. Jacoby, J.; Jaccard, J.J.; Currim, I.; Kuss, A.; Ansari, A.; Troutman, T. Tracing the impact of item-by-item information accessing on uncertainty reduction. *J. Consum. Res.* **1994**, *21*, 291–303. [CrossRef]
58. Hoque, A.Y.; Lohse, G.L. An information search cost perspective for designing interfaces for electronic commerce. *J. Market. Res.* **1999**, *36*, 387–394. [CrossRef]
59. Sharpe, K.; Staelin, R. Consumption Effects of Bundling: Consumer Perceptions, Firm Actions, and Public Policy Implications. *J. Public Policy Mark.* **2010**, *29*, 170–188. [CrossRef]
60. McCarthy, R.V.; Aronson, J.E. Competing in the Virtual World: E-commerce Factors that Affect the Property-Casualty Insurance Industry. Available online: http://aisel.aisnet.org/cgi/viewcontent.cgi?article=1557&context=amcis2000 (accessed on 8 July 2019).
61. Elliott, M.T.; Speck, P.S. Factors that affect attitude toward a retail web site. *J. Mark. Theory Pract.* **2005**, *13*, 40–51. [CrossRef]
62. Schaffer, E. A better way for web design. *Inf. Week* **2000**, *784*, 194.
63. Poddar, A.; Donthu, N.; Wei, Y. Web Site Customer Orientations, Web Site Quality, and Purchase Intentions: The Role of Web Site Personality. *J. Bus. Res.* **2009**, *62*, 441–450. [CrossRef]
64. Albarracin, D.; Wyer, R.S. The cognitive impact of past behavior: Influences on beliefs, attitude and future behavior decisions. *J. Personal. Soc. Psychol.* **2000**, *79*, 5–22. [CrossRef]
65. Taylor, S.E. On inferring one's attitude from one's behavior: Some delimiting conditions. *J. Personal. Soc. Psychol.* **1975**, *31*, 126–131. [CrossRef]
66. Tversky, A.; Kahneman, D. Judgment under uncertainty: Heuristics and biases. *Science* **1974**, *185*, 1124–1131. [CrossRef]
67. Soderlund, M. Customer familiarity and its effects on satisfaction and behavioral intentions. *Psychol. Mark.* **2002**, *19*, 861–879. [CrossRef]
68. Payne, C.R.; Hyman, M.R.; Niculescu, M.; Huhmann, B.A. Anthropomorphic responses to new-to-market logos. *J. Mark. Manag.* **2013**, *29*, 122–140. [CrossRef]
69. Alter, A.L.; Oppenheimer, D.M. Predicting short-term stock fluctuations by using processing fluency. *Proc. Natl. Acad. Sci. USA* **2006**, *103*, 9369–9372. [CrossRef]
70. Huberman, G. Familiarity breeds investment. *Rev. Financ. Stud.* **2001**, *14*, 659–680. [CrossRef]
71. Hoyer, W.D.; Brown, S.P. Effects of brand awareness on choice for a common, repeat-purchase product. *J. Consum. Res.* **1990**, *17*, 141–148. [CrossRef]
72. Novemsky, N.; Dhar, R.; Schwarz, N.; Simonson, I. Preference fluency in choice. *J. Mark. Res.* **2007**, *44*, 347–356. [CrossRef]
73. Garling, T.; Lindberg, E.; Mantyla, T. Orientation in buildings: Effects of familiarity, visual access, and orientation aids. *J. Appl. Psychol.* **1983**, *68*, 177–186. [CrossRef] [PubMed]
74. Desimone, R.; Miller, E.K.; Chelazzi, L.; Lueschow, A. Multiple memory systems in the visual cortex. In *Cognition Neurosciences*; Gazzaniga, M.S., Ed.; MIT Press: Cambridge, MA, USA, 1995; pp. 475–486.
75. Park, C.W.; Iyer, E.S.; Smith, D.C. The effects of situational factors on in-store grocery shopping behavior: The role of store environment and time available for shopping. *J. Consum. Res.* **1989**, *15*, 422–433. [CrossRef]
76. Ashby, F.G.; Valentin, V.V.; von Meer, S.S. Differential effects of dopamine-directed treatments on cognition. *Neuropsychiatr. Dis. Treat.* **2015**, *11*, 1859–1875. [CrossRef]
77. Daly, K. Corporate performance metrics to top board agendas: With heightened responsibilities and scrutiny, corporate boards are rethinking operations and finding that performance metrics are essential tools. *Financ. Exec.* **2011**, *27*, 50–54.
78. Swaminathan, V.; Lepkowska-White, E.; Rao, B.P. Browsers or buyers in cyberspace? An investigation of factors influencing electronic exchange. *J. Comput. Mediat. Commun.* **1999**, *5*, 1–23. [CrossRef]
79. Deighton, J.A. The future of interactive marketing. *Harvard Bus. Rev.* **1996**, *74*, 151–162.

80. Lepkowska-White, E.; Page, C.; Youndt, M. Web perception and young consumers: An empirical investigation of factors influencing perceptions of online companies. *J. Internet Commer.* **2004**, *3*, 53–77. [CrossRef]
81. Jin, B.; Park, J.Y. The moderating effect of online purchase experience on the evaluation of online store attributes and the subsequent impact on market response outcomes. *Adv. Consum. Res.* **2006**, *33*, 203–211.

brain sciences

MDPI

Article

Abnormal Emotional Processing and Emotional Experience in Patients with Peripheral Facial Nerve Paralysis: An MEG Study

Mina Kheirkhah [1], Stefan Brodoehl [1,2], Lutz Leistritz [3], Theresa Götz [1,3], Philipp Baumbach [4], Ralph Huonker [1], Otto W. Witte [2], Gerd Fabian Volk [5], Orlando Guntinas-Lichius [5] and Carsten M. Klingner [1,2,*]

1 Biomagnetic Center, Jena University Hospital, 07747 Jena, Germany; Mina.Kheirkhah-Rahimabadi@med.uni-jena.de (M.K.); stefan.brodoehl@med.uni-jena.de (S.B.); THERESA.GOETZ@med.uni-jena.de (T.G.); Ralph.Huonker@med.uni-jena.de (R.H.)
2 Hans Berger Department of Neurology, Jena University Hospital, 07747 Jena, Germany; Otto.Witte@med.uni-jena.de
3 Institute of Medical Statistics, Computer and Data Sciences, Jena University Hospital, 07740 Jena, Germany; lutz.leistritz@med.uni-jena.de
4 Department of Anesthesiology and Intensive Care Medicine, Jena University Hospital, 07747 Jena, Germany; Philipp.Baumbach@med.uni-jena.de
5 Department of Otorhinolaryngology, Jena University Hospital, 07747 Jena, Germany; fabian.volk@med.uni-jena.de (G.F.V.); orlando.guntinas@med.uni-jena.de (O.G.-L.)
* Correspondence: CARSTEN.KLINGNER@med.uni-jena.de

Received: 4 February 2020; Accepted: 2 March 2020; Published: 4 March 2020

Abstract: Abnormal emotional reactions of the brain in patients with facial nerve paralysis have not yet been reported. This study aims to investigate this issue by applying a machine-learning algorithm that discriminates brain emotional activities that belong either to patients with facial nerve paralysis or to healthy controls. Beyond this, we assess an emotion rating task to determine whether there are differences in their experience of emotions. MEG signals of 17 healthy controls and 16 patients with facial nerve paralysis were recorded in response to picture stimuli in three different emotional categories (pleasant, unpleasant, and neutral). The selected machine learning technique in this study was the logistic regression with LASSO regularization. We demonstrated significant classification performances in all three emotional categories. The best classification performance was achieved considering features based on event-related fields in response to the pleasant category, with an accuracy of 0.79 (95% CI (0.70, 0.82)). We also found that patients with facial nerve paralysis rated pleasant stimuli significantly more positively than healthy controls. Our results indicate that the inability to express facial expressions due to peripheral motor paralysis of the face might cause abnormal brain emotional processing and experience of particular emotions.

Keywords: classification; emotion; facial nerve paralysis; LASSO; MEG

---

1. Introduction

The human facial expressions are an essential part of communication. Eyes, mouth, and brows specific movements can show emotions that are universally understandable [1,2]. It is believed that facial expressions have a direct influence on subjective feelings, so that facial expressions strengthen our emotions while suppression of that weakens emotions [3]. This theory is called the facial feedback hypothesis (FFH), and Charles Darwin [4] was one of the first who suggested that. Several studies have supported the FFH. As reported earlier [5], receptors in the facial skin return information to the brain, and when this feedback attains consciousness, it is perceived as emotion. Izard [6,7] also argued that central neural activity in the brain stem, limbic cortex, and hypothalamus is activated by the perception of an emotional stimulus, and then a signal is sent from the hypothalamus to the facial muscles and subsequently to the brain stem, hypothalamus, limbic system, and thalamus. This concept is consistent with recent studies suggesting that deliberate imitation of facial expressions is linked to neuronal activation in limbic regions such as the amygdala [8–11], which is connected to the hypothalamus and brain stem regions [12].

As a result of the above conceptual discussion, facial expressions generate a feedback cycle to the brain, but what happens to this feedback cycle if a person cannot perform the facial expressions? The inability to perform facial expressions due to the facial nerve injury is called facial nerve paralysis [13]. The facial nerve is implicated in the control of facial asymmetries and expressions [14,15], which is mainly associated with the primary sensorimotor area [16,17]. The paralysis of the facial nerve leads to loss of facial movement feedback and breaks the integrity of the sensorimotor circuit, which results in impaired connectivity within the cortical facial motor network [18–21]. Such consequences of facial nerve paralysis raise the question of whether there are differences between the processing of emotional stimuli of healthy controls and patients with facial nerve paralysis. To answer this question, we consider one of the formulations of the FFH, the *necessity hypothesis*, which states that facial expressions are "necessary to produce emotional experience" [22]. If the "*necessity hypothesis*" is correct, a person who has total facial paralysis should not experience emotions [23]. In line with this, the inability of a woman with total facial nerve paralysis and normal intelligence to perform a facial expression recognition task was previously reported [24]. Then again, in another study, patients with facial nerve paralysis made at least three more incorrect judgments than the mean of the healthy controls in a facial expression recognition task but had no significant impairment [25]. In contrast, a case study of a woman with total facial paralysis showed no impairment in facial expression experience and recognition [23]. Even with more patients, 18 adults with total facial paralysis, another study [26] reported no widespread deficits in the facial expression recognition task.

Overall, these studies provide a wealth of information on proving or rejecting the *necessity hypothesis*. Nonetheless, none of these studies measured the brain signals of patients with facial nerve paralysis and healthy controls in response to emotional stimuli, and to our knowledge, differences between their brain emotional responses have not yet been reported. It is also unclear whether these patients with facial nerve paralysis have different brain frequencies compared to healthy subjects in response to emotional stimuli. In the present study, we investigate this question by applying a machine learning algorithm that classifies one second of brain activities (measured with MEG) belonging to either facial nerve paralysis patients or healthy controls. The selected machine learning technique in this study is the logistic regression with LASSO regularization, which is highly common in the classification of high-dimensional data and also showed high accuracies in the emotion classification studies (e.g., [27–29]). Using this method also showed higher accuracies compared to using the other classification methods in emotion classification studies. For instance, Kim and colleagues [27] reported equivalent or better emotion classification performances using logistic regression than related works using the support vector machine (SVM), and naïve Bayes. Moreover, another EEG study [28] found that logistic regression with LASSO regularization had better performance in emotion classification and less over-fitted results compared to only using logistic regression. They also found that their classification performances using logistic regression with LASSO regularization are higher than those reported by other studies using different classifiers like naïve Bayes, Bayes, and SVM. Caicedo and colleagues [29] also studied the classification of high vs. low valence and high vs. low arousal emotional responses of the brain considering EEG signals. They performed logistic regression with LASSO regularization, SVM, and neural network (NN) as classification methods, and they found that using logistic regression with LASSO regularization makes higher accuracies in both arousal and valence categories compared to SVM and NN. In addition to this strong evidence, using LASSO has the advantage of automatic feature selection by setting the regression coefficients of irrelevant predictors to zero, which is often more accurate and interpretable than achieved estimates produced by univariate or stepwise methods [30–32]. Hence, we decided to use the logistic regression with LASSO regularization in our study. The classifications are performed based on considering event-related fields (ERFs) and the power spectrums of five brain frequency bands. In addition, we assess the Self-Assessment Manikin (SAM; [33]) test to determine whether there are differences in the experience of different emotions in these two groups of subjects.

2. Materials and Methods

In order to classify the brain's emotional responses of healthy controls and patients with facial nerve paralysis in three categories (pleasant, neutral, and unpleasant), we proposed a methodology, which is described in the following section.

2.1. Subjects

Thirty-three subjects participated in the experiment: 17 healthy (11 females; aged 19–33 years; mean age 26.9 years) and 16 patients with facial nerve paralysis (14 females; age 26–65 years; mean age 45.8 years). Patients were recruited from the Department of Otorhinolaryngology of the Jena University Hospital. All subjects had a normal or corrected-to-normal vision, and healthy subjects had no history of neurological and psychiatric disorders. Beck Depression Inventory (BDI) [34] was measured for patients. The results of this inventory and further information about patients can be found in Table 1. All subjects gave their written informed consent, and the details of the study were approved by the local Ethics Committee of the Jena University Hospital (4415-04/15).

Table 1. Characteristics of the facial nerve paralysis patients in this study.

Patient Number.	Gender [1]	Side	Duration of Having Facial Paralysis in Month	Degree of Paralysis	Type of Paralysis	Reason for Facial Paralysis [2]	Becks Depression Inventory (BDI)	Depression's Severity According to BDI
1	W	Left	72	Complete	Chronic	3	10	Mild
2	W	Right	58	Complete	Chronic	1	12	Mild
3	W	Right	101	Complete	Chronic	1	1	Minimal
4	W	Left	40	Complete	Chronic	1	44	Severe
5	W	Left	29	Complete	Chronic	1	25	Moderate
6	W	Right	79	Complete	Chronic	1	3	Minimal
7	M	Left	35	Complete	Acute	2	6	Minimal
8	W	Right	23	Complete	Acute	1	7	Minimal
9	W	Right	71	Complete	Chronic	1	8	Minimal
10	W	Left	25	Complete	Chronic	1	13	Mild
11	W	Right	22	Complete	Chronic	2	3	Minimal
12	W	Right	21	Complete	Acute	1	17	Mild
13	M	Right	17	Complete	Chronic	1	2	Minimal
14	W	Left	99	Complete	Chronic	3	6	Minimal
15	W	Left	19	Complete	Acute	2	4	Minimal
16	W	Left	16	Complete	Chronic	3	15	Mild

[1] W: woman, M: man, [2] 1 = idiopathic, 2 = inflammation, 3 = post-surgical.

2.2. Stimuli and Design

The stimuli consisted of 180 color pictures that were selected from the International Affective Picture System (IAPS; [35]), consisting of three emotional categories (60 pictures each): pleasant, neutral, and unpleasant. The pictures were presented on a white screen in front of the subjects (viewing distance about 80 cm) and were divided into three blocks consisting of 20 pictures of each category in a pseudo-randomized order. Each picture was presented for 6000 ms, followed by varying inter-trial intervals between 2000 to 6000 ms. The three blocks were presented successively, and each block was followed by a short break that allowed the subject to relax. Subjects were asked to avoid eye blinks and eye movements during viewing the pictures and remaining motionless as much as possible. The entire recording process lasted about 45 min and was conducted in a magnetically shielded and sound-sheltered room in the bio-magnetic center of the Jena University Hospital.

After the measurement step, all 180 pictures were presented again in the same order as before, and subjects were requested to rate the level of arousal and valence of each picture. Pictures were rated using the Self-Assessment Manikin (SAM; [33]) with a seven-point scale indicating arousal (1 to 7, relaxed to excited) and valence (1 to 7, pleasant to unpleasant) levels. To find the differences between the ratings between patients and healthy controls, the median ratings of all healthy controls over one picture were compared with the median ratings of 14 patients over the same picture using the Wilcoxon rank-sum test. We did not consider the ratings of two patients because they did not fully participate in this step.

2.3. *Data Acquisition and Preprocessing*

MEG recordings were obtained using a 306-channel helmet-shaped Elekta Neuromag MEG system (Vectorview, Elekta Neuromag Oy, Helsinki, Finland), including 204 gradiometers and 102 magnetometers. In this experiment, only the information of the 102 magnetometers was analyzed. The reason for this is that we had a higher signal-to-noise ratio (SNR) when using magnetometers than when using gradiometers in our study. Moreover, since we used the SSS method, which estimates inside components with the 102 magnetometers and 204 magnetometers, taking magnetometers or gradiometers into account would lead to very similar result measures [36–38]. To define the Cartesian head coordinate system, a 3D digitizer (3SPACE FASTRAK, Polhemus Inc., Colchester, VT, USA) was used. MEG was digitized to 24 bit at a sampling rate of 1 kHz. All channels were on-line low-pass filtered at 330 Hz and high-pass filtered at 0.1 Hz. MaxFilter Version 2.0.21 (Elekta Neuromag Oy. Finland) using the signal-space separation (SSS) method [39] was applied on raw data with aligning of sensor-level data across all subjects to one reference subject which helped to achieve the same MEG channel positions for all subjects and quantify the robustness of sensors across all subjects. Then, 1000 ms before the stimulus onset and 1500 ms after the stimulus onset were pre-processed. Baseline correction was applied to the first 1000 ms of the epoch. Data were down-sampled to 250 Hz and band-pass filtered (1–80 Hz). Using the independent component analysis (ICA), eye artifacts (EOG), and artifacts caused by magnetic fields of heartbeat (ECG) were removed. Visual detection was used to identify and remove trials that had excessive movement artifacts. Finally, 45 to 55 trials remained for each stimulus category per subject. The artifact-free data were low-pass filtered at 45 Hz to calculate event-related fields (ERFs). Then the power spectrums of MEG data were calculated in five frequency bands: delta (1–4 Hz), theta (5–8 Hz), alpha (9–14 Hz), beta (15–30 Hz), and gamma (31–45 Hz). The entire analysis was performed using the Fieldtrip toolbox [40] and MATLAB 9.3.0 (Mathworks, Natick, MA, USA).

2.4. *Feature Extraction*

The feature sets used in this study can be categorized into two groups: features based on ERFs, and features based on power spectrums. These features and the classification method used in this experiment are explained in detail in the following section.

2.4.1. Features Based on ERFs

We took the mean values of event-related fields power (i.e., ERFs to the power of two) over one-second post-stimulus and all stimuli of each emotion category as observations for each subject. Thus, each subject provided three vector-valued observations: one for pleasant, one for neutral, and one for unpleasant. Each observation incorporates 102 (magnetometers) elements. Combining observations from all 33 subjects to define the feature matrix in one emotion category (e.g., pleasant), we obtained 33 observations with 102 predictors each. Therefore, based on ERF responses, we compiled three feature sets (according to three emotion categories), and each feature set had a dimensionality of 33×102.

2.4.2. Features Based on Power Spectrums

To generate features based on power spectrums, we took the mean values of the power spectrum (from a particular frequency band) over one-second post-stimulus and all stimuli of each emotion category as observations for each subject. Thus, each subject provided three vector-valued observations for each frequency band (5 bands): one for pleasant, one for neutral, and one for unpleasant. Each observation incorporates 102 (magnetometers) elements. Therefore, based on power spectrums, we compiled 15 feature sets (according to three emotion categories and five brain frequency bands) with a dimensionality of 33 × 102 each.

2.5. Feature Subset Selection and Classification

After extracting features, we had to select a subset of features that are mostly related to the emotion discrimination of these two groups of subjects and apply classification methods for that subset. The reason for selecting a subset is that from the statistical point of view, irrelevant features may decrease the classification accuracy [41]. However, exploring based on the entire feature set and identifying subsets of discriminative features is a very complex and lengthy process. Thus, using effective feature selection methods helps to avoid the accumulation of features that are not discriminative in the least amount of time possible.

Here, we employed regularized logistic regression with the most popular penalty, the least absolute shrinkage, and selection operator (LASSO; [42]), for feature subset selection and classification. LASSO is highly common in the classification of high dimensional data (a large number of predictors and small sample size) because it selects variables by forcing some regression coefficients to zero and provides high classification accuracies [43].

We defined the response variable of the logistic regression by one for healthy controls and zero for patients with facial nerve paralysis. Let $y_n \in \{0, 1\}$ be a vector with N elements, and let x_n be associate vectors with M predictors. The probability of being healthy (class 1) for the nth subject is estimated by Equation (1) [43]:

$$\pi_n = p(y_n = 1|x_n) = \frac{\exp\,(\beta_0 + \sum_{m=1}^{M} x_{nm}{}^{T}\beta_m)}{1 + \exp\,(\beta_0 + \sum_{m=1}^{M} x_{nm}{}^{T}\beta_m)} \qquad n = 1, 2, \ldots, N \tag{1}$$

where β_m and β_0 are the regression coefficients and the intercept, respectively. The goal of LASSO regression is to estimate the β_m and β_0 which are obtained by Equation (2) [43]:

$$\hat{\beta}_{LASSO} = \underset{\beta}{\text{argmin}}\left[-\sum\nolimits_{n=1}^{N}\{y_n \ln(\pi_n) + (1-y_n)\ln(1-\pi_n)\} + \lambda \sum\nolimits_{m=1}^{M}|\beta_m|\right] \tag{2}$$

The penalty term, $\lambda \sum_{m=1}^{M}|\beta_m|$, penalizes large regression parameters, where the regularization constant λ, is the positive tuning parameter that controls the balance between the model fit and the effect of the penalty term [44]. When $\lambda = 0$, maximum likelihood is reached and when λ tends towards infinity, it increases the impact of the penalty term on the parameter estimates, and the penalty term obliges all regression coefficients to be zero. To determine the optimal value of λ, we used a leave-one-subject-out cross-validation (33-fold). The optimal λ was selected according to the minimum cross-validation error under the constraint that at least two regression coefficients are not equal to zero. This constraint resulted from pilot investigations, which revealed that reliable discrimination of patients and healthy controls was not possible based on univariate features. Since we defined 18 feature sets, we had to determine 18 lambdas; exemplary, we show only one figure related to the lambda determination (see Figure 1). The optimal λ associated with each feature set was used for feature subset selection and classification. The classification performance was evaluated by accuracy, specificity, and sensitivity. The accuracy is the ratio of the correctly classified subjects to their total number. The ratio of correct positives (healthy controls classified as healthy controls) to the total number of healthy controls is called sensitivity or true positive rate. The ratio of correct negatives (patients classified as patients) to the total number of patients is called specificity or true negative rate. To assess our classification results, we performed 1000 16-fold-stratified cross-validations to estimate simultaneous 95%-confidence intervals for accuracy, sensitivity, and specificity (see Figure 2).

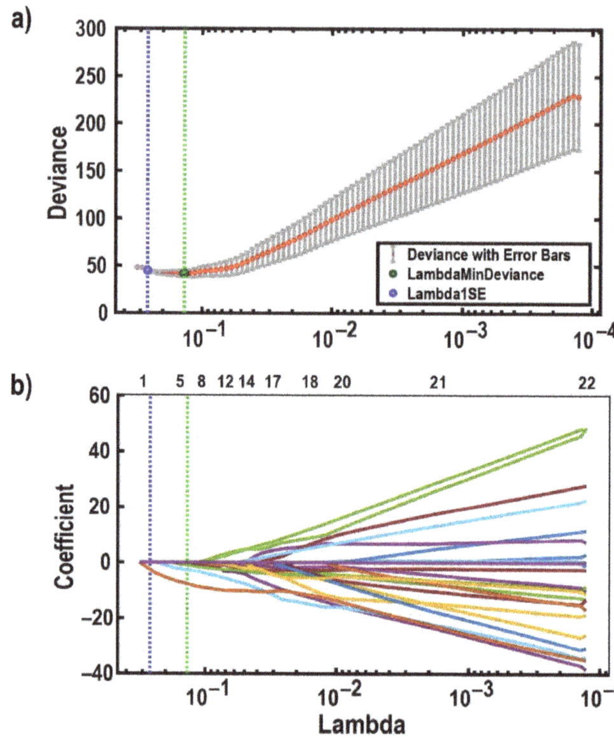

Figure 1. Effects of LASSO regularization tuning parameter λ on regression coefficients, and deviances. (**a**) A plot of the cross-validation deviance of the LASSO fit model against the λ. This figure shows leave-one-subject-out cross-validation results to determine the optimal value of λ. The *Y*-axis indicates the cross-validation deviance corresponds to the values of λ on the *X*-axis. The mean cross-validation deviance is shown by the red points in this figure, and each error bar shows ±1 standard deviation. The blue and green vertical dotted lines (in both figures) indicate the λ, which gives the minimum deviance with no more than one standard deviation (blue circle) and the minimum deviance (green circle), respectively. (**b**) The paths of the LASSO fit model's coefficients in dependence on λ. This figure shows how λ controls the shrinkage of LASSO coefficients. The numbers above the box show how many non-zero coefficients remain considering the corresponding λ values on the *X*-axis. The *Y*-axis illustrates the coefficients of classifiers. Each path refers to one regression coefficient. It is shown that when λ increases to the left side of the plot, the number of remaining non-zero coefficients gets close to zero.

3. Results

In this section, we assess the feasibility of classifying brain emotional responses of healthy controls and patients with facial nerve paralysis. To this end, we report the classification performances of choosing each feature set. Then we report the results of the comparison between the levels of arousal and valence rated by these two groups of subjects to determine whether there are differences between their experience of emotions or not.

3.1. Classification Results

Figure 2a depicts accuracies with 95% simultaneous confidence intervals for all feature sets. Simultaneous confidence intervals were determined at 99.2% of individual confidence levels in order to obtain a 95% simultaneous confidence level using Bonferroni correction for six hypotheses. As can be seen, it is possible to discriminate the brain responses of these two groups of subjects in each category:

in the category of pleasant based on ERFs as well as on delta-, theta- and gamma-band power; in the category of neutral based on ERFs as well as on beta- and gamma-band power; in the category of unpleasant based on alpha-band power. The highest accuracy of 0.79 (95% CI (0.70, 0.82), 99.2% CI (0.67, 0.85)) was obtained for pleasant stimuli in combination with a direct exploitation of ERFs. Comparing the three categories, by trend, the groups are best distinguishable for pleasant stimuli.

In order to elaborate that accuracy values are not dominated by one of the subjects' groups, sensitivities and specificities with 95% simultaneous confidence intervals for all feature sets are presented in Figure 2b,c, respectively. As expected, due to similar group sizes of 16 and 17, statistical significances with respect to sensitivity and specificity resemble the significance pattern of accuracy.

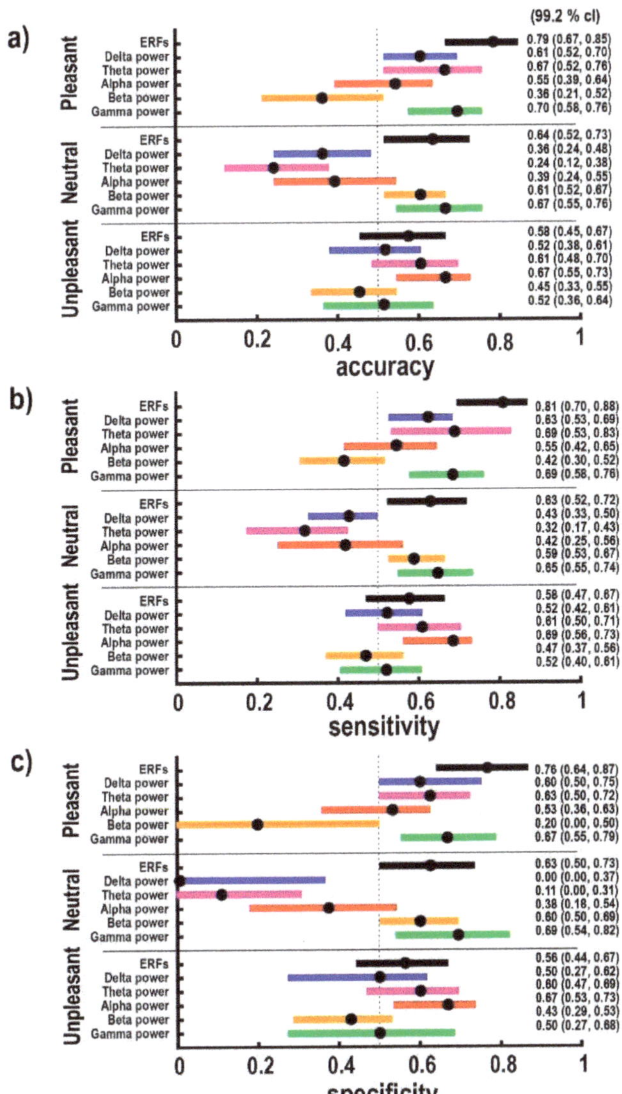

Figure 2. Evaluation of classifier performance for all feature sets based on 1000 16-fold-stratified cross-validations. Numerical values represent medians as well as 95% simultaneous confidence intervals for

the metrics (**a**) accuracy, (**b**) sensitivity, and (**c**) specificity. The median values considering 95% CI are represented by circles. The vertical dotted line displays results equal to random results. Considering features based on ERFs in the pleasant category, we achieved the highest classification performances.

3.2. Ratings Results

The results of the median ratings of patients and healthy controls for arousal and valence levels in three picture categories are indicated in Figure 3. To compare the median ratings between patients and controls, we performed the Wilcoxon rank-sum test, which is based on the null hypothesis of equal medians. We found no significant differences in the comparison of arousal ratings. In the comparison of the valence ratings, we found significant higher valence ratings only for pleasant stimuli in healthy subjects compared to patients ($p = 1 \times 10^{-6}$). This shows that patients rated pleasant images significantly more positively than controls, since, in the 7-point scale of valence, 1 indicates the highest positivity and 7 the highest negativity of an emotion. Except for some outliers, neutral stimuli showed no variation between subjects (median rating = 4).

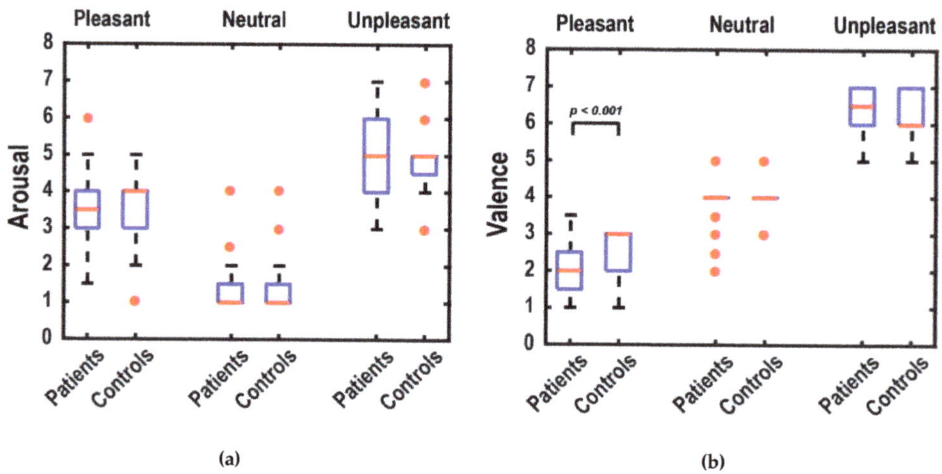

Figure 3. Boxplots of the arousal (**a**) and valence (**b**) ratings of patients and healthy controls for each picture category. Boxplots show the median ratings of subjects for each picture category. The red lines are the medians, and the red circles represent outliers. The valence ratings for pleasant stimuli are significantly higher for healthy controls compared to patients.

4. Discussion

Facial nerve paralysis is a common disorder of the main motor pathway, which causes an inability to perform facial expressions. In our present study, we investigated the automatic classification of brain responses of patients with facial nerve paralysis and healthy controls using MEG signals in response to three emotional categories of picture stimuli (pleasant, neutral, and unpleasant). We evaluated the feasibility of classifying brain emotional reactions of these two groups of subjects by computing several features based on ERFs and power spectrums in five brain frequency bands. Significant classification performances were obtained for all three emotional categories, and the highest was achieved when considering feature sets taken from ERFs in response to pleasant stimuli with the median of 0.79 (95% CI (0.70, 0.82)). These results demonstrate that patients with facial nerve paralysis might have different emotional brain responses compared to healthy controls. However, comparing the amplitude of brain responses between patients and controls, considering ERFs and power spectra in each frequency band, we found no significant differences. We propose that these differences might relate to the patterns of brain emotional responses. As a physiological explanation, since the loss of movement feedback in facial nerve paralysis influences the cortical motor network [18–21], which is responsible for the generation of patterned emotion-specific changes in several systems such as the limbic system [45]; it is possible that the produced patterns become different. To the best of our knowledge, there are no studies that report the differences between the brain's emotional responses of facial nerve paralysis patients and healthy controls. However, our results are consistent with the result of an earlier study that reported blocking facial mimicry of healthy subjects causes different neural activations in the amygdala in response to emotional stimuli [3]. Our results are also compatible with a very recent study that compared patients with facial nerve paralysis and healthy controls in resting state and found that the brain fraction amplitude of low-frequency fluctuation is abnormal in emotion-related regions [46].

Our classification accuracies obtained using logistic regression with LASSO regularization are not compatible with any study because, as mentioned above, to the best of our knowledge, our study is the first to classify the brain's emotional responses of patients with facial nerve palsy compared to the healthy controls. However, our results can be compatible with the results of emotion classification studies. The accuracies achieved in our study (the highest value: 0.79 (99.2% CI (0.67, 0.85))) are similar or higher than the results achieved with many studies. For instance, an EEG study [47] conducted SVM to classify valence and arousal in human emotions evoked by visual stimuli, and the classification accuracies were between 54.7% and 62.6%. Another EEG study [48] also used SVM to classify four emotion categories (joy, anger, sadness, and pleasure), and the best accuracies were obtained considering joy (86.2%). Using both SVM and the hidden Markov model, one EEG study [49] classified pleasant, unpleasant, and neutral emotion categories, and the highest mean accuracy was 62%. Classification using SVM was also performed in classifying joy, sadness, fear, and relaxed states, which resulted in an average accuracy of 41.7% [50]. Using naïve Bayes and Fisher discriminant analysis (FDA), the average accuracy of 58% was obtained for classifying three arousal categories of picture stimuli by another study [51]. In order to propose Bayesian network-based classifiers in classifying emotions, one EEG study achieved the highest accuracy of 78.17% [52]. To our knowledge, only one study [53] investigated MEG for the classification of human emotions. They performed linear SVM classifiers and achieved the highest classification accuracy of 84%. Our classification accuracies are also similar or higher than the results of other studies using the same classification methods as in our study. For instance, Kim and colleagues [27] reported accuracy of 78.57% performing logistic regression to classify positive versus negative emotions, and they also found that their results were more accurate than results of related works using SVM and naïve Bayes. Another EEG study [28] also reported the maximum accuracy of 78.1% when performing logistic regression with LASSO regularization in the classification of valence and arousal. They also noted that their results achieved by using logistic regression with LASSO regularization were higher than those achieved by logistic regression alone or compared with other studies using classifiers such as naïve Bayes, Bayes, and SVM. Caicedo and colleagues [29] also performed the logistic regression with LASSO regularization to classify arousal and valence. They also used SVM and NN classifiers and achieved an accuracy of 78.2% using logistic regression with LASSO regulation, which was higher than when using SVM and NN.

In our study, the classification accuracies obtained through brain responses to pleasant stimuli were higher than brain responses triggered by other stimuli. This finding indicates that the processing of pleasant emotions in facial nerve paralysis patients are significantly different from those in healthy controls, and this difference is more pronounced than differences between the brain responses evoked by unpleasant or neutral stimuli. However, why might paralysis of facial nerve cause different brain emotional responses to pleasant stimuli, more than to unpleasant stimuli? One possible explanation might be that people control their negative emotions more often than positive emotions [54]. Therefore healthy controls may refrain from performing facial expressions while having unpleasant emotions more than when experiencing pleasant emotions. Thus, there may not be vast differences between the feedback caused by facial expressions during unpleasant stimuli, and consequently, the brain responses triggered by that, in people who can perform (healthy subjects), and people who cannot perform facial expressions (patients with facial nerve paralysis).

In our emotion ratings task, we used the International Affective Picture System (IAPS; [35]), including a wide range of emotional scenes such as nature, war scenes, sports, and family, as opposed to previous studies that contained images of faces [23–26]. Using the Self-Assessment Manikin (SAM; [33]) test, we demonstrated that patients with facial nerve paralysis significantly rated lower valence levels for pleasant stimuli compared to healthy controls. Since valence is the positivity or the negativity conveyed by an emotion [55], the ratings obtained from subjects in this experiment imply that the effects of pleasant stimuli are more positive for patients than for healthy controls. Thus, our findings demonstrate that facial feedback plays an essential role in the normal experience of pleasant emotional images. This finding is in line with our previous findings regarding the highly significant different brain responses of these two groups of subjects in response to pleasant stimuli, which are reflected in the different experience of pleasant stimuli by these patients. Inconsistent with our results, from the suppression of emotional expressions in healthy controls, Davis and his colleagues [56] demonstrated that inhibiting facial expressions in healthy people makes no difference in positive emotional experiences, but weakens negative emotional experiences. The different emotional experience of patients with facial nerve paralysis and healthy controls has also been reported in earlier studies that evaluated facial expression recognition tasks. Calder and colleagues [25] studied three patients with total facial nerve paralysis and compared their emotion recognition with 40 healthy controls. They reported that patients made at least three times more wrong judgments than the average of the healthy controls, but there was no significant impairment. Giannini and colleagues [24] reported the complete inability of a woman with total facial nerve paralysis in performing a facial expression recognition task. However, some studies found no different emotion recognition by patients with total facial nerve paralysis compared to healthy controls [23,26]. Accordingly, such studies suggest that facial feedback is not necessary to recognize facial expressions, which might oppose the *necessity hypothesis*. Our study does not allow us to support or oppose the previously described *necessity hypothesis* because it requires that we study patients with total facial nerve paralysis. However, our study demonstrates that the paralysis of the facial nerve causes changes in the emotional responses of the brain, especially during pleasant stimuli and these results were also reflected in the ratings of pleasant emotion in these patients. This finding is a strong argument for the importance of the ability to perform facial expressions to have normal brain emotional processing and experience of particular emotions.

Considering different feature sets, we have demonstrated that the brain's responses to pleasant, unpleasant, and neutral stimuli in patients with facial nerve paralysis are significantly different from those in healthy controls. Moreover, we showed that these different brain responses are associated with the power spectrum of some frequency bands. No study to our knowledge has reported any differences between the frequency-bands of brain emotional responses in the comparison between healthy subjects and patients with facial nerve paralysis. However, we found some biological evidence that may explain some of these results. There is some evidence that gamma-band activity is associated with the activation of the sensorimotor cortex, and gamma event-related synchronization (ERS) occurs in the sensorimotor cortex during unilateral limb movements such as movements of fingers, toes, and tongue [57,58], thus unilateral facial movements might produce gamma activity in the sensorimotor cortex. Since patients with facial nerve paralysis cannot fully perform facial expressions, and because they have impaired connectivity within the sensorimotor cortex [18–21], their induced gamma activity might be different. Many recent experiments have also focused on the role of theta–gamma oscillations in cognitive neuroscience [59–63]. It is assumed that theta–gamma interactions are associated with cortical sensory processing [64], and a hierarchy of oscillations including delta, theta, and gamma oscillations arranges sensory functions [65]. Thus, impaired connectivity within the sensorimotor cortex caused by facial nerve paralysis can lead to a disruption of the delta–theta–gamma oscillations. Moreover, it has been demonstrated that when sensory and motor regions become engaged, the suppression of alpha power has been observed [63]. Given that the facial nerve is mainly associated with the primary sensorimotor area [16,17] and the paralysis of that results in reduced connectivity within the cortical facial motor network [18–21], it might be the reason for different alpha power in patients with paralysis of facial nerve compared to healthy controls.

Finding significant classification accuracies in the classification of brain neutral responses of these two groups of subjects were interesting, unexpected findings. Since it is assumed that neutral stimuli have non-emotional content, we did not expect to find different brain responses of these two groups of subjects during viewing neutral stimuli. However, we have shown that the brain ERFs of patients with facial nerve paralysis differ significantly from those of healthy controls and are associated with beta and gamma bands. Nonetheless, one possibility might be that mood changes when viewing affective pictures may influence the processing of neutral pictures, and the presentation of neutral images alone may lead to more accurate results [66].

5. Limitations in the Study

There are some limitations in this study that should be considered in further research. First, the mean age of patients in this study was greater than in healthy subjects. This was because most facial nerve paralysis patients were not interested in participating in the experiment. Therefore, we did not have many possibilities to consider the same mean age for both groups of participants. The reason for the unwillingness of these patients to participate in such studies might be that they feel reluctant to communicate with other people or to participate in public [67,68]. However, it might be beneficial to consider the same mean age in both groups of subjects in further research. The second issue that could be considered in future studies is to include other emotional categories such as anger, anxiety, or surprise to better classify all emotional states of these two groups of people. Third, in this study, we did not measure the brain activations of these two groups of subjects during the resting state. We would suggest that considering the data of the resting state in further studies would help to find the answer to these very important questions, namely whether these two groups of subjects have different brain activities even at baseline or whether some of the brain rhythms reflect the differences between these two groups of test subjects at baseline.

6. Conclusions

This study shows that the emotional experiences and the brain's emotional responses of patients with facial nerve paralysis are accurately separated from those in healthy controls in specific emotions. Our results suggest that the ability to perform facial expressions is necessary to have normal emotional processing and experience of emotions.

Author Contributions: Conceptualization, R.H., O.W.W. and C.M.K.; Data curation, M.K., L.L., P.B. and R.H.; Formal analysis, M.K., L.L. and P.B.; Funding acquisition, O.W.W. and C.M.K.; Investigation, M.K., S.B., L.L., T.G., P.B., R.H., O.W.W. and C.M.K.; Methodology, M.K., S.B., L.L., T.G., P.B. and C.M.K.; Project administration, O.W.W. and C.M.K.; Resources, R.H., O.W.W., G.F.V., O.G.-L. and C.M.K.; Supervision, O.W.W. and C.M.K.; Validation, M.K. and L.L.; Visualization, M.K.; Writing—original draft, M.K.; Writing—review & editing, M.K., S.B., L.L., T.G., P.B., R.H., O.W.W., G.F.V., O.G.-L. and C.M.K. All authors have read and agreed to the published version of the manuscript.

Funding: This research was funded by BMBF (IRESTRA 16SV7209 and Schwerpunktprogramm BU 1327/4-1).

Acknowledgments: The authors gratefully thank S. Heginger and T. Radtke for technical assistance and E. Künstler for her valuable comments.

Conflicts of Interest: The authors declare no conflict of interest.

References

1. Andrew, R.J. The origins of facial expressions. *Sci. Am.* **1965**, *213*, 88–95. [CrossRef] [PubMed]
2. Ekman, P.; Friesen, W.V.; O'Sullivan, M. Smiles when lying. In *What the Face Reveals*; Oxford University Press: New York, NY, USA, 1997; pp. 201–216.

3. Hennenlotter, A.; Dresel, C.; Castrop, F.; Ceballos-Baumann, A.O.; Wohlschläger, A.M.; Haslinger, B. The link between facial feedback and neural activity within central circuitries of emotion—New insights from Botulinum toxin–induced denervation of frown muscles. *Cereb. Cortex* **2008**, *19*, 537–542. [CrossRef] [PubMed]
4. Darwin, C.R. *The Expression of the Emotions in Man and Animals*; Appleton: New York, NY, USA, 1896.
5. Tomkins, S.S. Affect as amplification: Some Modifications in Theory. In *Theories of Emotion*; Academic Press: Cambridge, MA, USA, 1980; pp. 141–164.
6. Izard, C.E. *The Face of Emotion*; Appleton-Century-Crofts: New York, NY, USA, 1971.
7. Izard, C.E. Differential emotions theory and the facial feedback hypothesis of emotion activation: Comments on Tourangeau and Ellsworth's "The role of facial response in the experience of emotion". *J. Personal. Soc. Psychol.* **1981**, *58*, 487–498. [CrossRef]
8. Carr, L.; Iacoboni, M.; Dubeau, M.C.; Mazziotta, J.C.; Lenzi, G.L. Neural mechanisms of empathy in humans: A relay from neural systems for imitation to limbic areas. *Proc. Natl. Acad. Sci. USA* **2003**, *100*, 5497–5502. [CrossRef]
9. Wild, B.; Erb, M.; Eyb, M.; Bartels, M.; Grodd, W. Why are smiles contagious? An fMRI study of the interaction between perception of facial affect and facial movements. *Psychiatry Res. Neuroimaging* **2003**, *123*, 17–36. [CrossRef]
10. Dapretto, M.; Davies, M.S.; Pfeifer, J.H.; Scott, A.A.; Sigman, M.; Bookheimer, S.Y.; Iacoboni, M. Understanding emotions in others: Mirror neuron dysfunction in children with autism spectrum disorders. *Nat. Neurosci.* **2006**, *9*, 28. [CrossRef]
11. Lee, T.W.; Josephs, O.; Dolan, R.J.; Critchley, H.D. Imitating expressions: Emotion-specific neural substrates in facial mimicry. *Soc. Cogn. Affect. Neurosci.* **2006**, *1*, 122–135. [CrossRef]
12. LeDoux, J.E. Emotion circuits in the brain. *Annu. Rev. Neurosci.* **2000**, *23*, 155–184. [CrossRef]
13. Coulson, S.E.; O'dwyer, N.J.; Adams, R.D.; Croxson, G.R. Expression of emotion and quality of life after facial nerve paralysis. *Otol. Neurotol.* **2004**, *25*, 1014–1019. [CrossRef]
14. Spencer, R.C.; Irving, M.R. Causes and management of facial nerve palsy. *Br. J. Hosp. Med.* **2016**, *77*, 686–691. [CrossRef]
15. Hussain, A.; Nduka, C.; Moth, P.; Malhotra, R. Bell's facial nerve palsy in pregnancy: A clinical review. *J. Obstet. Gynaecol.* **2017**, *37*, 409–415. [CrossRef] [PubMed]
16. Sessle, B.J.; Yao, D.; Nishiura, H.; Yoshino, K.; Lee, J.C.; Martin, R.E.; Murray, G.M. Properties and plasticity of the primate somatosensory and motor cortex related to orofacial sensorimotor function. *Clin. Exp. Pharmacol. Physiol.* **2005**, *32*, 109–114. [CrossRef] [PubMed]
17. Svensson, P.; Romaniello, A.; Wang, K.; Arendt-Nielsen, L.; Sessle, B.J. One hour of tongue-task training is associated with plasticity in corticomotor control of the human tongue musculature. *Exp. Brain Res.* **2006**, *173*, 165–173. [CrossRef] [PubMed]
18. Klingner, C.M.; Volk, G.F.; Maertin, A.; Brodoehl, S.; Burmeister, H.P.; Guntinas-Lichius, O.; Witte, O.W. Cortical reorganization in Bell's palsy. *Restor. Neurol. Neurosci.* **2011**, *29*, 203–214. [CrossRef]
19. Klingner, C.M.; Volk, G.F.; Brodoehl, S.; Burmeister, H.P.; Witte, O.W.; Guntinas-Lichius, O. Time course of cortical plasticity after facial nerve palsy: A single-case study. *Neurorehabilit. Neural Rep.* **2012**, *26*, 197–203. [CrossRef]
20. Klingner, C.M.; Volk, G.F.; Brodoehl, S.; Witte, O.W.; Guntinas-Lichius, O. The effects of deefferentation without deafferentation on functional connectivity in patients with facial palsy. *Neuroimage Clin.* **2014**, *6*, 26–31. [CrossRef]
21. Klingner, C.M.; Brodoehl, S.; Witte, O.W.; Guntinas-Lichius, O.; Volk, G.F. The impact of motor impairment on the processing of sensory information. *Behav. Brain Res.* **2019**, *359*, 701–708. [CrossRef]
22. Fridlund, A.J. *Human Facial Expression: An Evolutionary View*; Academic Press: New York, NY, USA, 1994.
23. Keillor, J.M.; Barrett, A.M.; Crucian, G.P.; Kortenkamp, S.; Heilman, K.M. Emotional experience and perception in the absence of facial feedback. *J. Int. Neuropsychol. Soc.* **2002**, *8*, 130–135. [CrossRef]
24. Giannini, A.J.; Tamulonis, D.; Giannini, M.C.; Loiselle, R.H.; Spirtos, G. Defective response to social cues in Möbius' syndrome. *J. Nerv. Ment. Dis.* **1984**, *172*, 174–175. [CrossRef]
25. Calder, A.J.; Keane, J.; Cole, J.; Campbell, R.; Young, A.W. Facial expression recognition by people with Möbius syndrome. *Cogn. Neuropsychol.* **2000**, *17*, 73–87. [CrossRef]
26. Rives Bogart, K.; Matsumoto, D. Facial mimicry is not necessary to recognize emotion: Facial expression recognition by people with Moebius syndrome. *Soc. Neurosci.* **2010**, *5*, 241–251. [CrossRef] [PubMed]

27. Kim, S.; Li, F.; Lebanon, G.; Essa, I. Beyond sentiment: The manifold of human emotions. In Proceedings of the 16th International Conference on Artificial Intelligence and Statistics (AISTATS), Scottsdale, AZ, USA, 29 April–1 May 2013; Volume 31, pp. 360–369.
28. Fan, M.; Chou, C.A. Recognizing affective state patterns using regularized learning with nonlinear dynamical features of EEG. In Proceedings of the 2018 IEEE EMBS International Conference on Biomedical & Health Informatics (BHI), Las Vegas, NV, USA, 4–7 March 2018; pp. 137–140.
29. Caicedo-Acosta, J.; Cárdenas-Peña, D.; Collazos-Huertas, D.; Padilla-Buritica, J.I.; Castaño-Duque, G.; Castellanos-Dominguez, G. Multiple-instance lasso regularization via embedded instance selection for emotion recognition. In Proceedings of the International Work-Conference on the Interplay Between Natural and Artificial Computation, Almeria, Spain, 3–7 June 2019; pp. 244–251.
30. Meuleman, B.; Scherer, K.R. Nonlinear appraisal modeling: An application of machine learning to the study of emotion production. *IEEE Trans. Affect. Comput.* **2013**, *4*, 398–411. [CrossRef]
31. Kauppi, J.P.; Kandemir, M.; Saarinen, V.M.; Hirvenkari, L.; Parkkonen, L.; Klami, A.; Hari, R.; Kaski, S. Towards brain-activity-controlled information retrieval: Decoding image relevance from MEG signals. *NeuroImage* **2015**, *112*, 288–298. [CrossRef] [PubMed]
32. Addington, J.; Farris, M.; Stowkowy, J.; Santesteban-Echarri, O.; Metzak, P.; Kalathil, M.S. Predictors of transition to psychosis in individuals at clinical high risk. *Curr. Psychiatry Rep.* **2019**, *21*, 39. [CrossRef] [PubMed]
33. Lang, P.J. Behavioral treatment and bio-behavioral assessment: Computer applications. *Technol. Ment. Health Care Deliv. Syst.* **1980**, 119–137.
34. Beck, A.T.; Ward, C.H.; Mendelson, M.; Mock, J.; Erbaugh, J. An inventory for measuring depression. *Arch. Gen. Psychiatry* **1961**, *4*, 561–571. [CrossRef]
35. Lang, P.J.; Bradley, M.M.; Cuthbert, B.N. International affective picture system (IAPS): Technical manual and affective ratings. *Nimh Cent. Study Emot. Atten.* **1997**, *1*, 39–58.
36. Taulu, S.; Simola, J.; Kajola, M. Applications of the signal space separation method. *IEEE Trans. Signal Process.* **2005**, *53*, 3359–3372. [CrossRef]
37. Garcés, P.; López-Sanz, D.; Maestú, F.; Pereda, E. Choice of magnetometers and gradiometers after signal space separation. *Sensors* **2017**, *17*, 2926. [CrossRef]
38. García-Pacios, J.; Garces, P.; del Río, D.; Maestu, F. Tracking the effect of emotional distraction in working memory brain networks: Evidence from an MEG study. *Psychophysiology* **2017**, *54*, 1726–1740. [CrossRef]
39. Taulu, S.; Simola, J. Spatiotemporal signal space separation method for rejecting nearby interference in MEG measurements. *Phys. Med. Biol.* **2006**, *51*, 1759. [CrossRef] [PubMed]
40. Oostenveld, R.; Fries, P.; Maris, E.; Schoffelen, J.M. FieldTrip: Open source software for advanced analysis of MEG, EEG, and invasive electrophysiological data. *Comput. Intell. Neurosci.* **2011**, *2011*, 156869. [CrossRef] [PubMed]
41. Chandra, B.; Gupta, M. An efficient statistical feature selection approach for classification of gene expression data. *J. Biomed. Inform.* **2011**, *44*, 529–535. [CrossRef] [PubMed]
42. Tibshirani, R. Regression shrinkage and selection via the lasso. *J. R. Stat. Soc. Ser. B (Methodol.)* **1996**, *58*, 267–288. [CrossRef]
43. Algamal, Z.Y.; Lee, M.H. Penalized logistic regression with the adaptive LASSO for gene selection in high-dimensional cancer classification. *Expert Syst. Appl.* **2015**, *42*, 9326–9332. [CrossRef]
44. Friedman, J.; Hastie, T.; Tibshirani, R. Regularization paths for generalized linear models via coordinate descent. *J. Stat. Softw.* **2010**, *33*, 1–22. [CrossRef]
45. Gothard, K.M. The amygdalo-motor pathways and the control of facial expressions. *Front. Neurosci.* **2014**, *8*, 43. [CrossRef]
46. Han, X.; Li, H.; Wang, X.; Zhu, Y.; Song, T.; Du, L.; Sun, S.; Guo, R.; Liu, J.; Shi, S.; et al. Altered brain fraction amplitude of low frequency fluctuation at resting state in patients with early left and right Bell's palsy: Do they have differences? *Front. Neurosci.* **2018**, *12*, 797. [CrossRef]
47. Petrantonakis, P.C.; Hadjileontiadis, L.J. A novel emotion elicitation index using frontal brain asymmetry for enhanced EEG-based emotion recognition. *IEEE Trans. Inf. Technol. Biomed.* **2011**, *15*, 737–746. [CrossRef]
48. Lin, Y.P.; Wang, C.H.; Jung, T.P.; Wu, T.L.; Jeng, S.K.; Duann, J.R.; Chen, J.H. EEG-based emotion recognition in music listening. *IEEE Trans. Biomed. Eng.* **2010**, *57*, 1798–1806.

49. Schaaff, K.; Schultz, T. Towards emotion recognition from electroencephalographic signals. In Proceedings of the 2009 IEEE 3rd International Conference on Affective Computing and Intelligent Interaction and Workshops, Amsterdam, The Netherlands, 10–12 September 2009.
50. Takahashi, K. Remarks on emotion recognition from bio-potential signals. In Proceedings of the 2nd International Conference on Autonomous Robots and Agents, Palmerston North, New Zealand, 13–15 December 2004; pp. 1148–1153.
51. Chanel, G.; Kronegg, J.; Grandjean, D.; Pun, T. Emotion assessment: Arousal evaluation using EEG's and peripheral physiological signals. In Proceedings of the International Workshop on Multimedia Content Representation, Classification and Security, Istambul, Turkey, 11–13 September 2006; pp. 530–537.
52. Fan, X.A.; Bi, L.Z.; Chen, Z.L. Using EEG to detect drivers' emotion with Bayesian Networks. In Proceedings of the IEEE 2010 International Conference on Machine Learning and Cybernetics, Qingdao, China, 11–14 July 2010; pp. 1177–1181.
53. Abadi, M.K.; Subramanian, R.; Kia, S.M.; Avesani, P.P.I.; Sebe, N. DECAF: MEG-Based Multimodal Database for Decoding Affective Physiological Responses. *IEEE Trans. Affect. Comput.* **2015**, *6*, 209–222. [CrossRef]
54. Wallbott, H.G.; Scherer, K.R. Assessing emotion by questionnaire. In *The Measurement of Emotions*; Academic Press: Cambridge, MA, USA, 1989; pp. 55–82.
55. Kensinger, E.A. Remembering emotional experiences: The contribution of valence and arousal. *Rev. Neurosc.* **2004**, *15*, 241–252. [CrossRef] [PubMed]
56. Davis, J.I.; Senghas, A.; Ochsner, K.N. How does facial feedback modulate emotional experience? *J. Res. Personal.* **2009**, *43*, 822–829. [CrossRef] [PubMed]
57. Pfurtscheller, G.; Neuper, C.; Kalcher, J. 40-Hz oscillations during motor behavior in man. *Neurosci. Lett.* **1993**, *164*, 179–182. [CrossRef]
58. Crone, N.E.; Miglioretti, D.L.; Gordon, B.; Lesser, R.P. Functional mapping of human sensorimotor cortex with electrocorticographic spectral analysis. II. Event-related synchronization in the gamma band. *Brain A J. Neurol.* **1998**, *121*, 2301–2315. [CrossRef]
59. Schack, B.; Vath, N.; Petsche, H.; Geissler, H.G.; Möller, E. Phase-coupling of theta–gamma EEG rhythms during short-term memory processing. *Int. J. Psychophysiol.* **2002**, *44*, 143–163. [CrossRef]
60. Axmacher, N.; Henseler, M.M.; Jensen, O.; Weinreich, I.; Elger, C.E.; Fell, J. Cross-frequency coupling supports multi-item working memory in the human hippocampus. *Proc. Natl. Acad. Sci. USA* **2010**, *107*, 3228–3233. [CrossRef]
61. Voytek, B.; Canolty, R.T.; Shestyuk, A.; Crone, N.; Parvizi, J.; Knight, R.T. Shifts in gamma phase–amplitude coupling frequency from theta to alpha over posterior cortex during visual tasks. *Front. Hum. Neurosci.* **2010**, *4*, 191. [CrossRef]
62. Maris, E.; van Vugt, M.; Kahana, M. Spatially distributed patterns of oscillatory coupling between high-frequency amplitudes and low-frequency phases in human iEEG. *Neuroimage* **2011**, *54*, 836–850. [CrossRef]
63. Lisman, J.E.; Jensen, O. The theta-gamma neural code. *Neuron* **2013**, *77*, 1002–1016. [CrossRef]
64. Woolley, D.E.; Timiras, P.S. Prepyriform electrical activity in the rat during high altitude exposure. *Electroencephalogr. Clin. Neurophysiol.* **1965**, *18*, 680–690. [CrossRef]
65. Fujisawa, S.; Buzsáki, G. A 4 Hz oscillation adaptively synchronizes prefrontal, VTA, and hippocampal activities. *Neuron* **2011**, *72*, 153–165. [CrossRef] [PubMed]
66. Keil, A.; Bradley, M.M.; Hauk, O.; Rockstroh, B.; Elbert, T.; Lang, P.J. Large-scale neural correlates of affective picture processing. *Psychophysiology* **2002**, *39*, 641–649. [CrossRef] [PubMed]
67. Li, M.K.K.; Niles, N.; Gore, S.; Ebrahimi, A.; McGuinness, J.; Clark, J.R. Social perception of morbidity in facial nerve paralysis. *Head Neck* **2016**, *38*, 1158–1163. [CrossRef]
68. Nellis, J.C.; Ishii, L.E.; Boahene, K.D.; Byrne, P.J. Psychosocial Impact of Facial Paralysis. *Curr. Otorhinolaryngol. Rep.* **2018**, *6*, 151–160. [CrossRef]

MDPI
St. Alban-Anlage 66
4052 Basel
Switzerland
Tel. +41 61 683 77 34
Fax +41 61 302 89 18
www.mdpi.com

Brain Sciences Editorial Office
E-mail: brainsci@mdpi.com
www.mdpi.com/journal/brainsci

www.ingramcontent.com/pod-product-compliance
Lightning Source LLC
Chambersburg PA
CBHW061609210926
51850CB00009B/2266
9783036553788